Guide to Madagascar

For Peter, with love

Destiny is a chameleon at the top of a tree:
a child simply whistles and it changes colour.
The lake did not want to create mud,
but if the water is stirred, it appears.
There are many trees,
but it is the sugar cane that is sweet.
There are many grasshoppers,
but it is the *ambolo* that has beautiful colours.
There are many people,
but it is in you that my spirit reposes.

Guide to
Madagascar

5th edition

Hilary Bradt

Bradt Publications, UK
The Globe Pequot Press Inc, USA

First published in 1988 by Bradt Publications.
This fifth edition published in 1997 by Bradt Publications,
41 Nortoft Road, Chalfont St Peter, Bucks SL9 0LA, England.
Published in the USA by The Globe Pequot Press Inc, 6 Business Park Road,
PO Box 833, Old Saybrook, Connecticut 06475-0833.

British Library Cataloguing in Publication Data
A catalogue record for this book is available from the British Library
ISBN 1 898323 53 4

Library of Congress Cataloging-in-Publication Data
Bradt, Hilary
Guide to Madagascar / Hilary Bradt – 5th ed.
p. cm.
Includes index.
ISBN 1-898323-53-4
1. Madagascar–Guidebooks. I. Title.
DT469.M25873   1997
916.9104'53—dc21   96-52561
                                                                                CIP

Cover photographs
Front: Panther chameleon (Bill Love)
Back: Street kids (Hilary Bradt)
Colour photographs
Hilary Bradt (HB), Tertius Coetzee (TC), Elisabeth Cox (EC),
Nick Garbutt (NG), Mark Hannaford (MH), Roland Hejdström (RH),
Bill Love (BL), Kay Thompson (KT)
Illustrations   Hilary Bradt
Maps *Inside covers*: Steve Munns   *Others*: Hans van Well

Typeset from the author's disc by Patti Taylor, London NW10 1JR
Printed and bound in Spain by Grafo SA, Bilbao

CONTENTS

HAINTENY

How may I greet you?
I will greet you like the rice near a spring:
when the wind blows, it does not bend,
in the heat of the sun, it does not wither.

ACKNOWLEDGEMENTS

This guide has evolved from readers' experiences and letters and I owe them a debt of gratitude that can never be repaid. So many people have spent time and effort compiling new information, writing about their experiences, and keeping me up to date with happenings in obscure parts of Madagascar. In each edition there are correspondents who deserve a special mention: last time it was Chris Ballance, whose evocative and amusing descriptions have found their way into this edition, likewise Luc Selleslagh, adventurous traveller *par excellence*, whose descriptions of travelling in the south remain in the text. Philip Thomas's thoughtful comments on the anthropological aspects of the country have appeared again, as have some of the anecdotes from Henk Beentje of Kew Gardens.

As always this edition has gained from the mixture of experts, who share their knowledge so readily, and adventurous travellers who send me amazing quantities of both facts and anecdotes. Included in both categories are Jim Bond, who provided unique information on the Mikea people of the southwest and the baobab tree as well as travel nuggets, and Clare and Johan Hermans who keep me informed on orchids and the vagaries of travel. It was a particular pleasure to welcome back two of my most adventurous travellers from the last edition, Bishop Brock and John Kupiec, both from the USA, and both making a return visit to Madagascar. Between them they covered all the backroads of the east, north, and west of the country. John has also beaten the letter length record previously held by Luc Selleslagh: 41 pages. Thank you both, and please make a third trip! Other prolific writers include Anne Axel, Frances Kerridge and South Africans Jeremy Buirski and Lindie Meyer.

There is never a letter which does not add to my knowledge and understanding of the country. Some of the names below are well-known experts on Madagascar, others are ordinary travellers – and just as valued. Heartfelt thanks to all of you: John Buchan, Stephen Cartledge, Bjorn Donnis, Monica D'Onofrio, Robin Harris and Glynis Jackson (who so sadly died in 1996), Stinger Guala, Dean Gibson, Clare Hawkins, Jay Heale, Mark Hughes, Peter La Niece, Jytte Arnfred Larson, Paul and Sarah McBride, Alistair Marshall, Rupert Parker, Rick Partridge, Maggie Rush, Joy Shannon and Frederic Viaux. My apologies if I have missed anyone out.

Finally there are two stalwarts who keep me up to scratch with my information: Derek Schuurman's enthusiasm for writing about Madagascar regularly produces a virtual stair-carpet of faxed information and Nick Garbutt thrusts accurate maps and zoology updates into my hands during clandestine meetings in Madagascar and London.

On the production side I owe a special thank-you to my editor Janice Booth whose knowledge of and love for Madagascar have added so much to the quality of the book.

To everyone: *Misaotra*!

THE AUTHOR

Hilary Bradt has visited Madagascar about eighteen times since her first trip in 1976. She is a tour leader and lecturer for American, South African, Australian and British tour and cruise operators; and lectures, broadcasts and writes on the joys and perils of travelling in Madagascar and other countries. She is also proprietor of Bradt Publications.

CONTRIBUTORS

Ian Anderson (*The Music of Madagascar*) is the editor of the magazine *Folk Roots* and a regular broadcaster on the subject of folk music.

Marius Burger (*The Wild Trade in Reptiles*) is a research assistant at Eastern Cape Nature Conservation in South Africa, and leads herping trips to Madagascar.

Joanna Durbin (*The Environmental Action Plan*) works for the WWF and the Jersey Wildlife Preservation Trust in Madagascar.

Ed Fletcher (*Baobabs*) is a specialist in bonsai trees and is probably the only person growing baobabs in Great Britain.

Johan and Clare Hermans (*Orchids*) are award-winning orchid growers with a special interest in Madagascar.

Bill Love (Photographs and *The Wild Trade in Reptiles*) is a private breeder of reptiles and amphibians in Florida and, through Blue Chameleon Ventures, runs tours to Madagascar. He has a photo library of herpetology subjects.

Gordon and Merlin Munday (*Flora*) are a retired physicist/medical practitioner team, living in Switzerland, with a strong interest in botany.

Seraphine Tierney (*Famadihana Diary*) is the attaché at the Madagascar Consulate in London and runs the travel consultancy, Discover Madagascar.

Jane Wilson Howarth (*Health*) is a medical doctor with a degree in biology. She has researched and practised medicine in several tropical countries, writes about travellers' health for *Wanderlust* magazine, and is the author of *Bugs, Bites and Bowels* (Cadogan). She is currently writing a health guide for people travelling with children, to be published by Bradt.

Part One

GENERAL
INFORMATION

MADAGASCAR MOSAIC
Janice Booth

Two weeks after returning, I still feel my senses jangling. Images jerk through my mind like slides on an ancient projector.

On a night-walk at Périnet, tiny frogs shine like jewels in the beam of my torch, and high above me the eyes of a lemur gleam amber-orange out of the darkness.

A child hides from me by slithering beneath the slab of a dried-out drain, round eyes watchful and curious. In Malagasy I ask him his name and he tells me in a whisper, then dissolves into smiles at his own courage.

A fat little leech, full-to-bursting after a banquet of vazaha blood, flips and bounces on my palm before plopping to the ground.

The elderly president of a remote *fokontany* chats gently to me in rusty French about rice cultivation, rainfall, the effects of foreign travel – and the fact that he now has no teeth!

In a rainforest, I escape from the group and relax into the deep green velvet impenetrable silence – which is suddenly broken by the machine-gun clatter of wind shaking the leaves.

Two young fosas in a cage twist and leap and flirt sinuously with us as we watch, arching their spines and rolling on their backs like kittens. Their sleek coats shine with health. No they should not be there...but that's another story.

Breath rasping and blood drumming in my ears, I heave myself up the last stretches of a steep stony track; and the summit suddenly reveals a view so perfect that streaks of ice run down my spine and I panic, fearful of not remembering.

A serious young taxi-driver in Tana agrees a fare beforehand for the journey; then drives much further than expected as he gamely tries to locate the address. Unasked, I add a further 1000Fmg to my payment – and am rewarded by his sudden and dazzling smile of thanks.

I awake to a deserted beach beside a lake lying silver and empty in the morning light; and the reeds turn slowly golden as they catch the first rays of the sun.

A tame lemur in a nature reserve, lonely for others of its kind, clutches my neck with its tiny kid-gloved fingers, nuzzling my face and grunting companionably in my ear. Recalling the soft, leathery touch of its hands still makes my skin shiver.

'Some people love Madagascar and others hate it,' says Hilary carefully in *Chapter One*. I'm already saving to return.

Chapter One

The Country

PERSPECTIVES ON MADAGASCAR

'[Madagascar is] the chiefest paradise this day upon earth.'

Richard Boothby, 1630

'I could not but endeavour to dissuade others from undergoing the miseries that will follow the persons of such as adventure themselves for Madagascar ... from which place, God divert the residence and adventures of all good men.'

Powle Waldegrave, 1649

As it was in the 17th century, so it is today. Some people love Madagascar, others hate it. If this book helps to dissuade some from making an expensive trip that could leave them bitter and disappointed, I will have done a good job. If I recruit some more Madophiles I shall be happy.

My love affair with Madagascar has lasted 21 years and, like any lover, I tend to be blind to its imperfections and too ready to leap to its defence. I am therefore fortunate to receive so much feedback from travellers both new and experienced, wide-eyed or blasé, to help me appreciate why Madagascar is not for everyone. This is not a holiday island; it is not even a tourist island in that it lacks tangible tourist sights and events. As one disappointed traveller put it: 'I need to be hit in the face with garish temples, outrageous costumes, bizarre practices. I agree toying with Grandad's bones is pretty bizarre but what chance has a tourist like me of seeing a *famadihana*?'

In the late 1990s Madagascar faces the dilemma of many developing countries: its government is anxious to encourage tourism and there are a large number of potential visitors who have seen television programmes about the island's natural history or are looking for a new holiday destination. And yet this is one of the poorest countries in the world, getting to grips with the concept of democracy and trying to repair decades of financial mismanagement. Changes are not going to happen quickly. Furthermore, the Malagasy culture is based on respect for the past rather than anticipation of the future.

So why does Madagascar continue to work for me? Well, these are a few of my favourite things:

The natural history. I have seen spectacular wildlife in many parts of the world, but nothing to equal the surprises of Madagascar's small-scale marvels, such as the uroplatus, the spiny tenrec, the spiders with their golden webs, the weird and wonderful beetles. Nor have I seen any mammals more endearing than lemurs. For the anthropomorphic, gooey brigade they are winners!

The snorkelling. There are not a great number of good snorkelling places, but the underwater world around Nosy Tanikely (off Nosy Be) is so wonderful I have difficulty not gasping with delight and drowning. The area around Toliara is equally blessed.

The beauty of the Malagasy people. I remember sitting in a bus and gazing at the faces around me as though I was in an art gallery. I never get tired of their infinite variety. That it is combined with smiles and courtesy is an added delight.

The scenery. Always varied, often beautiful; from the air there's the tragic drama of the great red fissures in the overgrazed hillsides like terracotta fingers clawing the soft green landscape, and the emerald rectangles of rice paddies stacked like tiles up the mountain slopes. From the ground, the granite crags and domes that dominate the road to the south dramatically contrast with the small red-earth villages.

The food. The tiniest village or the humblest *hotely* is capable of producing an astounding meal. Even travellers on rock-bottom budgets write to me misty-eyed about some of the meals they ate.

Serendipity. Madagascar's size and former isolationist government have kept it free from many western influences. Wander away from the main tourist places in any town and you are likely to stumble across a market, a street fair, a group of musicians, or a gathering that brings home what we have lost in our culture: the ability to be joyful despite poverty, and a sense of wonder.

Now for the negative aspects, which irritate or depress all visitors, and are the last straw for some:

The towns. Excluding some of those in the highlands, there are few attractive Malagasy towns. All are shabby and some are in an advanced state of decay.

The poverty. Over 1,500 people in Antananarivo live exclusively off rubbish tips and there are many child beggars. Despite the ever-present laughter, seeing such deprivation is profoundly saddening to many visitors. Poverty has led to a rise in street crime against tourists.

Transport. Flights are sometimes delayed or cancelled and other public transport is more crowded and less reliable than in comparable countries. However fast the roads are improved they deteriorate with equal speed, so the situation is unlikely to change in the short term.

Let's turn to other travellers for some final words. Some love it...

'I could probably go on for a hundred more pages. In Madagascar each day something special happened to me; these on their own would have made the trip memorable but together they have left me permanently touched by all things Malagasy and constantly daydreaming about the trip. As one person told me: "You can't come to Madagascar just once, you will be back some day."'

'It was a truly memorable holiday. I don't think a person can be indifferent to Madagascar. It delights and offends, grabs and holds on. We are already planning our next trip.'

'Over much too quickly but with such wonderful memories of new and exciting places, people, animals and birds. I recall the smell of the forest, the blue of the ocean, the pure air. The sight of Venus, Jupiter and Mars in a velvet sky, and above all the feel of a lemur's hand as it took a banana – like the touch of a baby.'

And some are not so keen:

'We met people who had successfully travelled around in South America and Central Africa but, like ourselves, they had never encountered such nightmarish problems as we did in Madagascar. The authorities and the tourism infrastructure are totally, but totally, incompetent.'

'Tana and shit are synonymous... I want to tear out the page where you describe this dung-heap as one of the world's most beautiful capitals...'

'My advice is to see Madagascar before the Malagasy finish with it.'

Most independent travellers, however, reflect Stephen Cartledge, who wrote:

'We have travelled quite extensively in Africa and Asia but never quite encountered the problems we had in Madagascar. Emotions can fluctuate from elation at some of the fantastic scenery (at, for example, Isalo) to exasperation at the transport difficulties in getting there. You sometimes want to pick up the country and shake it, demanding that it gets its act together! But for all that, we have found the charm and openness of the Malagasy people, the wonder of the scenery and national parks, the delights of the small towns in the south simply wonderful. When you leave Madagascar, you leave a country that has touched you with its many problems but one that has also left indelible and lasting memories. Go with an open mind, with plenty of patience and a strong sense of humour. Then you will appreciate Madagascar for what it really is: a remarkable country!'

And even tour operators fall under its spell:

Some ten years, 29 trips, tremendous satisfaction, unbelievable aggravation – but Madagascar is still my favorite country.

SOME MALAGASY PROVERBS

Tantely tapa-bata ka ny foko no entiko mameno azy.
This is only half a pot of honey but my heart fills it up.

Mahavoa roa toy ny dakam-boriky.
Hit two things at once like the kick of a donkey.

Tsy midera vady tsy herintaona.
Don't praise your wife before a year.

Ny omby singorana amin' ny tandrony, ary ny olona kosa amin' ny vavany.
Oxen are trapped by their horns and men by their words.

Tondro tokana tsy mahazo hao.
You can't catch a louse with one finger.

Ny alina mitondra fisainana.
The night brings wisdom.

Aza manao herim-boantay.
If you are just a dung beetle don't try to move mountains.

Aza midera harena, fa niter-day.
Do not boast about your wealth if you are a father.

Ny teny toy ny fonosana, ka izay mamono no mamaha.
Words are like a parcel: if you tie lots of knots you will have to undo them.

HAINTENY

Reflect on regrets, Andriamatoa.
They do not look in at the door to be told 'enter!'
They do not sit to be told 'May I pass?'
They do not advise beforehand,
but they reproach afterward.
They are not driven along like sheep,
but they come following like dogs;
they swing behind like a sheep's tail.

FACTS AND FIGURES

Location	Madagascar, also known as the Malagasy Republic ('Malagasy' is the correct adjective, not 'Madagascan'), lies some 250 miles (400 kilometres) off the east coast of Africa, south of the equator. It is separated from Africa by the Mozambique channel and is crossed by the Tropic of Capricorn near the southern town of Toliara (Tuléar).
Size	The world's fourth largest island (after Greenland, New Guinea and Borneo), Madagascar is about 1,000 miles (1,580 kilometres) long by 350 miles (570 kilometres) at its widest point. Madagascar has an area of 227,760 square miles (590,000 square kilometres), 2½ times the size of Great Britain and a little smaller than Texas.
Topography	A chain of mountains runs like a spine down the east-centre of the island descending sharply to the Indian Ocean, leaving only a narrow coastal plain. These eastern mountain slopes bear the remains of the dense rainforest which once covered all of the eastern section of the island. The western plain is wider and the climate drier, supporting forests of deciduous trees and acres of savannah grassland. Madagascar's highest mountain is Maromokotro (9,450ft/2,876m), in the north of the island. In the south is the 'spiny forest' also known as the 'spiny desert'.
Climate	A tropical climate with rain falling in the hottest season – coinciding with the northern hemisphere winter. The amount of rainfall varies greatly by region: the wettest area in the east averages 140ins (355cm) annually; in the dry zone (south-west) the annual average is 12ins (30cm). It is hot and humid in low-lying areas. Temperatures can drop to freezing in Antananarivo (4,100ft/1,250m) and close to freezing in the extreme south during the coldest month of June.
Flora and fauna	A naturalist's paradise, most of the island's plants and animals are unique to Madagascar and new species and even new genera are being found by each scientific team that goes out there. Of the native plants 80% are endemic. All of the mammals are endemic, excluding those introduced by man; and half of the birds and well over 90% of the reptiles are found nowhere else. The incredible number of unique species is due to the island's early separation from the mainland some

165 million years ago, and to the relatively recent arrival of man (around 2,000 years ago).

History

It was first sighted by Europeans (the Portuguese) in 1500, but there were Arab settlements from about the 9th century. The name Madagascar comes from Marco Polo, who described (from other travellers' imaginative accounts) a land where a giant bird, the Roc, picked up elephants with ease. It was mostly united under one monarch from the early 19th century, a time of British influence through the London Missionary Society. It became a French colony in 1896 and regained independence in 1960.

Ethnic groups

The people of Madagascar, the Malagasy, are of Afro-Indonesian origin, divided into 18 'tribes' or clans. Other races include Indian/Pakistani, Chinese and European.

Government

From 1975 to the late 1980s the country followed its own brand of Christian-Marxism under President Didier Ratsiraka. He was forced to step down in 1991 following nation-wide strikes and demonstrations. A new parliamentary constitution in 1993 provided for a constitutional president with a prime minister elected by the National Assembly. But the new president, Albert Zafy, refused to accept the limitations on his role and in 1995 he won a referendum giving him the power to appoint the prime minister, thus becoming effectively head of the government. Increasing opposition to his leadership resulted in his impeachment in September 1996. Nevertheless, he stood for re-election in November 1996, along with ex-president Ratsiraka, who won the run-off election in January 1997.

Population

The population numbers about 13 million, nearly half of whom are under the age of 15. Formerly it was thought that 85% of the population lived in rural areas, but a new report shows it to be only 57%. Since independence the population of Antananarivo has grown by 4% per annum and per capita consumption has dropped by 45%. A third of this decline has taken place since 1993. Some 55% of Tana's population lives below the poverty line and 85% of the children are undernourished. The average mother has 6.6 children. The 'doubling time' of the population is approximately 22 years.

Religion

Christianity is the dominant organised religion, with the Catholic church slightly stronger than other denominations.

Islam and Hinduism are also practised, mainly by the Asian community, but to the majority of Malagasy their own unique form of ancestor worship is the most important influence in their lives.

Economy   Madagascar withdrew from the French Franc Zone in 1973 and set up its own central bank. After a promising recovery at the end of the 1980s, it has suffered from the political upheavals of the 1990s. However, inflation is down to 20% (from 60% at the end of 1994) and falling. Major exports are vanilla, coffee, meat and fish; and, increasingly, tourism. In the World Bank statistics of 1994, assessing poverty by Gross National Product per head of population, Madagascar came 183rd out of 203 countries.

Education   The reduction of public funding and shortage of teachers in rural areas have resulted in a fall in educational standards. A survey in 1993 showed that 49% of children were in primary schools and 17.8% in secondary schools or higher education; while 33.2% were receiving no education at all. The literacy rate is approximately 45% (although the government claims 65%).

Language   The first language is Malagasy, which belongs to the Malayo-Polynesian family of languages. French is widely spoken in towns, and is the language of business. Some English is spoken in the capital and major tourist areas.

Place names Since independence the colonial names of some towns have been changed. Many foreigners – and people who deal with foreigners – still use the easier-to-pronounce old names, however. I use the Malagasy names (apart from one or two cases where there is exceptional resistance to the change) but with the other name in parenthesis so as to avoid confusion: Tolagnaro (Fort Dauphin), Toliara (Tuléar), Andasibe (Périnet), Nosy Boraha (Île Sainte Marie), Antsiranana (Diego Suarez), Mahajanga (Majunga). Antananarivo (Tananarive) is often shortened to Tana.

Time   Greenwich Mean Time plus three hours.

Currency   The Malagasy franc (Franc Malgache, Fmg) floats against hard currencies so these rates (March 1997) are approximate only: £1 = 7,500Fmg, US$1 = 4,800Fmg, 1Ff = 860Fmg, 1DM = 2,800Fmg.

HISTORY

The first Europeans

The first Europeans to sight Madagascar were the Portuguese in 1500, although there is evidence of earlier Arab settlements on the coast. There were unsuccessful attempts to establish French and British settlements during the next couple of centuries; these failed due to disease and hostile local people. Hence a remarkably homogeneous and united country was able to develop under its own rulers.

By the early 1700s, the island had become a haven for pirates and slave-traders, who both traded with and fought the local kings who ruled the clans of the east and west coast.

The rise of the Merina Kingdom

The powerful Merina Kingdom was forged by Andrianampoinimerina (be thankful that this was a shortened version of his full name: Andrianampoinimerinandriantsimitoviaminandriampanjaka!). In 1794 he succeeded in conquering and uniting the various highland tribes. In many ways the Merina kingdom at this time paralleled that of the Inca empire in Peru: Andrian-

---

ROBERT DRURY

The most intriguing insight into 18th century Madagascar was provided by Robert Drury, who was shipwrecked off the island in 1701 and spent over 16 years there, much of the time as a slave to the Antandroy or Sakalava chiefs.

Drury was only 15 when his boat foundered off the southern tip of Madagascar (he had been permitted by his father to go to India with trade goods). The shipwreck survivors were treated well by the local king but kept prisoners for reasons of status. After a few days they made a bid for freedom by seizing the king as a hostage and marching east. They were followed by hundreds of warriors who watched for any relaxation in the guard; they were without water for three days as they crossed the burning hot desert, and just as they came in sight of the river Mandrare (having released the hostages) they were attacked and many were speared to death.

For ten years Drury was a slave of the Antandroy royal family. He worked with cattle and eventually was appointed royal butcher, the task of slaughtering a cow for ritual purposes being supposedly that of someone of royal blood – and lighter skin. Drury was a useful substitute. He also acquired a wife.

Wars with the neighbouring Mahafaly gave him the opportunity to escape north across the desert to St Augustine's Bay, some 250 miles away. Here he hoped to find a ship to England, but his luck turned and he again became a slave, this time to the Sakalava. When a ship did come in, his master refused to consider selling him to the captain, and Drury's desperate effort to get word to the ship through a message written on a leaf came to nothing when the messenger lost the leaf and substituted another less meaningful one. Two more years of relative freedom followed, and he finally got away in 1717, nearly 17 years after his shipwreck.

Ever quick to put his experience to good use, he later returned to Madagascar as a slave trader!

ampoinimerina was considered to have almost divine powers and his obedient subjects were well provided for; each was given enough land for his family's rice needs, with some left over to pay a rice tribute to the king, and community projects such as the building of irrigation canals were imposed through forced labour (though with bonuses for the most productive worker). The burning of forests was forbidden.

Conquest was always foremost in the monarch's mind, however, and it was his son, King Radama I, who fulfilled his father's command to 'Take the sea as frontier to your kingdom'. This king had a friendly relationship with Britain, which in 1817 and 1820 signed treaties under which Madagascar was recognised as an independent state. Britain supplied arms and advisers to help Radama conquer most of the rest of the island.

The London Missionary Society

To further strengthen ties between the two countries, the British Governor of Mauritius, which had recently been seized from the French, encouraged King Radama I to invite the London Missionary Society to send teachers. In 1818 a small group of Welsh missionaries arrived in Tamatave (now Toamasina). David Jones and Thomas Bevan brought their wives and children, but within a few weeks only Jones remained alive; the others had all died of fever. Jones retreated to Mauritius, but returned to Madagascar in 1820 to devote the rest of his life to its people, along with equally dedicated missionary teachers and artisans. The British influence was established and a written language introduced for the first time (apart from some ancient Arabic texts) using the Roman alphabet.

'The wicked queen' and her successors

Radama's widow and successor, Queen Ranavalona I, was determined to rid the land of Christianity and European influence, and reigned long enough (33 years) largely to achieve her aim. These were repressive times for Malagasy as well as foreigners. One way of dealing with people suspected of witchcraft or other evil practices was the 'Ordeal by Tangena' (see box on page 12).

It was during Queen Ranavalona's reign that an extraordinary Frenchman arrived in Madagascar: Jean Laborde, who, building on the work of the British missionaries, introduced the island to many aspects of Western technology. He remained in the queen's favour until 1857 – much longer than the other Europeans (see box on page 161).

The queen drove the missionaries out of Madagascar and many Malagasy Christians were martyred. However, the missionaries and European influence returned in greater strength after the Queen's death and in 1869 Christianity became the official religion of the Merina kingdom.

After Queen Ranavalona I came King Radama II, a peace-loving and pro-European monarch, who was assassinated after a two-year reign in 1863. There is a widely held belief, however, that he survived strangulation with a silk cord (it was taboo to shed royal blood) and lived in hiding in the northwest for many years (see box on page 316).

After the death of Radama II, Queen Rasoherina came to the throne, but the monarchy was now in decline and power shifted to the prime minister who shrewdly married the queen. He was overthrown by a brother, Rainilaiarivony, who continued the tradition by marrying three successive queens and exercising all the power. During this period, 1863–96, the monarchs (in title only) were Queen Rasoherina, Queen Ranavalona II and lastly Queen Ranavalona III.

The French conquest

Even during the period of British influence the French maintained a long-standing claim to Madagascar and in 1883 they attacked and occupied the main ports. The Franco-Malagasy War lasted thirty months, and was concluded by a harsh treaty making Madagascar a form of French protectorate. Prime Minister Rainilaiarivony, hoping for British support, managed to evade full acceptance of this status but the British government signed away its interest in the Convention of Zanzibar in 1890. The French finally imposed their rule by invasion in 1895. For a year the country was a full protectorate and in 1896 Madagascar became a French colony. A year later Queen Ranavalona III was exiled to Algeria and the monarchy abolished.

The first French Governor-General of Madagascar, Joseph Simon Gallieni,

---

TANGENA

When James Hastie, royal tutor, arrived in Madagascar in 1817 he witnessed and described one of the more barbaric tortures that King Radama I was using on his subjects: the Ordeal of Tangena. *Tangena* is a Malagasy shrub with a poisonous kernel in its fruit. This poison was used to determine the guilt or innocence of a suspected criminal. A 'meal' consisting of three pieces of chicken skin, rice, and the crushed *tangena* kernel was prepared. The suspect was then forced to drink large quantities of water to make him – or her – vomit. If all three pieces of chicken skin reappeared the person was innocent (but often died anyway as a result of the poison). If the skin remained in the stomach the unfortunate suspect was killed, usually after limbs, or bits of limbs and other extremities, had been lopped off first.

One of the successes of Hastie's influence on the king was that the monarch agreed that, although the Ordeal by Tangena should continue, dogs could stand in for the accused. This decision was ignored by Queen Ranavalona who used it freely on the Christian martyrs she persecuted with such enthusiasm. Sir Mervyn Brown (from whose book *A History of Madagascar* this information is extracted) estimates that several thousand Malagasy met their deaths through the *tangena* shrub during Queen Ranavalona's long reign. Even during this period of xenophobia the queen was reluctant to subject the Europeans under arrest to the ordeal because of the inevitable political repercussions. Prudently, the poison was administered to chickens; all but one promptly died (the 'innocent' chicken/ European was a bit too useful to condemn).

The Ordeal by Tangena was finally abolished by Queen Ranavalona's son, King Radama II, in 1861.

was an able and relatively benign administrator. He set out to break the power of the Merina aristocracy and remove the British influence by banning the teaching of English. French became the official language.

British military training and the two World Wars

Britain has played an important part in the military history of Madagascar. During the wars which preceded colonisation British mercenaries trained the Malagasy army to fight the French. The First World War saw 46,000 Malagasy recruited for the allies and over 2,000 killed. In 1942, when Madagascar was under the control of the Vichy French, the British invaded Madagascar to forestall the possibility of the Japanese Navy making use of the great harbour of Diego Suarez (see box on page 286).

In 1943 Madagascar was handed back to France under a Free French Government. An uprising by the Malagasy against the French in 1947 was bloodily repressed (some 80,000 are said to have been killed) but the spirit of independence lived on and in 1960 the country achieved full independence.

The first 30 years of independence

The first president, Philibert Tsiranana, was pro-French but in 1972 he stepped down in the face of increasing unrest and student demonstrations against French neo-colonialism. An interim government headed by General Ramanantsoa ended France's special position and introduced a more nationalistic foreign and economic policy.

In 1975, after a period of turmoil, a military directorate handed power to a naval officer, Didier Ratsiraka, who had served as Foreign Minister under Ramanantsoa. Ratsiraka established the Second Republic, changing the country's name from The Malagasy Republic to The Democratic Republic of Madagascar. He introduced his own brand of 'Christian-Marxism' and his manifesto, set out in a 'little red book', was approved by referendum. Socialist policies such as the nationalisation of banks followed. Within a few years the economy had collapsed and has remained in severe difficulties ever since. Ratsiraka was nevertheless twice re-elected, though there were claims of ballot rigging and intimidation.

The 1990s

In 1991 a pro-democracy coalition called the Forces Vives, in which the churches played an important part, organised a remarkable series of strikes and daily demonstrations calling for Ratsiraka's resignation. In August an estimated 500,000 demonstrators marched on the President's Palace. Though unarmed and orderly, they were fired on by the presidential guards and an estimated 100 demonstrators died. This episode further weakened Ratsiraka and at the end of the year he was compelled to relinquish executive power and agree to a referendum which approved a new constitution and fresh elections.

A transitional administration was formed with Professor Albert Zafy, who had led the Forces Vives opposition to Ratsiraka, at its head and a coalition government with Ratsiraka's nominee Guy Razanamasy as Prime Minister. Presidential elections took place in 1992/93 and were won by Albert Zafy. The Third Republic, born in 1993, soon ran into trouble. The new parliamentary constitution provided for a constitutional president with a prime minister elected by the National Assembly. But Albert Zafy refused to accept the limitations on his presidential role and in 1995 won a referendum which gave him, rather than the Assembly, the right to appoint the prime minister.

In 1996 opposition to Zafy's weak government came to a head when the National Assembly voted on July 26, by the required two-thirds majority, to impeach the president. Zafy carried on regardless. On September 5 the impeachment was confirmed by the Constitutional Court; and Zafy resigned and immediately declared himself a presidential candidate for the November elections, as did the other former president, Didier Ratsiraka.

With 13 other candidates splitting the opposition vote, Ratsiraka and Zafy came in first and second and qualified for a run-off election early in 1997 – a repeat of the 1993 run-off and described by a Malagasy newspaper as a choice between cholera and the plague. Ratsiraka won. As a friend commented: 'Only the Malagasy could be so forgiving!'

CLIMATE

Madagascar has a tropical climate: November to March – summer (wet season), hot with variable rainfall; April to October – winter (dry season), mainly dry and mild.

Southwest trade winds drop their moisture on the eastern mountain slopes and blow hot and dry in the west. North and northwest 'monsoon' air currents bring heavy rain in summer, decreasing southward so that the rainfall in Tolagnaro is half that of Toamasina. There are also considerable variations of temperature dictated by altitude and latitude. On the summer solstice of December 22 the sun is directly over the Tropic of Capricorn, and the weather is very warm. Conversely, June is the coolest month.

Average midday temperatures in the dry season are 77°F (25°C) in the highlands and 86°F (30°C) on the coast. These statistics are misleading, however, since in June the night-time temperature can drop to near freezing in the highlands and it is cool in the south. The winter daytime temperatures are very pleasant, and the hot summer season is usually tempered by cool breezes on the coast.

The east of Madagascar frequently suffers from cyclones during February and March and these may brush other areas in the north or west.

The map overleaf and chart below give easy reference to the driest and wettest months and regions, but remember – nothing is as unpredictable as weather, and even in the rainiest months there will be sunny intervals.

RAINFALL CHART

Region	Jan	Feb	Mar	Apr	May	Jun	Jul	Aug	Sep	Oct	Nov	Dec
West												
Highlands												
East												
Southwest												
North												
Northwest (Sambirano)												

Rain   Driest months   Fine but cool

Climatic regions

West

Rainfall decreases from north to south. Variation in day/night winter temperatures increases from north to south. Average number of dry months: 7 or 8. Highest average annual rainfall within zone (major town): Majunga, 152cm. Lowest: Tuléar, 36cm.

Central

Temperature and rainfall influenced by altitude. Day/night temperatures in Antananarivo vary by 14°C. The major rainy season starts end of November. Highest average annual rainfall within zone (major town): Antsirabe, 140cm.

East

In the northeast and central areas there are no months (or weeks) entirely without rain; but drier, more settled weather prevails in the southeast.

Reasonably dry months: May, September, October, November. Possible months for travel: April, December, January (but cyclone danger in January). Difficult months for travel (torrential rain and cyclones) are February, March. Highest annual rainfall in zone: Maroantsetra 410cm. Lowest: Fort Dauphin, 152cm.

Southwest

The driest part of Madagascar. The extreme west may receive only 5cm of rain a year, increasing to around 34cm in the east.

North

This is similar to the east zone except for the dry climate of the Diego Suarez region, which gets only 92cm of rain per year, with a long and fairly reliable dry season.

Northwest (Sambirano)

Dominated by the Massif of Tsaratanana, with Maromokotro the highest mountain, this region includes the island of Nosy Be and has a micro-climate with frequent heavy rain alternating with sunshine.

Chapter Two

The People

ORIGINS

Archaeologists believe that the first people arrived in Madagascar from Indonesia/Malaya about 2,000 years ago. A journey in a reconstructed boat of those times has proved that the direct crossing of the Indian Ocean – 6,400 kilometres – was possible, but most experts agree that it is much more likely that the immigrants came in their outrigger canoes via Southern India and East Africa, where they established small Indonesian colonies. The strong African element in the coastal populations probably derived from later migrations from these colonies since their language is also essentially Malayo-Polynesian with only slightly more Bantu-Swahili words than elsewhere in the island. The Merina people of the highlands retain remarkably Indonesian characteristics and may have arrived as recently as 500–600 years ago.

Later arrivals, mainly on the east coast, from Arabia and elsewhere in the Indian Ocean were also absorbed into the Malagasy-speaking population while leaving their mark in certain local customs clearly derived from Islam. The two-continent origin of the Malagasy is easily observed, from the highland tribes who most resemble Indonesians, to the African type characterised by the Bara or Makoa in the south. In between are the elements of both races which make the Malagasy so varied and attractive in appearance. Thus there is racial diversity but cultural uniformity.

BELIEFS AND CUSTOMS

The Afro-Asian origin of the Malagasy has produced a people with complicated and fascinating beliefs and customs. Despite the various tribes or clans the country shares not only a common language but a belief in the power of dead ancestors (*razana*). This cult of the dead, far from being a morbid preoccupation, is a celebration of life since the dead ancestors are considered to be potent forces that continue to share in family life. If the *razana* are remembered by the living, the Malagasy believe, they thrive in the spirit world and can be relied on to look after their descendants in a host of different ways. These ancestors wield considerable power, their 'wishes' dictating the behaviour of the family or community. Their property is respected, so great-grandfather's field may not be sold or changed to a different crop. Calamities are usually blamed on the anger of *razana*, and a zebu bull may be sacrificed in appeasement. Large herds of zebu cattle are kept as a 'bank' of potential sacrificial offerings.

Belief in tradition, in the accumulated wisdom of the ancestors, has shaped the Malagasy culture. Respect for their elders and courtesy to all fellow-humans is part of the tradition. But so is resistance to change.

Spiritual beliefs

At the beginning of time the Creator was *Zanihari* or *Andriananahary*. Now the Malagasy worship one god, *Andriamanitra*, who is neither male nor female. (*Andriamanitra* is also the word for silk, the fabric of burial shrouds).

Many rural people believe in 'secondary gods' or nature spirits, which may be male or female, and which inhabit certain trees or rocks (which are known as *ody*) or rivers. People seeking help from the spirit world may visit one of these sites for prayer. Spirits are also thought to possess humans who fall into a trance-like state, called *tromba* by the Sakalava and *bilo* by the Antandroy. Some clans or communities believe that spirits can also possess animals, particularly crocodiles.

The Malagasy equivalent of the soul is *ambiroa*. When a person is in a dream state it can temporarily separate from the body, and at death it becomes an immortal *razana*. Death, therefore, is merely a change and not an end. A special ceremony usually marks this rite of passage, with feasting and the sacrifice of zebu. The mood of the participants alternates between sorrow and joy.

FADY AND THEIR ORIGINS

The intruders and the geese During the rule of King Andrianampoinimerina, thieves once attempted a raid on the village of Ambohimanga. The residents, however, kept geese which caused a commotion when the intruders entered the compound, thus alerting the people who could take action. Geese are therefore not eaten in this part of Madagascar.

The onions and the hailstorm At the village of Antehiroko (near Tana) the crops were once devastated by a hailstorm. The farmers blamed this event on a stranger who was not part of the community but who planted onions in the area. The Merina do not now eat onions.

The baby and the drongo Centuries ago the communities of the east coast were persecuted by pirates who made incursions to the hills to pillage and take captives. At the warning that a pirate band was on its way the villagers would flee into the jungle. When pirates approached the village of Ambinanetelo the women with young children could not keep up with the others so hid in a thicket. Just as the pirates were passing them a baby wailed. The men turned to seek the source of the cry. It came again, but this time from the top of a tree: it was a drongo. Believing themselves duped by a bird the pirates gave up and returned to their boats. Ever since then it has been *fady* to kill a drongo in Ambinanetelo.

Fady

The dictates of the *razana* are obeyed in a complicated network of *fady*. Although *fady* (the plural is also *fady*) is usually translated as 'taboo' this does not truly convey the meaning: these are beliefs related to actions, food, or days of the week when it is 'dangerous to...'. *Fady* vary from family to family and community to community, and even from person to person.

The following are some examples related to actions and food among the Merina: it may be *fady* to sing while you are eating (violators will develop elongated teeth); it is also *fady* to hand an egg directly to another person – it must first be put on the ground; for the people of Andranoro it is *fady* to ask for salt directly, so one has to request 'that which flavours the food'. Also, Merina do not eat pork, goat, or onions. A *fady* connected with objects is that the spade used to dig a grave should have a loose handle since it is dangerous to have too firm a connection between the living and the dead.

Social *fady*, like *vintana* (see below), often involve the days of the week. For example, among the Merina it is *fady* to hold a funeral on a Tuesday, or there will be another death. Among the Tsimihety, and some other groups, it is *fady* to work the land on Tuesdays; Thursday is also a *fady* day for some people, both for funerals and for farming.

A *fady* is not intended to restrict the freedom of the Malagasy but to ensure happiness and an improved quality of life. That said, however, there are some cruel *fady* which Christian missionaries have been trying, over the centuries, to eliminate. One is the taboo against twins among the Antaisaka people of Mananjary. Historically twins were killed or abandoned in the forest after birth. Today this is against the law but still persists and twins may not be buried in a tomb. Catholic missionaries have established an orphanage in the area for the twins born to mothers torn between social tradition and maternal love. Many mothers who would otherwise have to suffer the murder or abandonment of their babies can give them to the care of the church.

Many *fady* benefit conservation. For instance the killing of certain animals is often prohibited, and the area around a tomb must be left undisturbed. Within these pockets of sacred forest, *ala masina*, it is strictly forbidden to cut trees or even to burn deadwood or leaf litter. In southeast Madagascar there are *alam-bevehivavy* (sacred women's forests) along a stretch of river where only women may bathe. Again, no vegetation may be cleared or damaged in such localities.

For an in-depth study of the subject try to get hold of a copy of *Taboo* (see *Further reading*).

Vintana

Along with *fady* goes a complex sense of destiny called *vintana*. Broadly speaking, *vintana* is to do with time – hours of the day, days of the week, etc – and *fady* usually involves actions or behaviour. Each day has its own *vintana* which tends to make it good or bad for certain festivals or activities. Sunday is God's day; work undertaken will succeed. Monday is a hard day, not a good day for work although projects undertaken (such as building a house) will last; Tuesday is an easy day – too easy for death so no burials take place – but all right for *famadihana* (exhumation) and light work; Wednesday is usually the day for funerals or *famadihana*; Thursday is suitable for weddings and is generally a 'good' day; Friday, *Zoma*, is a 'fat' day, set aside for enjoyment, but is also the best day for funerals; Saturday, a 'noble' day, is suitable for weddings but also for purification.

As an added complication, each day has its own colour. For example Monday

TOMB ARCHITECTURE AND FUNERARY ART

In Madagascar the style and structure of tombs define the different clans or tribes better than any other visible feature, and also indicate the wealth and status of the family concerned. Below is a description of the tombs that typify the main tribes (for the distribution and characteristics of each ethnic group see pages 29–34).

Merina In early times burial sites were near valleys or in marshes. The body would be placed in a hollowed-out tree trunk and sunk into the mud at the bottom of a marsh. These *fasam-bazimba* marshes were sacred. Later the Merina began constructing rectangular wooden tombs, mostly under the ground but with a visible structure above ground. In the 16th century the arrival of the Frenchman Jean Laborde had a profound effect on tomb architecture. Tombs were built with bricks and stone, no longer just from wood. It was Laborde's influence which led to the elaborate structure of modern tombs, which are often painted with geometric designs. Sometimes the interior is lavishly decorated.

Sakalava During the Vazimba period, the Sakalava tombs were simple piles of stones. As with the Merina the change occurred with the introduction of cement and a step design was added. At a later stage, wooden stelae, *aloalo*, were placed on the tombs, positioned to face east. These were topped with carvings of a most erotic nature. Since Sakalava tombs are for individuals and not families, there is no attempt at maintaining the stelae as it is believed that only when the wood decays will the soul of the buried person be released. Not all the carvings, however, are erotic – they may just depict scenes from everyday life or geometric paintings. Tomb construction commences only after the person's death and can take up to six weeks, the body meanwhile being kept in a house. While a tomb is under construction, many zebu are sacrificed to the ancestors. The Sakalava call their tombs *izarana*, 'the place where we are separated'.

Antandroy and Mahafaly The local name of these tombs is *fanesy* which means 'your eternal place'. Zebu horns are scattered on the tomb as a symbol of wealth (on Sakalava tombs, zebu horns are only a decoration, not an indication of status). The Antandroy and Mahafaly tombs have much the same architecture as those of the Sakalava, but are more artistically decorated. The *aloalo* bear figures depicting scenes from the person's life, and the entire length is often carved with intricate designs. These tombs are carefully maintained, and it is probably the Mahafaly tombs in the southern interior which are the most colourful and striking symbols of Malagasy culture.

is a black day. A black chicken may need to be sacrificed to avoid calamity, dark-coloured food should not be eaten, and people may avoid black objects. Other day-colours are: Tuesday multicoloured, Wednesday brown, Thursday black, Friday red, Saturday blue.

Tody and Tsiny

A third force shapes Malagasy morality. In addition to *fady* and *vintana*, there is *tody* and its partner *tsiny*. *Tody* is somewhat similar to the Hindu/Buddhist *kharma*. The word means 'return' or 'retribution' and indicates that for any action there is a reaction. *Tsiny* means 'fault', usually a breach of the rules laid down by the ancestors.

After death

Burial, second burial, and exhumation is the focus of Malagasy beliefs and culture. To the Malagasy, death is the most important part of life, when a person abandons his mortal form to become a much more powerful and significant ancestor. Since a tomb is for ever whilst a house is only a temporary dwelling, it follows that tombs should be more solidly constructed than houses.

Burial practices differ among the various tribes but all over Madagascar a ritual known as *sasa* is practised immediately after a death. The family of the deceased go to a fast-flowing river and wash all their clothes to remove the contamination of death.

Funeral practices vary from clan to clan. The Antankarana (in the north) and Antandroy (south) have 'happy' funerals during which they run, with the coffin, into the sea. An unusual ritual, *tranondonaky*, is practised by the Antaisaka of the southeast. Here the corpse is first taken to a special house where, after a signal, the women all start crying. Abruptly, after a second signal, they dance. While this is happening the men are gathered in the hut of the local chief from where, one by one, they go to the house where the corpse is lying and attach money to it with a special oil. The children dance through the night, to the beat of drums, and in the morning the adults wrap the corpse in a shroud and take it to the *kibory*. These tombs are concealed in a patch of forest known as *ala fady* which only men may enter, and where they deliver their last messages to the deceased. These messages can be surprisingly fierce: 'You are now at your place so don't disturb us any more' or 'You are now with the children of the dead, but we are the children of the living'.

More disturbing, however, is the procedure following the death of a noble of the Menabe Sakalava people. The body may be placed on a wooden bench in the hot sun until it begins to decompose. The bodily fluids which drip out are collected in receptacles and drunk by the relatives in the belief that they will then take on the qualities of the deceased.

It is *after* the first burial, however, that the Malagasy generally honour and communicate with their dead, not only to show respect but to avoid the anger of the *razana* who dwell in the tombs. The best-known ceremony in Madagascar is the 'turning of the bones' by the Merina and Betsileo people: *famadihana* (pronounced 'famadeean'). This is a joyful occasion which occurs from four to seven years after the first burial, and provides the opportunity to communicate with and remember a loved one. The remains of the selected relative are taken from the tomb, rewrapped in a new burial shroud (*lamba mena*), and carried around the tomb a few times before being replaced. Meantime the corpse is spoken to and informed of all the latest events in the family and village. The celebrants are not supposed to show any grief. Generous quantities of alcohol are consumed amid a festive atmosphere with much dancing and music. Women who are trying to conceive take small pieces of the old burial shroud and keep these under their mattresses to induce fertility.

By law a *famadihana* may only take place in the dry season, between June and September. It can last up to a week and involves the family in considerable expense, as befits the most important celebration for any family. In the *Hauts Plateaux* the practice of *famadihana* is embraced by rich and poor, urban and rural, and visitors fortunate enough to be invited to one will find it a strange but very moving occasion; it's an opportunity to examine our own beliefs and rituals associated with death. For an account of what *famadihana* means to a sophisticated London-based Merina woman, see page 24.

Variations of *famadihana* are practised by other tribes. The Menabe Sakalava, for example, hold a *fitampoha* every ten years. This is a royal *famadihana* in which the remains of deceased monarchs are taken from a tomb and washed in a river. A similar ritual, the *fanampoambe*, is performed by the Boina Sakalava further north.

Healers, sorcerers and soothsayers

The 'Wise Men' in Malagasy society are the *ombiasy*; the name derives from *olona-be-hasina* meaning 'person of much virtue'. Traditionally they were from the Antaimoro clan and were the advisors of royalty: Antaimoro *ombiasy* came to Antananarivo to advise King Andrianampoinimerina and to teach him Arabic writing.

The astrologers, '*mpanandro*' ('those who make the day'), work on predictions of *vintana*. There is a Malagasy proverb, 'Man can do nothing to alter his destiny'; but the '*mpanandro*' will advise on the best day to build a house, or hold a wedding or *famadihana*. Though nowadays *mpanandro* do not have official recognition, they are present in all levels of society. A man (or woman) is considered to have the powers of a *mpanandro* when he has some grey hair – a sign that he is wise enough to interpret *vintana*.

The Malagasy have a deep knowledge of herbal medicine and all markets display a variety of medicinal plants, amulets and talismans. The Malagasy names associated with these are *ody* and *fanafody*. Broadly speaking, *ody* refers to fetishes such as sacred objects in nature, and *fanafody* to herbal remedies – around 60% of the plants so far catalogued in Madagascar have healing properties.

Ody often encountered by travellers are the stones or trees that are sacred for a whole village, not just for an individual. Such trees are called *hazo manga*, 'good tree'. Another type of *ody* is the talisman worn for protection if someone has transgressed a *fady* or broken a promise. *Ody fiti* are used to gain love (white magic) but sorcerers also sell other forms of *ody* for black magic and are paid by clients with either money, zebu or poultry (a red rooster being preferred).

Mpamonka are witch doctors with an intimate knowledge of poison and *mpisikidy* are sorcerers who use amulets, stones, and beads (known as *hasina*) for their cures. Sorcerers who use these in a destructive way are called *mpamosavy*.

On their death, sorcerers are not buried in tombs but are dumped to the west of their villages, barely covered with soil so that feral dogs and other creatures can eat their bodies. Their necks are twisted to face south.

Thanks to Nivo Ravelajaona who provided much of the above information.

The way it is...

Visitors from the West often find the beliefs and customs of the Malagasy merely bizarre. It takes time and effort to understand and respect the richness of tradition that underpins Malagasy society, but it is an effort well worth making.

Leonard Fox, author of *Hainteny*, sums it up perfectly: 'Whoever has witnessed the silent radiance of those who come to pray... at the house of Andrianampoinimerina in Ambohimanga and has experienced the nobility, modesty, unobsequious courtesy, and balanced wholeness of the poorest Merina who has remained faithful to his heritage can have no doubt as to the deep integrative value of the Malagasy spiritual tradition.'

℘

'France, Spain, Italy and the Indie... must be ransackt to make sauce for our meat; while we impoverish the land, air and water to enrich our private table... Besides, these happy people have no need of any foreign commodity, nature having sufficiently supplied their necessities wherewith they remain contented. But it is we that are in want, and are compelled like famished wolves to range the world about for our living, to the hazards of both our souls and bodies, the one by the corruption of the air, the other by the corruption of religion'.
Walter Hamond, A Paradox Prooving that the Inhabitants of ... Madagascar ... are the Happiest People in the World, *Walter Hamond, 1640*

FAMADIHANA DIARY

By Seraphine Tierney Ramanantsoa, who attended her mother's famadihana *in August 1994*

I travelled across the seas to be here today. This day was long awaited, I would soon be in contact with my mother again. She had died seven years previously and I had not been able to be at her funeral. Tradition had always been so important to her so I knew she would be happy as I have come for her *famadihana.*

The meeting point is at 6am outside Cinema Soa in Antananarivo. My household woke up at about 4am to pack the food that had been prepared during the previous week. Drinks and cutlery are all piled into the car. A great number of people are expected as it is also the *famadihana* of the other members of my mother's family.

Fourteen cars and a big taxi-brousse carrying in all about 50 people, squashed one on top of the other, turn up. Everybody is excited. It is really great to see faces I haven't seen since my childhood. Everybody greets each other and exchanges news.

At 8am we all set off. We are heading towards Ifalimanjaka (meaning 'Joy Reigns Here'), in the *fivondronana* of Manjakandriana. Driving through villages with funny names like Ambohitrabiby (The Town of Animals) brings me back to the time when such names were familiar. We make one stop at Talatan'ny volon'ondry for a breakfast of rice cakes and sausages: another opportunity to re-acquaint myself with long lost cousins with whom I spent the long summer holidays as a child. We used to run around together playing games like catching grasshoppers and then finding carnivorous plants and dropping the insect in to see how long it took the plant to close its top to eat its prey.

10am. We arrive at the tombs. Faces are bright, full of expectancy. I ask what the day means to them. They all agree that it's a day for family togetherness, a day for joy, for remembrance.

We are in front of my mother's tomb. It is made out of stone and marble, very elegant. The family will have spent more money on keeping that tomb nice and well maintained than on their own house.

Everybody stands around in front of the tomb waiting for the main event to start: the opening of the tomb door. We have to wait for the president of the fokon'tany (local authority) to give permission to open the tomb. Although it had been arranged beforehand he cannot be found anywhere. This wait, after such anticipation, is taken patiently by all – just one of those things.

Mats are laid on the ground on one side of the tomb. The atmosphere of joy is so tangible! Music is blaring out. Permission is finally granted to enter the tomb. The *ray aman-dreny* (the elders) are the first to enter.

The inside of my mother's tomb looks very comfortable with bunk beds made out of stone. It is very clean. There are names on the side of the beds. The national flag is hoisted on top of the tomb as a sign of respect. The conversation goes on happily on the little veranda outside the tomb's door, people chatting about the event and what they have been doing in the last few days.

They start to take the bodies out. Voices could be heard above the happy murmur: 'Who is this one? This is your ma! This one your aunt! Here is your uncle! Just carry them around!' The closest relations carry the body but others could touch and say hello. When carrying them, they make sure that the feet go first and the head behind. Everybody carries their loved ones out of the tomb in a line, crying but happy.

When all the bodies are out, they are put on the ground on the front side of the tomb, the head facing east, with their immediate family seated around their loved one. This is a very important moment of the *famadihana*: the beginning of the wrapping of the body. The old shroud in which the body was buried is left on and the new silk shroud put on top of it, following the mummified shape and using baby safety pins to keep it in place. There are three new silk shrouds for my mother which have been donated in remembrance and gratitude. The belief is that she won't be cold and the top shroud befits her, being of top quality silk with beautiful, delicate embroidery. This is the time to touch her, give her something, talk to her. Her best friend is there, making sure that my mother is properly wrapped, as the ritual has to follow certain rules. Lots of touching as silent conversation goes on, giving her the latest news or family gossip, and asking for her blessing. Perfume is sprinkled on her and wishes made at the same time.

The music plays on, everyone happily sitting around the mummified bodies. Flowers are placed on the bodies. The feeling of togetherness and love is so strong. This occasion is not just for the immediate family, but for cousins, and cousins of cousins, uncles and aunts and everybody meeting, bonded by the same ties, belonging to one unique extended family.

Photographs of the dead person are now put on top of each body. There is a photograph of a couple on top of one body: they were husband and wife and are now together for ever in the same silk shroud.

Food is served in the forest area just next to the tombs. The huge feast and celebration begins.

Back to the bodies. We lift them, carrying them on our shoulders. We sing old rhymes and songs and dance in a line, circling the tomb seven times, moving the body on our shoulder and making it dance with us.

The last dance ends. The bodies have to be back inside the tombs by a precise time and the tomb is immediately closed after a last ritual cleaning. This moment of goodbye is very emotional. The next time the tomb will be opened will not be for happiness but grief because it will be for a burial. *Famadihana* only happens once every seven or ten years.

Everybody returns to the cars and drives to the next meeting place – my uncle's, where a huge party finishes the day. Everyone is happy at having done their duty, *Vita ny adidy*!

It has been a very special day for me. My mother was extremely traditional, spending endless energy and money during her lifetime to keep the traditions. It all makes sense now because this *famadihana* brought so much joy, a strong sense of belonging and identity, and giving a spiritual feeling that death is not an end but an extension into another life, linked somehow with this one.

Misaotra ry neny (thank you mum).

MALAGASY SOCIETY

The Malagasy have a strong sense of community which influences their way of life. Just as the ancestors are laid in a communal tomb, so their descendants share a communal way of life, and even children are almost considered common property within their extended family. Children are seldom disciplined but learn by example.

Marriage is a fairly relaxed union and divorce is common. There is no formal dowry arrangement or bride price, but a present of zebu cattle will often be made. In rural communities the man should bring his new wife home to his village (not vice versa) or he will lose face.

Most Malagasy (and all Christians) have only one wife, but there are exceptions. There is, for example, a well-known man living in Antalaha, in the northeast, who has 11 wives and 120 children. This arrangement seems to work surprisingly well, with each wife working to support her own children, and a head wife to whom the others defer. The man is wealthy enough to provide housing for all his family.

Malagasy society is a structured hierarchy with two fundamental rules: respect for the other person and knowing one's place. Within a village, the community is based on the traditional *fokonolona*. This concept was introduced by King Andrianampoinimerina when these councils of village elders were given responsibility for, among other things, law and order and the collection of taxes. Day-to-day decisions are still made by the *fokonolona*.

Part of the Malagasy culture is the art of oratory, *kabary*. Originally *kabary* were the huge meetings where King Andrianampoinimerina proclaimed his plans, but the word has now evolved to mean the elaborate form of speech used to inspire and control the crowds at such gatherings. Even rural leaders can speak for hours, using highly ornate language and many proverbs; a necessary skill in a society that reached a high degree of sophistication without a written language.

Rural Malagasy houses generally have only one room and the furniture is composed of mats, *tsihy*, often beautifully woven. These are used for sitting and sleeping, and sometimes food is served on them. There are often *fady* attached to *tsihy*. For example you should not step over a mat, particularly one on which meals are eaten.

Festivals and ceremonies

Malagasy Christians celebrate the usual holy days, but most tribes or clans have their special festivals.

Ala volon-jaza This is the occasion when a baby's hair is cut for the first time. With the Antambahoka people in the south the haircut is performed by the grandparents. The child is placed in a basin filled with water, and afterwards bathed. Among the Merina the ceremony is similar but only a man whose parents are still alive may cut a baby's hair. The family then have a meal of rice, zebu, milk and honey. Coins are placed in the bowl of rice and the older children compete to get as many as possible.

Circumcision Boys are usually circumcised at the age of about two; a baby who dies before this operation has been performed may not be buried in the family tomb.

Sambatra This is the mass-circumcision ceremony which takes place every seven years among the Antambahoka people of the southeast. The boys are aged from one to seven, and the exact date is determined by an *ombiasy*. The festivities last one to two weeks. A variation involves older boys, in the 'big house' or *trano be*. This is built specially for the purpose, with new mats and furniture. There is much celebrating; the women dance, groups of boys fight and the king makes a sacrifice; and, on the second last night, the boys are circumcised in the *trano be*. This is now done with a razor blade, but previously a sharpened piece of bamboo was used. Foreskins are either eaten by the grandparents or thrown on to the roof of the *trano be*.

Tsangatsaine This is a ceremony performed by the Antankarana. Two tall trees are tied together at a house of a noble family to symbolise the unification of the tribe, as well as the tying together of the past and present, the living and the dead.

Fandroana The Malagasy New Year celebrations used to take place in March. It was a time of feasting, with the best zebu being slaughtered and the choicest rump steak being presented to the village nobles. The French, however, changed the date to July 14, the date of the establishment of the French Protectorate. This caused major resentment among the Malagasy as effectively their traditional New Year was taken from them. After independence the date was changed to June 26 to coincide with Independence Day. These days, because of the cost of zebu meat and the value attached to the animals, the traditional meat has been replaced by chicken, choice portions again being given to the respected members of the community.

Music

Music infuses the lives of the Malagasy people, and like *Hainteny* it is the outward expression of their feelings towards nature and human relationships. Traditional musical instruments are often unadapted natural objects – dried reeds or gourds, rubbed together or shaken to the beat of the music – while the words reflect the spiritual essence of the culture. Pop music is encroaching on this tradition, of course, but worldwide there is a growing appreciation of Malagasy music. Several Malagasy groups now tour internationally (see box on page 116); Paddy Bush and the *valiha* player Justin Vali have formed a collaboration which has brought Malagasy music to a wider audience through Kate Bush's recording *The Red Shoes* and on television.

HAINTENY

References in this book to the Merina have hitherto been focused on their military abilities, but this tribe has a rich and complex spiritual life. Perhaps the shortest route to the soul of any society is through its poetry, and we are fortunate that there is now a book of the traditional Malagasy poetry, *Hainteny*. Broadly speaking, *hainteny* are poems about love: love between parent and child, between man and woman, the love of nature, the appreciation of good versus evil, the acceptance of death. Through the sensitive translations of Leonard Fox, the spiritual and emotional life of the Merina is made available to the reader who cannot fail to be impressed by these remarkable people. As Leonard Fox says: 'On the most basic level, *hainteny* give us an incomparable insight into a society characterised by exceptional refinement and subtlety, deep appreciation of beauty, delight in sensual enjoyment, and profound respect for the spiritual realities of life.'

There are two examples of *hainteny* below, and others are scattered throughout this book.

What is the matter, Raivonjaza,
That you remain silent?
Have you been paid or hired and your mouth tied,
That you do not speak with us, who are your parents?
~ I have not been paid or hired
and my mouth has not been tied,
but I am going home to my husband
and am leaving my parents,
my child, and my friends,
so I am distressed,
speaking little.
Here is my child, dear Mother and Father.
If he is stubborn, be strict, but do not beat him;
and if you hit him, do not use a stick.
And do not act as though you do not see him
when he is under your eyes, saying:
"Has this child eaten?"
Do not give him too much,
Do not give him the remains of a meal,
and do not give him what is half-cooked,
for I will be far and will long for him.

Do not love me, Andriamatoa, as one loves
the banana tree exposed to the wind,
overcome and in danger from cold.
Do not love me as one loves a door:
It is loved, but constantly pushed.
Love me as one loves a little crab:
even its claws are eaten.

ETHNIC GROUPS

This section was originally taken from A Glance at Madagascar *(written in 1973 and in the process of reprinting) and has subsequently been added to from a variety of sources.*

The Malagasy form one nation with one basic culture and language (though with many dialects), but there are 16 different 'tribes' or clans (formerly the number was given as 18, but some are accepted as splinter-groups). This division is based more upon old kingdoms than upon ethnic grouping.

Antaifasy (People-of-the-sands)
Living in the southeast around Farafangana they cultivate rice, and fish in the lakes and rivers. Divided into three clans each with its own 'king' they generally have stricter moral codes than other tribes. They have large collective burial houses known as *kibory*, built of wood or stone and generally hidden in the forest away from the village.

Antaimoro (People-of-the-coast)
These are among the most recent arrivals and live in the southeast around Vohipeno and Manakara. They guard Islam tradition and Arab influence and still use a form of Arab writing known as *sorabe*. They use verses of the Koran as amulets.

Antaisaka
Centred south of Farafangana on the southeast coast but now fairly widely spread throughout the island, they are an off-shoot of the Sakalava tribe. They cultivate coffee, bananas and rice – but only the women harvest the rice. There are strong marriage taboos amongst them. Often the houses may have a second door on the east side which is only used for taking out a corpse. They use the *kibory*, communal burial house, the corpse usually being dried out for two or three years before finally being put there.

Antankarana (Those-of-the-rocks)
Living in the north around Antsiranana (Diego-Suarez) they are fishers or cattle raisers whose rulers came from the Sakalava dynasty. Their houses are usually raised on stilts. Numerous *fady* exist amongst them governing relations between the sexes in the family; for example a girl may not wash her brother's clothes. The legs of a fowl are the father's portion, whereas amongst the Merina, for instance, they are given to the children.

Antambahoaka (Those-of-the-people)
The smallest tribe, of the same origin as the Antaimoro and living around Mananjary on the southeast coast. They have some Arab traits and amulets are used. They bury in a *kibory*. Group circumcision ceremonies are carried out every seven years.

Antandroy (People-of-the-thorns)
Traditionally nomadic, they live in the arid south around Ambovombe. A

Map labels:
Antsiranana (Diego Suarez)
ANTANKARANA
BETSIMISARAKA
Mahajanga
TSIMIHETY
MAKOA
SAKALAVA
MERINA
ANTANANARIVO
SIHANAKA
BEZANOZANO
Toamasina
BETSIMISARAKA
VEZO SAKALAVA
MIKEA
BETSILEO
Fianarantsoa
BARA
ZAFIMANIRY
TANALA
ANTAMBAHOAKA
ANTAIMORO
ANTAIFASY
ANTAISAKA
Toliara
MAHAFALY
ANTANOSY
ANTANDROY
Tolagnaro

DISTRIBUTION OF ETHNIC GROUPS

dark-skinned people, they wear little clothing and are said to be frank and open, easily roused to either joy or anger. Their women occupy an inferior position. The villages are often surrounded by a hedge of cactus plants. They do not eat much rice but subsist mostly on millet, maize and cassava. They believe in the *kokolampo*, a spirit of either good or bad influence. Their tombs are similar to those of the Mahafaly tribe. Sometimes it is *fady* among them for a child to say his father's name, or to refer by name to parts of his father's body. Thus he may say *ny fandiany* (the-what-he-moves with) for his feet, and *ny amboniny* (the-top-of-him) for his head.

Antanosy (People-of-the-island)

The island is a small one in the Fanjahira river. They live in the southeast principally around Tolagnaro (Fort Dauphin). Their social structure is based on clans with a 'king' holding great authority over each clan. There are strict *fady* governing relationships in the family. For example, a brother may not sit on or step over his sister's mat. As with many other tribes there are numerous *fady* regarding pregnancy: a pregnant woman should not sit in the doorway of the house; she should not eat brains; she should not converse with men; people who have no children should not stay in her house overnight. Other *fady* are that relatives should not eat meat at a funeral and the diggers opening a tomb should not wear clothes. When digging holes for the corner posts of a new house it may be *fady* to stand up so the job must be performed sitting down.

Bara

Originally in the southwest near Toliara, these nomadic cattle raisers now live in the south-central area around Ihosy and Betroka. Their name has no special meaning but it is reputed to derive from an African (Bantu) word. They may be polygamous and women occupy an inferior position in their society. They attach importance to the *fatidra* or 'blood pact'. Cattle stealing is regarded as proof of manhood and courage, without which a man cannot expect to get a wife. They are dancers and sculptors, a unique feature of their carved wooden figures being eyelashes of real hair set into the wood. They believe in the *helo*, a spirit that manifests itself at the foot of trees. In the past a whole village would move after somebody died owing to the fear of ghosts. They use caves in the mountains for burial. It is the custom to shave the head on the death of a near relative.

Betsileo (The-many-invincibles)

They are centred in the south of the *Hauts Plateaux* around Fianarantsoa but about 150,000 of them also live in the Betsiboka region. They are energetic and expert rice-producers, their irrigated, terraced rice-fields being a feature of the landscape. *Famadihana* was introduced to their culture by the Merina at the time of Queen Ranavalona I. It is *fady* for the husband of a pregnant woman to wear a lamba thrown over his shoulder. It may be *fady* for the family to eat until the father is present or for anyone to pick up his fork until the most honourable person present has started to eat.

Betsimisaraka (The-many-inseparables)

They are the second largest tribe and live on the east coast in the region between Toamasina and Antalaha. Their culture has been influenced by Europeans, particularly pirates. They cultivate rice and work on vanilla plantations. Their clothes are sometimes made from locally woven raffia. Originally their society included numerous local chiefs but they are not now important. The *tangalamena* is the local official for religious rites and customs. The Betsimisaraka have many superstitious beliefs: *angatra*, ghosts, *zazavavy andrano*, mermaids, and *kalamoro*, little wild men of the woods, about 25 inches high with long flowing hair, who like to slip into houses and steal rice from the cooking pot. In the north coffins are generally placed under a shelter, in the south in tombs. It may be *fady* for a brother to shake hands with his sister, or for a young man to wear shoes while his father is still living.

Bezanozano (Many-small-plaits)

The name refers to the way in which they do their hair. They were probably one of the first tribes to become established in Madagascar, and live in an area between the Betsimisaraka lowlands and the Merina highlands. Like the Merina, they practise *famadihana*. As with most of the coastal tribes their funeral celebrations involve the consumption of considerable quantities of *toaka*, rum.

Mahafaly (Those-who-make-taboos or Those-who-make-happy)
The etymology of the word is sometimes disputed but the former meaning is generally regarded as being correct. They probably arrived around the 12th century, and live in the southwest desert area around Ampanihy and Ejeda. They are farmers, with maize, sorgho and sweet potatoes as their chief crops; cattle rearing occupies a secondary place. They kept their independence under their own local chiefs until the French occupation and still keep the bones of some of their old chiefs – this is the *jiny* cult. Their villages usually have a sacrificial post, the *hazo manga*, on the east of the village where sacrifices are made. Some of the blood is generally put on the foreheads of the people attending.

The tombs of the Mahafaly attract a great deal of interest. They are big rectangular constructions of uncut stone rising some three feet above the ground and decorated with *aloalo* and the horns of the cattle slain at the funeral feast. The tomb of the Mahafaly king Tsiampody has the horns of 700 zebu on it. The *aloalo* are sculpted wooden posts set upright on the tomb, often depicting scenes from the person's life. The burial customs include waiting for the decomposition of the body before it is placed in the tomb. It is the practice for a person to be given a new name after death – generally beginning with 'Andria'.

The divorce rate is very high and it is not at all uncommon for a man to divorce and remarry six or seven times. It is very often *fady* for children to sleep in the same house as their parents. Their *rombo* (very similar to the *tromba* of the Sakalava) is the practice of contacting various spirits for healing purposes. Amongst the spirits believed in are the *raza* who are not real ancestors and in some cases are even supposed to include *vazaha* (white foreigners), and the *vorom-be* which is the spirit of a big bird.

Mikea
The Mikea are an off-shoot of the Sakalava. The name refers not so much to a tribe as to a lifestyle. They subsist by foraging in the dry forests of the west and southwest. Various groups of people up the west coast are called *Mikea*, although their main area is the Forêt des Mikea between Morombe and Toliara. The Mikea are Malagasy of various origins, having adopted their particular lifestyle (almost unique in Madagascar) for several reasons, including fleeing from oppression, taxation etc exerted on them by various powers: Sakalava, French, and the Government of the 2nd Republic. (Information from Dr J Bond)

Makoa
Mainly of African origin, and generally lowly regarded by other Sakalava groups, the Makoa live in the northwest (Ambongo) region. They are probably

descended from African slaves and are said to be the most primitive group in Madagascar.

Merina (People-of-the-Highlands)
They live on the *Hauts Plateaux*, the most developed area of the country, the capital being 95% Merina. They are of Malayo-Polynesian origin and vary in colour from ivory to very dark, with straight hair. They used to be divided into three castes: the *Andriana* (nobles), the *Hova* (freemen) and the *Andevo* (serfs); but legally these divisions no longer exist. Most Merina houses are built of brick or mud; some are two-storey buildings with slender pillars, where the people live mainly upstairs. Most villages of any size have a church – probably two, Catholic and Protestant. There is much irrigated rice cultivation, and the Merina were the first tribe to have any skill in architecture and metallurgy. The *famadihana* is essentially a Merina custom.

Sakalava (People-of-the-long-valleys)
They live in the west between Toliara and Mahajanga and are dark skinned with Polynesian features and short curly hair. They were at one time the largest and most powerful tribe, though disunited, and were ruled by their own kings and queens. Certain royal relics remain – sometimes being kept in the northeast corner of a house. The Sakalava are cattle raisers, and riches are reckoned by the number of cattle owned. There is a record of human sacrifice amongst them up to the year 1850 at some special occasion such as the death of a king. The *tromba* (trance state) is quite common. It is *fady* for pregnant women to eat fish or to sit in a doorway. Women hold a more important place amongst them than in most other tribes.

Sihanaka (People-of-the-swamps)
Their home is the northeast of the old kingdom of Imerina around Lake Alaotra and they have much in common with the Merina. They are fishers, rice growers and poultry raisers. Swamps have been drained to make vast rice-fields cultivated with modern machinery and methods. They have a special rotation of *fady* days.

THE VAZIMBA

Vazimba is the name given to the earliest inhabitants of Madagascar, pastoralists of the central plateaux, who were displaced or absorbed by later immigrants. Once thought to be pre-Indonesian aboriginals from Africa, it is now generally accepted that they were survivors of the earliest Austronesian immigrants who were pushed to the west by later arrivals.

Vazimba come into both legends and history of the Malagasy. Vazimba tombs are now places of pilgrimage where sacrifices are made for favours and cures. It is *fady* to step over such a tomb. Vazimba are also thought to haunt certain springs and rocks, and offerings may be made here. They are the ancestral guardians of the soil.

Tanala (People-of-the-forest)
These are traditionally forest-dwellers, living inland from Manakara, and are rice and coffee growers. Their houses are usually built on stilts. The Tanala are divided into two groups: the Ikongo in the south and the Menabe in the north. The Ikongo are an independent people and never submitted to Merina domination, in contrast to the Menabe. Burial customs include keeping the corpse for up to a month. Coffins are made from large trees to which sacrifices are sometimes made when they are cut down. The Ikongo usually bury their dead in the forest and may mark a tree to show the spot.

Some recent authorities dispute that the Tanala exist as a separate ethnic group.

Tsimihety (Those-who-do-not-cut-their-hair)
The refusal to cut their hair (to show mourning on the death of a Sakalava king) was to demonstrate their independence. They are an energetic and vigorous people in the north-central area and are spreading west. The oldest maternal uncle occupies an important position.

Vezo (Fishing people)
More usually referred to as Vezo-Sakalava, they are not generally recognised as a separate tribe but as a clan of the Sakalava. They live on the coast in the region of Morondava in the west to Faux Cap in the south. They use little canoes hollowed out from tree trunks and fitted with one outrigger pole and a small rectangular sail. In these frail but stable craft they go far out to sea. The Vezo are also noted for their tombs, which are graves dug into the ground surrounded by wooden palisades, the main posts of which are crowned by erotic wooden carved figures.

Zafimaniry
A clan of some 15,000 people distributed in about 100 villages in the forests between the Betsileo and Tanala areas southeast of Ambositra. They are known for their wood carvings and sculpture, and are descended from people from the *Hauts Plateaux* who established themselves there early in the 19th century. The Zafimaniry are thus interesting to historians as they continue the forms of housing and decoration of past centuries. Their houses, which are made from vegetable fibres and wood with bamboo walls and roofs, have no nails and can be taken down and moved from one village to another.

St Marians
The population of Île Ste Marie (Nosy Boraha) is mixed. Although Indonesian in origin there has been influence from both Arabs and European pirates of different nationalities.

In the last few years there have been several anthropological books published in English about the people of Madagascar. See *Further reading*.

The tribes may differ but a Malagasy proverb shows their feeling of unity: *Ny olombelona toy ny molo-bilany, ka iray mihodidina ihany*; 'Men are like the lip of the cooking pot which forms just one circle'.

LANGUAGE

The Indonesian origin of the Malagasy people shows strongly in their language which is spoken, with regional variations of dialect, throughout the island. (Words for domestic animals, however, are derived from Kiswahili, indicating that the early settlers, sensibly enough, did not bring animals with them in their outrigger canoes.) Malagasy is a remarkably rich language, full of images, metaphors and proverbs. Literal translations of Malagasy words and phrases are often very poetic. 'Dusk' is *Maizim-bava vilany*, 'Darken the mouth of the cooking pot'; 'two or three in the morning' is *Misafo helika ny kary*, 'When the wild cat washes itself'. The richness of the language means that there are few English words that can be translated to a single word in Malagasy, and vice versa. An example given by Leonard Fox in his book on the poetry of Madagascar, *Hainteny*, is *miala mandry*; *miala* means 'go out/go away' and *mandry* means 'lie down/go to sleep'. Together, however, they mean 'to spend the night away from home, and yet be back in the early morning as if never having been away'! No wonder there is no practical Malagasy/English dictionary for travellers!

There is, however, an excellent cassette and accompanying phrase book which will enable you to learn the rudiments of the language without becoming

---

MORE THAN JUST WORDS

Janice Booth

At Nosy Komba I was the first off the boat when it hit shore; and was still in the water when a girl – about eight years old – waded up and started trying to sell me little clay birds. She was expressionless, running through obviously familiar 'patter' in very basic French. I bought one.

After I'd been on the island for a few hours she came back, not recognising me from the first sale, and tried again. I explained slowly, in a mixture of simple French and sign language, that I'd already bought a bird, that I liked it, and that I didn't need another. She listened intently, her eyes locked on mine, absorbing every word and gesture. I could see the effort she was making to understand – she really *wanted* to. When I'd finished, just to make sure she'd got it right, she pointed a small finger questioningly at herself, as if to ask 'and was it really *my* bird that you bought?' When I nodded she broke into a most radiant smile, eyes still holding mine, as if we had become conspirators in some shared pleasure. She was so happy to have understood, and skipped away, still smiling.

On our way back from seeing the lemurs, girls were emerging from every alley with tablecloths, pestering us to buy. One spoke reasonable French and we were a little apart from the crowd, so I asked if she could tell me something – on my walk I'd heard some creature cry, but I couldn't identify it. I made the sound; and she unfolded one tablecloth and pointed to an embroidered bird. Trees and fruit were also embroidered on the cloth, and she pointed them out and named them for me one by one. I said the island was beautiful, and she glowed. I explained that I really didn't want a tablecloth but was so pleased to have the information and felt it was lucky that I'd asked someone knowledgeable. She looked so much happier with this than if I'd been 'just another tourist' buying goods.

helmed by its complexities: *Malagasy Basics* by Rasoanaivo Hanitrarivo. The author is better known as Hanitra Anderson, the leader of Tarika, the internationally known group of Malagasy musicians. *Malagasy Basics* is available from Bradt Publications or from FMS in London; tel: 0181 340 9651, email: froots@cityscape.co.uk. Another very useful book is *Guide to Communication: Malagasy, Français, English* by James Yount. This is available in the Librairie de Madagascar in Antananarivo.

Learning, or even using, the Malagasy language may seem a challenging prospect to the first-time visitor. Place-names may be 15 characters long (because they usually have a literal meaning, such as Ranomafana: Hot water), with erratic syllable stress. However, as a courtesy to the Malagasy people you should learn a few Malagasy words and phrases rather than communicating in the language of their former colonial rulers. That is not to say that a reasonable grasp of French won't ease your travels considerably, and will also enable you to communicate with the educated Malagasy. For rural people and children, however, a smattering of Malagasy works wonders. Frances Kerridge writes: 'I attempted to learn some Malagasy using *Malagasy Basics*. I found the excellent book and cassette a tremendous help. Just being able to pronounce Malagasy names, and to use and recognise nouns, impressed my hosts and friends, and endeared me to strangers that I met who I felt were all too used to impatient tourists shouting English or French.'

See page 346 for some Malagasy vocabulary.

DID YOU KNOW?

· Earthquakes mean the whales are bathing their children.
· If a woman maintains a bending posture when arranging eggs in a nest, the chickens will have crooked necks.
· If the walls of a house incline towards the south, the wife will be the stronger one; if they incline towards the north it will be the husband.
· Burning a knot on a piece of string causes the knees to grow big.

Chapter Three

Natural History

Most people are drawn to Madagascar by its flora and fauna. This is 'nature's laboratory', where evolution has taken a different route.

The reason so many endemic species have evolved in Madagascar goes back to the dawn of history. It is thought that in the early Cretaceous era a huge land-mass known as Gondwanaland began to break up and form the present continents of Africa and Madagascar, Asia, South America and Australasia. The phenomenon of continental drift explains why some Malagasy plants and animals have their closest relatives in South America and Asia but not Africa. The boas, for instance, occur only in South America and

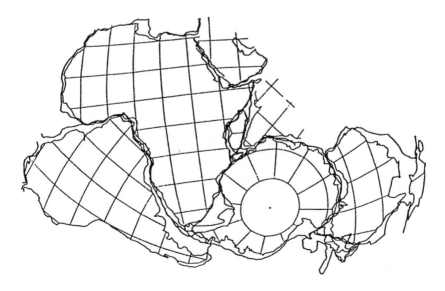

Gondwanaland and the fit of the southern continents

Madagascar, and the urania moth and six plant families are also limited to these two places.

Madagascar broke away from Africa as much as 165 million years ago, during the time of the dinosaurs. It is thought to have reached its present position about 120 million years ago. No one knows what reptiles and other early forms of life were the original inhabitants but mammals had yet to evolve, so the lemurs, tenrecs, and other unique families most probably arrived on rafts of vegetation. Not many made it – notable absentees are the large carnivores such as big cats, dogs or bears, and their prey: deer, antelope and other hoofed animals.

Once these original colonists had established themselves there was little need for evolutionary change since there were no large carnivores to threaten their existence and the thickly forested island provided food without competition. Thus many of Madagascar's unusual creatures are referred to as 'living fossils'.

Man arrived some 2,000 years ago. Only 1,000 years later nearly two dozen species of fauna were extinct. Of these, 15 were lemurs, some the size of gorillas, hanging from the trees like sloths or browsing on the forest floor. There were dwarf hippos, tortoises larger than any known today, and the elephant bird (*Aepyornis maximus*) which stood ten feet high. Man was probably largely responsible for the extinction of these animals through hunting and destruction of habitat, although climatic changes also played their part.

Madagascar has an amazing percentage of endemic species: it is said that of the 200,000 living things so far identified there, 150,000 are found nowhere else. Of the world's 400 flowering plant families, 200 grow only here. There

The rukh (roc), as visualised by an artist in 1595.

are seven species of baobab (compared with one in Africa), and new b
and zoological discoveries are being made every year. Most scientific
expeditions to Madagascar find new species and many discover new genera:
I used to try to give exact numbers in this guide but have given up – it keeps
changing. There are approximately 50 different lemurs, around 300 species
of reptile and the same number of frogs... but one thing you can rely on:
whatever species you are observing in Madagascar, you are unlikely to have
seen it elsewhere.

GEOLOGY

The main geological features of Madagascar are a Pre-Cambrian crystalline
basement (eastern two-thirds of the island) overlaid with laterite, a sedimentary
region in the south and west (Jurassic, Cretaceous and Tertiary) and volcanic
outcrops. The Ankaratra mountains near Antananarivo are of volcanic origin.
There are no active volcanoes but in the highlands there are many hot springs,
craters and ash cones.

Millions of years of weathering have produced the smooth granite mountains
of the southern highlands, the eroded sandstone shapes of Isalo in the southwest,
and the extraordinary spikes of the *tsingy* or limestone karst.

A great variety of precious and semi-precious gemstones are found in
Madagascar, including several types of tourmaline, amethyst, citrine, rhodonite,
celestine, amazonite, Labradorite (moonstone), iolite, kornerupine, sphene,
spinel, chrysoberyl, rose quartz, milky quartz, and grossular garnets (known
as cinnamon stone in Madagascar). There is a rare, dark blue variety of
aquamarine (beryl); and the finest Morganite in the world comes from
Madagascar. The largest crystal ever found was in Madagascar: a beryl measuring
18 metres long and 3.5 metres in diameter; it weighed about 380 tons.

This enormous diversity of beautiful minerals may be found in the markets
and shops of Madagascar in the form of colourful Solitaire sets and similar
souvenirs. There are tours available specialising in minerals and gemstones;
well worth considering if you are a rock-hound.

TYPES OF VEGETATION

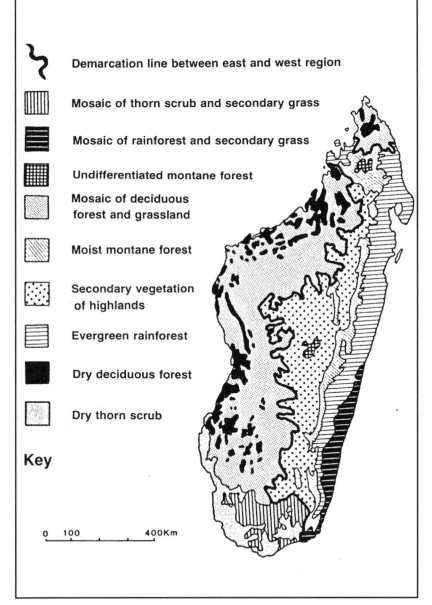

Key

Demarcation line between east and west region.

Mosaic of thorn scrub and secondary grass

Mosaic of rainforest and secondary grass

Undifferentiated montane forest

Mosaic of deciduous
forest and grassland

Moist montane forest

Secondary vegetation
of highlands

Evergreen rainforest

Dry deciduous forest

Dry thorn scrub

0   100   400Km

FLORA

A glance at the statistics will warm a botanist's heart: Madagascar has around 10,000 species whilst Great Britain has only 1,750. The large number of species is due to the dramatically different climatic zones, and around 80% of the flora is found nowhere else in the world. Unlike the fauna, however, which looks unique even to the unscientific eye, a large proportion of Madagascar's vegetation appears familiar to the non-botanist. Having worked out a successful blueprint in other parts of the world, Nature has come up with the same basic design to fit the different climates: water-retaining plants for arid zones and tall trees with buttress roots for the rainforest.

The account below is extracted from a more detailed survey of Madagascar's flora, kindly written by Gordon and Merlin Munday.

Flora: an overview

You may be surprised to discover that you already know a few Madagascar plants – many house or florist's plants come from Madagascar. These include 'crown of thorns' (*Euphorbia millii*), with its bright red flowers and sharp spines, 'flaming Katy' (*Kalanchoe blossfeldiana*) with brilliant red and long-lasting flowers, 'panda plant' (*Kalanchoe tomentosa*), 'Madagascar dragon tree' (*Dracaena marginata*), 'Madagascar jasmine' (*Stephanotis floribunda*) – the bridal bouquet with waxy, white, heavily scented flowers, the 'polka dot' plant (*Hypoestis phyllostachya*), and 'velvet leaf' (*Kalanchoe beharensis*). Then there is the poinciana (*Poinciana regia*) or flamboyant with its brilliant orange flowers.

Few of Madagascar's many unusual species have been given English names, but one Malagasy plant name has made its way into our language: raffia. The palm *Raphia pedunculata* has been a mainstay for craft workers and gardeners.

Of about 400 flowering plant families worldwide almost 200 are known to occur in Madagascar. There are eight endemic families and 18% of the genera and nearly 80% of the species are also endemic.

Evidence suggests that primitive flowering plants (Angiosperms) originated in the western part of Gondwanaland, probably in the early Cretaceous period, and that subsequently they spread north while diversifying, leading to the establishment of flora in the two large supercontinents. Africa has many genera in common with Madagascar, but individual species are quite distinct. For example, none of the 300 African aloe species is found in Madagascar, and the 60 found in Madagascar are endemic; and the 'succulent' euphorbias are here more woody than succulent. Africa has only a few hundred species of orchid, whilst Madagascar claims around a thousand. Nevertheless, many plants such as the African violet (*Viola abyssinica*) and *Cardamine africana* are widely distributed and common to both land masses. Mangroves, as one would expect of water disseminated plants, are all identical with those found on the East African coast, whereas Madagascar's endemic palms – 16 genera – almost all show affinities with those of Asia and South America.

ORCHIDS IN MADAGASCAR

Johan and Clare Hermans
Illustrated by Cherry-Anne Lavrih

Like so many other living things on the island, the orchids of Madagascar are extremely varied and most are endemic. Well over 800 different species have been recorded so far and pressure on their habitats may cause many to expire before ever being found. The orchids have adapted to every possible habitat, including the spiny forest and the cool highland mountain ranges.

Compared with the tropical cloud forests of South and Central America, orchids are not very easily found in Madagascar; good habitat sites are scarce, and even there plants will not be plentiful; also many are small if not insignificant. The main flowering season is during January, February and March, just when the climate is less benevolent to visitors. However something will be flowering most times of the year and their scarcity will enhance the delight of finding an intricate, fragrant *Angraecum* orchid in its natural environment.

Plant taxonomists have not made it easy to learn the different orchid names: *Angraecum*, *Aeranthes* and *Aerangis* are all too easily confused in the big mass of white, star-shaped flowers found in Madagascar. The following may help to unravel some of the initial confusion.

The eastern coastal area

A great number of truly exciting orchids can be seen in this area; it is the habitat of large *Angraecums*, *Eulophiellas* and *Cymbidiellas*. Most orchids here are epiphytes – they live on tree branches or stems with their roots anchoring the plants and although they scramble over their host, collecting moisture and nutrients, they are not parasites.

Angraecum eburneum is frequently seen in flower from September to May. The thick leathery leaves form a half metre wide fan shape; the flower stems reach above the leaves carrying a number of large greenish white fragrant flowers. Our first close encounter with a Malagasy orchid was a gigantic

Angraecum flowering plant of *eburneum* planted in front of our bungalow at Hotel Soanambo on Nosy Boraha (Île St. Marie). Aeroflot jet-lag promptly vanished.

The Comet Orchid, *Angraecum sesquipedale*, is one of the most striking: it flowers from June to November; the plants are similar to *eburneum* but slightly more compact. Individual flowers can be almost 26cm across and over 30cm long, including its long nectary spur at the back of the flower. The spur is characteristic for the *Angraecoid* orchids. The flower was described by Charles Darwin at the end of the 19th century when he predicted that there would be a moth with a very long tongue that could reach down to the nectar at the bottom of the spur. This idea was ridiculed by his contemporaries but in 1903 a moth with a proboscis of over

Aeranthes

30cm was found in Madagascar!

Aeranthes plants look similar to *Angraecum*. Their spider-like greenish flowers are suspended from a long thin stem, gently nodding in the seabreeze. Most *Aeranthes* flower in January–February.

Eulophiella roempleriana (L'Orchidée Rose) is now extremely rare. One of the few remaining, gigantic, almost two metre high plants can be seen on Île aux Nattes (Nosy Natto) a small island off Île Sainte Marie, where one of the local entrepreneurs will show you the site for a small fee. The large, deep-pink flowers normally appear from October onwards.

Cymbidiella orchids are also very striking, they generally flower from October to January; *Cymbidiella pardalina* with its huge crimson lip, cohabits with a stag-horn fern; *Cymbidiella falcigera*, with large black spotted yellow flowers, prefers the exclusive company of the raffia palm.

Cymbidiella

The highlands

The Highlands of Madagascar with their cooler and more seasonal climate are inhabited by numerous terrestrial orchids, growing in soil or leaf litter; underground tubers produce deciduous leaves and flower stems.

Cynorkis is a semi-epiphyte growing in moist shady places; the squat plants carrying bright pinkish-purple flowers on the roadside by the Ranomafana reserve are a fine representative of the genus. The flowers are not to be confused with a *Streptocarpus* growing on the same dripping rocks. Epiphytic orchids like *Angraecum* and *Aeranthes* are also common in the Highlands.

Jumellea

Aerangis plants are instantly recognisable by their shiny, dark green foliage. The flowers superficially resemble those of *Angraecum* but they are often much smaller, carried on elegant racemes. The plants are commonly seen in the wet shade of the rainforest reserves of Perinet and Ranomafana.

Aerangis

Jumellea are again similar but have a more narrow, folded-back single flower on thin stems.

Bulbophyllum orchids are easily missed by the untrained eye; their rounded, plump pseudo-bulbs are often seen on moss covered trees, they are always worthwhile investigating; small gem-like blooms may be nestled amongst the foliage.

Oeonia with its huge white lip and two red dots in its throat can sometimes be seen rambling amongst the undergrowth.

The apparently bare higher peaks of the *Hauts Plateaux*, like Ibity near Antsirabe, also contain a very specialised community of orchids; the thick-leaved, sun-loving *Angraecoid* and *Bulbophyllum* species share the rock faces with succulents.

One of the best and easiest places to see orchids, such as *Angraecum*, *Cymbidiella* and *Phaius*, is in hotel and private gardens but one must be aware that these domesticated collections may contain the odd foreign interloper; orchids from the Orient and South America are grown for their aesthetic value, the flowers being often bigger and brighter than the native plants.

Bulbophyllum

It is very important to stress that on no account should plants be collected or bought from street traders; the orchids are unlikely to survive and export is also restricted. The customs officers at Ivato have no trouble detecting plants.

It is only possible to give a taste of the subject in these few pages; more information on the native orchids of Madagascar can be obtained from more specialised literature.

Where to find orchids

Phaius

Orchid hunters recommend the following places: Manjakatompo forest station (a day trip from Tana); recommended orchid guide: Edward. Périnet; guide: Desiré (Desy). Mahavalona (Foulepointe); this is the only recommended place in the Toamasina area, apart from Pangalanes. Île Sainte Marie and Île aux Nattes. Montagne d'Ambre.

Orchids for export

Orchid enthusiasts may contact Alfred Razafindratsira, a botanist who grows and exports a large variety of Malagasy orchids from his orchid nursery in Antananarivo. He will arrange all necessary export permits. His address is BP 198, Antananarivo 101.

Further reading

Flore de Madagascar. Henri Humbert, Editor. Tanarive Imprimerie Officielle, Madagascar, 1941. 49e. Famille. – Orchidées by H Perrier de La Bathie. Now very difficult to obtain and incomplete.

An Introduction to the Cultivated Angraecoid Orchids of Madagascar.
Fred E Hillerman & Arthur W Holst. Timber Press, Oregon: 1986. 302pp, 95 line drawings, 36 colour plates, maps. Large tome on a small selection of Malagasy plants.

The Orchid Review. Johan & Clare Hermans. RHS. 1994-95. Various articles.

Malagasy Orchids, an annotated Bibliography. J & C Hermans. Privately published, 1994. For the seriously addicted (available from Bradt Publications).

Regional flora and vegetation and where to see them

The island's vegetation falls naturally into two regions: East and West. Botanists further divide the country into Domains (an uneasy translation of the French *domaine*) giving a broad classification in terms of geography, climate and vegetation.

The eastern region

This coincides with the climatic eastern region but includes the Sambirano Domain and Nosy Be. The Central Domain is also included; this is the backbone of the island with erosion creating deep gullies, or *lavaka*. Heavy storms carry away the soil – thin clay over friable sedimentary layers – made vulnerable by tree clearance. Vegetation of the region is classified as evergreen forest, mosaic of rainforest and secondary grass, moist montane forest, secondary vegetation of the highlands, and montane bushland and scrub.

Evergreen forest Occurs below 800m. The rainfall is generally over 2,000mm and in some places up to 3,500mm. The vegetation is stratified into layers; the upper canopy is dense allowing little light to penetrate. Thus competition on the forest floor is intense and the understorey sparse. Many trees have buttress roots or stilt-like aerial roots. Epiphytes, including orchids and ferns, are abundant.

The Madagascar rainforest is distinct from corresponding forests in Africa in having a higher species diversity, a lower main canopy and an absence of large emergent trees. Tree density is also three times greater than comparable rainforests in other continents. Families that form part of the upper canopy include Euphorbiaceae (nearly all with milky latex sap), Sapindaceae (woody lianas), Rubiaceae (including wild coffee), Ebenaceae, including the genus *Diospyros* (with 97 species, one of which is the true ebony), and palms (Palmae).

Tourist-accessible lowland rainforest can best be seen on the Masoala Peninsula and Nosy Mangabe.

Île Sainte Marie is botanically rewarding. Here you can see the spectacular comet orchid, *Angraecum sesquipedale* (see page 42). Features of the coastal landscape on the island are large Barringtonia trees on the shoreline, with 'bishop's hat' fruits, and coconut palms leaning into the sea which disperses their fruit.

Mosaic of rainforest and secondary grass An outstanding example of a successful indigenous secondary forest tree is the traveller's palm or traveller's tree (*Ravenala madagascariensis*), the symbol of Madagascar and the logo of Air Madagascar. It gets its name from the relief it affords a thirsty traveller: water is stored in the base of its leaves and can be released with a panga blow. The fan arrangement of the leaves is extremely decorative. The Ravenala is, in fact, not a palm but is related to the *Strelitzia* or bird-of-paradise flower. It often occurs in combination with Pandanus (screw pine), which is somewhat like a palm, and Typhonodorum, which grows in or by water and has huge spinach-like leaves.

Other indigenous vegetation does less well in competition with introduced grasses, ferns and shrubs which take over after fire. Indigenous forest species able to colonise the edges of cut forests include some useful to man such as *canarium*, a valuable all-purpose wood and a source of essential oils; croton, from which drugs are derived; and two guavas, *Psiadia altissima* and *Haronga madagascariensis*, which is also the source of a valuable drug, Harunganin, used for stomach disorders.

This type of vegetation (unfortunately) can be seen anywhere near inhabited places by the east coast, where the landscape is degraded as a result of fire and dominated by grass. There are few trees.

Moist montane forest Also called montane rainforest, this generally occurs between 800m and 1,300m but can go as high as 2,000m if the conditions are right. The canopy is about 5m lower than the lowland forest, and there is more undergrowth, including some temperate genera such as *Labiatae* and *Impatiens*. There are abundant epiphytes, ferns and mosses, and large lianas and bamboo. As the altitude increases, so the height of the canopy decreases, letting in more light and permitting the growth of epiphytes and shrubby, herbaceous undergrowth with an abundance of moss. Leaves become tougher, with a thicker cuticle to help retain water.

Trees at this altitude include *Dalbergia* (rosewood) and *Weinmannia*, a useful light timber; species of palm and tree fern grow in lower areas.

The most accessible example of medium-altitude moist montane forest is Périnet. The upland variety can best be seen in Montagne d'Ambre National Park, and high-altitude moist montane forest is best shown on the slopes of the Marojejy massif (not open to tourists).

SCIENTIFIC CLASSIFICATION

Since many animals and plants in Madagascar have yet to be given English names, I have made much use of the Latin or scientific name. For those not familiar with these and the associated terminology, here is a brief guide:

Having been separated into broad **classes** like mammals (mammalia), angiosperms (angiospermae) – flowering plants – etc, animals and plants are narrowed down into an **order**, such as Primates or Monocotyledons. The next division is **family**: Lemur (*Lemuridae*) and Orchid (*Orchidaceae*) continue the examples above. These are the general names that everyone knows, and you are quite safe to say 'in the lemur family' or 'a type of orchid'. There are also sub-families, such as the 'true lemurs' and 'the indri sub-family' which includes sifakas. Then come **genera** (**genus** in singular) followed by **species**, and the Latin names here will be less familiar-sounding. It is these two names that are combined in the scientific name precisely to identify the animal or plant. So *Lemur catta* and *Angraecum sesquipedale* will be recognisable whatever the nationality of the person you are talking to. We call them ring-tailed lemur and comet orchid, the French say maki and orchidée comète. With a scientific name up your sleeve there is no confusion.

Highland vegetation (the Central Domain) The forest that formerly covered the *Hauts Plateaux* has been replaced by grassland. This is relieved by granite outcrops which harbour succulents. These hills are called 'Inselbergs'. Pachypodium species occur in this environment, with, among others, aloes and euphorbia.

The most rewarding accessible area is probably the Ibity range of mountains near Antsirabe.

High-altitude montane forest Beginning at 1,300m and extending to 2,300m, the vegetation here is shaped by lower, more varied temperatures, wind, sun and rain. The forest resembles tall scrub with small, tough leaves. Moss and lichens clothe branches and cover the ground up to 30cm, and provide anchorage for epiphytic ferns and orchids. Ericaceous species predominate in the undergrowth.

The massifs of Marojejy and Andringitra provide the best example, along with the botanical reserve of Ambohitantely.

Tapia forest This is the local name for the dominant species *Uapaca bojeri*, a tree with a thick, creviced bark which is fire resistant. The forest is on the western slopes of the central highlands, with a drier climate than the Eastern Domain's. The impenetrable vegetation appears similar to Mediterranean cork oak forests. There are few epiphytes or ground mosses.

Isalo National Park has tapia groves and also various succulents on its sandstone outcrops.

Montane bushland and thicket Characterised by a single stratum, up to six metres, of impenetrable branching evergreen woody plants growing above 2,000m, and interesting for trees belonging to the daisy family (Compositae).

None of Madagascar's high mountains is easily accessible. Andringitra offers the best possibility for a visit.

The western region
Dry deciduous forest The flora is extensive and varied but of lower density and less rich than in the moister eastern forests. Deciduous trees grow to a height of 12 to 15m with some emergent trees up to 25m. There are abundant lianas, and shrubby undergrowth, but no ferns, palms or mosses covering the forest floor, and few orchids.

Dry deciduous forest grows on clay or sandy soil. The latter includes the luxuriant gallery forests along rivers where tamarind trees predominate. Away from water, it is the baobabs that take precedence. A third environment, calcareous plateaux, produces a lower forest canopy with fewer lianas and evergreens. Trees and shrubs with swollen trunks or stems (*pachycauly*) are much in evidence.

The Forestry Station of Ampijoroa is an easily accessible area of dry deciduous forest, as is Kirindy. Harder to reach, but rewarding when you get

BAOBABS, AUSTRALIA AND GONDWANALAND

The Australian baobab is closely related to the Madagascar species. Some botanists think that the Australian *Adansonia gibbosa* survived on this continent when Gondwanaland broke up, but it is now generally believed that the baobab evolved after the continents broke up and that the seeds spread east on Indian Ocean tides. Botanical evidence of the links between Australia and Madagascar have also been discovered in the Undara Lava Tubes in the Gulf Savannah country of Queensland. These huge channels are all that remain of the largest volcanic explosion ever to occur on earth – 200,000 years ago – and are the closest thing on earth to the sinuous ridges of the moon. Inside the tubes are plants found only in Madagascar and Australia.

The baobab

Ed Fletcher

Baobabs occur in Madagascar, Africa and Australia: one species in Australia, one in Africa, and seven in Madagascar (including the African species). Many myths and much folklore have been created about baobabs; in Africa it is commonly called the upside-down-tree, the legend being that the devil plucked up the baobab, thrust its branches into the earth and left its roots in the air. It has been described as 'A Caliban of a tree, a grizzled distorted old goblin with a girth of a giant, the hide of a rhinoceros, twiggy fingers clutching at empty air'.

Baobabs can reach an age of several hundred years. Age calculations have been carried out on mature baobabs using a formula of rate of growth, size and growing conditions in areas of low rainfall; some baobabs could be over 2,000 years old.

Like some other 'bottle trees', the baobab is a succulent and able to store water in its trunk.

The baobab has many traditional uses: bark fibre is used to make rope, baskets, snares, fibre cloth, musical instrument strings, and waterproof hats. One characteristic of the baobab, which most other trees do not possess, is that stripping the bark will not usually kill the tree: the bark is highly resistant to trauma, particularly fire, and will regenerate if left for five to ten years. Wood pulp makes strong coarse paper, floats, trays and platters. The fresh leaves are sometimes used as a medicinal infusion. Seeds are a source of food high in protein and oil, and may be pounded into a paste similar to peanut-butter, or traded for oil extraction. The seed pulp is commonly eaten and is high in vitamin C; the empty husks can be used for various utensils.

Listed below are the species of baobab found in Madagascar; all except *A. digitata* are endemic.

Adansonia grandidieri Malagasy name: *Reniala* (mother of the forest).
These are very large trees which, when mature, have an almost cylindrical trunk with reddish-grey bark. (When young they are shaped somewhat like an upside-down parsnip.) The characteristic horizontal branches produce a noticeably flat-topped crown, emerging high above the canopy of undisturbed forest, so that bats can easily fly in to pollinate them. Flowering is in the dry season, May to August, producing a large white upturned flower with yellow stamens. It has a restricted distribution in deciduous forests particularly on flood plains and on river banks in southwest Madagascar. The Sakalava regard the fruits as a valuable source of food, harvesting them and also the edible seeds which produce a valuable oil. The sheer vertical trunks are scaled by means of wooden spikes driven into the bark. The best-known

examples of these baobabs are those growing near Morondava, notably the 'Avenue of the Baobabs'. This area is heavily cultivated, but many large baobabs also remain in the fields. The best surviving populations are in the vicinity of Morombe, particularly between the Mangoky river and Lac Ihotry.

Adansonia madagascariensis Malagasy names: *Bozy, M'bois, Renida, Za, Zabe.*
This is one of the most beautiful of all baobab species. Its trunk generally has little swelling, being cylindrical or tapering from the base to the branches. The tree ranges from 10 to 30 metres in height. Flowering is in March to April, when it produces dark red flowers. This baobab is distributed from northwest to north Madagascar in dry deciduous forests. Around Antsiranana it can be found within metres of the coastal high-water mark, on the road to Ramena and in the town itself close to the abattoir.

Adansonia perrieri Malagasy name: *Bozy.*
The trees vary from 5 to 30 metres in height. The trunk is usually cylindrical or tapering, with greyish smooth bark, and has a yellow flower. It was only discovered in 1960 on the plateau of Ankarana, growing in mid-altitude rainforest and deciduous forests.

Adansonia rubrostipa (formerly *A. fony*) Malagasy names: *Fony, Boringy, Ringy, Za, Zamena, Reniala.*
Trees vary from 3 to 25 metres in height, the trunk usually bottle-shaped, with a marked constriction beneath the branches and reddish-brown bark. The leaves have a characteristic serrated margin. These baobabs grow in the dry deciduous forests of the west and south. Close to Lac Tsimanampetsotsa and Ifaty they are found in spiny forest but further north, close to Morondava, they are the dominant species in the western deciduous forests of Andranomena, Marofandelia, and Kirindy.

Adansonia suarezensis Malagasy name: *Bozy.*
This species has a smooth trunk, usually tapered from the base and swelling at the branches. The height varies from 20 to 30 metres. The flowers are large and white. The trees are distributed in an extremely restricted area in the deciduous forests around the Bay of Antsiranana (Diego-Suarez), growing close to the sea in degraded scrubland. They are also found in the Beantely forest close to Antsahampano. The conservation status of this baobab is critical.

Adansonia za Malagasy names: *Bontona, Bozy, Za,* and *Zabe.*
The cylindrical trunk tapers from the base to the top, making it easily confused with *A. madagascariensis.* The height varies between 10 and 39 metres and the flower is yellow tinged with red. Flowering occurs from November to January. It is the most widespread of the Malagasy species, and very variable in appearance, growing in arid conditions from extreme south to northwest Madagascar. This baobab is sometimes used for the zebu cattle of the area in times of severe drought. After the tree is felled, the bark is peeled off to enable the zebu to feed on the water-saturated fibre (the wet weight of this baobab is 56lb/cu ft, whilst the dry weight is 13lb/cu ft).

Adansonia digitata Malagasy names: *Bontona, Ringy, Za, Zabe, Sefo* and *Vontona* (which means 'the swollen one').
This is the baobab that Madagascar has in common with Africa. It has a large trunk up to 15 metres in diameter which can contain up to 30,000 gallons of water. It is a very large spreading tree with an irregular crown and a large, white flower. It is thought to have been introduced from Africa by Arab traders who moved extensively around the Indian Ocean during the 14th and 15th centuries, perhaps carrying the baobab fruit to prevent scurvy. It is often found in the central square of Sakalava villages; there is a famous one in Mahajanga, reputed to be 700 years old.

there, is Ankarana which has a dense combination of dry forest, savannah, and plants specially adapted to the pinnacles, or calcareous karst (*tsingy*).

Deciduous thicket ('spiny forest') Madagascar's most strikingly different landscape comes into this category, where Didiereaceae, an endemic family, are associated with tree Euphorbias. There are some evergreens here, probably because of sea mists bathing the plants. Heavy morning dews are a boon to the local people who collect the precious water with 'dew ladles'. Thickets vary in height from three to six metres, and with their thorns are impenetrable. Emergent trees are mostly baobabs.

Didiereaceae show some resemblance to the Boojum cactus (Fouquieriaceae) of the southwest USA and Mexico. There are four genera, exclusive to the west and south of Madagascar: *Alluaudia* (six species), *Alluaudiopsis* (two species), *Didierea* (two species), and *Decaryia* (one species). Examples of the tree euphorbia of the thicket are *E stenoclada* (thorny, the latex used for caulking pirogues), *E enterophora* (thornless, up to 20 metres), and *E plagiantha*, also thornless, and characterised by peeling yellowish-brown bark.

Very conspicuous are the 'barrel' and 'bottle' trees with their massive trunks adapted for water storage. *Adansonia*, *Moringa*, and *Pachypodium* are the genera.

Leaf succulents are well represented, with several species of tall (three to four metre) aloes. The shrivelled redundant leaves wrap the stem and give some resistance to fire. Look also for the genus *Kalanchoe*. One of the most interesting species, *K beauverdii* (two to three metres long), forms buds around the leaf margins, each of which then becomes a tiny daughter plant, thus giving it great survival powers.

These are only a few examples from well over a thousand species belonging to genera of widely different plant families, which nevertheless show much resemblance to one another in their methods of circumventing drought. After rain, leaves and flowers form fast and in some species the flowers even form before rain, giving maximum time for fruit formation and dispersal before the next drought.

The best place to view the spiny forest is near Toliara along the Tolagnaro–Ambovombe road, and in Berenty reserve. Beza-Mahafaly is also an excellent example of this type of forest.

Secondary grassland After the excitement of the spiny forest this is inevitably a let-down, but inescapable as about 80% of the western region is covered with secondary or wooded grassland, burnt annually. Two species of palm, *Medemia nobilis* and *Borassus madagascariensis* (both riverside species), have settled in this habitat.

Mangrove This is an environment of shrubs or small trees growing in muddy lagoons, river deltas, bays or shores, their roots washed by salt or brackish water. Mangroves are found mainly on the west coast and are characterised by stilt-like roots, some of which emerge above the water to take in oxygen.

Some have another advantage because their seeds germinate in the fruit while remaining on the tree (viviparity); the fruit then drops into the mud with its plantlet well on the way to independence. There are three families (nine species) in Madagascar. In the Toliara region the contrast of spiny vegetation inland and a bright green band of mangroves is particularly striking. Mangroves are economically important to the people for various aspects of fish or shellfish farming. The wood is hard and very dense but not very durable, and is used for poles and planks and also firewood. The bark is good for tanning leather.

Apart from the Toliara region, there is a population of *Avicennia marina* in the Betsiboka estuary and Nosy Be has the same species in a much smaller area.

ETHNOBOTANY IN MADAGASCAR

Ethnobotany is the study of the traditional knowledge and uses of plants by local peoples, for example for food, medicines, fibre.

Already mentioned in this book (page 48-9) are some of the many uses for various parts of the baobabs. The wealth of palm species on the island are equally valuable, providing wood and thatch for house construction, and leaf fibre for basketry, hat-making and raffia cloth. Some have edible palm-hearts and fruit, and other uses such as for medicine, irrigation pipes, brooms, blowpipes, etc.

Most Malagasy today still rely to some extent on wild-harvested plants for their medicines. However, with increasing deforestation, urbanisation and an aspiration to Western values, many are now turning to modern drugs which they can ill afford, and which are often inappropriately prescribed by street vendors. Meanwhile much of the traditional plant lore is in danger of being lost. Since ethnobotanists have a joint interest in both the people and the plants that they study, they are well-placed to apply their research to help meet the needs of local communities through education, health-care and marketing in a way which promotes conservation of the plants and their habitats. Among the ethnobotanical projects now under way in Madagascar are:

The Manangarivo Project WWF-funded health-care service, using a combination of traditional and Western medicine to treat disease, and to evaluate the efficiency of this treatment. Contact Nat Quansah, WWF, BP 8511, Antananarivo.

Masoala Project Ethnobotanical studies taking place in conjunction with the establishment of the new National Park. Contact Philip Gallery, Wildlife Conservation Society, BP 27, Antalaha 206.

Ankaranfantsika Project An ethnobotanical inventory of the Strict Nature Reserve, funded by Conservation International. BP 5178 Antananarivo.

Projet Renala Working, in association with the Royal Botanic Gardens (Kew), with the Mikea people of the southwest. Among the plans are a mobile, integrated health-care service and various local conservation initiatives. Contact Jim Bond, Manguzi Hospital, P/Bag X301, KwaNgwanase, 3973 South Africa.

A LAYMAN'S GUIDE TO LEMURS

Unless you are a keen natural historian, sorting out Madagascar's 50 varieties *(taxa)* of lemur is challenging. The information below, together with the scientific classification (see box on page 46), should help you put names to faces; and if you know in which region/reserve the most common species are found you'll be better able to decide what that leaping animal high in the trees is likely to be.

DIURNAL LEMURS (active during the day)
The largest and the easiest to identify, these are usually found in groups of between three and twelve individuals.

Ring-tailed lemurs *Lemur catta* Recognisable by their banded tails, and more terrestrial than other lemurs, these are seen in troops of around 20 animals in the south and southwest, notably in Berenty reserve.

Ruffed lemurs These are large lemurs (genus *Varecia*) and commonly found in zoos but seldom seen in the wild. There are two species: black-and-white ruffed lemur and red ruffed lemur. Both live in the eastern rainforest.

True lemurs This family has only recently been grouped under a new generic name, *Eulemur*. They are all roughly cat-sized, have long noses, and live in trees. A confusing characteristic is that males and females of each species are coloured differently. The best-known *Eulemur* is the **black lemur**, *E. macaco* (called *maki* by the Malagasy), of northwest Madagascar, notably Nosy Komba. Only the males are black; females are chestnut brown. Visitors to Ranomafana usually see the **red-bellied lemur**; the male has white 'tear-drop' face markings. In the northern reserves you'll find the **crowned lemur**, *Eulemur coronatus*.

   Brown lemurs *(Eulemur fulvus)* present the ultimate challenge. There are six subspecies and, since the males mostly look quite different from the females, you have 12 animals to sort out. Fortunately for you their ranges do not overlap. Two neighbouring brown lemurs have beautiful cream or white eartufts and side whiskers: **Sanford's brown lemur** (*E. f. sanfordii*) is found in the northern reserves; the **white-fronted brown lemur**, *E. f. albifrons* (the males have bushy white heads and side whiskers of almost Santa Claus proportions), in the northeast. Moving south you'll find the **common brown lemur** (*E. f. fulvus*) in the east and also the

FAUNA
Mammals

There are five orders of land mammals on the island: Primates (lemurs), Insectivora (tenrecs), Chiroptera (bats), Carnivora (carnivores) and Rodentia (rodents). Of these it is the five families of lemur that get the most attention so it is worth describing them in some detail.

Lemurs

Once upon a time there were lemur-type animals all over the world. Known as prosimians, these creatures evolved from an ancestral primate that eventually gave rise to all primates including ourselves. The early prosimians had some monkey-like characteristics but retained a foxy face and long nose indicating a highly developed sense of smell. Lemurs have changed little since the Eocene

west. The **red-fronted brown lemur** (*E. f. rufus*) lives in the southeast and southwest. Females all look pretty much the same – boring and brown.

Bamboo lemurs (genus *Hapalemur*) These are smaller than the 'true lemurs', with short muzzles and round faces. They occur in smaller groups (one to three animals), cling to vertical branches, and feed on bamboos. You may see these in the eastern reserves of Périnet and Ranomafana; the commonest species is the **grey bamboo lemur** (*Hapalemur griseus*), although in Ranomafana you could see the **golden bamboo lemur**, *H. aureus*.

Indri The largest of the lemurs, and the only one without a tail, this black-and-white 'teddy bear' lemur is unmistakable. It is seen in Périnet.

Sifakas (genus *Propithecus*) The sifakas (sometimes pronounced Shee-fahk) belong to the same family as the indri, sharing its characteristic of long back legs; sifakas are the 'dancing lemurs' that bound upright over the ground and leap spectacularly from tree to tree. The commonest sifakas are white or mainly white and so are unlike any other lemur. The **white sifaka** (*P. verreauxi verreauxi*) shares its southern habitat with the ring-tailed lemur, and its cousin the **Coquerel's sifaka** (*P. v. coquereli*), which has chestnut arms and legs, is seen in Ampijoroa, in the northwest. You may also see the dark-coloured **Milne-Edwards sifaka** in Ranomafana.

NOCTURNAL LEMURS

Two genera of nocturnal lemur helpfully sleep or doze in the open so are regularly seen by tourists: **sportive lemurs** (lepilemurs) and **woolly lemurs** or avahis (guides may use both popular and generic names). Most species of lepilemur spend the day in a tree-hole from which they peer drowsily, and the woolly lemur sleeps in the fork of a tree or shrub.

During guided night walks you may see the eyes of **dwarf lemurs** – most likely the greater dwarf lemur at Périnet. The tiny **mouse lemurs** are quite common, and easiest to see at Ranomafana or Berenty.

You're very unlikely to see an unplanned **aye-aye**, but check the description on page 54 if you think you did...

See *Appendix Four* for a check list of lemurs and where to find them.

period 58–36 million years ago. Other descendants of the ancestral primate evolved into monkeys; faced with competition these developed a greater intelligence and better eyesight. An acute sense of smell became less important so their noses lost their physical prominence.

Lemurs are the only surviving prosimians apart from the bushbabies and pottos of Africa, and the lorises and tarsiers of Asia. From their faces it's hard to believe they are our relatives, but quoting from *Defenders of Wildlife* magazine (April 1975) 'One needn't be a scientist to look at a lemur's hand... and feel the thrill of recognition across a gap of 60 million years'.

Most experts now agree that there are 50 species and subspecies of lemur. New discoveries are still being made, however, both in the field and in the laboratory, so this figure is by no means final. Four species were discovered or rediscovered within a decade, proving the vital importance of preserving habitats which no doubt harbour thousands of unclassified living things.

In recent years primatologists have divided the genus *Lemur* into two: *Lemur* and *Eulemur*. The latter include the various subspecies of brown lemur, *Eulemur fulvus*; and the familiar black lemur, *Eulemur macaco* of Nosy Komba.

The majority of lemurs are active during the day (diurnal) so are easily seen; dedicated lemur-watchers can look for nocturnal animals with the help of a headlamp. The diurnal lemurs that are common in certain nature reserves are described in those sections: ring-tails and sifakas in *Berenty*, indri in *Andasibe* and black lemurs in *Nosy Be*. However, there are some generalities which are interesting. Diurnal lemurs live in family groups or troops where the females are usually dominant (which is rare in primates, where males are generally larger) and they sunbathe in the morning to raise the body temperature. Lemurs have slow metabolism, and need a bit of help from the sun for their daily quota of energy.

The strangest lemur is the aye-aye, *Daubentonia madagascariensis*. It took a while for scientists to decide that it was a lemur at all: for years it was thought to be a peculiar type of squirrel. Today it is classified in a family of its own, Daubentonidae. The aye-aye seems to have been assembled from the leftover parts of a variety of animals. It has the teeth of a rodent (they never stop growing), the ears of a bat, the tail of a fox, and the hands of no living creature since the middle finger is like that of a skeleton. It's this finger which so intrigues scientists as it shows the aye-aye's adaptation to its way of life. In Madagascar it seems to fill the ecological niche left empty by the absence of woodpeckers. The aye-aye evolved to use its skeletal finger to winkle grubs from under the bark of trees. It has added the skill (shown by the Chinese when using chopsticks to eat soup) of flicking coconut milk into its mouth; coconuts are now a favoured food. The aye-aye's fingers are unique among lemurs in another way – it has claws not fingernails (except on the big toe). When searching for grubs the aye-aye taps on the wood with its finger, its enormous ears pointing like radar dishes to detect a cavity. It can even tell whether this is occupied by a nice fat grub.

Another anatomical feature of the aye-aye that sets it apart from other primates is that it has inguinal mammary glands. In other words, its teats are between its back legs. This fascinating animal was long considered to be on the verge of extinction, but recently there have been encouraging signs that it is more widespread than previously supposed. Although destruction of habitat is the chief threat to its survival, it is also at risk because of its supposedly evil powers. Rural people believe the aye-aye to be the herald of death. If one is seen near a settlement it must be killed, and even then the only salvation may be to burn down the village. Nevertheless there are several places where you are likely to see wild aye-ayes: Mananara is the easiest, and Nosy Mangabe if you are fortunate. Being strictly nocturnal, aye-ayes can only be watched with the help of a torch (flashlight); so for a prolonged session with these amazing animals treat yourself to a visit to Jersey Zoo where the purpose-built 'night-into-day' aye-aye house allows you to watch their behaviour to your heart's content, or pay your fee for a night-time visit at Tana's zoo, Tsimbazaza.

Other mammals

Madagascar is also celebrated for its **tenrecs**. These insectivores are considered by some zoologists to be the most primitive of all mammals and have diversified into at least 26 species. There are two sub-families, the spiny tenrecs, some of which look like European hedgehogs, and the furred tenrecs which are furtive and furry, mostly resembling shrews. In the former group is the guineapig-sized common tenrec (*Tenrec ecaudatus*), which is a popular food item so it is fortunate that it is the most prolific of all mammals: up to 32 babies may be born at one time. Not all survive, so the female's 24 nipples are sufficient. The smallest of the spiny group is the striped tenrec (*Hemicentetes* spp). They have rows of specialised spines which they can vibrate and strike together, producing a sound (inaudible to humans) called stridulation, which is used to call the young when they scatter to feed. Apart from the 16 or so shrew-like furred tenrecs, there is a startlingly different aquatic tenrec (*Limnogale mergulus*) which swims around in streams.

Some species of tenrec aestivate (go into a torpor) during the dry season when food is scarce.

Bats have not been studied extensively in Madagascar. The most visible are the fruit bats or flying foxes (*Pteropus rufus*), an endemic species closely related to those of Asia. There are six families of smaller, mainly insectivorous bats but only one is endemic. It contains a single species, the sucker-footed bat (*Myzopoda aurita*), which uses its specially adapted feet and wrists (with suction pads) to hang from the smooth leaves of palms in the eastern rainforest.

The eight species of Malagasy carnivore all belong to the family **Viverridae**, and are related to the mongooses, civets and genets of Africa and Asia. The largest is the cat-like fosa (*Cryptoprocta ferox*), which is also spelt fossa. Although rarely seen it is not uncommon. The fosa is an expert tree climber, and the only serious predator (apart from hawks) of the larger lemurs. It has sandy-brown fur, a long body and a very long tail, short strong jaws, retractable claws, and is about the size of a large domestic cat.

The spelling 'fossa' brings confusion with the smaller nocturnal *Fossa fossana* or fanaloka, also known as striped civet, which is easy to see at Ranomafana. The similarly named falanouc (*Eupleres goudotii*) is extremely secretive and little studied. It feeds on invertebrates such as earthworms.

Of the mongooses the most frequently seen is the ring-tailed mongoose, *Galidia elegans*, which is chestnut brown with a striped tail. It frequents the eastern and northern rainforests. There are several differences between it and African or Asian mongooses: *Galidia* has webbed feet, retractable claws, and teats between its back legs.

Madagascar has about 20 endemic species of **rodent** (along with introduced rats and mice), of which the rabbit-sized giant jumping rat (*Hypogeomys antimena*) is the most interesting – and charming: it leaps like a wallaby in the forests north of Morondava.

BIRDING IN MADAGASCAR

Derek Schuurman

Birding is becoming very popular in Madagascar, and with good reason: there are 110 endemics on the island and another 25 shared with the Comoros and Aldabra. It's a case of quality, rather than quantity, as none of these is numerous and the species diversity in Madagascar is quite low.

To see a reasonable selection of the Malagasy endemics, one should plan a trip encompassing visits to at least one site in each of the three prime habitats: the eastern rainforests, the western deciduous forests and the southern semi-arid spiny bush. Each of these floristic/climatic zones boasts its own endemics. Below are the best sites.

Eastern rainforests

Andasibe/Périnet For those who have very little time, this is ideal being near to Antananarivo. Specials in the reserve include blue and red-fronted couas; velvet and sunbird asitys. Of the vangas there are Chabert's, blue, nuthatch, and red-tailed. You may also find the Madagascar flufftail.

Ranomafana Much the same as Périnet but some rarer species include the pitta-like, short-legged and rufous-headed ground-rollers, the Pollen's vanga, forest rock-thrush, brown mesite, Crossley's babbler, white-throated and yellow-browed oxylabes, brown and grey emutails, and the grey-crowned greenbuls.

Masoala Peninsula This is for hard-core birders who wish to see the region's specials: the red-breasted coua, scaly ground-roller, helmet and Bernier's vangas. The elusive brown mesite is there too, as is Henst's goshawk, Madagascar pratincole and the very rare red-tailed newtonia. Birds common in the eastern rainforests are seen here such as the nelicourvi weaver, red forest fody, blue and green pigeons. You may also see 'Tylas', formerly Tylas Vanga, but now classified as an oriole.

Western deciduous dry forests

Ampijoroa Forestry Station The birding is exceptional here: red-capped, Coquerel's and crested couas; Chabert's, sicklebill and hook-billed vangas, as well as rufous, blue and the very rare Van Dam's vanga. The elusive Schlegel's asity is present. The white-breasted mesite is common here and Madagascar fish eagles frequent the lake area; raptor enthusiasts may find the rare banded kestrel.

Ankarana Special Reserve Much the same as Ampijoroa, including the Madagascar pygmy kingfisher, the crested ibis and the banded kestrel. But there are no asity or Van Dam's vangas.

Southern semi-arid spiny bush and dry gallery forest

Berenty and Amboasary-Sud There is rewarding birding here; specials of the region include the giant coua, the white-browed owl, and the littoral rock-thrush.

Spiny forests near Ifaty This is the place to search for the three specials of the south: the long-tailed ground-roller, the subdesert mesite and the Lafresnaye's vanga. Also found are the running and verreaux's coua.

Zombitse Forest The only locality for the Appert's greenbul. Other species include the giant coua, Frances's sparrow-hawk and the Madagascar partridge. At nearby Isalo National Park is found Benson's rock-thrush.

Birds

Compared with mainland Africa Madagascar can at first appear disappointing for birdwatchers, with even the forests eerily silent as a traveller in 1942 noted: 'Had it not been for the fact that my porters kept up an incessant chatter, telling each other stories and folk tales...I should have been struck by the uncanny stillness of the forest, the apparent absence of animal life and the scarcity of birds.'

Here, however, it is quality not quantity that draws the enthusiasts; there are 36 endemic genera – more than any country in the Africa region. Of the 202 resident species, 110 are endemic and 25 are shared with Aldabra and the Comoro Islands. The five endemic families comprise mesites (similar to rails), ground-rollers, the cuckoo-roller, asitys and sunbird asitys, vangas, and there is also an endemic sub-family of couas. These are a striking group (nine species) which have long, broad tails and resemble the African touracos. The family that most fascinate ornithologists are the vangas. The 14 species remind us of Darwin's finches in the Galapagos Islands, having evolved a variety of different beaks to deal most efficiently with the food available in the different niches they occupy. Unlike the finches, however, the vangas differ from each other in colour and size as well.

Frogs and reptiles

Madagascar is particularly rich in this group of fauna – there are several hundred species of **frog** (the only amphibians here, there are no toads, newts or salamanders), and new species are regularly added to the list. There are

---

LEECHES

Few classes of invertebrates elicit more disgust than leeches. Perhaps some facts about these extraordinarily well-adapted animals will give them more appeal.

Terrestrial leeches such as those found in Madagascar are small (1-2cm long) and find their warm-blooded prey by vibrations and odour. Suckers at each end enable the leech to move around in a series of loops and to attach itself to a leaf by its posterior while seeking its meal with the front end. It has sharp jaws and can quickly – and painlessly – bite through the skin and start feeding. When it has filled its digestive tract with blood the leech drops off and digests its meal. This process can take several months since leeches have pouches all along their gut to hold as much blood as possible – up to ten times their own weight. The salivary glands manufacture an anticoagulant which prevents the blood clotting during the meal or period of digestion. This is why leech wounds bleed so spectacularly. They also inject an anaesthetic which is why you don't feel them biting.

Leeches are hermaphrodite but still have pretty exciting sex lives. To consummate their union they need to exchange packets of sperm. This is done either the conventional way via a leechy penis or by injection, allowing the sperm to make its way through the body tissues to find and fertilise the eggs.

Readers who are disappointed with the small size of Malagasy leeches will be interested to hear that an expedition to French Guiana in the 1970s discovered the world's largest leech: at full stretch 18 inches long!

some delightful little tree frogs and the brilliantly coloured genus *Mantella*. These are very similar to the poison arrow frogs of South America. Reptiles number some 300 species. Of the many types of lizard in Madagascar, the iguanids are interesting since other members of this family are found not in Africa but in South America: they were probably inhabitants of Gondwanaland. There are two genera in Madagascar, *Chalaradon* and *Oplurus*. The lizards that most interest tourists (and film-makers) are the **chameleons** (see separate box below). The world's smallest and largest chameleon species are found in Madagascar: Oustalet's chameleon (*Furcifer oustaleti*) which can exceed 60cm in length, and the nose-horned chameleon (*Calumma nasutus*) which barely stretches to 10cm. Even smaller is the tiny *Brookesia minima*, of the genera of stump-tailed chameleons which live on the forest floor.

The real masters of the art of camouflage are the **fringed geckos** (also called leaf-tailed geckos) of the genus *Uroplatus*. These reptiles blend so perfectly into the bark of the trees on which they spend the day, that when I pointed one out on Nosy Mangabe (particularly rewarding for *Uroplatus*) my companions failed to see it until I had encouraged it to gape in self defence. Not only does the lizard's skin perfectly match the bark, but its sides are fringed so no shadow

---

CHAMELEONS

Everybody thinks they know one thing about chameleons: that they change colour to match their background. Wrong! You have only to observe the striking *Calumma parsonii*, commonly seen at Périnet, staying stubbornly green while transferred from boy's hand to tree trunk to leafy branch to see that in some species this is a myth. Many chameleons are cryptically coloured to match their preferred resting place (there are branch-coloured chameleons, for instance, and leaf-coloured ones) and some do respond to a change of background, but their abilities are mainly reserved for expressing emotion. An anxious chameleon will darken and grow stripes and an angry chameleon, faced with a territorial intruder, will change his colours dramatically. The most impressive displays, however, are reserved for sexual encounters. Chameleons say it with colours. Enthusiastic males explode into a riot of spots, stripes, and contrasting colours, whilst the female usually responds by donning a black cloak of disapproval. Only on the rare occasions that she is feeling receptive will she present a brighter appearance.

Chameleons use body language more than colour to deter enemies. If you spot a chameleon on a branch you will note that his first reaction to being seen is to put the branch between you and him and flatten his body laterally so that he is barely visible. If you try to catch him, he will blow himself up, expand his throat, raise his helmet (if he has one) and hiss. His next action will be to either bite, jump, or try to run away. Fortunately they must be the slowest of all lizards, are easily caught, and pose for the camera with gloomy resignation (who can resist an animal that has a constantly down-turned mouth like a Victorian headmistress?). This slowness is another aspect of the chameleon's defence: when he walks, he moves like a leaf in the wind. This is fine when the danger is an animal predator, but less effective when it is a car. In a tree, his best protection is to keep completely still. He can do this by having feet shaped like pliers and a prehensile tail so he can effortlessly grasp a branch, and eyes shaped like gun-turrets which can swivel 180 degrees

is cast on the tree; even its eye is flecked like bark. It is truly almost invisible. There are ten species of *Uroplatus* and not all look like bark – some are leaf-mimics.

In complete contrast to the *Uroplatus* are the almost iridescent green day geckos of the genus *Phelsuma*.

None of Madagascar's 85 or so species of land **snake** is dangerous; or to be accurate the six genera of venomous snakes are back-fanged so cannot inflict a venomous bite. Boas, like iguanids, are found in Madagascar and South America. Two species are easily seen: the ground boa, *Acrantophis madagascariensis*, and the 'tree boa' (which doesn't spend much time up trees), *Sanzinia madagascariensis*. The giant hog-nosed snake (*Leioheterodon madagascariensis*) is also quite common, and easily identified by its black and yellow markings.

It is interesting that despite the harmlessness of the island's snakes, the local population still hold them in fear and myths abound. It is thought, for instance, that the long, slim *fandrefiala* (*Ithycyphus perineti*) can spear a zebu by dropping down from a tree, tail first. They say this devilish creature measures its aim by dropping a couple of leaves before it falls. The Malagasy name for

---

independently of each other, enabling him to view the world from front and back without moving his head. This is the chameleon's true camouflage.

The family Chamaeleonidae is represented by three genera, the 'true chameleons' *Calumma* and *Furcifer*, and the little stump-tailed chameleons, *Brookesia*. Unlike the true chameleons, the *Brookesia*'s short tail is not prehensile.

In chameleons there is often a striking colour difference between males and females. Many males have horns (occasionally used for fighting) or other nasal protuberances. Where the two sexes are the same you can recognise the male by the bulge of the scrotal sac beneath the tail, and a spur on the hind feet.

It is interesting to know how the chameleon achieves its colour change. It has a transparent epidermis, then three layers of cells – the top ones are yellow and red, the middle layer reflects blue light and white light, and the bottom layer consists of black pigment cells with tentacles or fingers that can protrude up through the other layers. The cells are under control of the autonomic nervous system, expanding and contracting according to a range of stimuli. Change of colour occurs when one layer is more stimulated than others, and patterning when one group of cells receives maximum stimulation.

In the early 17th century there was the firm conviction that chameleons subsisted without food. A German author, describing Madagascar in 1609, mentions the chameleon living 'entirely on air and dew' and Shakespeare refers several times to the chameleon's supposed diet: 'The chameleon ... can feed on air' (*Two Gentlemen of Verona*) and 'of the chameleon's dish: I eat the air promise-crammed' (*Hamlet*). Possibly at that time no-one had witnessed the tongue flash out in a quarter of a second to trap an insect.

The name apparently comes from Greek: *chamai leon*, dwarf lion. I suppose a hissing, open-mouthed reptile *could* remind one of a lion, but to most visitors to Madagascar they are one of the most appealing and bizarre of the 'strange and marvellous forms' on show.

the tree boa is *Kapilangidro*, 'lemur's plate'. They say that this snake will coil itself into a bowl to tempt lemurs to approach for a drink.

There are four species of endemic land **tortoise** but these are threatened by introduced wild animals such as the bushpig, which eats the eggs and young hatchlings. Several are in danger of extinction so captive breeding programmes have been established to ensure their future. The plow-share tortoises or *Angonoka* (*Geochelone yniphora*) are being raised at Ampijoroa reserve, under the auspices of the Jersey Wildlife Preservation Trust, which is also breeding the attractive little flat-tailed tortoise, *Pyxis planicauda*.

THE WILD TRADE IN REPTILES AND AMPHIBIANS IN MADAGASCAR: TWO POINTS OF VIEW

Marius Burger

The trade in live amphibians and reptiles ('Herps') for the exotic pet markets has become a lucrative business worth millions of dollars.

Malagasy herpetofauna were poorly represented in the exotic pet market until the mid 1980s. Consider the recent export figures for day geckos (*Phelsuma* spp): nearly 145,000 specimens of 17 different species between 1986 and 1991. Another popular group is the chameleons: 38,325 specimens comprising 21 species (CITES figures). In one year the legal export of *Mantella* frogs rose from 230 specimens to 11,058. These figures are an underestimation since they do not include illegal trading nor mortalities prior to exportation.

Herp dealers often try to justify their business by claiming that they are in actual fact saving species which would otherwise have become extinct due to habitat destruction. There is a fraction of truth in this statement, ie, a few species have benefited from captive propagation, but the overwhelming majority of herp keepers have contributed nothing to the conservation of the species in their collections. In fact, by purchasing these animals, they have created a demand which in some cases may lead to the over-exploitation of particular species.

Comparing a relatively lesser threat (collecting of live specimens) with a worse one (habitat destruction) in no way justifies the former. The exotic pet trade represents an additional threat for some species. And as for the so-called 'saving' of species by breeding them in captivity, this is mostly futile if not done in conjunction with a specific Species Survival Programme which incorporates genetic and pathological considerations. That does not necessarily mean that the trade in wild herps for the exotic pet market is an absolute no-no. Most species could probably sustain a reasonable measure of harvest. However, the current uncontrolled trade is increasing at an alarming rate and, coupled with a paucity of essential biological and distributional data for the various species, it is of conservation concern.

Very often the extreme rarity of a specific species causes it to be in particularly great demand, and thus fetch high prices. This leads to greed and unscrupulous dealings. A case in point is the theft of 75 specimens of the world's rarest tortoise, the *Anganoka*, from the breeding centre in Ampijoroa in May 1996.

The unacceptable levels of discomfort and mortality often incurred during the capture, transport and subsequent housing of specimens are distressing. Chameleons, in particular, suffer great losses when collected from the wild. In short, the exotic pet trade generally has a bad name within conservation circles and it needs to clean up its act. But the trade is a reality and, in fact, it is also an opportunity. A reversal in conservation priorities from protection to utilisation can work if the

Invertebrates

Loosely catagorised as 'creepy-crawlies' by many visitors, the insects, spiders, and other arthropods provide enthusiasts with endless surprises and delights. There are extraordinary flatworms, eight-inch long millipedes, golf-ball sized pill-bugs, bizarre stick insects and mantids disguised as leaves, huge hissing cockroaches, brilliantly-coloured giant grasshoppers, little hopping nymphs dressed in imitation feathers, beetles and spiders of all shapes and colours, and, of course, butterflies.

Madagascar has around 300 species of butterfly and 4,000 moths. Moths

profits of sustainable harvesting are equitably distributed to the people whose survival currently depends on cutting and burning the forest.

Bill Love
The number of herps exported from Madagascar is merely a drop in the bucket compared to those permanently lost to habitat destruction. Animals are renewable resources that can replenish themselves if their environment is not severely disturbed or cleared. The ability to be naturally prolific has evolved as part of their survival strategy to counter wildfire, disease, predation, etc.

Local people collecting small animals typically take them from places where populations are dense to ensure profitable catches. As numbers dwindle, the effort becomes unprofitable and is quickly abandoned. Most animals such as lizards and frogs bounce back in numbers quickly.

Not all exported animals end up simply as pets. Some go to experienced modern breeders who dedicate vast amounts of time and effort in studying them to unravel their reproductive biologies. This, in turn, leads to self-sustaining captive colonies of less-stressed, parasite-free, healthy animals that will eventually nullify the need for continued large-scale importation of wild-origin stock.

Breeding farms are also under development in Madagascar. While there is no excuse for overcrowding, malnutrition, poor transportation methods, etc, these problems are being corrected, and can be viewed as regrettable consequences of a learning process to discover the 'recipes' for captive reproduction.

People don't care about things for which they feel no familiarity or passion. People purchasing live animals, and learning from the experience, gain a broader love and appreciation of wildlife generally. This leads to concern for nature later when their vote or donation could benefit conservation causes.

Attacking the live animal trade is a substitute for dealing with the seemingly intractable mega-problem of saving whole environments, or slowing the human population growth that is putting the intense pressure on the land and resources. If the same zeal focused against the pet trade was redirected there, accelerated progress would occur in protecting *all* species.

The demand for exotic pets will continue as surely as the Malagasy people's need to utilise their natural resources. The relatively new sustainable harvest concept may be the best solution since it recognises both factors. Human nature will surely find ways to fill its needs even if total 'hands-off' style legislation is enacted. The opportunity now exists to create new laws to take this predictable factor into account, and instead create a mutually beneficial system that recognises the interwoven relationship between commercialism and conservation, allowing both to coexist and work hand in hand toward a common goal.

pre-date butterflies in evolutionary terms so probably existed on Gondwanaland, but butterflies are likely to have flown or been blown over from East Africa. Many Malagasy species have counterparts in Africa. However, there is a swallowtail, *Atrophaneura anterior*, whose nearest relative is in Asia, and the Urania moth *Chrysiridia madagascariensis* is very similar to the one found in South America.

The most spectacular moth is the comet (*Argema mittrei*), one of the largest in the world (one third larger than its African counterpart), with a beautiful silver cocoon. They are still relatively common and a captive breeding programme in Mandraka provides mounted specimens for the tourist trade.

DRAGONFLIES

Kay Thompson

Dragonflies are among the earth's oldest living insects. They have existed, virtually unchanged, for 350 million years although fossils show that these early forms were much larger: *Meganeura monyi* had a wingspan of 75cm. There are more than 5,000 species of dragonfly in the world; the hotter the climate the more species there are – although there are records of dragonflies surviving night frosts of -8° centigrade and waiting for the sun to thaw off the frozen dew.

The scientific name for dragonflies is Odonata. This order consists of two sub-orders: true dragonflies, the Anisoptera; and damselflies, the Zygoptera. Damselflies are generally smaller insects with narrow, delicate bodies and four similar-shaped wings. They are not strong flyers, and flutter among the marginal vegetation of a pond or fly close to the water's surface. When settled the wings of damselflies are usually folded together down their backs. The eyes are separated. True dragonflies are more robust; they have thicker bodies and compound eyes that meet, or almost meet, at the top of their heads. Their wings are always held at 90° to their body.

Dragonflies are formidable fliers. They can reach speeds of 30kph and can hover, loop the loop, and fly backwards. They also feed and mate on the wing. Their diet consists of insects and cannibalism is common.

The female dragonfly lays her eggs into the water or on vegetation above or below the water. Depending on the species, the egg may remain dormant through the winter or hatch within two to six weeks of being laid. The larva outgrows its skin (instar) 10 to 15 times before it reaches adult size and is ready to climb out into the air and complete its metamorphosis into the flying jewel we are familiar with.

CONSERVATION
An age-old problem

When people first settled in Madagascar, the culture they brought with them depended on rice and zebu cattle. Rice was the staple diet and zebu the spiritual staple, the link with the ancestors. Rice and zebu cannot be raised in dense forest, so the trees were felled and the undergrowth burned.

Two hundred or so years ago King Andrianampoinimerina punished those of his subjects who wilfully deforested areas. The practice continued, however. In 1883, 100 years later, the missionary James Sibree commented: 'Again we noticed the destruction of the forest and the wanton waste of trees.' The first efforts at legal protection came as long ago as 1927 when ten reserves were set aside by the French colonial government, which also tried to put a stop to the burning. Successive governments have tried – and failed – to halt this devastation.

Since independence in 1960, Madagascar's population has more than doubled (to almost 13 million) and the remaining forest has been reduced by half. Only about 10% of the original cover remains and an estimated 2,000 square kilometres is destroyed annually. Yet the population density averages only 21 people per square kilometre, while in Great Britain it is 228. The pressure on the forests is because most of Madagascar is sterile grassland and bare, eroded laterite. Here, forests are destroyed not by timber companies (although there have been some culprits) but by impoverished peasants clearing the land by the traditional method of *tavy*, slash and burn, and cutting trees for fuel or to make charcoal. There is still some 'wanton destruction'; burning has been illegal for so long, defying this law has become a means of defying authority.

The race against time

Madagascar has more endangered species of mammal than any other country in the world. The authorities are not unaware of this environmental crisis: as long ago as 1970 the Director of Scientific Research made this comment in a speech during an international symposium on conservation: 'The people in this room know that Malagasy nature is a world heritage. We are not sure that others realise that it is *our* heritage.' Resentment at having outsiders make decisions on the future of their heritage without proper consultation with the Malagasy was one of the reasons there was little effective conservation in the 1970s and early 1980s. This was a time when Madagascar was demonstrating its independence from Western influences.

Things changed in 1985, when Madagascar hosted a major international conference on conservation for development. The Ministry of Animal Production, Waters and Forests, which administered the protected areas, went into partnership with the World Wide Fund for Nature. Their plan was to evaluate all protected areas in the country, then numbering 37 (2% of the country), and in their strategy for the future to provide people living near the reserves with economically viable alternatives. They have largely achieved their aims. All the protected areas have been evaluated and recommendations for their management made. They are now the responsibility of the National Association for Management of Protected Areas (Association Nationale pour la Gestion des Aires Protégées, ANGAP) which was established under the auspices of the Environmental Action Plan (EAP), sponsored by the World Bank. Among their successes are a three-year 'Debt for Nature' swap negotiated by the WWF with the Central Bank of Madagascar.

The WWF funds a number of projects in Madagascar. Other outside agencies

---

TAVY

Jamie Spencer

Slash and burn farming, or in Malagasy *tavy*, is blamed for the permanent destruction of the rainforest. Those practising *tavy* agree with this. They also respect this forest and they can see that *tavy* greatly jeopardises the future for the next generations. So why destroy what you love and need?

One answer to a very complex question is the practical need. The poverty is extreme and there are few options. Life's priority is to feed your family and children. Rice, the food staple, is grown both on the flat ground in sustainable paddy fields, and on the steep slopes of slashed and burned forest. The last cyclone washed away much of the paddy rice crop and wiped out the earth dams and irrigation waterways built at great cost and effort. Some farmers had recently invested a life-time's savings employing labour for their construction. So if floods strike, people rely on the hill rice. Fertility in these fields is not replenished as in paddies where nutrients are carried in the water. The soil quickly becomes unproductive so new slopes must be cut after a few years.

The cultural explanation for *tavy* is less obvious. The people of Sandrakely are Tanala, meaning 'people of the forest'. The forest is their world and to survive in this surprisingly harsh environment they clear the land with fire – the ancient agricultural technique brought by the original immigrants from Indonesia perhaps 2,000 years ago. In more recent history the Tanala were forced into the forest by warring neighbours and colonial occupants of more fertile areas.

As the traditional means of survival and provision *tavy* can be seen as central to society's make-up and culture. The calendar revolves around it, land ownership and hierarchies are determined by its practice, and politics is centred on it. It is the pivot and subject of rituals and ceremonies. The forest is the domain of the ancestors and site of tombs and religious standing stones. *Tavy is* an activity carried out between the living and the dead: the ancestors are consulted and permit its execution to provide for the living. The word *tavy* also means 'fatness', with all the associations of health, wealth and beauty.

If they have the choice many people are happy to pursue the sustainable kind of agriculture and so *Feedback* is ready to help them. But the practical and cultural context must always be respected. The new alternatives must be rock solid when people's lives are at stake and to be truly enduring they must be accommodated within the culture by the people themselves. It is they who understand the problems and know the solutions that are acceptable. They must not be forced.

Jamie Spencer runs the charity Feedback Madagascar; see page 127.

involved in conservation are the Jersey Wildlife Preservation Trust, Conservation International, Missouri Botanical Gardens, and the Peregrine Fund; also USAID (US Agency for International Development), La Coopération Suisse, UNDP (United Nations Development Programme) and UNESCO.

The stated aims of the WWF and other conservation agencies working in Madagascar are to: 'Ensure the conservation of Malagasy biodiversity and ecological processes by stopping, and eventually reversing, the accelerating environmental degradation, and by helping to build a future in which humans live in harmony with nature.'

During the Earth Summit in Rio in 1992, Madagascar expressed its commitment There areto international conservation, and signed both the Biodiversity and Climate Change conventions.

How you can help

• Support the organisations listed in *Chapter Seven*.
• Do not interrupt the work of scientists in the reserves.
• Do not encourage the illegal trade in endangered species by admiring or paying to photograph pet animals.
• Pay the full park/reserve fee with a good grace. The money is used for conservation.
• Do not berate the Malagasy for destroying their forests: understand the underlying reasons (see box opposite).

"There are fewer and fewer forests, the rivers are drying up, the wild creatures are becoming extinct, the climate is ruined, and every day the earth is growing poorer and more hideous... I realise that the climate is to some extent in my power, and that if, in a thousand years man is to be happy, I too shall have had some small hand in it. When I plant a birch tree and see it growing green and swaying in the wind, my soul is filled with pride ..."
Anton Chekhov, Uncle Vanya, 1899

Antsiranana

FORÊT D'AMBRE ⊕

⊕ MONTAGNE D'AMBRE
⊕ ANALAMERA

Lokobe □

⊕ ANKARANA

MANONGARIVO ⊕   Tsaratanana
□

□ Marojejy

⊕ ANJANAHARIBE-SUD

Mahajanga
⊕ BORA

Lac Kinkony   Katsepy

⊕ MASOALA
NOSY MANGABE

Baie de Baly/Soalala ▽   ▽

⊕ MANANARA

Ankarafantsika ⊕

⊕ AMBATOVAKY

□ Namoroka

⊕ KASIJY   Lac ▽
Alaotra

MAROTANDRANO
TAMPOKETSA-
ANALAMAITSO

MANINGOZA-⊕
BEMARIVO'-⊕

Zahamena □   □ Betampona

AMBOHIJANAHARY ⊕

Toamasina

AMBOHITANTELY
⊕

MANGERIVOLA

□ Bemaraha   ⊕

▽ Lac Bemamba
Lac Ilasy   Tana   ⊕ ANDASIBE
▽   ⊕ ANALAMAZAOTRA

ANALABE

▽ Kirindy CFPF   ✦ MANJAKOLOMPO

⊕ ANDRANOMENA

⊕ RANOMAFANA

Morondava
Fianarantsoa ⊘

Lac Ihotry ▽   ISALO ⊕   □ Andringitra

Vohibasia ▽   ⊕ IVOHIBE

○ ZOMBITSE   ⊕ MANOMBO

Andrevo ▽
(PK 32)

⊕ KALAMBATRITRA

Toliara   BEZA-
⊕ MAHAFALY   ○ MIDONGY-SUD

Tsimanampetsotsa

Andohahela
□

BERENTY ■

Hatokaliotsy ▽   ▽   Tolagnaro

Lac
Anony

CAP STE MARIE

⊕ NATIONAL PARK   ▽ Site of biological interest
⊕ SPECIAL RESERVE   ○ CLASSIFIED FOREST
□ Strict nature reserve   ✦ FORESTRY STATION
■ PRIVATE RESERVE   ⊘ City or town

NATIONAL PARKS AND RESERVES

NATIONAL PARKS AND RESERVES
Categories
There are six categories of protected area, of which the first three have been established to protect natural ecosystems or threatened species:

1. Réserves Naturelles Intégrales (strict nature reserves)
2. Parcs Nationaux (national parks)
3. Réserves Spéciales (special reserves)
4. Réserves de Chasse (hunting reserves)
5. Forêts Classées (classified forests)
6. Périmètres de Reboisement et de Restauration (reafforestation zones).

1. Four of the *reserves* in this category are mentioned in this book, although only areas outside the park or in the 'buffer zone' may be visited: Tsingy de Bemaraha, Andringitra, Andohahela and Lokobe.

These reserves protect representative ecosystems, and are open only to authorised scientific research.

2. As in other countries, *national parks* protect ecosystems and areas of natural beauty, and are open to the public (with permits). There are now six national parks: Ranomafana, Montagne d'Ambre and Isalo are the best known, with the equally famous Périnet-Analamazaotra and Mantadia joining the ranks as Andasibe National Park. Less known and difficult to visit are Mananara and the newest arrival (1996) Masoala.

3. There are 20 or so *special reserves*, of which Ankarana, Cap Sainte Marie, Beza-Mahafaly, Andranomena, Anjanaharibe-Sud, and Nosy Mangabe are described. These reserves are for the protection of ecosystems or threatened species. Not all are supervised. Access may be limited to authorised scientific research.

4. Four lakes (including Kinkony and Ihotry) are duck-hunting *reserves*.

5 and 6. The 158 *classified forests* and 77 *reafforestation zones* conserve forests and watersheds using accepted forestry principles. Zombitse classified forest (now a protected area) is described in this book.

There are also some private reserves, the most famous of which is Berenty, with the Swiss-administered Kirindy in second place.

Ecotourism
Ecotourism, or 'discovery tourism' (as opposed to mass tourism), was part of the National Environmental Action Plan set up in 1990. The aim was that tourism should generate about a third of the funding for protected area maintenance by the end of the century. However, tourist numbers have fallen short of the expected figure (the target for 1995 was 77,000) and of these visitors only 20% visited a national park or reserve. Only four national parks

THE ENVIRONMENTAL ACTION PLAN: PAST RESULTS AND FUTURE PLANS

Joanna Durbin

The integrated conservation and development projects in Madagascar (for example, Ranomafana National Park) were always intended to be experimental, and it is only to be expected that some development initiatives would be successful and others would be less so. They were funded during the first phase of the National Environmental Action Plan (1990–1996) in order to test the hypothesis that providing alternatives and improvements to the standards of living of local people would take pressure off protected areas and promote sustainable management of natural resources.

After periods of three to five years these projects are being evaluated, and although there are some promising results, there is a general feeling that they have not been as successful as originally anticipated. This is probably partly due to the fact that changes in attitudes and resource use cannot be expected within such short time frames. A justified criticism of such projects is that they have generally been very expensive in relation to their achievements. It has been recognised that some smaller projects such as the DEF/ANGAP/WWF Zombitse-Vohibasia project and the DEF/JWPT Angonoka project have had relatively good success. Their small size and budget have worked in their favour as they do not create big self-sufficient technical development departments, but must work closely with partners, including government services and other NGOs, and must rely on motivation from the villagers themselves. The emphasis is on finding locally appropriate, non-technological solutions, and negotiating agreements about resource use between different interest groups. The small project teams have to build up good communication and good relations with all their various partners. This good communication is an important prerequisite for learning about the resource issues relevant to the region and developing, together with the partners, more sustainable forms of management. One could also argue that such projects are more likely to have long-lasting impacts and to be sustainable in the long term as they have not become reliant on large-scale external inputs (such as money, materials and technical expertise).

There is a move towards this smaller-scale type of project in the proposals for the second phase of the Environmental Action Plan (1997–2002). It must still be recognised that conservation and development problems in Madagascar will not be solved within a few years. We should hope to improve the chances of maintaining the extraordinary and magnificent Malagasy biodiversity in some areas, while also trying to help improve productivity of natural resources upon which the vast majority of the Malagasy population rely for their livelihoods.

– Isalo, Montagne d'Ambre, Ranomafana and Andasibe/Périnet – are easy to visit, and these generate 60% of the total revenue from entrance fees.

Some reserves with hitherto restricted access are being opened up or reclassified as national parks, but the supporting infrastructure will take time to develop. Planned facilities are the creation of access roads, nature trails, accommodation, education and visitor centres.

Joanna Durbin, of the JWPT in Madagascar, writes: 'Tourism, if sensitively and respectfully managed, can help to give a value to Malagasy wildlife and forests. By just visiting and being willing to pay the entrance fee (half of which goes to ANGAP to help manage the parks network throughout Madagascar and half of which goes to a fund for local communities), by buying some local handicrafts, and by staying in a local hotel and eating local produce, visitors are contributing to the local economy and helping to provide reasons for conservation of the forest.'

Permits

Permits to visit the reserves and national parks cost foreigners 20,000Fmg per person per reserve. In September 1997 the fee is likely to go up to 50,000Fmg. Half of this entrance fee goes to ANGAP and half to local communities, so each visitor is playing his or her part.

Permits are now available at the park/reserve entrance (be sure to get a receipt) but you may wish to visit the ANGAP office in Antananarivo (see page 153) for the latest information.

Hiring guides

There has been much confusion on the subject of guides and their fees, with an unstructured system of tips causing anger and resentment in guides and tourists alike. Fees are now becoming standardised and are listed in this book under the appropriate reserve. Changes in the fees should be posted at the entrance of all protected areas open to the public.

If the guide has been exceptional, by all means add a tip or present to the fee, but do not feel that it is obligatory.

CORAL

Only the upper two centimetres or so of a lump of coral is alive. The reefs around Madagascar are composed of the skeletons of dead coral, and the black 'rocks' found on the Malagasy shores are mostly old coral.

Coral spawns once a year in October during full moon. The larvae are like tiny jellyfish and are so numerous they make the sea look milky. These larvae collect in same-species groups and settle in one place. Coral also reproduces by budding, and this is how coral grows; it is a slow process and coral is easily damaged.

All over the world coral is threatened. Although the anchors of tourist boats and careless divers' feet will kill it, in Madagascar the silt-laden rivers are likely to be the main cause of the disappearance of once plentiful coral. Some rivers carry six milligrams of soil per litre of water, and all this ends up in the sea. Coral feeds on minute particles of organic matter and inert substances like silt 'clog up the works'. Human contamination is also a factor. As visitors soon find out, beaches are latrines and coral cannot survive if the water becomes over-enriched with organic matter; seaweed flourishes and smothers the coral. Near villages coral is further damaged during the search for edible sea creatures or for shells to sell to tourists.

Chapter Four

Planning and Preparations

WHEN TO GO

Read the section on climate in *Chapter One* before deciding when to travel. Broadly speaking, the dry months are in the winter between April and September, but rainfall varies enormously in different areas. The months you may want to avoid are August and during the Christmas holidays, when popular places are crowded, and February and March (the cyclone season) when it will rain. However, the off-peak season can be rewarding, with cheaper international airfares and accommodation and fewer other tourists. Botanists will want to go in February when many of the orchids are in flower, and herpetologists will also prefer the spring/summer because reptiles are more active – and brightly coloured – during those months. September is nice, but very windy in the south. My favourite months are October and November, when the weather is fine but not too hot, the jacarandas are in flower, the lemurs have babies, and lychees are sold from the roadside.

RED TAPE

Visas

A visa is required by everyone (except citizens of Malawi and Lesotho) and is normally issued for a stay of 30 or 90 days, valid for travel within six months of the date of issue. (For a brief period in early 1996 the Malagasy government decided to limit visas to 30 days; fortunately they bowed to pressure and 90-day visas are again available.) Applications from some professions, such as journalists, may have to be referred to Head Office. Business visitors need a letter of recommendation. Visa prices vary from country to country.

Long-term visas are usually available for stays of more than 90 days, but need authorisation from Antananarivo so can take about two months to process. Travellers who apply for a visa extension during their stay are usually successful.

The completed visa form must be accompanied by four photos. You may also be asked to show evidence of a return ticket; a letter from the travel agent dealing with your flights is sufficient.

Note: The visa situation is fluid. Check with your nearest embassy/consulate.

Embassy and consulate addresses

Australia Consulate. Floor 7, 19-31 Pitt St, Sydney, NSW 2000. Tel: 02 9252 3770. Fax: 02 9247 8406. Hours 09.00–13.00. Visas are issued within 48 hours and cost AUS\$38. The consul-general, Anthony Knox, is very enthusiastic and helpful. He is also the agent for Air Madagascar.

Austria Consulate. Pötzleindorferstr. 94-96, A-1184 Wien. Tel: 47 41 92 & 47 12 73.

Belgium Embassy. 276 Ave de Tervueren, 1150 Bruxelles. Tel: 770 1726 & 770 1774.

Canada *Embassy.* 649 Blair Rd, Gloucester, Ontario K1J 7M4. Tel: 613 744 7995. Fax: 613 744 2530.
Honorary Consulate. 8530 Rue Saguenay, Brossard, Québec, J4X IM6. Tel/fax: 514 6720 353.
Honorary Consulate. 335 Watson Ave, Oakville, Toronto, L6J 3V5. Tel: 416 845 8914.

Denmark c/o DZ Holding, Skodsborgvej 242, Naerum. Costs 400 DKr.

France Embassy. 4 Ave Raphael, 75016 Paris. Tel: 145 04 62 11. Visas take three days and cost 70Ff.

Germany Consulate. Rolandstrasse 48 (Postfach 188), 5300 Bonn 2. Tel: 0228 331057.

Great Britain Honorary Consulate. 16 Lanark Mansions, Pennard Rd, London W12 8DT. Tel: 0181 746 0133. Fax: 0181 746 0134. Hours 09.30–13.00. Visas supplied immediately or by post (add £1.50 for recorded delivery); very helpful. £35 (single entry) or £45 (double entry) tourist visa. £50 business visa.

Italy Embassy. Via Riccardo Zandonai 84/A, Roma. Tel: 327 7797 & 327 5183.

Kenya Visas are obtainable from Air Madagascar on the second floor of the Nairobi Hilton (PO Box 41723). Tel: 25286/26494. Allow 24 hours.

Mauritius Embassy. Ave Queen Mary, Port Louis. Tel: 6 50 15 & 6 50 16.

La Réunion Consulate. 73 Rue Juliette Dodu, 97461 Saint Denis. Tel: 21 05 21/21 65 58. Visas cost the same as in France.

South Africa Consulate. PO Box 786098; Sandton, 2146.
14 Greenfield Rd, Greenside, Johannesburg 2193. Tel: 011 646 4691. Fax: 011 486 2403. Also in KwaZulu/Natal (Hon Consul, David Fox): PO Box 1976, Durban, 4000 (201 Percy Osborn Rd, Durban). Tel/fax: 031 23 9704. Visas issued for 30 or 90 days; R140 or R180.

Spain Honorary Consulate; Avda Diagonal 432, 08037 Barcelona. Tel: 416 0936.

Switzerland Birkenstr. 5, CH-6000 Lucerne. Tel: 01 211 2721. Also Kappelgasse 14, CH-8022 Zürich. Tel: 01 211 2324.

United States The most accommodating and helpful source of visas is Jean-Marie de la Beaujardière in California (see below), but the following places also issue visas:

Embassy. 2374 Massachusetts Ave NW, Washington DC 20008. Tel: 202 265 5525. Visas also available from the Permanent Mission of Madagascar to the United Nations, 801 Second Ave, Room 404, New York, NY 10017. Tel: 212 986 9491. But for some reason they charge almost double the normal price for visas.

Honorary Consulate. 123 South Broad St, Philadelphia, PA 19109. Tel: 215 893 3067.
Honorary Consulate. 229 Piedmont Ave, Berkeley, CA 94720. Tel: 800 856 2721.
'Annex': 3707 Acosta Rd, Fairfax, VA 22031. Tel: 703 319 0731. Mr de la Beaujardière gives far more than just a visa: advice, enthusiasm, and an excellent information leaflet.

Visas in the US cost US$33.45 for a one-entry visa.

Extending your visa

A visa extension is usually easy to obtain. As early in your trip as possible go to the Ministry of the Interior, five minutes from the Hilton Hotel in Antananarivo. For your *prolongation* you will need three photos, a photocopy of your currency declaration, a typewritten declaration (best done at home) of why you want to stay longer, a *Certificat d'Hébergement* from your hotel, your passport, your return ticket, and 180,000Fmg (£30/US$45). Every provincial town has an immigration office, or at least a *Commissariat de Police*, so in theory you can extend your visa anywhere but some places are much more cooperative than others.

Currency restrictions and other requirements

Independent travellers are expected to spend at least 2,000Ff (£235/US$350) during their stay, and may be checked on departure. You may be given a form for recording all exchange transactions including credit card payments (this seems to be arbitrary). Keep all bank receipts. You may not bring in any Malagasy currency, nor can you exchange it back into hard currency at the end of your trip.

Spending requirements do not apply to children under 12 years, foreigners with a work permit, business visitors with proof of an invitation from a local business, and tourists on organised visits.

A yellow-fever vaccination certificate is no longer required but you may be asked to show one if you are coming from a fever area (eg Africa).

The international airport tax is payable in hard currency only: Ff80 (or equivalent) to Indian Ocean destinations (including South Africa), Ff100 for other places.

Film-makers

Making a film in Madagascar is becoming increasingly expensive. Even amateurs must declare their camcorder when they pass through customs on arrival, and will be asked to pay a high charge if filming in the zoo. Professionals get the works: to film the aye-aye in Tsimbazaza costs one million francs! (That's £166/US$250.) Eight copies of permit applications must be filled in, and eight copies of the final film must be donated to the Madagascar Ministry of Tourism. Your local Madagascar consulate should be able to give you more details, and you should book your trip through one of the specialist tour operators listed below who will be able to help you with the paperwork.

GETTING THERE
By air
If you are planning to take several domestic flights during your stay, Air Madagascar should be the international carrier since they offer an Air Touristic Pass which gives up to 50% discount on flights between the most popular destinations in Madagascar, providing visitors also book their international flight on Air Madagascar. This pass is only valid for visitors staying one to four weeks; those on an extended visit pay the full rate.

From Europe
Air Madagascar This is now the airline of choice – indeed it is with some regret that I have to report that Air Mad is becoming sane, at least for international flights. I haven't seen a poodle romping down the aisles for some years! Part of this normality, and a cause for rejoicing, is that the airline is now represented in Britain by Aviareps who are both efficient and helpful and have brought prices down to a level that is not far above Aeroflot. Contact Air Madagascar, Première House, Betts Way, Crawley, West Sussex RH10 2GB. Tel: 01293 523 958 or 596 665. Fax: 01293 512 229.

There are, as yet, no Air Madagascar flights from London – it is necessary to fly to Paris and connect with the Air Mad flight from CDG Airport (section 2a). 1996 air fares from Paris range from £640 (low season) to £850 (high season) but there are often special promotions with lower fares. Specialist tour operators such as Discover Madagascar and Reef and Rainforest Tours (see below) are also able to get lower fares for their clients.

Flight schedules are reviewed half-yearly. At the time of writing (January 1997) they leave Paris on Saturdays and Thursdays. The Saturday flight goes via Munich and the Thursday flight via Rome; both flights stop at Nairobi for refuelling. These flights are overnight, taking approximately 14 hours. Madagascar is three hours ahead of GMT.

Flight arrangements may also be made via tour operators such as Reef and Rainforest Tours (tel: 01803 866965) or Discover Madagascar, which is run by Seraphine Tierney. This very helpful and knowledgeable Malagasy woman can arrange international and domestic flights and give advice on travel arrangements. Phone (weekday afternoons, after 2.30) 0181 995 3529 or fax 0181 742 0212.

Travellers from mainland Europe will want to contact the nearest Air Madagascar office: the address of the head office, in Paris, is 29, Rue des Boulets, Paris 75011. Tel: 43 79 74 74. Fax: 43 79 30 33. There are also Air Madagascar offices in Frankfurt (tel: 069 690 72700, fax: 690 59206), Munich (tel: 089 2900 3940, fax: 2900 3946), Geneva (tel: 022 732 42 30, fax: 731 16 90), Zürich (tel: 01 810 85 84, fax: 810 91 19), Milan (tel: 02 801 437, fax: 720 01670) and Rome (tel: 06 474 7368, fax: 48 25 711).

Aeroflot For backpackers who will not be taking internal flights, the cheapest way of getting to Madagascar from Britain is with Aeroflot. Despite Russia's current problems these flights still seem to be fairly reliable, but now that Air Madagascar has a British representative the saving of about £150 may not seem worth the extra hassle. However, most readers are favourably surprised by the Aeroflot experience and besides, the airline puts you in the right frame of mind for Madagascar – anything can happen!

There is an eight-hour wait in Moscow for the onward flight. Frances Kerridge writes: 'It is worth pointing out to readers that the transit lounge at Moscow airport is upstairs (so don't queue downstairs with returning Muscovites). A free meal is available upstairs in the dining area. You must have a meal coupon which, if not handed to you when you check in, is available in the transit lounge... I was finally rewarded with a lukewarm frankfurter, some cold pasta which had bonded itself into an amorphous mass, and two pieces of stale bread.'

It is now just as quick and easy to book direct through Aeroflot, but you can also use one of their agents in London such as WEXAS, Sam Travel (tel: 0171 636 2521 or 0171 434 9561), or World Travel and Tours (tel: 0181 673 4434).

On most airlines serving Madagascar there are low-season and high-season rates. Low season is from January to the end of June, and mid-September to mid-December. The exception is Aeroflot.

In November 1996 the Air France/Air Mad monopoly was broken by the introduction of scheduled and charter flights from Paris to Madagascar by AOM and CORSAIR. This is expected to have far-reaching effects on the profitability of Air Mad.

From other Indian Ocean islands

You may be able to pick up a cheap flight from Paris to **La Réunion** from where there are almost daily Air Madagascar flights to Antananarivo, and also to Toamasina (Tamatave) on the east coast with Air Madagascar. Air Mad's new rival, TAM, operates between La Réunion and Nosy Be. There are far fewer formalities when arriving at one of these smaller airports, so it's an option to be considered seriously.

Air Mauritius flies between **Mauritius** and Antananarivo three times a week, and there are several flights from the Comoro Islands.

From Africa

From **Kenya** there are several flights per week (Air Madagascar and Air France) from Nairobi. With so many cheap flights from London to Nairobi, this may be a good option – if you can stand the departure time of 02.50 Thursday morning and 06.00 Sunday morning, and the danger of the planes being overbooked since they are coming from Europe. Current (1996) fares for a 21-day excursion are US$424, but for over 21 days it goes up to US$706.

Flights go twice a week from **South Africa**. Air Madagascar (tel: 011 784 7724) flies from Johannesburg on Sundays at 08.30, returning on Saturdays at

17.05; and Inter Air (tel: 011 397 1445) flies on Tuesdays at 08.30, returning on Wednesdays. The flight takes four hours and, at a discounted rate through a tour operator, costs about R1,600. Air Austral (tel: 011 880 9039) flies from Durban or Johannesburg to La Réunion, from where you can get a flight to Nosy Be.

South Africans are lucky; they have Unusual Destinations to make all their arrangements (see advert opposite). They are particularly strong on specialised natural history tours, and their knowledge of the country and understanding of its hassles are second to none in Africa. Unusual Destinations, PO Box 11583, Vorna Valley, SA 1686. Tel: 011 805 4833/4. Fax 011 805 4835.

From the USA

Madagascar is about as far from California as it is possible to be. Indeed, San Francisco and the southern town of Toliara *are* as far apart as it is possible to be. Understandably, therefore, the published fare from the USA is expensive – US$4242 from LA in the high season, and US$3760 from New York. However, there is a specialist tour operator who combines reasonably-priced flights on Air France and Air Madagascar with individualised land arrangements and a great knowledge of, and love for, Madagascar: Monique Rodriguez, Cortez Travel Services, 124 Lomas Santa Fe Dr, Solano Beach, CA 92075. Tel: 619 755 5136 or (toll free) 800 854 1029. Fax: 619 481 7474. Email: cortez-usa@mcimail.com. Another agency with similarly priced flights is M & H Travel. Tel: 310 338 1171. Round-trip flights through these people are as low as US$1850 from NY or US$2200 from LA. Occasional low-season specials go down to US$1250 from NY.

The General Sales Agent for Air Madagascar can be reached toll free on 800 821 3388, fax: 619 792 5280.

From Australia

The specialist tour operator here is Hartley's Safaris/Africa Travel Centre, with branches in Perth, Sydney and Melbourne. Air Madagascar has an office in the same building as the Sydney Consulate. There are no direct flights; you have a choice of going from Melbourne or Perth to Mauritius (Air Mauritius) and connecting with an Air Madagascar flight to Antananarivo, or flying from Perth via Johannesburg.

Arrival in Antananarivo

See *Chapter Eight* for the rather complicated arrivals and departure procedure.

By sea

There is now a regular cargo line from Durban (South Africa) which takes up to ten passengers. Phone 031 301 1225.

Getting to Madagascar by yacht from South Africa is becoming very popular. Try the following:

Yacht clubs

Royal Natal Yacht Club, PO Box 2946, Durban 4000. Tel: 031 301 5425. Fax: 307 2590.

Point Yacht Club, PO Box 2224, Durban 4000. Tel: 031 301 4787. Fax: 305 1234.

Richards Bay Yacht Club, PO Box 10387, Meer'en'see 3901. Tel: 0351 32704. Fax: 31784.

Royal Cape Yacht Club, PO Box 777, Cape Town 8000. Tel: 021 211 354. Fax: 216 028.

Many yachts sail from Natal to Madagascar and the Durban consulate was set up to cope with their visas. It takes six to seven days to sail to Anakao, the most popular port (south of Toliara). Most stop en route at Europa island, where a French garrison will advise on the next stage. Experienced sailors and divers will want to reach the atoll of Bassas da India which offers superb diving but has been responsible for the shipwreck of numerous vessels.

Boat charters

Andrew Wright. Tel/fax: 031 708 5664.

SA Cruising Association. Dennis Wiggins. Tel: 031 305 2125.

WHAT TO BRING

Luggage

A sturdy duffel bag or backpack with internal frame is more practical than a suitcase (and you may not be allowed to take a suitcase on a Twin Otter plane). Backpackers should consider buying a rucksack with a zipped compartment to enclose the straps when using them on airlines. Or – a cheaper option – roll up the straps and bind them out of the way with insulating tape. Bring a light folding nylon bag for taking purchases home, and the largest permissible bag to take as hand baggage on the plane. Pack this with everything you need for the first four or so days, especially if travelling by Aeroflot. Then, if they lose your luggage, you won't be too inconvenienced.

Clothes

Before deciding what clothes to pack, take a look at the climate section on page 15. There is quite a difference between summer and winter temperatures, particularly in the highlands and south where it is distinctly *cold* at night between May and September. A fibre-pile jacket or a body-warmer (down vest) is useful in addition to a sweater. At any time of the year it will be hot during the day in low-lying areas, and very hot between October and March. Layers of clothing – T-shirt, sweatshirt, light sweater – are warm and versatile, and take less room than a heavy sweater. Don't bring jeans, they are too heavy and too hot. Lightweight cotton or cotton mix trousers such as Rohan Bags are much more suitable. The Bags have a useful inside zipped pocket for security. At any time of year you will need a light showerproof jacket, and during the wet season, or if spending time in the rainforest, appropriate rain gear and perhaps a small umbrella. A light cotton jacket is always useful for breezy evenings by the coast. Don't forget a hat.

For footwear, trainers (running shoes) and sandals are usually all you need. 'Sports sandals' which strap securely to the feet and are waterproof are better than flip-flops. Hiking boots may be required in places like Ankarana and Isalo but are not necessary for the main tourist circuits.

Give some thought to beachwear if you enjoy snorkelling. You may need an old pair of sneakers (or similar) to protect your feet from sea urchins, and a T-shirt and shorts to wear while in the water to prevent sunburn.

Toiletries

Supplies in Madagascar are erratic so bring what you need, especially insect repellent, sunscreen, skin creams, and so on. You should also bring a roll of toilet paper, although you can usually buy adequately soft toilet paper in supermarkets. Don't rely on the local loos supplying anything.

Women should bring enough tampons to last the trip (the brands without an applicator take up less luggage space). Men (and women) should bring condoms if there is any chance of a sexual encounter (although Madagascar is addressing the problem of AIDS with enthusiasm: in the drawer of my posh Tana hotel was Gideon's Bible and a condom).

Bring as many baby-wipes as you can. Apart from the pleasure of being able to freshen up during a long trip, these are essential for washing hands when there is no water and will help you avoid traveller's diarrhoea.

Some toilet articles have several uses: dental floss is excellent for repairs as well as for teeth, and a nail brush gets clothes clean too.

Don't take up valuable space with a bath towel – a hand towel is perfectly adequate.

Women (and men) should leave all valuable jewellery at home. Apart from the high risk of theft, such items have to be declared on arrival and may even be weighed to make sure you don't sneakily sell a link or two of your gold chain!

Protection against mosquitoes

With malaria on the increase, it is vital to be properly protected. There are a lot of products on the market, one of the most useful being Buzz-Bands (made by Traveller International Products). These slip over the wrists and ankles (mosquitoes' favourite area) and really do the job. A reader's tip is that Avon's Skin-so-Soft bath oil is a natural mosquito repellent.

For hotel rooms, pyrethrum coils which burn slowly through the night and repel insects with their smoke are available all over Madagascar. The brand name is Big-Tox. They really do work.

If you expect to be using C category hotels, or sleeping outside, it is sensible to have a mosquito net, preferably a self-standing one. The best I know are made by Long Road, USA, (see advert on page 102) whose Indoor Travel Tent is sturdy enough to use outdoors and has a built-in groundsheet giving protection from bed bugs and fleas as well as mosquitoes. This means, however, that you must use your own sleeping bag inside it. Of the conventional nets which need to be hung from the wall or ceiling, the one sold by SafariQuip is recommended: lightweight and small, and easy to erect. Bring insulating tape, and to be on the safe side pack a couple of cup-hooks to screw into a convenient crack in the wall. SafariQuip, The Stones, Castleton, Sheffield, S30 2WX. Tel: 01433 620320. Fax: 01433 620061.

Rough travel equipment

Basic camping gear gives you the freedom to travel adventurously and can add a considerable degree of comfort to overland journeys.

The most important item is your backpack: this should have an internal frame and plenty of pockets. Protect it from oil, dirt, and the effluent of young or furry/feathered passengers with a canvas sack or similar adapted covering. The plastic woven rice sacks sold outside the Marché Artisanal in Tana are ideal for this purpose (bring a large needle and dental floss to do the final custom-fitting in Tana).

In winter (June to August) a lightweight sleeping bag will keep you warm in cheap hotels with inadequate bedding, and on night stops on – or off – 'buses'. A sheet sleeping bag plus a light blanket or space blanket is ideal for the summer months (October to May) and when the hotel linen is missing or dirty.

An air-mattress or pillow pads your bum on hard seats as well as your hips when sleeping out. One of those horseshoe-shaped travel pillows lets you sleep sitting up (which you'll need to do on taxi-brousses).

A lightweight tent allows you to strike out on your own and stay in nature reserves, on deserted beaches and so forth. It will need to have a separate rain fly and be well-ventilated. A bivi-sac or the Long Road Travel Tent is sufficient for the occasional night out.

Most people forgo a stove in order to cut down on weight, but if you will be camping extensively bring a stove that burns petrol (gasoline) or paraffin (kerosene). Meths (*alcohol à bruler*) is usually available as well. There are always fresh vegetables for sale in the smallest village so bring some stock cubes to make vegetable stew.

Take your own mug and spoon (and carry them with you always). That way you can enjoy roadside coffee without the risk of a cup rinsed in filthy water, and market yoghurt without someone else's germs on the spoon. Milk powder tastes (to most people) better in tea or coffee than condensed milk. You can buy it locally, or bring it from home. Don't forget a water-bottle. The sort that has a belt attached – or can be attached to a belt – is ideal.

Give some thought to ways of interacting with the locals (see *Show and tell items* below). Bring the Malagasy phrase-book and cassette (see page 35) and practise your language skills on fellow passengers. Take along some playing cards or dominoes. And how about 'Pigs'? This game, which involves throwing three plastic pigs, like dice, and scoring according to how they land, wins you instant friends and gaming partners.

A good book allows you to retreat from interaction for a while (but you won't be able to read on a taxi-brousse). If you want to read at night, buy a 100-watt bulb (bayonet type) to substitute for the 40-watt one supplied by Category C hotels.

Finally, and most important of all, don't forget to carry a photocopy of your passport information page and Madagascar visa at all times. Then you can leave your passport safely locked in a hotel and still have something to show at road checks (if asked, which is rare). Also take photocopies of all your air tickets before leaving home. The airline will then refund them more easily if lost.

Photography

Ordinary print film is available in Madagascar, but it is safer to bring plenty. It can be competently developed at the photo shop near the Colbert. Slide film is hard to find; all you need should be brought with you – and you need twice as much as you think.

You will not need a telephoto lens for the lemurs of Berenty and Nosy Komba (wide-angle is more useful for these bold animals) but you'll want a long lens plus very fast film (400 ASA) and a flash for most forest creatures. For landscapes 64 or 100 ASA is ideal. A macro lens is wonderful for all the weird insects and reptiles. Don't overburden yourself with camera equipment – there's no substitute for the eye/brain combination!

Miscellaneous

Some random tips: bring a transparent pouch (the sort you carry maps in) to hang round your neck at the airport to cope with all those papers and documents. Bring a roll of insulating tape or – better still – gaffer/duck tape which is very versatile. A Swiss Army knife (or similar) is essential. A rubber wedge will secure your hotel door at night, and a combination lock is useful in a variety of ways (see the section on safety in *Chapter Five*). Many readers report (and I agree) that a small tape recorder/Walkman is a great asset during lone evenings in dingy hotel rooms or on an all-night taxi-brousse (but beware of exciting too much envy from your fellow-passengers). Earplugs are just about essential, to block out not only the sounds of the towns but those of enthusiastic nocturnal animals when camping in reserves! (Personally I think it's worth being kept awake by these, but it can pall after several nights.) A large handkerchief or bandana has many uses and protects your hair and lungs from dust, and the uses for a *lamba* (Malagasy sarong) are too numerous to list.

If you are a keen snorkeller you would be safer to bring your own mask and snorkel; they are not always available at the resorts, even in Nosy Be.

Checklist

Small torch (flashlight) with spare batteries and bulb, or headlamp (for nocturnal animal hunts), travel alarm clock (or alarm wristwatch), penknife, sewing kit, scissors, tweezers, safety pins, insulating tape or Sellotape

(Scotchtape), felt-tipped pen, ballpoint pens, a small notebook, a large notebook for diary and letters home, envelopes, plastic bags (all sizes, sturdy; Zip-loc are particularly useful), universal plug for baths and sinks, elastic clothes line or cord and pegs, concentrated detergent (available in tubes in camping stores) and biodegradable soap for camping, ear plugs, insect repellent, sunscreen, lipsalve, spare glasses or contact lenses, sun glasses, medical and dental kit (see *Chapter Five*), dental floss, a water container, water purifying tablets or other sterilising agent. Compact binoculars, camera and film, books, miniature cards, Scrabble/pocket chess set, French dictionary and Malagasy phrasebook.

Goods for presents, sale or trade

This is a difficult area. In the past tourists have handed out presents to children and created the tiresome little beggars you will encounter in the popular areas (if you don't now know the French for pen or sweets, you soon will). They have also handed T-shirts to adults with similar consequences. There are, however, plenty of occasions when a gift is appropriate, although as Will Pepper points out 'On a number of occasions people said this souvenir of Ireland is all well and good but I would prefer cash'. Giving money as a 'present' in return for services is entirely acceptable so in rural areas it's best to pay cash and refrain from introducing a new consumer awareness.

In urban areas or with the more sophisticated Malagasy people, presents are a very good way of showing your appreciation for kindness or extra good service. Goods can also be used instead of cash for hotel rooms, transport, etc. Will Pepper says: 'Trade samples of perfume (small bottles) were such a hit with women and husbands that I got free accommodation and meals on two occasions. Music cassettes were a huge hit with taxi-brousse drivers, and also mean that you can listen to good quality music on long trips.' Frances Kerridge points out that you'd better like pop music – Elton John, Bryan Adams, Whitney Houston etc – to gain points on a taxi brousse. It's worth bringing some duty-free cigarettes, however much you disapprove of the habit. Clothes, especially trendy T-shirts, are often requested by those with an appetite for the 'Western' look, and you will always find a home for trainers (running shoes).

If you want to contribute something a little more intellectually satisfying, here is a suggestion from Dr Philip Jones, who travelled in Madagascar on behalf of the charity Money for Madagascar. 'I was asked several times for an English Grammar, so any such books would be valued gifts. If visitors take a French-English dictionary, why not leave it in Madagascar?' Frances Kerridge suggests English-language tapes as an alternative to books: 'Almost everyone seems to want to learn English.'

Show and tell items

In previous editions I wrote: 'Better than presents are the things you can bring which allow you to interact with the locals: postcards of your country, picture books, paper and a knowledge of origami, string and a knowledge of cat's cradles. Simple conjuring tricks go down a treat. Photos of your family will be pored over gratifyingly or, if you haven't got a family, the Royal Family will do. If you're unfortunate enough to come from a country that doesn't have a Royal Family, film stars are a good substitute – particularly the male muscle-bound type, preferably scowling. Any colour picture is an attraction; I've been told that the photos in this book drew about 50 viewers at one time! Frisbees and balls all add to the fun. However, to call yourself a real traveller you should be capable of being entertaining without the use of props.'

This last sentence drew the following response from a reader: 'Let me take you to task over a sentence which seemed not to fit with the rest of the book... I've travelled for a few years in a few countries; and I've never felt that I needed to be entertaining in order to interact. How about learning from the people? Finding out what *they* can contribute? By all means suggest that we have some interactive "props" to use with the relatively sophisticated people we may meet on public transport or in the cities; but please please don't ask us to insult the more remote villagers by assuming that *we* should lead *them* in the interaction. I have so often been made aware of – and humbled by – how much *they* have to teach *us*, in terms of human qualities and courtesies.'

MONEY

How much money to take is covered in *Chapter Six*, but give some thought to *how* to take it.

Bring your money in US dollar or pound sterling travellers cheques. Money may only be changed at 'accredited establishments' – banks, some hotels, and some travel agents. It is useful to bring some cash – French francs, dollars or sterling banknotes are equally good – for those occasions when you want to change a small amount of money or haven't got your passport with you. Do not bring US$100 bills – these are not being accepted because of the large number of counterfeit ones doing the rounds. The same problem may occur with 500Ff notes.

Some of the large hotels accept credit cards, but there are some notable exceptions, such as the Dauphin in Tolagnaro. However, credit cards may be used to draw cash, but with restrictions. The Banque Malgache de l'Océan Indien accepts Visa cards only, and Madagascar Air Tours is the agent for American Express. The French for Visa card is *Carte Bleue*.

Independent travellers who are not on a tight budget may run into problems such as those experienced by Joy Shannon: 'Financing our holiday was a large cause of stress and delay on our first day and a continuing cause for worry right up to departure.' The problem was the requirement to pay for airfares and upmarket hotels in foreign currency with little opportunity to pay with credit cards, especially outside the main cities. Malagasy money may not be changed back into hard currency at the airport.

The answer, probably, is to bring a large amount of money in travellers cheques, and to pay in advance when possible.

WAYS AND MEANS

Madagascar... Are you sure?

With the right planning almost everyone can enjoy Madagascar. It will not be a cheap holiday, however, so if you have serious doubts about your ability to adapt to its ways you would do better not to go.

Having decided that you have the enthusiasm and flexibility to make your trip a success consider the options below.

What sort of traveller are you?

Deciding what's best for your budget and inclinations is as important as planning where to go in this huge island. Consider which of the following options suits you best.

Expedition cruising

This is the softest option in that you know that you will sleep in a comfortable bed each night and eat familiar food. It is thus ideal for the adventurous at heart who are no longer able to take the rigours of land travel. It is also sometimes the only way of getting to remote off-shore islands and for snorkelling over some of the best reefs in the world. Since I accepted (without too much delay) an offer to lecture on the ships chartered by Noble Caledonia (UK) and Special Expeditions (US) I have become a convert – indeed, I've had some of my best Madagascar experiences ever from the *Caledonian Star* and the *Professor Khromov*. Contact Noble Caledonia Ltd, 11 Charles St, London W1X 7HB (tel: 0171 491 4752) or Quark Expeditions, 980 Post Rd, Darien, CT 06820, USA (tel: 800 356 5699). In South Africa try Starlight Cruises, tel: 011 884 7680 (Alan Foggitt).

Group travel

Cruising aside, this is the easiest option for the person with only limited time available, and who is happy to leave the arrangements to someone else. Group travel is usually a lot of fun, ideal for single people who do not wish to travel alone, and if you choose the tour company and itinerary carefully you will see a great deal of the country, gain an understanding of its complicated culture and unique wildlife, and generally have a great time without the need to make decisions.

Many tour operators in Britain and America do set departures to Madagascar; some of them have advertised in this book.

One tour operator that should be mentioned because it's different is **Earthwatch**. This non-profit organisation involves paying volunteers in scientific projects. Among other things in Madagascar you can work with Dr Alison Jolly or Josephine Andrews on lemur research. Addresses: Belsyne Court, 57 Woodstock Rd, Oxford OX2 6HU, England, tel: 01865 311600; and 680 Mt Auburn St, PO Box 403, Watertown, MA 02272-9104, USA.

Tailor-made tours

This is the ideal option for a couple or small group who are not restricted financially. It is also the best choice for people with special interests or strong ideas, who like things to go as smoothly as possible. You will be the decision-maker and will choose where you want to go, but the logistics will be taken care of. Although a good travel agent can make these arrangements, you are strongly recommended to use a specialist such as Cortez Travel in the USA or Unusual Destinations in South Africa, or their associates in Britain, Reef and Rainforest Tours.

Some sample tours are: fishing, diving, trekking, river journeys, sailing, mineralogy, speleology, birdwatching, herpetology, botany (which can be further split into orchids and succulents), and entomology.

If you have a fax machine or email and are willing to persevere with Madagascar's erratic telecommunications (which are rapidly improving), you can save money by dealing directly with a tour operator in Madagascar. The best ones are listed later in this chapter.

Independent travel

Independent travellers usually have a rough idea of where they want to go and how they will travel, but are open to changes of plan dictated by local conditions, whim and serendipity. Independent travellers are not necessarily budget travellers: those that can afford to fly to major towns, then rent a vehicle and driver, can eliminate a large amount of hassle and see everything they set out to see – providing they set a realistic programme for themselves. What they miss out on is contact with the local people, and some of the smells, sounds, and otherness of Madagascar.

The majority of independent travellers (and users of this book) go by public transport and stay in B or C Category hotels. They are exposed to all Madagascar's joys and frustrations and most seem to love it, even if they agree that they have never travelled in a country that is so difficult to get around in. The key here is not to try too much. *Chapter Six* tells you about the trials and tribulations of travelling by taxi-brousse: no problem providing you allow time for delays.

The seriously adventurous

Madagascar must be one of the very few countries left in the world where large areas are not yet detailed in a guidebook. I have deliberately kept it that way, occasionally leaving out a traveller's description of the fantastic road he (or she) cycled down or the village he walked into. For the seriously adventurous, a study of the standard 1:2,000,000 map of Madagascar reveals some mouth-watering possibilities, and a look at the more detailed 1:500,000 maps confirms the opportunities for people who are willing to walk or cycle. In my very thick Readers' Letters file I have some wonderful accounts from travellers such as Anne Axel, Frances Kerridge, Bishop Brock and John Kupiec who did just that. Not everyone is courageous enough to step or pedal into the unknown like this, but in fact it's one of the safest ways to travel: the Malagasy that you meet will, once they have got over the shock of seeing you, invariably be welcoming and hospitable. The risk of crime is very low. It's how I first saw Madagascar and why I fell in love with the place.

Tour operators in Madagascar

There are many tour operators in Madagascar. This is by no means a complete list, just a selection of those that I can recommend. The Maison du Tourisme de Madagascar in Antananarivo puts out a comprehensive list.

Madagascar Airtours Hilton Hotel, Antananarivo. BP 3874. Tel: 341 92. Fax: 343 70. They now have an address in the city centre: 33 Ave de l'Indépendance. The most experienced agency, with offices in most major towns, they can organise a wide variety of specialist tours including natural history, ornithology, speleology, trekking, mineralogy, river trips, sailing, etc.

SETAM Ave 26 de Juin, Antananarivo. Tel: 272 49. Fax: 2347 02. Extremely helpful and efficient. Excellent English spoken. Recommended.

Boogie Pilgrim 40 Ave de l'Indépendance, Antananarivo 101. Tel: 258 78. Fax: 251 17. Email: bopi@bow.dts.mg. Organise tours of every sort, including some by light aircraft. Owners of Bush House (Pangalanes). Recommended.

Malagasy Tours Tel/fax: 261 2 356 07. The owner, Olivier Toboul, runs specialised itineraries for ethnobotany (amongst other things) using local people who can explain the complexities of the Malagasy culture. Good for off-the-beaten-track exploration, too.

Transcontinents 10 Ave de l'Indépendance, Antananarivo. BP 541. Tel: 223 98.

Voyages Bourdon 15 Rue P Lumumba, Antananarivo. Tel: 296 96.

Tropica Touring 41 Lalana Ratsimilaho. BP 465. Tel: 222 30 or 276 80. Fax: 349 01.

Highlights and itinerary suggestions

One of the hardest decisions facing the first-time visitor to a country as diverse as Madagascar is where to go. Even a month is not long enough to see everything so itineraries must be planned according to interests and the degree of comfort wanted. Here are some suggestions for tours lasting three to four weeks.

Reliability and comfort

Now that top-class hotels have been built near key reserves and national parks, comfort-loving visitors can be fairly sure of a proper holiday as well as getting a good overview of the country and its wildlife. All the following places have hotels of international standard: Antananarivo, Andasibe (Périnet) Reserve, Antsirabe, Toliara (Tuléar) with a side trip to Isalo, Tolagnaro (Fort Dauphin) and Berenty, Nosy Be. The stretches between Antananarivo and Antsirabe, and Toliara and Isalo, should be done by taxi or private car, and the rest by plane.

Nature reserves in moderate comfort

These are accessible by good road and have good-to-moderate accommodation: Andasibe (Périnet), Ampijoroa (as a day trip from Mahajanga), Montagne d'Ambre (as a day trip from Antsiranana), Lokobe (Nosy Be), Berenty, Ivoloina (near Toamasina).

The best reserves, comfort immaterial

Use the index to check out the following: Andasibe (Maromizaha, Mantady), Ampijoroa (camping), Montagne d'Ambre (camping), Ankaranana (camping), Ranomafana, Nosy Mangabe and the Masoala Peninsula, Beza Mahafaly (camping), Kirindy (camping), Zombitse Forest.

Birding

See *Chapter Three* for full details, but these cover all the different habitats: Ampijoroa (and along the road from Mahajanga), Ranomafana, Masoala Peninsula, Forest of Ambohetantely, spiny forest north of Toliara, Zombitse forest.

Landscape, people and tombs

For those whose interest lies more in the people and the countryside, a journey overland is recommended. RN7 from Antananarivo to Toliara gives a wonderful overview from rice-paddies in the highlands to the lovely town of Ambalavao and its magnificent granite mountains, and the small villages between Ihosy and Toliara. It also gives you a chance to see Isalo National Park. The journey is best done in a private vehicle so you can stop and look; there are good hotels at the main towns.

A more adventurous alternative (but still on a good road) is by train or bus to Toamasina then north by public transport to Soanierana-Ivongo and by boat to Nosy Boraha (Île Sainte Marie). Another east-coast journey is from Fianarantsoa to Manakara by train (if it's running), then south to Farafangana. Probably the most challenging west coast trip is to Morondava by road then overland to Toliara.

For the seriously adventurous

Find a place that is not described in the guidebooks – and have it to yourself!

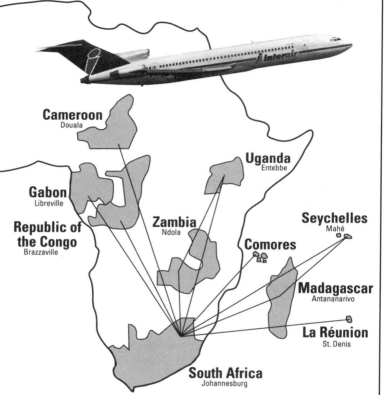

FLORA
Left: *A tall stand of didiera trees, near Tolagnaro* (HB)
Above right: *Pitcher plants,* Nepenthes madagascariensis (KT)
Below right: *One of Madagascar's most striking endemic orchids,* Eulophiella
roempleriana, *which is found only on Île aux Nattes, off Île Sainte Marie* (HB)

THE MOST COMMONLY SEEN LEMURS
Above left: *Male Sanford's brown lemur* (NG) Above right: *Male crowned lemur* (NG)
Both species are found at Montagne d'Ambre and Ankarana
Below left: *Ring-tailed lemur with twins, Berenty* (HB)
Below right: *Female black lemur, Nosy Komba* (MH)
Centre: *Indri and young, Périnet* (NG)

SIFAKA
Above: *The white sifaka,* Propithecus verreauxi verreauxi, *also known as Verreaux's sifaka, is common in Berenty and other southern reserves.* (BL)
Below: *The most beautiful lemur of all, the golden crowned sifaka (Propithecus tattersalli), is confined to a tiny area in the north.* (NG)

WEIRD AND WONDERFUL

Above left: *Tomato frog,* Dycophus antongili (NG)

Centre left: *Giraffe weevil* (KT)

Below left: *Unidentified caterpillar* (NG)

Above right: *Leaf-tailed gecko,* Uroplatus ebenaui (NG)

Centre right: *Unidentified weevil* (KT)

Below right: *Hedgehog tenrec,* Echinops telfairi (BL)

Chapter Five

Health and Safety

HEALTH

The health section is written by Dr Jane Wilson Howarth, who led two expeditions to Ankarana. She has studied bilharzia in western Madagascar and has worked as a health adviser in South East Asia for the last nine years. She is the author of Bugs, Bites and Bowels *(Cadogan).*

Before you go
Malaria prevention
About 2,000 travellers a year return to Britain with malaria; ten or a dozen subsequently die of it. This is the most common serious tropical disease that affects international travellers, and it is reckless to ignore the risk of contracting it. You should start taking malaria prophylaxis tablets one week before leaving for Madagascar and continue for four weeks after returning home.

At the time of writing, two chloroquine (Nivaquine) weekly and two proguanil (Paludrine) daily were recommended. Mefloquine (Larium) is an excellent weekly prophylactic, but some people get unpleasant dreams or other unacceptable side effects; take a couple of doses well before travelling, to see if the side effects will bother you. Up-to-date advice is available from the Malaria Reference Laboratory in London. Phone 0891 600 350 for a recording of where malaria is a problem and what tablets to take, or 0891 600 274 for advice on avoiding bites.

Malaria tablets are best taken with or soon after food (or milk or a couple of biscuits), when they are least likely to cause the side effect of nausea which troubles some people. It is safe to take chloroquine during pregnancy and breast feeding. Proguanil is also safe in pregnancy, but you should then take Folic Acid – a vitamin supplement – with it. Fansidar is *not* a safe drug to take as a prophylaxis, but if you are travelling far from reliable medical facilities you should carry three Fansidar tablets for emergency treatment of malaria. Take plenty of insect repellent (DEET-based are best), long-sleeved shirts, long trousers, and consider carrying a mosquito net (see page 79). Nets are most effective if treated with Permethrin or a similar contact insecticide. Kits are sold at British Airways Travel Clinics, etc.

Immunisations

Disease patterns and international health regulations change, so it's worth taking special advice. Travel clinics such as those operated by the Berkeley Street Clinic and British Airways (phone 0171 831 5333 for the nearest of the 36 BA clinics) offer constantly updated health briefs as well as immunisations. It's important that your immunisations for tetanus, polio and typhoid are up to date. A highly effective vaccine against Hepatitis A, Havrix, is recommended for those travelling for several months. Two shots provide protection for ten years.

It's also worth having a Schick Test to check that your childhood immunisation for diphtheria is still protective. An 'ordinary' intramuscular shot against rabies is now available, and may be worth arranging if you think you are at risk. The disease is a problem in Madagascar because of the half-wild dogs found in many parts of the island.

Remember that 'live' vaccines cannot be given within a fortnight of each other, so plan well ahead. There is a list of vaccination centres at the end of this section.

If you are coming from Africa you may be required to show a vaccination certificate for yellow fever; these are not required for passengers arriving from Europe or the USA.

Teeth

Have a dental check-up before you go. There is now a Dental Emergency Kit on the market (if you can't get it at Boots, ask your dentist). Amongst other things it contains emergency fillings.

Insurance

Make sure you have insurance covering the cost of an air ambulance and treatment in La Réunion or Nairobi, which offer more sophisticated medical facilities than are available in Madagascar. Europ Assistance International, which has an office in Antananarivo, gives cover for scuba diving.

Water sterilisation

Although the standard advice on water sterilisation in the tropics is to boil it for 20 minutes, merely bringing water to the boil kills all bugs and renders it safe. This means that tea, coffee, *ranovola*, etc bought in *hotelys* are probably the most convenient drinks to take when travelling.

If you're worried about water not being boiled properly, you can take a thermos flask; almost-boiling water kept in this for 15 minutes will be thoroughly sterilised. *Eau Vive* or mineral water is not always available and can be quite expensive, and studies in other countries suggest it may be contaminated. It's often better to purify your own tap water. Silver-based sterilising tablets (sold in Britain under the tradename Micropur) are tasteless so recommended. A cheaper and effective sterilising agent is iodine (preferable to chlorine because it kills amoebic cysts), which is available in liquid or tablet form. To make treated water more palatable, bring packets of powdered drink. An alternative is a water filter such as the Pur system. It gives safe water with no unpleasant flavour, but is expensive. Another possibility is a plug-in immersion heater, so that you can have a nice hot cuppa (if you bring teabags).

Note that most travellers acquire diarrhoea from inadequately heated, contaminated food – salads, ice, ice-cream, etc – rather than from disobeying the 'don't drink the water' rule.

Some travellers' diseases
Malaria and insect-borne diseases

Tablets do not give complete protection from malaria, although they should make it less serious if it does break through; it's important to protect yourself from being bitten, especially since there are also other mosquito-borne infections (eg Rift Valley Fever). The mosquitoes which give you malaria usually bite in the evening (from about 5 pm) and throughout the night, so it's wise to dress in long trousers and long-sleeved shirts, and to cover exposed skin with insect repellent. *Anopheles* mosquitoes generally hunt at ankle level, and tend to bite the first piece of exposed flesh they encounter, so DEET-impregnated ankle bands are a surprisingly effective protection.

Malaria transmission is rare in urban environments, but it does occur around Antananarivo; the altitude there is insufficient to limit the malaria mosquito. Cerebral malaria is a problem, and is presumably caught by people bitten by mosquitoes which breed in the paddy fields around the city; malaria mosquitoes can fly five kilometres from their breeding grounds.

At night, protect yourself by sleeping under a mosquito net, preferably one treated with Permethrin, or by burning mosquito coils. And be sure to take your malaria tablets meticulously. Mosquito coils and nets are available in Antananarivo, but treatment kits are not.

Even if you have been taking your malaria prophylaxis carefully, there is still a slight chance of contracting malaria. The symptoms are fevers, chills, joint pain, diarrhoea and headache – in other words the symptoms of many illnesses including flu. Bear in mind that malaria can take as little as seven days to develop. However, if you become ill within a week of arriving in Madagascar it is unlikely to be malaria, and the delay between being infected and the symptoms appearing may be several months so always consult a doctor (mentioning that you have been abroad) if you develop a flu-like illness within a year of getting home. The life-threatening cerebral malaria will become apparent within three months.

Mosquitoes pass on not only malaria but also elephantiasis, dengue fever and a variety of other unpleasant viral fevers. By avoiding mosquito bites you also avoid these serious diseases, as well as those itching lumps which so easily become infected. Once you've been bitten, tiger balm, calamine lotion or calamine-based creams help stop the itching.

Travellers' diarrhoea

Diarrhoea is very common in visitors to Madagascar, and you are more likely to suffer from this if you are new to tropical travel. Tourists tend to be obsessed with water sterilisation, but contrary to popular belief, travellers' diarrhoea usually comes from contaminated food not contaminated water. Ice-cream, sadly, is particularly risky: a survey in Antananarivo showed that 100% of home-made and 60% of factory-made ice-creams contained the faecal bacteria which cause diarrhoea. So if you want to stay healthy avoid ice-cream, and also ice, untreated water, salads, fruit with lots of crevices such as strawberries, uncooked foods and cooked food that has been hanging around or has been inadequately reheated. Sizzling hot street food is likely to be far safer than the food offered in buffets in expensive hotels, however gourmet the latter may look. Yoghurt is usually safe, as are sorbets.

The way to the quickest recovery from travellers' diarrhoea is to reduce your normal meals to a few light items, avoid milk and alcohol and drink lots of clear fluids. You need to replace the fluids lost down the toilet, and those containing salt and sugar are most easily absorbed. Add a little sugar to a salty drink, such as Marmite or Oxo, or salt to a sugary drink like Coca-Cola. Sachets of rehydration mixtures are available commercially, but you can make your own by mixing a rounded dessert spoon (or four teaspoons) of sugar with a quarter-teaspoon of salt and adding it to a glass of boiled and cooled water. Drink two glasses of this every time you open your bowels – more often if you are thirsty. Substituting glucose for sugar will make you feel even better. If you are in a rural area drink the 'milk' from young coconuts, which is an effective and safe rehydration fluid, as is *ranovola* (water boiled in the pot that rice is cooked in).

Hot drinks and iced drinks cause a reflex emptying of the bowel, so avoid these while the diarrhoea is at its worst; they will make the belly ache worse, too.

Once the bowel has ejected the toxic material causing the diarrhoea, the symptoms will settle quite quickly and you should begin to feel better again after 24–48 hours. Should the diarrhoea be associated with passing blood or slime, it would be sensible to have a stool check at some stage, but provided you continue to drink clear fluids, no harm will come from waiting for a few days.

Holiday schedules often make it impossible to follow the 'sit it out' advice. When a long bus journey or flight is anticipated you will have to take a blocker such as Imodium. Just remember that such drugs slow up the action of the bowel so you tend to feel ill for a longer period of time. Safer and far more effective is the antibiotic Ciprofloxacin. It can be taken as a single (500mg) dose if the symptoms are mild or as a three-day course (500mg twice daily) if the symptoms are more severe. Discuss this with your doctor or travel clinic. This drug must not be given to children, or where fluid intake is inadequate.

If you are worried or feel very sick, seek local medical advice, but as long as you keep well hydrated you should come to no harm and the symptoms will usually settle without further treatment. Even bacillary dysentery and cholera will resolve within a week without treatment, as long as you drink plenty of rehydration fluids.

Other bowel beasties

There is a high prevalence of tapeworm in Malagasy cattle, so I would recommend eating your steaks well done. If you do pass a worm, this is alarming but treatment can wait, and indeed travellers often carry only one and so need no treatment.

Bilharzia

This is a nasty, debilitating disease which is a problem in much of lowland Madagascar. It is caught by swimming or paddling in clean, still or slow-moving water (not fast-flowing rivers) where an infected person has defecated or urinated. The parasite next infects pond snails and then people, by penetrating the skin, where it causes 'swimmer's itch'. Since it takes at least ten minutes for the worm to infect you, a quick wade across a river, preferably followed by vigorous towelling off, should not put you at risk. Bilharzia is cured with a single dose of Praziquantel, but the parasites are acquiring resistance to this medicine. If you think you may have been exposed to the disease, ask your doctor to arrange a blood test when you get home. This should be done more than six weeks from the last exposure.

Sexually transmitted diseases

These are common in Madagascar and AIDS is on the increase. If you enjoy nightlife, male or female condoms will make encounters less risky.

Rabies and animal bites

Bites from pet lemurs and habituated animals are on the increase in Madagascar and even the smallest danger of the animal being rabid has to be taken seriously. Do not try to stroke wild or captive animals. Should you be unfortunate enough to be bitten by any mammal, wild or domesticated, you are at risk from both rabies and tetanus. If you're not immunised against tetanus, you must seek medical help speedily. The risk of rabies should also be taken seriously if you haven't been immunised, particularly if you have been bitten by a dog. Whether immunised or not, you should immediately scrub the wound under running water for five minutes, then flood it with alcohol or iodine.

Once the rabies virus enters the body, it migrates slowly along the nerves, and the dramatic symptoms of hydrophobia, etc, do not appear until the virus has reached the brain. Symptoms will begin after perhaps two weeks if the bites have been to the face, but may be delayed by as much as two years if the bite is to the foot. Once symptoms have appeared, rabies is untreatable and almost invariably fatal. Before the onset of symptoms, the disease can be prevented by a simple course of injections into the arm (the painful ones in the abdomen have long been superseded). Although it's wise to seek medical help as soon as possible after you are bitten (and bites to the face must be attended to within ten days) it may not be too late to do so after you get home.

Immunisation against tetanus and rabies before you travel is strongly recommended if you're venturing off the beaten track. Even if you have been immunised, it is advisable to seek medical attention if the bite is severe, or if the wound is dirty or deep. A rabies booster is sensible after any suspect bite.

Infection and trivial breaks in the skin

The skin is very prone to infection in hot, moist climates, so anything that makes even the slightest break to its surface is likely to allow bacteria to enter and so cause problems. Mosquito bites – especially if you scratch them – are probably the most common route of infection, so apply a cream to reduce the itching. Toothpaste helps if you are stuck for anything better. Cover any wounds, especially oozing wounds, so that flies don't snack on them.

Fairly major infections can arise through even a small nick in the skin. Antiseptic creams are not advised, since they keep the wounds moist and this encourages further infection. A powerful antiseptic which also dries the skin is potassium permanganate crystals dissolved in water. Another alternative is diluted tincture of iodine (which you should be carrying anyway as a water steriliser). Bathe the wound twice a day, more often if you can, by dabbing with cotton wool dipped in dilute potassium permanganate or iodine solution.

Bathing in sulphur springs cures mild skin infections.

Sunburn

Light-skinned people burn remarkably quickly near the equator, especially when snorkelling. Wearing a shirt, preferably one with a collar, protects the neck and back, and long shorts can also be worn. Use a sunscreen with a high protection factor (up to 25) on the back of the neck, calves and other exposed parts.

The nasty side of nature
Animals

Malagasy land-snakes are back-fanged, and so are effectively non-venomous. **Sea-snakes**, although venomous, are easy to see and usually – but not always – unaggressive.

Particularly when in the dry forest, it's wise to be wary of scorpions and centipedes. Neither is fatal, but they are very unpleasant. **Scorpions** are nocturnal, but they often come out after rain; they like hiding in small crevices during the day. If you are camping in the desert or the dry forest, it's not unusual to find they have crept into the pocket of a rucksack – even if you have taken the sensible precaution of suspending it from a tree. Scorpion stings are very painful for about 24 hours, but are not life-threatening. After a sting on the finger, I had an excruciatingly painful hand and arm for several days. The pain was only eased with morphine. My finger had no feeling for a month, and over ten years later it still has an abnormal nerve supply.

Madagascar has some very unpleasant (15cm) **centipedes**, though they are rarely seen; large **spiders** can be dangerous – the Black Widow is found in Madagascar, as well as an aggressive hairy spider with a nasty bite. Navy digger **wasps** have an unpleasant sting, but it's only the scorpions that commonly cause problems, because they favour hiding places where one might plunge a hand without looking. If you sleep on the ground, isolate yourself from these creatures with a mat, a hammock or a tent with a sewn-in ground sheet.

Leeches can be a nuisance in the rainforest, but are only revolting, not dangerous (AIDS cannot be spread via leeches). They are best avoided by covering up, tucking trousers into socks and applying insect repellent (even under the socks and shoes – but beware, DEET dissolves plastics). Once leeches have become attached they should not be forcibly removed or some mouth parts may remain causing the bite to itch for a long time. Either wait until they have finished feeding (when they will fall off) or encourage them to let go by applying a lit cigarette or salt. A film canister is a convenient salt container. The wound left by a leech bleeds a great deal, and may become infected if not kept clean. For more on leeches see box on page 57.

Beware of strolling barefoot on damp, sandy river beds. This is the way to pick up **jiggers**. These are female sand fleas, which resemble maggots and burrow into your toes to feed on your blood while incubating their eggs. Remove them, using a sterilised needle, by picking the top off the boil they make and teasing them out (this requires some skill, so it's best to ask a local person to help). Disinfect the wound thoroughly to prevent infection.

Plants

Madagascar has quite a few plants which cause skin irritation. The worst one I have encountered is a climbing legume which has pea-pod-like fruits that look furry. This 'fur' penetrates the skin as thousands of tiny needles, which must be painstakingly extracted with tweezers. Prickly pear fruits have the same defence. Relief from the secretions of other irritating plants is obtained by bathing. Sometimes it's best to wash your clothes as well, and immersion fully clothed may be the last resort!

Medical kit

Apart from personal medication taken on a regular basis, it's unnecessary to weigh yourself down with a comprehensive medical kit, as many of your requirements will be met by the pharmacies.

The list below is the absolute maximum an ordinary traveller needs to carry (I always carry less). Expeditions or very adventurous travellers should contact MASTA (see *Useful addresses*, below).

Malaria tablets; lots of plasters (Band-Aid/Elastoplast) to cover broken skin, infected insect bites, etc; antiseptic (potassium permanganate crystals to dissolve in water are best); small pieces of sterile gauze (Melonin dressing) and sticky plaster; soluble aspirin – good for fevers, aches and for gargling when you have a sore throat. Lanosil or some kind of soothing cream for sore anus (after diarrhoea) – also useful in cases of severe diarrhoea where a cough or sneeze can be disastrous are sanitary pads; Canestan for thrush and athlete's foot; foot powder; Vaseline or Heel Balm for cracked heels. A course of Amoxycillin (or Erythromycin if you're penicillin-allergic) which is good for chest infections, skin infections and cystitis; Cicatrin antibiotic powder for infected bites, etc; antibiotic eye drops; anti-histamine tablets; travel sickness pills (for those winding roads and taxi-brousses); tiger balm or calamine lotion for itchy bites; pointed tweezers for extracting splinters, sea-urchin spines, small thorns and coral.

Useful addresses
Britain
The Berkeley Street Clinic, 32 Berkeley Street, London W1 (near Green Park tube station). Tel: 0171 629 6233.

British Airways Travel Clinic and Immunisation Service. There are now BA clinics all around Britain. To find your nearest one, phone 0171 831 5333. The central London British Airways clinic is at 156 Regent Street W1, tel: 0171 439 958. This place also sells travellers' supplies and has a branch of Stanfords travel book and map shop.

Trailfinders Immunisation Centre, 19 Kensington High Street, London W8 7RG. Tel: 0171 938 3999. Also 254-284 Sauchiehall St, Glasgow G2 3EH. Tel: 0141 353 0066.

Travel Clinic and Vaccination Centre, Hospital for Tropical Diseases, 4 St Pancras Way, London NW1 (09.00–11.00 only). Also 1st Floor, Queens House, 182 Tottenham Court Road, London W1 (Warren Street tube station). Tel: 0171 637 9899. It sells many useful things, such as dental first aid kits.

MASTA (Medical Advisory Service for Travellers Abroad), Keppel St, London WC1E 7HT. Tel: 0171 631 4408. They can provide an individually tailored Personal Health Brief or a cheaper standard one. For this service phone 0891 224 900. MASTA also does a mail order service selling basic tropical supplies, mosquito anklets and a medical equipment pack with sterile syringes, etc.

USA and Canada
North American travellers looking for further information should phone the Center for Disease Control in Atlanta, Georgia. The hotline there provides information on a range of subjects: malaria, vaccinations, disease outbreaks in specific regions, etc. Tel: (404) 332 4559.

As a postscript, Dr Jane comments on a study she did in Indonesia. Village mothers were given soap and an explanation of the need for hand-washing after using the toilet and before eating, to protect their children from faecal-oral diarrhoea. The reduction in diarrhoea during the study was 89%, and two years later it was still down 75%!

Readers' comments on health problems

'An ordinary little scratch becomes a big infected wound after three days. Once I couldn't walk for several days after a scratched open mosquito bite became infected. I never had this problem before.' Luc Selleslagh

'Kem-o-dene, which is available in South Africa, is recommended for diarrhoea and digestive disorders of all sorts. I have also been told by an expatriate that bed bugs and other nasties don't like vanilla – put some pods in your bed in the morning and by evening all the bugs will have left!' Derek Schuurman

'I managed to get stung by a scorpion on my left middle finger. This nearly gave me a heart attack, since I remembered Jane Wilson's description and that she had quite a hard time of it. So my heart beat like a robotics factory, and I did not know whether this was from the poison or just scaredness! It turned out to be the latter. It hurt like blazes for about five hours – especially since I tried to keep it cool with my hand in the air outside the car window. Later in Tana I discovered you have to keep it warm...Then there were a few hours of prickly feelings (like tasting a 9V battery) and that was the last of it. No scars, no after effects...' Henk Beentje

---

CLOSE ENCOUNTERS OF THE TURD KIND

The surf sparkled in the early morning sun and the sand was firm underfoot as the tourist strode along the beach, revelling in the freedom of miles and miles of eastern coastline. As he approached the picturesque fishing village of bamboo and reed huts he saw people on the beach: the villagers, wrapped in their lambas, were squatting near the water. He approached, curious to see every aspect of their daily lives, and the men greeted him politely. Then he saw what they were doing. Turning away in acute embarrassment and disgust, he headed quickly back to the hotel. His morning's walk was spoiled.

Even the most basic pit toilets are unknown to most rural Malagasy. This lack of concern over one of the west's most taboo bodily functions is rightly disturbing. No rationalisation can diminish the disgust we feel when confronted by a neat pile of human faeces in a rural beauty spot. And disgust turns to anxiety when we consider the role that flies play in spreading disease.

The tourist involved in the beach experience asked a Malagasy why they do not bury their faeces. He was told that this would be *fady* because the dead (ie ancestors) are interred in the earth. Dr Jane Wilson, who studied schistosomiasis and intestinal parasites in western Madagascar, made the following observations in *Journal of Tropical Medicine and Hygiene*. 'It is common to find human faeces within 10 metres of houses. It is *fady* for Sakalavas to use latrines, or to defaecate in the same place as siblings of the opposite sex. There are several well-defined areas for defaecation, and also places where it is *fady* – but usually out of respect for the ancestors rather than for reasons of public health.'

Much as I support the adherence to local customs and traditions, this is one that I hope disappears soon.

SAFETY

Sadly, the widening gap between rich and poor in Madagascar has produced a sharp rise in crime against tourists. Robbery is now a danger in all large towns, especially Antananarivo. There it pays to be paranoid, but remember that the vast majority of Malagasy are touchingly honest; often you will have people call you back because you have overpaid them (while still unfamiliar with the money) and every traveller can think of a time when his innocence could have been exploited – and wasn't. In my experience, too, hotel employees are, by and large, trustworthy. So try to keep a sense of proportion. Like health, safety is often a question of common sense. Keep your valuables hidden, keep alert in potentially dangerous situations, and you will be OK. Remember, thieves have to learn their profession so theft is only common where there are plenty of tourists to prey on. In little-visited areas you can relax and enjoy the genuine friendliness of the people.

Crime prevention

Violent crime is still relatively rare in Madagascar, and even in Antananarivo you are probably safer than in a large American city. The response to a potentially violent attack is the same in Madagascar as anywhere: if you are outnumbered or the thief is armed, it is sensible to hand over what they want.

You are far more likely to be robbed by subterfuge. Razor-slashing is very popular (with the thieves) and is particularly irritating since your clothes or bag are ruined, maybe just for the sake of the used tissue that caused the tempting-looking bulge in your pocket. When visiting crowded places avoid bringing a bag (even a day-pack carried in front of your body is vulnerable);

'MADAGASCAR: ISLAND OF EXCITEMENT!'

Henk Beentje

We spent three days in Farafangana, collecting palms in the Manombo Forest [Henk is employed by Kew Gardens]. On leaving we were mobbed by about 200 irate locals who accused my Malagasy companion and me of being *voleurs de sang* and of abducting young maidens. On the advice of my companion we reported to the police, who thought this was quite funny but advised us to leave town all the same. We were escorted out of town by the Chief of Police himself, who was careful to use the side streets. Two days later we were back at Ranomafana. As we got into our Landcruiser we were stopped by three *gendarmes*, one of whom was toting a submachine gun. We were arrested and taken to the *Gendarmerie*. There had been an 'all points bulletin' to arrest two *vazaha* (one Merina, one white) in a red Landcruiser. We were accused of having abducted no fewer than three girls from Farafangana, and to have put them in sacks at the back of the vehicle (this clearly referred to my palm collection, indeed esconced in large sacks). It took us four hours to regain our freedom and I was very glad we had reported to the Farafangana police, because after a request from us they were contacted and could confirm our story. Who said you cannot have adventures any more in this streamlined world of ours?

bring your money in a money belt under your clothes, or in a neck pouch. Women have advantages here: the neck pouch can be hooked over their bra so no cord shows at the neck and a money belt beneath a skirt is safe since it needs an unusually brazen thief to reach for it! If you must have a bag, make sure it is difficult to cut.

Passengers in taxis may be the victims of robbery: the thief reaches through the open window and grabs your bag.

Having escorted dozens of first-timers through Madagascar, I've learned the mistakes the unprepared can make. The most common is wearing jewellery ('But I always wear this gold chain'), carelessness with money, etc ('I just put my bag down while I tried on that blouse'), and underestimating the value of clothes ('It's not as though it was an expensive T-shirt..').

Tips for avoiding robbery

• Remember that most theft occurs in the street not in hotels; leave your valuables hidden in a locked bag in your room or in the hotel safe.

• Bring a rubber wedge to keep your door closed at night in cheap hotels. If you can't secure the window put something on the sill which will fall with a clatter if someone tries to enter.

• Lock your bag when travelling by plane or taxi-brousse; combination locks are more secure than small padlocks. Make or buy a lockable cover for your backpack.

• Leave your valuable-looking jewellery at home. You do not need it in Madagascar. Likewise your fancy watch; buy a cheap one.

• Carry your cash in a money belt, neck pouch or deep pocket. Make these yourself by cutting the bottom off existing pockets and adding an extra bit. Fasten the 'secret' pocket with velcro. Wear loose trousers that have zipped pockets. Keep emergency cash (eg a 100 dollar bill) in a Very Safe Place.

• Divide up travellers cheques so they are not all in one place. Keep a note of the numbers of your travellers cheques, passport, credit cards, plane ticket, insurance, etc in your money belt. Keep photocopies of the above in your luggage.

• Remember, what the thief would most like to get hold of is money. Do not leave it around (in coat pockets hanging in your room, in your hand while you concentrate on something else, in an accessible pocket while strolling in the street). If travelling as a couple or small group have one person stand aside to keep watch while the other makes a purchase in the street.

• Avoid carrying a handbag or daypack in cities where it is an obvious target for thieves. In a restaurant never hang it on the back of a chair or lay it by your feet (unless you put your chair leg over the strap).

• For thieves, the next best thing after money is clothes. Avoid leaving them on the beach while you go swimming (in tourist areas) and never leave swimsuits or washing to dry outside your room near a public area.

• Bear in mind that it's impossible to run carrying a large piece of luggage. Items hidden at the bottom of your heaviest bag will be safe from a grab and

THE BEST OF TIMES AND THE WORST OF TIMES

This box is a tribute to the courage of Anne Axel who, at the age of 25, travelled alone through Madagascar, much of it by bicycle. What I admire so much is that she did it despite her fears and anxieties, and that she travelled so well, so perceptively and so happily. These are some quotes from her diaries.

Anne begins with a description of a cycle ride on Christmas day in the pouring rain. 'As I ascended the long, windy hill I noticed a young man up ahead on a bicycle. I pedalled a little faster and came up behind him. He was riding a one-speed bike but at times I found myself struggling to keep up with him on my mountain bike. Nevertheless we paced each other for the entire trip back to Ambatolampy. The heavy rain continued. The red dirt road had turned to oozing mud and my legs were covered with it. My fellow biker and I did not speak; there seemed to be an unspoken understanding between us – it felt as if words would break the spell. We rode together for about 45 minutes and never once did the rain let up. In town I waved goodbye to my companion and turned off towards the ranch.'

'The man in the back of [the private truck] kept asking me personal questions (not unusual) and then started asking about pornographic films. The woman in the front was drunk, and she and the others began asking if I had any camera equipment (I lied). Eventually the driver stopped the vehicle in the middle of nowhere for no apparent reason, and the men in the back got out and talked to the driver. We started off again and when we passed a taxi-brousse we pulled off the road again, and everyone in the other vehicle got out to peer into the truck at me. I was quite nervous. It all ended OK, but I think maybe I was just lucky.'

'The pirogue snaked through the mangroves, the scenery remaining unchanged for 30 minutes. Then I heard the sound of an ocean breeze. A five-minute walk over sand brought us to the Indian Ocean. There are no words to describe the colour of the water but I shall try. Clear at the water's edge, crystal clear and a brilliant shade of green just beyond with patches of deep blue woven throughout. I left Francis under a shade tree and set out for a three-hour walk along the beach. You cannot imagine the beauty. I passed a handful of fishermen, but there were no other tourists. I ate lunch under a small grove of trees on the edge of the beach all the while staring with wonderment at that green water. Then I turned and walked back.'

'My ride to Fianar was fraught with mechanical difficulties. The wheel lugs were stripped, and the driver couldn't keep the tyre on the car. He fiddled with it on and off for four hours, driving several miles only to stop again. We began having serious problems when he was negotiating dangerous curves, and I began making mental preparations for finding another means of transportation, when he finally stopped in a small town and refused to go any further. He found rides in other vehicles (most of them private) for all of the passengers. What service! I landed a ride with two businessmen in a sporty little car that the large driver sped round blind curves at an incredible rate. I, however, was simply too happy to be out of the previous deathtrap to pay any mind to this driver's bad habits.'

'Madagascar is a special place – one moment you will be delighted and exhilarated, while the very next you might be sickened and frustrated. It's difficult sometimes to keep all your emotions in check.'

run thief. Couples or small groups can pass a piece of cord through the handles of all their bags to make them one unstealable unit when waiting at an airport or taxi-brousse station.

• Avoid misunderstandings – genuine or contrived – by agreeing on the price of a service before you set out.

• Enjoy yourself. It's preferable to lose a few unimportant things and see the best of Madagascar than to mistrust everyone and ruin your trip.

...and what to do if you are robbed

Have a little cry and then go to the police. They will write down all the details then send you to the chief of police for a signature. It takes the best part of a day, but you will need the certificate for your insurance. If you are in a rural area, the local authorities will do a declaration of loss.

Unsafe areas

In the opinion of expatriates and others with long experience in Madagascar, the following areas may be unsafe for lone travellers: Antsirabe, Fianarantsoa, Ranomafana and environs, Isalo, Vohibasia and Zombitse forests. These places are along or near to the popular tourist route of RN7 where thieves have become bold. They are also some of the most worthwhile places to visit and the vast majority of travellers come to no harm (of the many people who write to me, very few have been hurt or even threatened by robbers). It's up to you.

The bandit regions of Ambohetantely and Tsaratanana are best not visited alone. Travel in a small group or bring a local guide.

Women travellers

Things have changed in Madagascar. During my independent travels in the country my only experience of sexual harassment (if it could be called that) was when a small man sidled up to me in Nosy Be and asked: 'Have you ever tasted Malagasy man?'.

Sadly, with the increase of tourism comes the increase of men who think they may be on to a good thing. A firm 'no' is usually sufficient; try not to be too offended: think of the image of Western women that the average Malagasy male is shown via the cinema or TV. The south of Madagascar is said to be worse than other regions for sexual harassment, probably because the men are more assertive.

A woman Peace Corps volunteer gave me the following advice for women travelling alone on taxi-brousses: try to sit in the cab, but not next to the driver; if possible sit with another woman; if in the main body of the vehicle, establish contact with an older person, man or woman, who will then tend to look after you. Frances Kerridge adds 'I always say that I am married, even though I never wear a ring, and am usually believed.'

The final word should come from solo traveller Anne Axel: 'I personally would feel comfortable returning to Madagascar alone. However, as I did before, I would check with others before venturing off with strangers or into areas by myself on my bike. I would encourage other women to travel alone in Madagascar. The few times I felt uncomfortable I was usually in a city. I found it possible to meet other travellers in cities when I wanted companions for safety reasons. I never went out alone at night, and would suggest the same for others. I especially enjoyed travelling alone in the rural areas – on the couple of occasions I was with others I never felt the full impact of the experience. Being alone I was able to interact fully with the Malagasy people.'

Men travellers

Judging from the letters from some of my most adventurous male readers, being pursued by women happens everywhere (whilst women are usually only pursued by men in tourist spots). John Kupiec writes: 'I was constantly fighting off women wherever I went. One night in Fort Dauphin I actually had to run away!' He was also offered the mother of the Président du Fokontany in one village. Saying you're married is considered irrelevant...

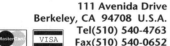

Chapter Six

In Madagascar

MONEY
Cost of travel

The Malagasy currency is unstable; the Malagasy government is unstable; the Malagasy people have learned how readily some tourists will part with their dollars. These factors mean that Madagascar is not a particularly cheap country, even for budget travellers. For those travelling mainly by bus or taxi-brousse and staying in Category C hotels, £25/US$38 per day for a couple is about average, and allows for an occasional splurge. Note that couples can travel almost as cheaply as singles, since most hotels charge by the room (with double bed). Rupert Parker, who spent three weeks in Madagascar around Christmas 1996, writes:

'Hotels vary from 25,000 to 70,000Fmg (£3.50–£10), for those which accept local currency, and meals are around 15,000 to 20,000Fmg (£2–£3). I reckoned on spending around 150,000Fmg (£20) a day for two people, with two good meals with beer and wine, and staying in middle of the range hotels. You could get by on far less if you ate at *hotelys* and stayed in the cheapest rooms. Wine in restaurants is now around 20,000Fmg per bottle, and beer varies between 4,500 to 8,000Fmg.'

The easiest way to save money on a day-to-day basis is to cut down on bottled water: a bottle of *Eau Vive* costs over £1/US$1.50 in most hotels. Bring a water container and sterilising agent.

Malagasy francs

Madagascar's currency has always been difficult to cope with. Here is an extract from an account written 100 years ago:

'The French five-franc piece is now the standard of coinage in Madagascar; for small change it is cut up into bits of all sizes. The traveller has to carry a pair of scales about with him, and whenever he makes a purchase the specified quantity of this most inconvenient money is weighed out with the greatest exactness, first on his own scales, and then on those of the suspicious native of whom he is buying.'

Ariary confusion

Madagascar's unit of currency is the *franc malgache* (Fmg). With recent inflation one rarely sees the small lower-denomination brass coins of 5, 10, and 20 francs (which are practically worthless), but there are silver coins which look, at face value, to be for 10 and 20 francs. Closer inspection reveals that they are *ariary*; one ariary is five francs, so they are worth 50 and 100 francs respectively. At least in the past this confusion only applied to coins: banknotes stated the ariary value in Malagasy and only the franc value in figures. Tourists look at figures not words so there was no problem. Now the cunning Treasury has issued new banknotes for 500 and 5000 ariary. The franc value (2,500Fmg and 25,000Fmg) is also stated but in much smaller figures. It almost seems a deliberate ploy to catch out unsuspecting tourists, and many a happy porter has received a tip of US$6 from a harassed new arrival who thought he was giving a dollar or so.

The colour of money

Keep the following in mind: big green = 5000 ariary/25,000Fmg; pink and green = 500 ariary/2,500Fmg; brown = 10,000Fmg; purple = 5000Fmg; blue = 1000Fmg. Filthy brown = once green = 500Fmg. (Some of the old large notes are still in circulation – you're on your own here.)

Learn too the approximate value of each colour. At the 1996 exchange rate it was convenient to think of 25,000Fmg (big green) as £4/$6 and 5,000Fmg as roughly a pound or a dollar; 15 per cent out but near enough when making quick calculations while bargaining.

Exchange rate

The Malagasy franc floats against hard currencies and this, plus inflation, means that the March 1997 exchange rates given below should be used as a rough guide only.
£1 = 7,510Fmg
US$1 = 4,800Fmg
Ff = 860Fmg
DM1 = 2,800Fmg

Changing money

This has been made easier with the abolition of currency declaration forms. In previous years money could be changed only in an accredited hotel or a bank. These days you are permitted to make purchases using dollars – indeed, the tourist-aware vendors in places visited by cruise ships are quite unhappy if offered Malagasy francs. Always carry some dollars with you (in a safe place) for emergencies. John Kupiec writes: 'The presence of a bank does *not* guarantee the changing of money. Two BTM banks in the west refused to change money in any form. Fortunately I had some US dollars which I was able to change with a Canadian priest (!) and a local merchant.'

Exchange rates at hotels are higher than at banks, but don't be fooled by all those zeros. In the end 200Fmg is only 3p/5c and changing money at a bank can be *very* time consuming.

Transferring funds

Now that you can draw cash from many BTM banks using your credit card you are less likely to need money transferred from home. If you are staying a long time in Madagascar, however, it's best to make the transfer arrangement beforehand. The best bank for this is Banque Malgache de l'Océan Indien, Place de l'Indépendance, Antananarivo. Its corresponding bank in the UK is Banque Nationale de Paris, King William St, London.

TRANSPORT

You can get around Madagascar by rail, road, air and water. If there is a motor involved, however, you'd better learn the meaning of *en panne*; it is engine trouble/breakdown. During these *en panne* sessions one can't help a certain nostalgia for the pre-mechanised days when Europeans travelled by *filanzana* or palanquin. These litters were carried by four cheerful porters who, by all accounts, were so busy swapping gossip and telling stories that they sometimes dropped their unfortunate *vazaha* in a river. The average distance travelled per day was 30 miles – not much slower than a taxi-brousse today! The *filanzana* was used for high officials as recently as the 1940s. To get around town the locals depended on an earlier version of the current rickshaw, or *pousse-pousse*. The *mono-pousse* was a chair slung over a bicycle wheel. One man pulled and another pushed. The more affluent Malagasy possessed a *boeuf-cheval*: a zebu trained to be ridden. (I've seen a photo; the animal looks rather smug in its saddle and bridle.)

By rail

There are only four railway lines in Madagascar, and these have deteriorated dramatically in the last few years. The lines have been damaged by cyclones, and the locomotives and rolling-stock allowed to deteriorate. Derailments are common. Despite all this, train travel is always enjoyable providing you can cope with the delays.

The four lines are Antananarivo to Toamasina (Tamatave), Moramanga to Ambatondrazaka, Antananarivo to Antsirabe, and Fianarantsoa to Manakara.

Keep an eye out for the *Micheline*. This luxury, white 'rail-bus' runs on and off between Antananarivo and Toamasina. At present it's off, but it may reappear. Enquire at the station in Tana.

By road

'If I make roads, the white man will only come and take my country. I have two allies – *hazo* [forest] and *tazo* [fever]...' (King Radama I)

Coping with the 'roads' is one of the great travel challenges in Madagascar. It's not that the royal decree has lasted 180 years but there's a third ally that the king didn't mention – the weather: torrential rain and cyclones destroy roads as fast as they are constructed. But they *are* being repaired and reconstructed, mostly with foreign aid. At the time of writing many of the most important roads (the *Routes Nationales*) are either paved or in the process of being paved. The others are dreadful, but then...that's Madagascar. Here's a comment from a Belgian traveller: 'A good example of how the Malagasy maintain their roads comes before Rantobe [east coast]. A huge tree fell over the road. Instead of cutting the log in two they made a big hole under the tree in the road!'

Taxi-brousse is the generic name for public transport in Madagascar. *Car-brousse* and *taxi-be* are also used, but they all refer to the 'bush taxis' which run along every road in the country. And I doubt if there is any country in the world offering more crowded, less reliable transport. If you think you're a well-seasoned traveller, wait until you try Madagascar! If you don't believe me read some readers' stories on page 108. On the other hand... you may be like Frances Kerridge who took taxi-brousses along all the popular routes 'none of which ever broke down or had a puncture' so obviously things *are* improving. Next edition I may even have to remove the horror stories! Frances became a dab hand at taxi-broussing and provided much of the information below.

Travelling by taxi-brousse: the vehicles

Taxi-brousses are generally minibuses or Renault vans with seats facing each other so no good view out of the window (a *baché* is a small van with a canvas top). More comfortable are the Peugeot 404s or 504s sometimes known as taxi-be (although some people call the 25-seater buses taxi-be) designed to take nine people, but often packed with 14 or more. A car-brousse is usually a 'Tata' sturdy enough to cope with bad roads. Breakdowns are still frequent in remote areas, but more reliable buses are being introduced on the most-travelled routes, and there are even 'luxury buses' running between the capital and Toliara and Toamasina.

Travelling by taxi-brousse: the practicalities

Vehicles leave from a *gare routière* on the side of town closest to their destination. You should try to go there a day or two ahead of your planned departure to check times and prices, and for long journeys you should buy a ticket in advance (from the kiosk – don't give your money to a ticket tout). 'Don't be embarrassed to ask to see the vehicle, the Malagasy do. Reserve your seat – they will write your name on a hand-drawn plan in an exercise book – and get them to write your place on the ticket. Once you have anything written on a piece of paper it is regarded as law and once it is typed it must be gospel! The best seats in a car are in the front, either next to the driver if you have short legs (you'll be sitting where the hand brake should be) or next to the window if you have long legs – but beware of the sun cooking your right arm. In the front you have the added advantage that you can turn down the volume of the stereo when the driver is not looking.' (FK)

'Never be late for a taxi-brousse. Some of them do leave on time, especially on popular journeys or if the departure time is horrendous, eg 2am. Get there early to claim your seat, then read your book, write your diary or whatever. Be ready with soap and towel for a bath stop. Follow the women and children to get some degree of privacy.' (FK)

Frances advises not to bring anything flashy like a Walkman since such things are indicators of extreme wealth and therefore invite envy.

On short journeys and in remote areas, vehicles simply leave as soon as they fill up. Or if they have a schedule expect them to leave hours late, and always be prepared (with warm clothing, fruit, water, etc) for a night trip, even if you thought it was leaving in the morning.

There is no set rate per kilometre; fares are calculated on the roughness of the road and the time the journey takes. They are set by the government and *vazahas* are only occasionally overcharged. Ask other passengers what they are paying. In 1996 some sample fares for journeys on rough roads are 15,000Fmg (£2.50/US$3.75) for four hours, and 40,000Fmg (£6.50/US$9.75) for a ten-hour journey. Faster journeys over paved roads may be a bit more expensive. Passengers are occasionally charged for luggage that is strapped on to the roof.

Drivers stop to eat, but usually drive all night. If they do stop during the night most passengers stay in the vehicle or sleep on the road outside.

There is much that a committed overland traveller can do to soften his/her experiences on taxi-brousses – see *What to bring* on page 80. In addition to basic camping equipment, bring a good book or cards to while away the time during breakdowns, or games that do not involve verbal communication to help you 'bond' with your fellow passengers. If you're prepared for the realities, an overland journey can be very enjoyable and gives you a chance to get to know the Malagasy and practise character-building. As one reader says: 'When a taxi-brousse driver joins two wires together to start his vehicle one needs a sense of humour – but one arrives.'

Note: For the last edition several readers stressed the need to point out that it is unwise to use taxi-brousses if on a tight schedule: vehicles break down or just fail to leave. This is no longer true for popular routes, but it is still risky in the more remote areas. Unless you have lots of time, alternatives such as hiring a car or joining a tour should be considered. The challenge is even greater if you do not have an adequate command of French. Or even if you have. Stephen Cartledge advises: 'One has to remember that "*Sûrement*" means "Never", and "*Maintenant*" means in five hours! Then one is equipped to travel in Madagascar by taxi-brousse.' I would add that when a driver says 'Pas de problème' I get worried.

Car hire

With public transport so unreliable, more visitors have been renting cars or 4WD vehicles in recent years. You would need to be a competent mechanic to

VIVE LE TAXI-BROUSSE!

'At about 10 o'clock we (two people) went to the taxi-brousse station. "Yes, yes, there is a car. It is here, ready to go." We paid our money. "When will it go?" "When it has nine passengers." "How many has it got now?" "Wait a minute." A long look at notebooks, then a detailed calculation. "Two." "As well as us?" "No, no including you." It finally left at about 7 o'clock.'
Chris Ballance

'To go from Morondava to Tana by taxi-brousse took us over 22 hours, and for most of the way the Peugeot 504 had more than 12 people (17 for several hours). And all our luggage. And one man was taking a huge clothing stall to market. And, of course, the woman who was carrying her plough home with her...'
Chris Ballance

'After several hours we picked up four more people. We couldn't believe it – the driver had to sit on someone's lap!'
Stephen Cartledge

'The taxi-brousse from Tana to Majunga was supposed to leave in the early afternoon. At 4.00pm we left (all ten of us) and went to a furniture stall to buy pineapples – well it makes sense. At 6.00pm we had the first of seven punctures. The driver pushed his tyre two kilometres down the road to get it mended... We drove all night (four punctures) and as the light rose over the countryside we – well, you guessed – had a puncture. Now we had no spare and no airpump. A lorry eventually passed and helped to repair the tyre. At 11.00am we had another puncture... I took my rucksack off the car roof and hitchhiked into Majunga.'
Jonathan Miller

'At last we were under way. I had my knees jammed up against the iron bar at the back of the rows in front where sat a very sick soldier, who spent most of the journey with his head out of the window spewing lurid green bile at passers-by like something from a horror-movie... After about 20 minutes we had to stop at a roadside stall to buy mangoes. Since I was now on the sunny side of the vehicle the temperature of my shirt rose to what, had it been made of polyester, would have been melting point. Our next stop was Antsirabe where we were surrounded by about 50 apple vendors and all and sundry went absolutely beserk. I hadn't seen so many apples since...since we left Ambositra. At about 5.00pm the radio was turned on so we could listen to two men shouting at each other at a volume which would have caused bleeding of the eardrums in Wembley Stadium. When one passenger complained our driver managed to find a few extra decibels. At about 6.00pm it started to get decidedly brisk, and since the ailing squaddie in front of me showed no sign of having rid himself of toxic enzymes I now had to endure an icy blast in my face. Our next stop was for grapes. We now had enough fruit on board to start a wholesale business in Covent Garden, and I was a bit tetchy.'
Robert Stewart

hire a self-drive car in Madagascar, and generally cars come with chauffeurs (providing a local person with a job and you with a guide/interpreter). A few days on Madagascar's roads will cure you of any regret that you are not driving yourself. Night-time driving is particularly challenging: headlights often don't work, or are not switched on. Your driver will know that the single light bearing down on you is more likely to be a wide truck than a narrow motorbike and react accordingly. The Merina Highway Code (informal version) decrees that drivers must honk their horns after crossing a bridge to ensure that the spirits are out of the way.

There are car-hire firms in most large towns. The Maison du Tourisme in Antananarivo has a comprehensive list. I have personal recommendations for the following in Antananarivo: Locaut, 52 Ave du 26 Juin (BP 8150); tel: 219 81, fax: 248 01. Aventour, 55 Route de Majunga; tel: 317 61, fax 272 99. Eurorent, BP 5282; tel: 297 66, fax: 297 49. They have a desk at Ivato airport. Rahariseta, BP 3779 (located next to Lake Behoririka); tel: 257 70, fax: 224 47. There is also Avis, 3 Rue P Lumumba; tel: 340 80, fax: 216 57 (they have an office at the Hilton hotel) and Hertz, but these tend to be more expensive.

Prices currently work out at about £50/US$75 per day, including fuel and driver, for a small saloon car driving around Antananarivo. For a week's hire of a 4WD you should expect to pay about £750/US$1125.

Mountain bicycle

The experience An increasingly popular means of touring Madagascar is by the most reliable transport: mountain bike. Bikes can be hired in Antananarivo, Antsirabe, Tolagnaro (Fort Dauphin), Antsiranana (Diego Suarez) and Nosy Be. Or you can bring your own. You can do a combination of bike and taxi-brousse or bike and plane, or you can set out to cycle the whole way. Don't be overambitious; dirt roads are so rutted you will make slow progress, and tarred roads can be dangerous from erratic drivers.

Bishop Brock, who toured for ten weeks by mountain bike in 1992, wrote in the last edition: 'Madagascar is an excellent country for cycle touring, definitely one of my favourite places in the world, and I've taken my holidays by bicycle for the last 13 years. Route 7 now has a good-to-excellent surface most of the way and there are lots of opportunities for interesting side trips. Having a bike gave me access to places that otherwise can only be reached on foot. If I had to advise a prospective cyclist with limited time I would say that Fianar to Manakara and Fianar to Sakaraha were the favourite parts of my trip. I should add that it's not a problem to put the bike on a train or taxi-brousse after payment of a small fee.' Bishop returned to Madagascar in 1996 and cycled through much of the west, having an equally good time, and taking his bike without problem on various planes. He is a little doubtful if a Twin Otter would take a bike, however, but does not rule out the possibility.

There are some suggested bike routes around the Highlands in *Chapter Eight* (page 159).

Preparation, equipment and spares Bring a spare tyre, tubes, spokes, spanners and tools, puncture kit, and – very important – a Teflon-based lubricant that does not attract dust. The sandy, dusty roads play havoc with the gear system. Anne Axel installed sealed hubs and headset on her bike which cut down the amount of maintenance she had to do. She also carried extra cables and spokes, storing some extra tools and spare parts in Tana. And she took a repairs manual. Thus prepared she had no problems when touring with her own bike (but plenty on a rented bike).

Bishop Brock adds: 'Carry a compass and a cyclometer as the roads often take a different course to those shown on the map; locking cleats are dangerous on sandy roads – use toe clips or dual purpose pedals.' He also recommends that cyclists stay at the Tana hotel *Relais des Pistards* since the owner, M Colney, is an avid cyclist and can offer advice.

A bike as unaccompanied luggage Cyclists are unanimous: *Don't do it!* You *must* travel with your bike, whatever the excess baggage charge. Reader Rick Partridge is still too upset to recount his 'Trying-for-four-weeks-to-get-my-bike-out-of-customs' story, and Anne Axel is only just recovering from the ordeal of retrieving hers from Nairobi airport to where it was shipped as cargo.

Safety when cycling In 1996 a Peace-Corps volunteer was murdered 'while cycling'. It is worth pointing out that this horrible crime – which deeply upset the Malagasy – was perpetuated by people she knew. She was not the victim of random violence.

Even so, a cyclist is obviously more vulnerable than other travellers but I've yet to have a report of anyone being harmed while travelling this way. Some, like Anne Axel, have been put off cycling notoriously dangerous routes (in her case, from Antsiranana to Mahajanga) while others defied the warnings and had a marvellous time. Bishop Brock cycled from Tsiroanomandidy to Maintirano. 'Many Malagasy were amazed that I had survived this ride without being killed by *dahalo* (bandits). However, all of the gendarmes I spoke to told me I really didn't have anything to worry about. The *dahalo* are not hijackers who work the roads, but cattle thieves who tend to stay in the hills and valleys. It was actually rare for me to meet *anyone* out there, and no one I met seemed like a bandit, just a truck driver or a cattle herder.'

You must make your own decisions. All I can recommend is to cycle off the beaten track. Here you will meet only hospitality and curiosity, and will be in no danger – intentional or unintentional – from other road-users. But what I really want to say is 'Go for it!'.

By air
Air Madagascar started its life in 1962 as Madair but understandably changed its name after a few years of jokes. Most people now call it Air Mad. It serves 59 destinations, making it the most efficient way – and for some people the

only way – of seeing the country. Foreigners must pay their fares in hard currency, and only the Tana office accepts credit cards. Here are some sample one-way fares (1997) from Antananarivo: Mahajanga £32/US$48, Nosy Be £50/US$75, Antsiranana (Diego Suarez) £54/US$81, Toliara (Tuléar) £50/US$75, Toamasina (Tamatave) £20/US$30, Nosy Boraha (Île Sainte Marie) £28/$42. These prices have come down substantially in the last three years and, furthermore, with the new Air Touristic Pass, you get a 33% discount on domestic flights providing you chose Air Mad as your international carrier.

The recent rise in tourism in Madagascar has brought more passengers than Air Mad can cope with, particularly at peak holiday times. Try to book in advance through one of their agents (see *Chapter Four*) or through a Tana tour operator. If you are doing your bookings once you arrive, avoid the crush by getting to the Air Mad office when it opens in the morning. Often flights which are said to be fully booked in Antananarivo are found to have seats when you reapply at the town of departure. In any case, you should reconfirm your next flight as soon as you arrive at your destination (at the Air Mad office in town). You can very often get on fully booked flights if you go standby (as I learned to my cost when our group checked in 15 minutes late. Our seats had been given away). Paying with cash dollars may find you a seat.

There are no numbered seats or refreshments on internal flights, although on longer flights you'll be given a drink and a sweetie. Smokers sit at the back of the plane, so if you are a non-smoker board at the front. It is useful to know that *Enregistrement Bagages* is the check-in counter and *Livraison Bagages* is luggage arrival.

Frances Kerridge gives this advice for flying by Twin Otter:
'The check-in is hilarious – they weigh you as well as your luggage, so a bit of dieting between flights will cover those extra souvenirs you've bought! I recommend getting there early – about an hour before they say – to check in as there will be lots of Malagasy, each trying to cart a market-stall equivalent of whatever goods are a speciality of that region. The smaller your bag, the more popular you will be as other passengers eagerly claim your unused luggage allowance.' She goes on to emphasise that luggage should be locked, but that airport thieves know how to pick locks so keep your luggage in sight for as long as possible.

Air Mad schedules are reviewed twice-yearly at the end of March and the end of October (maddening: in the peak travel month) but are subject to change at any time and without notice.

There is an airport tax on domestic and international flights. See *Chapter Eight*.

Air Madagascar have the following planes: Boeing 747 (jumbo) on the Paris to Antananarivo route, Boeing 737 (flying to the larger cities and Nosy Be), the smaller Hawker Siddeley 748, and the very small and erratic Twin Otter and Piper which serve the smaller towns. There is a danger that service to these unprofitable destinations may be cut due to the anticipated financial difficulties following the loss of Air Mad's monopoly on flights from Paris (see *Chapter Four*).

With a shortage of aircraft and pilots, planes are often delayed or cancelled. Almost always there is a perfectly good reason: mechanical problems, bad weather. Sometimes, however, it is better for your blood-pressure not to know why... But to give credit where it's due, Air Mad is improving and on the whole they provide as safe and reliable a service as one can expect in a poor country. Indeed, it has improved so much in the last year that I confess to nicking one of their marvellous Safety Instructions cards which tell you to 'Sit on the thrush and skid feet first'. I have a nasty feeling that those thrushes may soon be extinct!

TAM, who used only to provide charter flights (see below), now have some scheduled departures. They tend to be expensive, but are worth contacting in times of crisis.

Private charters

For a small group this is a viable option and not as expensive as you may think. TAM (Travaux Aériens de Madagascar) offer light aircraft for one to seven passengers. Prices range from about US$150 per flying hour for a two-seater to US$700 per flying hour for a seven-seater. The cost of fuel must be added: US$40 to US$170 per flying hour. Bigger planes fly faster, so they may not end up being more expensive. Some flying-time examples for a six-seater Piper: Antananarivo–Sainte Marie–Antananarivo, 1 hr 46 mins; Antananarivo–Fort Dauphin–Antananarivo, 5hrs 20 mins. Remember there is no such thing as a one-way flight – you still have to pay for the pilot to return to Antananarivo. More sensible to pay him to spend the night.

TAM's address is 31 Avenue de l'Indépendance, Antananarivo. Tel: 222 22. They also have an operations office at Ivato airport.

There are, however, other companies so shop around. Madagascar Air Services is one that has been recommended.

Some tour operators, such as Boogie Pilgrim (see page 86), have small planes and can organise special trips such as flights over the *tsingy*.

By boat

The Malagasy are traditionally a seafaring people (remember that 6,000km journey from Indonesia) and in the absence of roads, their stable outrigger canoes are used to cover quite long sea distances. *Pirogues* without outriggers are used extensively on the rivers and canals of the watery east. Quite a few adventurous travellers use pirogues for sections of their journeys. You will read their accounts in the relevant chapters of this guide. Romantic though it may be to sail in an outrigger canoe, it can be both uncomfortable and, at times, dangerous.

Ferries and cargo boats travel to the larger islands. These provide a different version of discomfort.

River rafting is becoming increasingly popular as a different way of seeing the country. This is not the hair-raising white-water variety, but a gentle float down the wide, lazy rivers of the west. For more information see *Chapter Fourteen*, page 340.

Transport within cities

There are **taxis** in all cities. Their rates are reasonable – usually a fixed price for the centre of town – and they will sometimes pick up other passengers. They have no meters, so agree on the price before you get in. Some major cities have Japanese **buses**.

Rickshaws, known as *pousse-pousses* ('push-push' – said to originate from the time they operated in the capital and needed an additional man behind to push up the steep hills), are a Madagascar speciality and provide transport in Antsirabe, Mahajanga, Toamasina and some other coastal towns. Occasionally you see them in Antananarivo, but they are mostly used for transporting goods.

Many western visitors are reluctant to sit in comfort behind a running, ragged, bare-foot man and no-one with a heart can fail to feel compassion for the *pousse-pousse* pullers. However, this is a case of needing to abandon our own cultural hang-ups. These men want work. Most rickshaws are owned by Indians to whom the 'drivers' must pay a daily fee. If they take no passengers they will be out of pocket – and there's precious little *in* their pockets. Bargain hard (before you get in) and make sure you have the exact money. It would be optimistic to expect change. For most medium-length journeys 2,000Fmg is generous payment. *Pousse-pousse* pullers love carrying soft-hearted tourists and have become quite cunning in their dealings with *vazahas*. On the other hand, remember how desperately these men need a little luck – and an innocent tourist could make their day!

✆

THE GLOBETROTTERS CLUB

An international club which aims to share information on adventurous budget travel through monthly meetings and *Globe* magazine. Published every two months, *Globe* offers a wealth of information from reports of members' latest adventures to travel bargains and tips, plus the invaluable 'Mutual Aid' column where members can swap a house, sell a camper, find a travel companion or offer information on unusual places or hospitality to visiting members. London meetings are held monthly (Saturdays) and focus on a particular country or continent with illustrated talks.

Enquiries to: Globetrotters Club, BCM/Roving, London WC1N 3XX.

'Madagascar only requires the advent of railways and roads to make it one of the most prosperous commercial countries of the world'.
Capt E W Dawson, Madagascar: its Capabilities and Resources, *1895*

ACCOMMODATION

Hotels in Madagascar are classified by a national star system – five star being the highest – but in my experience this indicates price, not quality. In this book I have used three categories: A, B and C. Five and four star hotels must usually be paid for in hard currency, and the hotels print their rates in French francs.

Outside the towns, hotels in the form of a single building are something of a rarity. Accommodation is usually in bungalows which are often constructed of local materials and are quiet, atmospheric and comfortable.

A word about bolsters. Visitors who are not accustomed to the ways of France are disconcerted to find a firm, sheet-covered sausage anchored to the top of the bed. In the better hotels you can usually find a pillow hidden away in a cupboard. Failing that, I make my own pillow with a sweater stuffed into a T-shirt.

Hotel prices rose in 1996 because of the imposition of a room tax, *vignette touristique*, of 3,000Fmg (50p/75c) for three-star hotels, 2,000Fmg for two-star, etc. It's not the tax that pushed up the prices as much as the concept that tourists would be willing and able to pay more.

What you get for your money
Category A
Up to international standard in the large towns and tourist areas, but sometimes large and impersonal and usually foreign-owned. There has been a boom in hotel building during the last few years, and there are now some very good Malagasy-owned hotels in this category, so the difference between A and B has become somewhat blurred. Prices range from 150Ff (£20/US$35) to 1,000Ff (£125/US$188) double. Outside the main cities Category A hotels cost much less and can usually be paid for in Fmg.

Category B
These are often just as clean and comfortable, though you may occasionally find a gecko in your room. There will be no TV beaming CNN into your bedroom, but you should have an en suite toilet, and comfortable beds although bolsters are the norm. The hotels are often family-run and very friendly. The average price is £10/US$15.

Category C
In early editions I described these as 'Exhilaratingly dreadful at times' until a reader wrote: 'We were rather disappointed by the quality of the Category C hotels... We found almost all the beds comfortable, generally acceptably clean, and not one rat. We felt luxuriously cheated!' It *is* a bit disappointing (another sign of the 'normalisation' of Madagascar), but the persistent can still find rats and cockroaches in abundance as well as other surprising features, though you now have to get well off the beaten track and try the little *hotelys*, or

choose rock-bottom in a big town.

Apart from resident fauna in these places the pillows are filled with sisal and the double beds can be quite amazingly uncomfortable with lumpy mattresses sagging like hammocks so that couples are thrown companionably together in the centre. Some hotels have basins and/or bidets in the room, but the toilet is likely to be a stinking hole or – better – out in the bushes. Ask for the WC ('dooble vay say'), not *toilette* which means shower or bathroom.

In these hotels (and some B ones too) used toilet paper should not be thrown into the pan but into the box provided for it. Not very nice, but preferable to a clogged loo.

Many – indeed, most – of the C hotels in this book are clean and excellent value, only earning the C because of their price. Almost always they are run by friendly Malagasy who will rustle up a fantastic meal. In an out-of-the-way place you will pay as little as £1/US$1.50 for the most basic room, although £3/US$4.50 or £4/US$6 would be more usual.

Hotely usually means a restaurant/snack bar rather than accommodation, but it's always worth asking if they have rooms.

Many B and C hotels will do your washing for you at a very reasonable price. In A hotels laundry is expensive.

Hotel prices listed in this book

After some thought I have decided to print the prices for the Category A hotels in French francs (Ff) because that's the hard currency quoted by the hotels, but have converted them to US dollars at the 1996 rate of US$1.00 = Ff8.50 for the convenience of the majority of my readers. Where pounds sterling are also quoted I have taken the exchange rate to be £1.00 = $1.50. For hotels that can be paid for in Malagasy francs I have given the price (when known) in Fmg along with the date if not recent. By the time you read this the Fmg prices may have doubled, but it's worth taking the risk for the convenience of travellers who have become accustomed to thinking in francs. Where there is no price you can guess the approximate cost by the Category listing.

How would you like to see this dealt with in future editions? Do let me know.

✆

'One of the great evils arising from [slavery] is the dignifying of idleness as belonging to freedom, and the degrading of labour by making it the badge of slavery'.
Rev W. Ellis, The Martyr Church, *1869*

THE MUSIC OF MADAGASCAR: A BRIEF INTRODUCTION

Ian A Anderson

The music of Madagascar is like the island itself – owing many things to other parts of the world, but unique.

The Malagasy are very fond of harmony singing, varying from Polynesian style (the Merina) to almost East African on the west coast. Traditional musical instruments include the celebrated *valiha*, a member of the zither family with 21 strings stretched lengthways all around the circumference of a hollow bamboo tube (there's also a box variety called the *marovany*), the *sodina*, an end-blown flute that can work magic in the hands of a master like Rakotofra (find his picture on the old 1000Fmg note); the *kabosy*, a small guitar with paired strings and partial frets; the *jejy voatavo* with a gourd resonator and two sets of strings on adjacent sides of the neck; the *lokanga bara*, a 3-string fiddle; and a great variety of percussion instruments.

You'll also find most western instruments, successfully adapted to local music. Visit Ambohimanga, for example, to hear one of several generations of blind accordion players. Catch one of the *hiragasy* troupes and they'll be using ancient brass instruments and clarinets. Visit a nightclub or a larger concert and a modern band such as Jaojoby, Mily Clement or Tianjama will have electric guitars, synthesisers, and kit drums and might play one of the wild Malagasy dance styles such as *salegy*, *balesa*, *watsa watsa* or *sega*. Malagasy music has also enjoyed a big explosion of outside interest in recent years. The artists who have gained the most success touring abroad in the mid '90s have been Tarika, the Justin Vali Trio, Jaojoby, Njava and guitarist D'Gary.

Finding live music in Madagascar is a hit-and-miss affair; don't expect the real thing to be laid on for tourists in hotels. Keep an eye open for concert posters, and check out clubs used by local people.

The local cassette market has greatly expanded in recent years, though tapes are of variable quality. There are now even a few locally marketed CDs, but Malagasy music on record is still best purchased in Europe or North America where there is now a huge CD selection. A regularly updated Madagascar CD-ography can be found on the Internet at http://www.cityscape.co.uk/froots/madagcd/html. The following small sample is a good starting point:

Tarika: *Son Egal* (Xenophile XENO 4042) (USA)

The Justin Vali Trio: *Ny Marinal The Truth* (Real World CDRW51) (UK)

Jaojoby *Salegy!* (Xenophile XENO 4040) (USA)

Various: *Madagascar Open Notes – Fruits de Voyages* (Musikela ELA 102) (France)

Various: *The Marovany of Madagascar* (Silex Y 225224) (France)

Various: *Madagasikara 2 – Current Popular Music* (GlobeStyle CDORBD 013) (UK)

Various: *Madagaskar 3 – Sounding Bamboo* (Feuer & Els FUEC 712) (Germany)

Various: *A World out of Time* (Shanachie 64048)

A good source for these Malagasy CDs in London is Stern's African Record Shop, 293 Euston Road, London W1P 5PA.

FOOD AND DRINK
Food
Eating well is one of the delights of Madagascar, and even the fussiest tourists are usually happy with the food. International hotels serve international food, usually with a French bias, and often do special Malagasy dishes. Lodges and smaller hotels serve local food which is almost always excellent, particularly on the coast where lobster, shellfish and other seafood predominates. Meat lovers will enjoy the zebu steaks, although they are usually tougher than we are used to. Outside the capital, most hotels offer a set menu (*table d' hôte*) to their guests. Where the menu is *à la carte* it is a help to have a French dictionary, preferably one with a food section.

The national dish in Madagascar is *romazava* (pronounced 'roomaz<u>ahv</u>), a meat and vegetable stew, spiced with ginger and containing *brèdes* (pronounced 'bread'), tasty, tongue-tingling greens. Another good local dish is *ravitoto*, shredded manioc leaves with fried pork.

Independent travellers will find Chinese restaurants in every town; these are almost always good and reasonably priced. *Soupe Chinoise* is available almost everywhere, and is filling and tasty. The Malagasy eat a lot of rice so away from the tourist routes most dishes are accompanied by a sticky mound of the stuff. It's bland and flavourless, but sops up the tasty sauces.

In *hotelys*, often open-sided shacks, the menu may be chalked up on a blackboard:

Henan-omby (or *Hen' omby*) – beef.
Henan-borona (or *Hen' akoho*) – chicken.
Henan-kisoa – pork.
Henan-drano (or *Hazan-drano*) – fish.

The menu may add *Mazotoa homana*. This is not a dish, it means *Bon appétit!*

Along with the meat or fish and inevitable mound of rice (*vary*) comes a bowl of stock. This is spooned over the rice, or drunk as a soup.

Thirst is quenched with *ranovola* obtained by boiling water in the pan in which the rice was cooked. It has a slight flavour of burnt rice, and since it has been boiled for several minutes it is safe to drink.

For do-it-yourself meals there is a great variety of fruit and vegetables, even in the smallest market. A selection of fruit is served in most restaurants, along with raw vegetables or *crudités*. From June to August the fruit is mostly limited to citrus and bananas, but from September there are also strawberries, mangoes, lychees, pineapples and loquats. Slices of coconut are sold everywhere, but especially on the coast where coconut milk is a popular and safe drink, and toffee-coconut nibbles are sold on the street, often wrapped in paper from school exercise books.

Madagascar's dairy industry is growing. There are now some good, locally produced cheeses and Malagasy yoghurt is excellent and available in the smallest shops. Try the drinking yoghurt, *yaourt à boire*.

Drink

The most popular drink, Three Horses Beer (THB), is wonderful on a hot day. I think it's wonderful on a cold day, too. The price goes up according to the surroundings: twice as much in the Hilton as in a *hotely* and there is always a hefty deposit payable on the bottle. In most hotels you would pay 6,000Fmg (£1/US$1.50) for a large (2-litre) bottle. The Star Brewery which makes THB has introduced a new brand, Queens (which most people think is inferior to THB), and there is also Gold. Why does Star give its beer English names that the Malagasy can't pronounce? And why horses and queens when the country has few of either (and not much gold)? I don't know.

Madagascar produces its own wine in the Fianarantsoa region, and some is excellent. L'azani Betsileo (*blanc* or *gris*, *reservé*)) is recommended.

A pleasant aperitif is *Maromby* (the name means 'many zebu') and I have been told that *Litchel*, made from lychees, is good. Rum, *toaka gasy*, is very cheap and plentiful, especially in sugar-growing areas such as Nosy Be; and fermented sugar-cane juice, *betsabetsa* (east coast), or fermented coconut milk, *trembo* (north), make a change. The best cocktail is *punch au coco*, with a coconut-milk base, which is a speciality of the coastal areas. Yummee!

'Fresh' is an agreeable shandy, and 'Tonic' is – you guessed it – tonic water. The good but rather expensive spring-water is called 'Eau Vive' and, of course, there are Coca-Cola and other popular soft drinks. The locally produced *limonady* sadly bears no resemblance to lemons, and Bon Bon Anglais is revolting (although I do know one anglaise who rather likes it!).

Caffeine-addicts have a problem. The coffee is OK if drunk black, but usually only condensed milk is available. It's best to bring your own powdered milk – for the coffee. I find that one quickly regresses to childhood and surreptitiously spoons the condensed milk not into the coffee but into the mouth.

The locally-grown tea is very weak, the best quality being reserved for export. A nice alternative is *citronelle*, lemon-grass tea, which is widely available.

HANDICRAFTS AND WHAT TO BUY

You can buy just about everything in the handicrafts line in Madagascar. Most typical of the country are wood carvings, raffia work (in amazing variety), crocheted and embroidered table-cloths and clothes, semi-precious stones (the solitaire sets are typical and most attractive), leather goods, carved zebu horn, Antaimoro paper (with embedded dried flowers), and so on. The choice is almost limitless, and it can all be seen in the artisans' market (*Marché Artisanal*) in Antananarivo.

In the south you can buy very nice heavy silver bracelets that are traditionally worn by men. In the east and north (Nosy Be) you will be offered vanilla pods (although strictly speaking you are limited to 100 grams), peppercorns, cloves and other spices, and honey.

Do not buy products from endangered species. That includes tortoiseshell, snake skins (now crocodiles are farmed commercially, their skins may be sold legally) and, of course, live animals. Also prohibited are endemic plants, fossils and any genuine article of funerary art.

To help stamp out the sale of endangered animal products, tourists should make their feelings – and the law – known. If, for instance, you are offered tortoise or turtle shell, tell the vendor it is *interdit*; and to push the point home you can say it is *fady* for you to buy such a thing.

The luggage weight-limit when leaving Madagascar is normally 20kg (30kg if you are going direct to Paris which manages to count as a 'national' flight!). Bear this in mind when doing your shopping.

Permits

Some purchases need, in theory, an export permit, but the rule is seldom enforced with tourists – indeed, looking at the official list which contains every item tourists are likely to buy, it would be impossible to enforce it. If you are taking a lot of minerals, you can get an export permit at the airport providing you have a receipt from the vendor. For other goodies, use your judgement: if you are planning to take home a rosewood wardrobe or an *aepyornis* egg you'd do well to get the paperwork; if it's a carved bookend, I wouldn't bother.

Export permits for major craft items are obtained from the Ministère de la Culture et de la Communication, Antsahavola. Tel: 270 92. You will need to list your purchases and have receipts. Leave the list in the morning and pick up your permits in the afternoon. For animal products such as mounted butterflies apply to the Direction des Eaux et Forêts.

To avoid all this hassle, if in doubt check the latest regulations with the Maison du Tourisme.

MISCELLANEOUS
Tipping

During the Marxist era tipping was frowned on and there were too few tourists (who always tip, whatever) to make much difference. These days a service charge is added to most restaurant meals so tipping is not strictly necessary, but waiters in tourist hotels expect it. About 5–10% is ample. Before you give a dollar to the doorman for carrying your bag from the taxi to the hotel lobby, bear in mind that a labourer earns that for a half-day's work, and a doctor charges about US$15 for a private consultation. That said, the porters in posh hotels make their disgust very clear if you tip as a local would (about 1000Fmg).

Electrical equipment

The voltage in Madagascar is 110 or 220 (it varies in different parts of the country). Assume 220 to avoid wrecking your electrical gadget. Outlets (where they exist) take 2-pin round plugs. If you use a 3-pin fused plug plus adapter, bring a spare fuse for the plug.

Business hours
Most businesses open 08.00–12.00 and 14.00–18.00. Banks are open 08.00–16.00, and are closed weekends and the afternoon before a holiday.

Communications: keeping in touch
In the past Madagascar has had woeful telecommunications. Until a couple of years ago, getting through to Antananarivo from the outside world could take many hours of perseverance, and within the country it was mostly impossible. Telephones did not even exist in important resorts such as Nosy Be. All this is changing, and by the end of 1997 the whole country should be linked up by satellite or radio phones. It will make an enormous difference to the tourist infrastructure.

International **telephone** calls are hideously expensive. Tell your nearest and dearest that you won't be phoning to say you arrived safely. If you must telephone do it from the post office; hotels add up to 50%.

The **mail** service is reasonably efficient and letters generally take about two weeks to reach Europe and a little longer to the USA. The smaller post offices often run out of stamps, but some hotels sell them. Clare Hermans adds: 'Malagasy stamps are a meal in themselves! Bring a sponge or dunk in the nearest puddle.'

If you want to receive mail, have your correspondent address the envelope with your initial only and your surname in capitals, and send it to you c/o Poste Restante in whichever town you will be in. It will be held at the main post office. If you are an Amex member the Amex Client Mail Service allows you to have letters sent to their office in the Hilton Hotel. They keep mail for a month.

BP in an address is *Bôite Postale* – the same as PO Box.

PUBLIC HOLIDAYS

January 1 New Year's Day
March 29 Commemoration of 1947 rebellion
Easter Monday (movable)
May 1 Labour Day
Ascension Day (movable)

Whit Monday (movable)
June 26 Independence Day
August 15 Feast of the Assumption
November 1 All Saints' Day
December 25 Christmas Day
December 30 Republic Day

When these holidays fall on a Thursday, Friday will be tacked on to the weekend.

'The mercies of God [be bestowed on] this people, whose simplicity hath herein made them more happy than our too dear-bought knowledge hath advantaged us'.

Walter Hamond, 1640

The stone-cutter and his child, Maromizaha (HB)

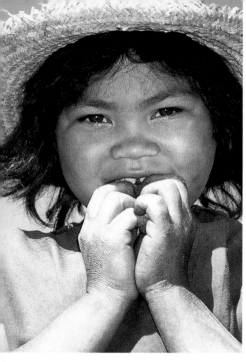

THE CHILDREN OF MADAGASCAR
Above left: *Merina girl* (EC)
Below left: *Backflip in Nosy Be* (MH)

Above right: *Girl from Mahajanga* (RH)
Below right: *Boy with homemade 'camera',
Tolagnaro* (HB)

WEARY DAYS IN THE MARKET
Above: *Zoma, Antananarivo* (HB)
Below: *Mahajanga* (RH)

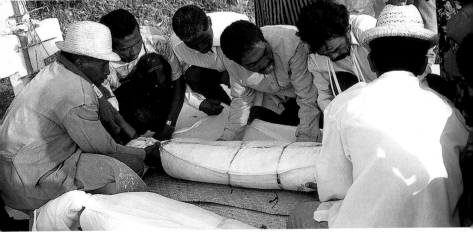

AFTER DEATH
Above left: *Erotic Sakalava tomb carving* (BL)   Above right: *Mahafaly aloalo* (TC)
Centre: *Modern Mahafaly tomb, near Toliara* (HB)
Below: *Bone-turning ceremony or* famadihana (HB)

Chapter Seven

Madagascar and You

Tsihy be lambanana ny ambanilantra
'All who live under the sky are woven together like one big mat.'

Malagasy saying

In recent years there has been a welcome shift of attitude among visitors to developing countries from 'What can I get out of this trip?' to 'How can I minimise the damage I do?' This chapter addresses those issues, and suggests ways in which you can help this marvellous, but often tragic, country.

THEY DO THINGS DIFFERENTLY THERE

I once caught our Malagasy guide scowling at himself in the mirror. When I teased him he said: 'As a Malagasy man I smile a lot. I can see that if I want to work with tourists I must learn to frown.' He had learned that the group considered him insufficiently assertive. Tolerance and the fear of causing offence is an integral part of Malagasy social relationships. So if a tourist expresses anger in a way that is entirely appropriate in his or her own culture, it is counter-productive in Madagascar. It is deeply unsettling to the person at the receiving end who often giggles in response, thus exacerbating the situation. If you are patient, pleasant and keep your temper, your problem will be solved more quickly.

Avoid being too dogmatic in conversation (you do not have exclusivity of the truth). Make use of 'perhaps' and 'maybe'. Be excessive in your thanks. The Malagasy are very polite; we miss the nuances by not understanding the language. Body language, however, is easier to learn. For instance, 'excuse me, may I come through?' is indicated by a stooping posture and an arm extended forward. Note how often it is used.

Part of responsible tourism is relinquishing some of our normal comforts. Consider this statistic: by the end of the century in Madagascar, fuelwood demand is likely to outstrip supply by two million metric tons a year. Wood and charcoal are the main sources of energy. Do you still feel that hot water is essential in your hotel?

Madagascar's shortcomings can be maddening. Sometimes a little reflection reveals the reasons behind the failure to produce the expected service, but sometimes you just have to tell yourself 'Well, that's the way it is'. After all, you are not going to be able to change Madagascar, but Madagascar may change you.

ASPECTS OF RESPONSIBLE TOURISM

Photography

Lack of consideration when taking photos is probably the most common example of irresponsible tourist behaviour – one that each of us has been guilty of at some time. It is so easy to take a sneak photo without first establishing contact with the person, so easy to say we'll send a print of the picture and then not get round to it, so easy to stroll into a market or village thinking what a wonderful photo it will make and forgetting that you are there to *experience* it.

The rules are not to take people's photos without permission, and to respect an answer of 'no'. Give consideration to the offence caused by photographing the destitute. Be cautious about paying your way to a good photo; often a smile or a joke will work as well, without setting a precedent. People *love* to receive pictures of themselves. If you are travelling on an organised tour your guide is sure to visit that area again so can deliver the prints that you send to him. If you are travelling independently write down the addresses and honour your promise (see page 124).

Philip Thomas writes: 'A Malagasy, for whom a photograph will be a highly treasured souvenir, will remember the taking of the photograph and your promise to send them a copy, a lot longer than you might. Their disappointment in those who say one thing and do another is great, and so if you think you might not get it together to send the photograph then do not say that you will.'

A responsible attitude to photography is so much more *fun*! And it results in better pictures. It involves taking some time getting to know the subject of your proposed photo: making a purchase, perhaps, or practising your Malagasy greetings (if that doesn't draw hoots of laughter nothing will!).

Beggars

Whether to give to professional beggars is up to you. I believe that it is wrong to give to the little ragamuffin children who follow you around because it is better to give to the charities (see *Tourist Aid*) that work with them. Actually, the same applies to all age-groups. My policy is to give to the elderly and I also single out 'beggar days' when I fill my pockets with small change and give to everyone who looks needy and over school age. And if I make some trickster's day, so be it.

It is important to make up your mind about beggars before you hit the streets so you can avoid standing there looking through a conspicuously fat wallet for a low-denomination bill.

The effects of tourism on local people

The impact of foreigners on the Malagasy was noted as long ago as 1669 when a visitor commented that formerly the natives were deeply respectful of white men but were changed 'by the bad examples which the Europeans have had, who glory in the sin of luxury in this country...'.

In developing countries tourism has had profound effects on the inhabitants, some good, some bad. Madagascar seems to me to be a special case – more than any other country I've visited it inspires a particular devotion and an awareness of its fragility, both environmental and cultural. Wildlife is definitely profiting from the attention given it and from the emphasis on ecotourism. For the people, however, the blessings may be very mixed: some able Malagasy have found jobs in the tourist industry, but for others the impact of tourism has meant that their cultural identity has been lost, along with some of their dignity and integrity. Village antagonisms are heightened when one or two people gain the lion's share of tourist revenue and gifts, leading in one case to murder, and hitherto honest folk have lapsed into corruption or thievery.

The gap between the affluent Malagasy who work with tourists and their impoverished neighbours who spend long hours labouring in the fields or factories is growing ever wider. Consider this: the fee set by ANGAP for a half-day guided walk in Isalo National Park is 20,000Fmg. Our guide slouched along telling us nothing unless requested to, and left us to find our own way back while he chatted to his friends. Had he done his job better he would have received another 5,000Fmg or so in a tip. That 25,000Fmg (US$6.00) would be two weeks' pay in a factory, and even that is a lot more than most rural Malagasy earn: the average annual income is $200. What we, as tourists, can do about it is unclear.

Giving presents

This continues the theme above, and is a subject often discussed among experienced travellers who cannot agree on when, if ever, a present is appropriate. Most feel that giving presents is only appropriate when it is in exchange for a service. Many tourists to the developing world, however, pack sweets and trinkets 'for the children' as automatically as their sunglasses and insect repellent.

My repeat visits to Madagascar over the course of 20 years have shaped my own view: that giving is usually self-gratification rather than generosity, and that one thoughtless act of giving can change a community irreparably. I have seen the shyly inquisitive children of small communities turn into tiresome beggars; I have seen the warm interaction between visitor and local turn into mutual hostility; I have seen intelligent, ambitious young men turn into scoundrels. What I haven't sorted out in my mind is how much this matters. Thieves and scoundrels make a good living and are probably happier than they were in their earlier state of dire poverty. Should we be imposing our cultural views on the Malagasy? I don't know.

But consider our walk through a series of small communities near Andapa (described on page 249). We will remember this experience for the rest of our lives. The people we encountered on the way will also recall it with joy and laughter. We were amazingly good entertainment: a complete change from the normal, predictable day. Had we given out presents, or polaroid photos, or even paid tourist rates for a local guide, would those young men still have

'PLEASE SEND ME A PHOTO'

It is not always easy to keep a promise. Of course we intend to send a print after someone posed cheerfully for the photo, but after we get home there are so many other things to do, so many addresses on torn-out pages of exercise books. I now honour my promises. Here's why.

I was checking my group in to a Nosy Be hotel when the bell boy asked if he could speak to me. He looked nervous, so suspecting a problem with the bookings I asked him to wait until everyone was in their rooms.

When we were alone he cleared his throat and recited what was obviously a carefully prepared speech: 'You are Mrs Hilary Bradt. Ten years ago you gave your business card to the lady at Sambava Voyages and she gave it to a schoolboy who wrote to you. But you were away so your mother answered the letter. She wrote many letters. My name is Murille and I am that boy. And now I want to talk to you about Janet Cross and Brian Cross and Andrew and...' There followed a list of every member of my family. As I listened, incredulous, I remembered the original letter. 'We love England strongly,' he wrote, 'especially London, Buckingham, Grantham, Dover...' I remembered passing it to my mother saying I was too busy for such a correspondence but maybe she'd like to write. She kept it up for several years, answering questions such as 'How often does Mrs Hilary go to Grantham and Dover?' and she sent a photo of the family gathering at Christmas, naming every member on the back of the photo.

This brought an indignant letter from a cousin. 'I have seen your photo. It is a very nice one. I asked Murille if he would lend it for one day only because we all study English so we must have photo of English people more to improve this language, but he refused me strongly because they are only his friends not mine...'

Murille brought out the treasured photo. It had suffered from the constant handling and tropical heat and was peeling at the edges. He wanted to trim it, he explained, 'but if I do I will have to cut off a bit of your mother's beautiful chair and I can't do that.'

Later that year I sent Murille a photo album filled with family photos. I never heard from him again – that's the way it is in Madagascar – but the story has a twist to its tail.

I recently went back to Sambava, twelve years after the original visit, and found myself addressing a classroom of eager adult students of English and their local teacher. Searching for something interesting to say, I told them about the time I was last in Sambava and the series of letters between Murille and my mother. And I told them about the cousin who also wrote to her. 'I think his name was Patrice,' I said. The teacher looked up. 'I'm Patrice. Yes, I remember writing to Janet Cross...'

agreed to give their labour to their community, because their community mattered, or would they in future have looked to tourists for their income? Would the children race up to future visitors with shrieks of delight mixed with apprehension, or approach with outstretched hands? I know the answer and I know that we would all have been losers in the long run.

My views over present-giving are backed up by Laura Benson, who spent several weeks researching government, church and private programmes to help the poor. She wrote: 'I am convinced now that giving to children directly is only hurting the situation, and that if you really want to help then a donation to an organisation is the best way. Giving pens, etc can have an even worse effect, especially if you only have one to give. I saw many fights started among children over who got the pen or the empty Coke bottle.'

More and more...

Visitors who have spent some time in Madagascar and have befriended a particular family often find themselves in the 'more and more and more' trap. The foreigner begins by expressing appreciation of the friendship and hospitality he or she received by sending a gift to the family. A request for a more expensive gift follows. And another one, until the luckless *vazaha* feels that she is seen as a bottomless cornucopia of goodies. The reaction is a mixture of guilt and resentment.

Understanding the Malagasy viewpoint may help you to come to terms with these requests. You may be considered as part of the extended family, and family members often help support those who are less well-off. You will almost certainly be thought of as fabulously wealthy, so it is worth dispelling this myth by giving some prices for familiar foodstuffs at home – a kilo of rice, for instance, or a mango. Explain that you don't have servants, that you pay so much for rent, and that you have a family of your own that needs your help. Don't be afraid to say 'no' firmly.

Off the beaten path

Travellers venturing well off the beaten path will want to do their utmost to avoid offending the local people, who are usually extremely warm and hospitable. Unfortunately, with the many *fady* prohibitions and beliefs varying from area to area and village to village, it is impossible to know exactly how to behave, although *vazahas* (white foreigners) and other outsiders are exempt from the consequences of infringing a local *fady*.

Sometimes, in very remote areas, Malagasy will react in sheer terror at the sight of a white person. This probably stems from their belief in *Mpakafo* (pronounced 'mpakaf<u>oo</u>'), the 'stealer of hearts'. These pale-faced beings are said to wander around at night ripping out people's hearts, an understandable reason for rural Malagasy not going out after dark – and a problem when you are looking for a guide. The arrival of a pale-faced being in their village is understandably upsetting. In the southeast it is the *Mpangalak' aty*, the 'taker of the liver', who is feared.

Villages are governed by the *Fokonolona*, or People's Assembly. On arrival at a village you should ask for the *Président du Fokontany*. Although traditionally this was the village elder, these days it is more likely to be someone who speaks French – perhaps the schoolteacher. He will show you where you can sleep (sometimes a hut is kept free for guests, sometimes someone will be moved out for you). You will usually be provided with a meal. Now travellers have penetrated most rural areas, you will be expected to pay. If the *Président* is not available, ask for *Ray aman-dreny*, an elder.

Philip Thomas, a social anthropologist who has conducted research in the rural southeast, points out several ways that tourists may unwittingly cause offence. 'People should adopt the common courtesy of greeting the Malagasy in their own language. *Salama*, *manahoana* and *veloma* are no more difficult to say than their French equivalents, and to insist on using French displays an ignorance of Madagascar's colonial past.

'*Vazaha* sometimes refuse food and hospitality, putting up tents and cooking their own food. But in offering you a place to sleep and food to eat the Malagasy are showing you the kindness they extend to any visitor or stranger, and to refuse is a rejection of their hospitality and sense of humanity. You may think you are inconveniencing them, and this is true, but they would prefer that than if you keep to yourselves as though you were not people (in the widest sense) like them. It may annoy you that it is virtually impossible to get a moment away from the gaze of the Malagasy, but you are there to look at them and their activities anyway, so why should there not be a mutual exchange? Besides, you are far more fascinating to them than they are to you, for their view of the world is not one shaped by mass education and access to international images supplied by television.

'It is perfectly acceptable to give a gift of money in return for help. Gifts of cash are not seen by the Malagasy as purchases and they themselves frequently give them. Rather, you give as a sign of your appreciation and respect. But beware of those who may try to take advantage of your position as a foreigner (and you may find these in even the remotest spot), those who play on your lack of knowledge of language and custom, and their perception of you as extremely wealthy (as of course you are by their standards).

'You may well see memorial sites by the side of the road or tombs marked on maps, especially in the southeast. Do *not* think it is OK to visit these or photograph them if no-one is around to ask. Seek out someone, a male elder being best, and ask if you can be allowed to visit the site and under what terms. More often than not your request will be accepted. But what annoys people here is that *vazaha* see something beside the road then trample all over it, photographing it, then carry on with their journey as if they cared nothing for the feelings of those that own the site. To do so shows little respect, as the Malagasy understand it, neither to themselves nor to the dead commemorated there.'

Both Henk Beentje and Philip Thomas recommend presenting yourself and your passport to the *Gendarmerie* if you are staying in a small village. Apart from being good manners, this could avoid problems for both you and your Malagasy hosts (see box page 98).

TOURIST AID: HOW YOU CAN HELP

There *are* ways in which you can make a positive contribution. By making a donation to local projects you can help the people – and the wildlife – without creating new problems. My favourite is the Streetkids Project, which was started by a couple of English teachers, Jill and Charlie Hadfield. Visiting a charity run by the Sisters of the Good Shepherd in the capital, they could see where a little money could go a long way. The nuns, Irish and Sri Lankan, run – amongst other things – a preparatory school for the very poor. When the children are ready to go on to state school, however, the parents can't afford the £15 a year they must pay for registration, uniform and books, so the children were condemned to return to the streets as beggars. The Streetkids Project raises money to continue their education.

Visiting this centre is an intensely moving and inspiring experience. Apart from the school and preschool groups, there is a mother and baby programme involving 260 families where the health and weight of the infant are monitored on a regular basis, a feeding programme, and many other projects. So if you want to help Madagascar by helping the poor, give a donation of money, clothes (especially clothes for new-born babies), medicines, or school supplies to the Centre Fihavanana at St Joseph's church in Antananarivo. The nuns can usually be reached at phone number 299 81 (their house). Ask for Sister Lucy or Sister Anna. The full address is Soeurs du Bon Pasteur, 58 Lalana S. Stephani, Amparibe, Antananarivo 101. Do remember how busy they are, and be prepared to fit in with their timetable.

In Britain the Streetkids scheme is administered by Money for Madagascar (see below) so you may prefer to send them your donation.

The organisations and charities listed below are all working with the people of Madagascar, and, by extension, habitat conservation. Other charities work specifically for wildlife.

Charities assisting Madagascar
People

Money for Madagascar 29 Queen's Rd, Sketty, Swansea SA2 0SB, Great Britain. This long-established small charitable trust may be in the process of winding down, now that other organisations are doing similar work with rural communities. However, they still administer the Streetkids Education Scheme described earlier, so this is the contact address for British-based readers wishing to make a contribution to the Scheme.

The Sedgwick Trust Moresdale Hall East, Lambrigg, Kendal, Cumbria LA8 0DH. Administered in England by a former LMS missionary in Madagascar, Dr James Pottinger. Like Money for Madagascar, they work with local organisations at village level to promote self-help projects in health, agriculture and education.

SAF Both the above charities work with the development organisation of the United Protestant Church of Madagascar. SAF organises and runs a large variety of projects, from emergency relief following natural disasters such as the 1994 cyclone, to irrigation, potable water supplies, tree nurseries, small agricultural projects, village pharmacies and so on. They are indispensable for the smooth running of many of the British charities.

Feedback Madagascar Ashfield House, by Balloch, Dunbartonshire, G83 8NB. Tel: 01389 752805. A small but highly effective Scottish charity which bases its activities on feedback from the local Malagasy who identify and agree on development and conservation projects (see box on page 130). These have included irrigation dams, the rebuilding of a school, and a 'school reserve' near Ranomafana. Other schemes are a women's market-gardening cooperative and a reforestation project near Ambalavao.

The Azafady Group 306a Portobello Rd, London W10 5TA. Tel: 0181 960 0110; fax: 0181 960 0488. A well-organised new charity funding a variety of projects in Madagascar, mainly in the southeast. Initiatives include a tree nursery near Tolagnaro, a variety of projects for the villages of Anosibe and Evatra, and support for the Libanona Ecology Centre in Toliara.

STARFISH PO Box 1915, Cleveland, OH 44106, USA. Tel: (216) 932 2438. Fax: (216) 932 7403; Email: JFSellers@aol.com. The acronym is for Society Taking Active Responsibility for International Self-help; the aim is to provide the tools and training for local people to do their jobs. The emphasis is on medical help. Projects have included surgery training for student doctors and nurses, village health projects (working in conjunction with the WWF in villages adjoining reserves), the establishment of pharmacies, and the provision of bicycles to allow doctors and nurses to reach remote villages.

Jim Sellers, who runs the Madagascar projects for STARFISH, sells Antaimoro paper, greetings cards, etc as a means of fundraising. Contact him at the above address.

MOSS 3 Peterborough Mansions, New King's Rd, London SW6 4SF. The Madagascan Organisation for Saving Sight (MOSS) was set up in 1993 to help develop ophthalmic and general health services in Madagascar, where 300,000 people suffer blindness from treatable and preventable causes. MOSS is funding a Landrover equipped for ophthalmic fieldwork which can reach the rural population most in need.

The Dodwell Trust A British registered charity running a radio project designed to help rural villagers, through the production and broadcast of a radio drama series for family health, family planning and welfare. The programmes are in Malagasy, by Malagasy, and based in Malagasy tradition.

To enhance this 3½-year programme the Dodwell Trust also runs a solar radio project, and a clockwork or wind-up radio project which aims to put these radios into rural and rainforest villages. The Baygen clockwork radio needs only 20 seconds' wind-up to play for 30 minutes. This radio is British-invented and won the Design Award for 1996.

Andrew Lees Memorial Trust c/o Friends of the Earth, 26–28 Underwood St, London N1 7BR. Set up in memory of the FOE campaigner who died while researching the possible impact of a mining project on the forests of the southeast, the Trust helps fund environmental, research and educational programmes in that area. The Libanona Ecology Centre is one of their successes (see box on page 215).

The Valiha Project FMS, PO Box 337, London N4 ITW. Tel: 0181 340 9651. This is not a registered charity but a project to maintain the musical traditions of Madagascar, instigated by the leader of the world-acclaimed Malagasy group, Tarika. Hanitrarivo Rasoanaivo was depressed at the influence of foreign cultures on the young people of Madagascar and the violent or pornographic videos which are now their preferred entertainment. She writes: 'I would like to make it possible for children to be taught the most famous traditional musical instrument, the *valiha*. Not only will this teach them a useful skill and an enjoyable leisure activity, it will also revive a pride in Malagasy culture. Lessons will be free of charge and pupils will be given a valiha each to practise at home. Eventually there will be music competitions and prizes.' Donations to the project will go towards the cost of buying the instruments, training teachers, and for prizes.

Zaza Faly (Mission Aid for Children). Elke Driese, Oberonstr 8a, 13129 Berlin, Germany. Local address: Lot 233-B bis, Amparatanana, Fenoarivo-Est 509. A nonreligious charity that works with local people to help the street children of Fenoarivo, on the east coast.

Wildlife
World Wide Fund for Nature (UK) Avenue du Mont-blanc, 1196 Gland, Switzerland (International Office).
Panda House, Weyside Park, Godalming, Surrey GU7 IXR, England.
1250 24th St NW, Washington DC 20037-1175, USA.
Aires Protégées, BP 738, Antananarivo 101, Madagascar.

Madagascar Fauna Group Two of the main supporters are The Jersey Wildlife Preservation Trust, Les Augres Manor, Jersey, Channel Islands, Great Britain; and San Francisco Zoo (director David Anderson), 1 Zoo Rd, San Francisco, CA 94132-1098. Tel: 415 753 7061. Fax: 681 2039.

Conservation International (USA) 1015 18th St NW, Washington DC, 20003, USA.

Black Lemur Forest Project c/o 53 Priory Way, North Harrow, Middx HA2 6DQ, England. A small but effective project in Nosy Be, helping to protect the habitat and survival of one of Madagascar's most popular lemur species. See page 130.

Organisations promoting responsible tourism
Tourism Concern Froebel College, Roehampton Lane, London SW15 5PJ, England. With the slogan 'putting people back in the picture', Tourism Concern 'promotes tourism that takes account of the rights and interests of those living in the world's tourist areas'. They put pressure on governments or companies which promote harmful tourism, run meetings and conferences, and publish an informative and interesting newsletter.

Center for Responsible Tourism PO Box 827, San Anselmo, CA 94979, USA. Full title: The North America Coordinating Center for Responsible Tourism (NACCRT). 'Exists to change attitudes and practices of North American travelers, to involve North Americans in the struggle for justice in tourism and to work for tourism practices that are compatible with a sustainable global society.'

Finally, if on your return to Britain you want to keep connections with Madagascar, how about joining the **Anglo-Malagasy Society**? The London consulate will give you the current secretary's address.

FROM LITTLE ACORNS...

Jamie Spencer is an anthropologist who first visited Madagascar at the age of 22 to write his university dissertation. He was so moved by the poverty yet joyfulness of the Tanala people, and their kindness to a stranger when he was ill, that he resolved to repay the debt by returning to help the Malagasy. Funding for the first trip was raised by a sponsored cycle-ride. He took with him a microscope donated by the local pathologist and a sack full of medicines begged from hospitals and chemists, and headed for the eastern rainforest. Thus *Feedback Madagascar* was born.

All along the local people were the driving force: it was they who identified the projects they most cared about, then enlisted *Feedback*'s support to make them happen. The first major project was to build irrigation dams for the village of Sandrakely (resulting in 100 acres of sustainable rice-fields), and then to rebuild a school destroyed by Cyclone Geralda. The children also have their very own forest reserve. This 'School Reserve' was the first of its kind in Madagascar. Twelve hectares of rainforest were donated by the village chief. Though small, it is the home of four species of lemur and also provides a vital reservoir of water for Sandrakely. The only people allowed access to the forest are the government foresters and the schoolchildren themselves, who are being aided in their environmental studies by the WWF.

Josephine Andrews also studied anthropology (and geography). She fulfilled her dream of visiting Madagascar when she won a Winston Churchill Scholarship to do a survey of Madagascar's environmental problems. Like Jamie she fell in love with the island and its people, and determined to go back. The Black Lemur Forest Project was established in Nosy Be, using funds begged from a variety of businesses. The aim was to conserve the remaining untouched forests of Lokobe, the black lemurs' dwindling habitat, by working with the local people to find alternative means of support, particularly through Nosy Be's thriving tourist industry. After several years of working on a shoestring budget, Josephine and her Malagasy husband were awarded the Whitely Award for Conservation. Most recent developments include a community centre in the village of Ambanoro on the western edge of Lokobe Reserve, which encompasses a Visitor Centre for tourists and a shop for locally made handicrafts.

Liz Caldicott is a very ordinary tourist who briefly visited Madagascar off a cruise ship. Going ashore in Nosy Komba she was disappointed to find that the handicrafts did not truly reflect the island's main attraction: lemurs and chameleons. She wanted to see soft toys for sale and wondered why the local women did not make such saleable items. 'They don't know how to' came the answer. So she enlisted the help of Josephine. Back in England Liz worked 'like a factory' producing a series of sample toys – a lepilemur, black lemurs of both sexes, and a panther chameleon – from locally available materials. These are now in production in Ambanoro, giving the islanders a reliable income from their sales, and tourists a delightful souvenir to take home with them.

Three ordinary people with extraordinary perseverance, united by their love for Madagascar.

Part Two

THE HIGHLANDS

In October 1996 James Clarke, a columnist for the Johannesburg newspaper The Star, *ran a competition for the best humorous poem about Madagascar. Famadihana proved the winning theme: here is the winning entry and the runner-up.*

Famadihana

Carol McIlraith

Don't dig me up again today
Cried Grandpa in distress
Last time you turned my ancient bones
You left me in a mess.

My head was put back upside down
My foot was in my ear
It is no fun being rearranged
Year after blooming year.

Famadihana is to blame
Why can't they let me be?
Oh to have been an Englishman
And not Malagasy!

Dead again in Madagascar

Craig Cook

If in death it is action you crave,
Madagascar's the place for a rave,
For if you're deceased
They won't leave you in peace
You'll be literally turned in your grave!

There's no point in their looking ahead,
They have ancestor worship instead –
You'll be lucky to see
This great ceremony
But for God's sake don't tell them they're dead.

Chapter Eight

Antananarivo and Area

INTRODUCTION

Looking down from the plane window as you approach Antananarivo you can see how excitingly different this country is from any of its near neighbours. Clusters of red clay houses and steepled churches stand isolated on the hilltops overlooking a mosaic of green and brown paddy fields. Old defence ditches, *tamboho*, form circles around villages or estates, and dotted in the empty countryside are the white concrete Merina tombs from where the dead will be exhumed in the *famidihana* ceremony.

Most people stay only a day or so in Tana, but there is plenty to see in the city and the surrounding *Hauts Plateaux*. A week would not be too long to experience the cultural, historical and natural sites which lie within a day's excursion of the capital. The Kingdom of Imerina thrived for over a century before French colonisation, so it is here that the rich and fascinating history and culture of the Merina people are best appreciated.

HISTORY

The recorded history of the Merina people (characterised by their Indonesian features) begins in the 1400s with a chief called Andriandraviravina. He is widely thought to have started the Merina dynasty that became the most powerful in Madagascar, eventually conquering much of the country.

Key monarchs in the rise of the Merina include Andrianjaka, who conquered a Vazimba town called Analamanga built on a great rock thrusting above the surrounding plains. He renamed it Antananarivo and ordered his palace to be built on its highest point. With its surrounding marshland, ideal for rice production, and the security afforded by its high position, this was the perfect site for a Merina capital city.

In the 18th century there were two centres for the Merina kingdom, Antananarivo and Ambohimanga. The latter became the more important and around 1787 Ramboasalama was proclaimed king of Ambohimanga and took the name of Andrianampoinimerina. The name means 'the prince in the heart of Imerina' which was more than an idle boast: this king was the Malagasy

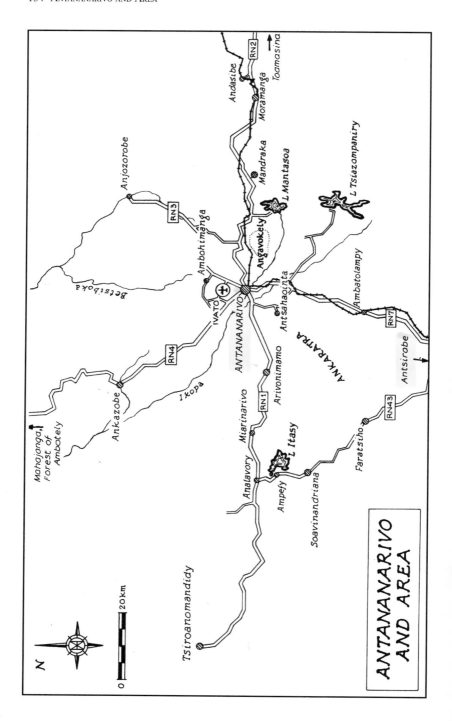

ANTANANARIVO AND AREA

counterpart of the great Peruvian Inca Tupac Yupanqui, expanding his empire as much by skilful organisation as by force, and doing it without the benefit of a written language (history seems to demonstrate that orders in triplicate are not essential to efficiency). By his death in 1810 the central plateau was firmly in control of the Merina and ably administered through a mixture of old customs and new. Each conquered territory was governed by local princes, answerable to the king, and the system of *fokonolona* (village communities) was established. From this firm foundation the new king, Radama I, was able to conquer most of the rest of the island.

Antananarivo means 'City of the Thousand', supposedly because a thousand warriors protected it. By the end of the 18th century, Andrianampoinimerina had taken Antananarivo from his rebellious kinsman and moved his base there from Ambohimanga. From that time until the French conquest in 1895 Madagascar's history centred around the royal palace or *rova*, the modest houses built for Andrianjaka and Andrianampoinimerina giving way to a splendid palace designed for Queen Ranavalona I by Jean Laborde and James Cameron. The rock cliffs near the palace became known as Ampamarinana, 'the place of the hurling', as Christian martyrs met their fate at the command of the Queen.

There was no reason for the French to move the capital elsewhere: its pleasant climate made it an agreeable place to live, and plenty of French money and planning went into the city we see today.

IVATO AIRPORT
Arriving
In the Good Old Days Ivato was like the cottage of a wicked witch, seducing innocent visitors through its beguiling doors. Once inside, only the good and the brave emerged unscathed. During the rebuilding and enlarging of the airport it became, if anything, more chaotic. Now (sigh) it is much the same as other international airports in the developing world.

On arrival the procedure is as follows:

1. Fill in the arrivals form. This should be handed to you on the plane and takes a Malagasy interest in your ancestry.
2. Join one of three 'queues' for passport control where you hand in the form and your visa is checked.
3. Pick up luggage. The few trolleys that exist are porter-operated and usually commandeered by groups. Independent travellers not wanting to pay a porter (who will expect US$1) should carry their own bags.
4. Pass through customs. If you are carrying a video camera or something of value such as jewellery or a lap-top computer you should pass through the red channel and declare it. Failure to do this may cause problems on departure. Still cameras need not be declared (note that in French *camera* means a video camera; a still camera is *appareil*). If queueing for the green 'Nothing to Declare' channel, try to get behind other tourists who are usually waved through

without needing to open their bags. Luggage belonging to Malagasy arrivals is thoroughly searched.

Leaving

This is no longer a two-hour nightmare, but it is still a somewhat testing experience. For international flights be prepared for the following:

1. Arrive at the airport three hours before the flight, with all or most of all your Malagasy money spent. Remember that you cannot change your Fmg back into hard currency. Also, the check-in counter is *after* you leave the main airport area (with shops). Once you have checked in there is nowhere to spend your Fmg.

2. Pay your departure tax at the kiosk marked Adema. Only hard currency is accepted (no travellers cheques): 100Ff, DM30 or US$20 for flights to Europe, 80Ff, DM25 or US$17 for 'regional' destinations on the Indian Ocean, which include South Africa. The receipt will be stapled on to your air ticket.

3. Collect and fill in a departure form from a window to the left of the kiosk (or at the kiosk itself).

4. Join the queue with your luggage; prepare for a certain amount of jostling.

5. When you reach the doorway show your ticket and passport, and pass through baggage security. If the X-ray machine is working you're unlikely to be asked to open your bags but have the keys ready. If you're carrying only a small amount of baggage, officials may 'encourage' you to take additional packages on behalf of their friends. Don't do it.

6. Proceed to the check-in counter. Any orderly queue will have disintegrated by now as people compete for priority. If the computer is working your seat will be assigned here.

7. Passport control. Hand in your departure form.

8. Departure tax check.

9. Final passport check, hand-luggage X-ray, and you're through into the departure lounge! There are souvenir shops here (hard currency only) and a bar. It is sometimes possible to change the Malagasy money you've belatedly found in your pocket into hard currency with the ladies who supervise the toilets.

Internal flights

The domestic building is separated from the main airport. If you are connecting to an internal flight immediately on arrival in Madagascar, you can pass directly down a linking corridor on the right of the main hall. However, there is no bank in the domestic building. The domestic airport tax is 3,300Fmg. These flights are distinctly no-frills. Boarding passes are carefully recycled and there are no seat assignments. Sometimes, for security reasons, you have to identify your luggage from a pile on the runway.

Lost luggage

Sometimes your luggage doesn't arrive. Most people are on a tight schedule and cannot hang around waiting for the next flight. If you are on an organised tour your guide will handle it, but if on your own it can be a bit of a challenge. For someone else to pick up your luggage you will need to get a proxy form with a signature that is legalised in the town hall. The only alternative is to meet every international flight (assuming it was lost on the way to Madagascar) in the hope that your bag is on it. Unclaimed bags are put under lock and key, and finding *le responsable* may not be easy.

Transport to the city centre (12km)

In the past there was an airport bus service, Air Routes Service, but at the time of writing this is not running. Official taxis cost about 55,000Fmg (£9.00/ US$14.00), but if you walk purposefully across the carpark you will find some lurking unofficial taxis for around 40,000Fmg. Experienced travellers can go for the local bus which stops at the road junction about 100m from the airport. In 1996 it cost 850Fmg (about 25 cents) and you can pay for an extra seat for your luggage. This takes you to the Vasakosy area behind the train station.

ANTANANARIVO (TANA) TODAY

From the right place, in the right light, Antananarivo (Tana for short) is one of the most attractive capitals in the developing world. In sunshine it has the quality of a child's picture book, with brightly coloured houses stacked up the hillsides, and mauve jacarandas and purple bougainvillea against the dark blue of the winter sky. Red crown-of-thorn euphorbias stand in rows against red clay walls, rice paddies are tended right up to the edge of the city, clothes are laid out on the river bank to dry, and zebu-carts rumble along the roads on the outskirts of town. It's all deliciously foreign, and can hardly fail to impress the first-time visitor as he or she drives in from the airport. Indeed, this drive is one of the most varied and interesting in the Highlands. The good impression is helped by the climate – during the dry season the sun is hot but the air pleasantly cool (the altitude is between 1,245m and 1,469m).

Sadly, for many people this wonderful first impression does not survive a closer acquaintance. Tana can seem squalid and dangerous, with conspicuous poverty, persistent beggars, and a rising crime rate.

The geography of the city is both simple and confusing. It is built on two ridges which combine in a V. On the highest hill, dominating all the viewpoints, is the ruined Queen's Palace. Down the central valley runs a broad boulevard, Avenue de l'Indépendance (sometimes called by its Malagasy name Fahaleovantena), which terminates at the station. It narrows at the other end to become Avenue du 26 Juin, then dives through a tunnel to reach Lake Anosy and the Hilton Hotel. The Avenues de l'Indépendance and du 26 Juin (district Analakely) are the focal point of the Lower Town, lined with shops, offices and hotels, and crammed with market stalls and lower-class bustle, but the 'centre of town' could just as easily refer to the Upper Town (district Isoraka) where the President's Palace, the Hotel Colbert, the main post office and other assorted businesses are located. This is where you will find the most expensive boutiques, posh offices and the main supermarket.

The confusing part is that pedestrians use the many flights of stairs to reach their destinations on the hills while cars go through tunnels or crawl and stall on traffic-choked circuitous roads. Finding your way on foot is made worse by streets being unnamed, changing name several times within a few hundred metres, or going by two different names (when reading street names it's worth knowing that *Lalana* means street, *Arabe* is avenue, and *Kianja* is a square). Wandering lost but happy is, unfortunately, no longer advisable (see *Safety* below). The city is divided into small districts. When taking a taxi or finding your way on foot it will help to have the name of the district written down.

The population of Tana is about two million and growing fast.

Getting around

Get to know the city on foot during the day (but carry nothing of value); use taxis for long distances, unknown destinations, and always at night. Taxis do not have meters so agree on the price before you get in. Expect to pay more than the locals, but avoid the exorbitant *vazaha* price charged by the taxis serving the big hotels. Battered Renaults and Citroens will be cheaper – around 5,000Fmg (90p/US$1.40) for city destinations. In such vehicles you can have an interesting time watching the street go by through the hole in the floor, or being pushed by helpful locals when the vehicle breaks down or runs out of petrol.

The great advantage of not having meters is that if the driver gets lost (which frequently happens) you will not pay any more for the extra journey. In my experience Tana taxi drivers are honest and helpful and can be trusted to get you to your destination – eventually.

Buses are much cheaper, but sorting out the destinations and districts can be challenging. Often it's best to take a taxi to your destination and a bus back.

Safety

Sadly, violent robbery has become quite common in Tana. Leave your valuables in the hotel (preferably in a safe deposit or locked in your bag) and carry as little as possible. The *zoma* area and Avenue de l'Indépendance are particularly risky. The current scam is the 'Ballet of the Hats'. Kids wearing or carrying wide-brimmed straw hats encircle you and, using the hats to obscure your view, work through your pockets, money-belt, neck pouch or whatever. Unless you are confident of your ability to handle such a situation, or are in a small group so you can keep an eye on each other, it may be best to avoid the *zoma* altogether. There are other, safer, markets in Madagascar.

Do not risk taking the path over Lake Anosy to the World War I memorial, and if possible avoid wandering around the area near the Gare du Nord which has the highest incidence of muggings in the city.

Be careful when taking a taxi to keep your bag on the floor by your feet. Thieves sometimes grab handbags through the open window.

Always keep in mind that thieves are looking for valuables, and are rarely out to harm you physically. If you are not carrying anything they want, and have no bulging pockets to attract them, you can still enjoy exploring this serendipitous city on foot.

Where to stay

New hotels and restaurants are opening all the time in Tana. This selection is by no means complete – be adventurous and find your own!

Category A

Hilton Hotel Near Lake Anosy. Tel: 260 60. Fax: 260 51. One of Tana's skyscrapers (as you'd expect), very comfortable with good meals. Its advantages are the offices and shops in the building and the swimming pool. In the pleasantly hot sun of the dry season this is a real bonus. It is some way from the centre of town (although the walk in is enjoyable). 1110Ff double, 920Ff single. Most credit cards accepted.

Palace Hotel A smart newish hotel at the lower end of the Avenue de l'Indépendance. Tel: 256 63. Fax: 339 43. No restaurant, but enormous studio apartments with kitchens. 630Ff double, 595Ff single, 950Ff apartment.

Tana Plaza Avenue de l'Indépendance, near the station. Formerly the Terminus and popular with *vazahas* in the 1980s, this is now an upmarket hotel with small but good rooms for 240Ff.

Hotel Colbert Lalana Printsy Ratsimamanga. Tel: 202 02. Fax: 340 12. Very French, usually full, my choice of the posh Tana hotels for its good location in the Upper Town, nice atmosphere and excellent food. 550–1,550Ff per room (double room to studio apartment). Most credit cards accepted.

La Résidence (Complexe Hoteliers d'Ankerana). BP 265. Tel: 417 48/201 01. Fax: 417 86. A very smart, newly opened hotel in a converted colonial house/school in the Nanisana district (northeast Tana). Large garden, spacious rooms, three excellent restaurants with live music (jazz or Malagasy groups). From 800Ff (luxury apartments) to 250Ff. Breakfast 25Ff.

Radama Hotel 22 Ave Grandidier, Isoraka (near the Colbert). Tel: 319 27. Fax: 353 23. A very nice small (30 rooms) hotel with excellent food. Impractical for groups because there is no parking for tour buses, but ideal for business people (there is a conference room) or independent travellers. No lift (elevator). 360–560Ff (double room to studio apartment). Most credit cards accepted.

Hotel Shanghai 4 Lalana Rainitovo (near US Embassy and opposite the Radama Hotel). Tel: 314 72. Room rates are highly competitive, with a double room at £15/$25. A breakfast of eggs, yoghurt and tea is a little over £1/$1.55.

Hotel de France 34, Avenue de l'Indépendance. Tel: 213 04. Fax: 201 08. Ask for an inside room or it tends to be noisy. 250Ff/$50 per room. Gaining popularity because of its central location and good restaurants, but there is no lift and the service is not up to the level of the other hotels in this category.

Hotel Gregoire Mahavoky, Besarety, near the Marché Artisanal. Tel: 222 66. Fax: 292 71. Used mainly by groups. US$76 single, US$82 double. Quiet, comfortable, friendly and efficient, with two very good restaurants, L'Aquarium and Le Rotonde.

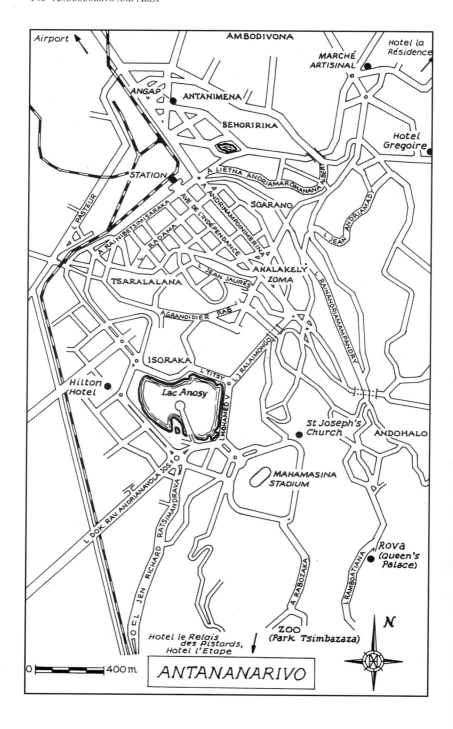

ANTANANARIVO

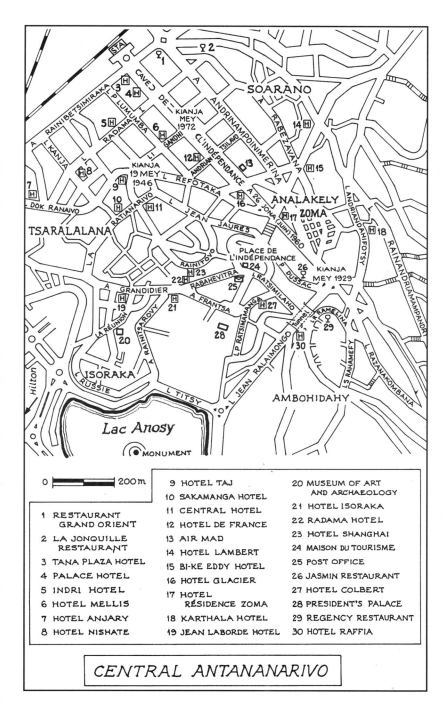

CENTRAL ANTANANARIVO

0 — 200m

1 RESTAURANT GRAND ORIENT
2 LA JONQUILLE RESTAURANT
3 TANA PLAZA HOTEL
4 PALACE HOTEL
5 INDRI HOTEL
6 HOTEL MELLIS
7 HOTEL ANJARY
8 HOTEL NISHATE

9 HOTEL TAJ
10 SAKAMANGA HOTEL
11 CENTRAL HOTEL
12 HOTEL DE FRANCE
13 AIR MAD
14 HOTEL LAMBERT
15 BI-KE EDDY HOTEL
16 HOTEL GLACIER
17 HOTEL RÉSIDENCE ZOMA
18 KARTHALA HOTEL
19 JEAN LABORDE HOTEL

20 MUSEUM OF ART AND ARCHAEOLOGY
21 HOTEL ISORAKA
22 RADAMA HOTEL
23 HOTEL SHANGHAI
24 MAISON DU TOURISME
25 POST OFFICE
26 JASMIN RESTAURANT
27 HOTEL COLBERT
28 PRESIDENT'S PALACE
29 REGENCY RESTAURANT
30 HOTEL RAFFIA

Le Hintsy Hotel de l'Ikopa 4 Route Digue d'Ambohimanambola (RN 58B, 20 minutes from the town centre, close to l'Ikopa river). BP 8421. Tel: 264 14 or 263 79. This newly opened hotel/restaurant has 13 twin-bedded bungalows and 8 single rooms, all with bath, mini-bar, hot water and TV. It also boasts two conference/reception rooms and a 300-seat restaurant.

Category B

Jean Laborde Hotel 3 Rue de Russie, Isoraka. Tel: 330 45. Fax: 327 94. A walk uphill from Ave de l'Indépendance. Six beautiful, pine-furnished rooms, all en-suite, at 120,000Fmg (about £20/US$30). Excellent French restaurant. Frequently booked up, so make room or restaurant reservations in advance.

Indri Hotel 15 Rue Radama, Tsaralalana. Tel/Fax: 209 22. Comfortable, medium-sized hotel near the *zoma* with a cocktail bar, live entertainment and gift shop. Bedrooms have TV, telephone and mini-bar. One caution: recent reports mention caged lemurs kept in poor conditions, with the owners unwilling to rectify matters. As a result at least one tour operator boycotts the hotel.

Hotel Raffia Lalana Ranavalona III (just beyond the Aeroflot office in the Upper Town). A nice new (1997) hotel with lovely views over Lake Anosy. 50,000–65,000Fmg.

Hotel Mellis Lalana Indira Gandhi. Tel: 234 25. Once the most popular *vazaha* hotel, and still praised by recent visitors although the hot water is said to be unreliable. From 80,000 to 90,000Fmg (for a room with a bath).

Central Hotel 7 Rue Rajohnson (continuation of Indira Gandhi). Tel: 227 94. Fax: 357 04. A good and friendly hotel with newly renovated rooms. 45,000–85,000Fmg (£7/US$10–£15/US$23).

Hotel le Résidence Zoma 43 Ave du 26 Juin (next to Bata store). Tel: 231 13. Fax: 348 35. A room with two beds, bath and TV is 80,000Fmg. Breakfast 10,000Fmg. Clean and comfortable, but can be noisy, says reader M. Hughes, especially on *zoma* days.

Sakamanga Rue A Ratianarivo, near the Central. Tel: 35 809. Ten rooms and one apartment. Double 55,000Fmg – with shower and WC, 78,000Fmg. French run, very pleasant (though noisy) but almost always full. There is an excellent, lively French restaurant, with main dishes 8,000–16,000Fmg, also heavily booked. For room reservations write to them at Lot IBK 7B1S, Ampasamadinika, Antananarivo 101.

Hotel Anjary Lalana Razafimahandry and Dr Ranaivo. Tel: 244 09. Clean, large, secure, friendly. Hot water. From 40,000Fmg double. Recommended.

Karthala Hotel 48 Lalana Andriandahifotsy, BP 912 (near the Adventist church, Mandrosoa, 100m from the *zoma*). Tel: 248 45 or 298 30. Mrs Rafalimanana speaks good English. About 30,000–45,000Fmg, including breakfast. 'Wonderful – and quiet' (Maggie Rush)

Le Relais des Pistards Lalana Fernand Kasanga (same road as Tsimbazaza), about 1km beyond the zoo. BP 3550. Tel: 291 34. A friendly, family-style hotel run by Florent and Jocelyn Colney. Double with breakfast 60,000Fmg (about £10/US$15), single with breakfast 40,000Fmg, double demi-pension 90,000Fmg, single demi-pension 60,000Fmg. Pleasant communal dining room, and excellent cooking, but rooms vary. Florent Colney is an avid mountain biker, so a stay here is a must for those planning to cycle in Madagascar. His advice will be invaluable.

Hotel l'Etape Five minutes' walk from Tsimbazaza. Some English spoken. Clean, helpful. Doubles 35,000–50,000Fmg (shared WC and bath with hot water). Set meals at around 10,000Fmg. Anne Axel, who spent several months travelling alone in Madagascar, says l'Etape is her favourite hotel in Tana, with a kind and helpful owner and very friendly staff.

Taj Hotel 69 Rue Dr Razafindranovona, Tsaraikiana (near Kianja 19 Mey 1946). Tel: 305 40. Fax: 245 57. Comfortable rooms with hot water. 130,000–170,000Fmg (with extra bed).

Auberge du Cheval Blanc BP 23, Ivato. Tel: 446 46. Near Ivato airport. Convenient when you have a late arrival and early departure the following morning, but there are other nearby hotels that may be better. 65,000Fmg single/double. Breakfast 9,000Fmg, meals (mediocre) 15,000–25,000Fmg. MasterCard and Visa accepted.

Hotel Refuge Another hotel near the airport which is worth checking out. It is signposted to the right, as you approach Tana, just after a house with an intriguing balcony of carved soldiers on your left.

Category C
Hotel Isoraka 11, Ave Grandidier, past the Radama Hotel. Formerly the Valiha, this is one of the few budget hotels in the Upper Town. Clean, with hot water. Communal bathroom. 35,000Fmg single.

Hotel Lambert Through the *zoma* and towards the top of the steps on the Ambondrona side of town. Basic, clean, convenient. Good value and popular, but be prepared to climb a lot of stairs! 25,000–30,000Fmg. Readers speak highly of the *patron*, Henri Ferblantier, who goes out of his way to be helpful.

Hotel Nishate Lalana Razafimahandry. Has hot water and toilet in room.

Bi-ke Eddy Rue Rabezavana. Friendly, basic, central. Room 9 is the only one with private shower and bidet. 35,000Fmg.

Hotel Glacier Ave de l'Indépendance, near the Hotel de France. One of the oldest – and shabbiest – hotels in Tana, but it is conveniently located, has a lively bar (full of prostitutes) and low-priced rooms at 37,500–60,000Fmg.

Lapasoa au Bolidor Ave Andrianampoinimerina. The activities of the other guests may keep you awake, but it's cheap at 25,000Fmg.

Le Manoir Rouge Near the airport, and recommended by Jim Bond as 'definitely the best value I've come across around Ivato: 29,000–36,000Fmg I think. Good food, too'.

Other hotels on the road from the airport, which are probably **Category C** but not checked out, include **Hotel Sitara** (tel: 450 64) and, side by side, **Hotel Emeraude** and **Hotel Saphir.** The latter are likely to be the least expensive. Staying near Ivato saves the taxi fare into town if you are arriving on a late flight or leaving early in the morning.

Business visitors or study groups

For a long stay you are recommended (by Christina Dodwell) to contact Eddy Rasoamanana (BP 4376; tel: 257 62) who has four self-contained studios with their own bathrooms, kitchenette and phone for £10–£12 per night. Eddy can also supply efficient and reasonably-priced bilingual office facilities, and look after mail and phone calls.

Where to eat

Hotel restaurants

Most of the better hotels serve good food. Expats and Malagasy professionals favour the **Colbert**. The 'all you can eat' Sunday buffet is good value (but beware of the health risks of eating cold buffets). There are two restaurants at the Colbert; the Taverne is the smartest and imposes a dress-code on its diners. Phone 202 02 for reservations. Bring your French dictionary – menus are not translated.

The **Hilton** does a whole series of buffets – each lunch-time there is a 'businessman's buffet' with a 'gourmet buffet' on Sundays. Evenings are the time to try different nationalities. Sundays: Chinese, Tuesdays: Alsace, Thursdays: Italian. These cost around 50,000Fmg (1996).

The restaurant at the **Radama** is very good, with excellent French and Malagasy cooking. A meal for two, with two or three dishes, wine, coffee and service charge is less than £25/US$38.

The O! Poivre Vert at the **Hotel de France** is described by a reader as 'the hottest new place in town'.

Upper and middle range restaurants

Le Restaurant 65, Rue Emile Ranarivelo, Behoririka. Tel: 282 67. A lovely colonial house with a terrace overlooking superb gardens. Excellent food, attentive service. Highly recommended.

Au Grille du Rova Lot VX29, Avaradrova. About 100 metres down from the ruins of the Queen's Palace. Tel/Fax: 356 07. Excellent food, eaten indoors or outside, with a view over the city. Regular *Musique Malgache* evenings. Good English spoken. Recommended by several readers. The owner, Olivier Toboul, runs Malagasy Tours (see page 86).

Le Regency 15, Rue Ramelina, Ambatonakanga. Tel: 210 13. French owned and run with flair and elegance. Lovely atmosphere and super food.

Le Coupe de Paté Near Le Regency, probably on Lalana Ramelina (our correspondent, Bradley Rink, was so bowled over he didn't get the address!). A small, friendly Italian restaurant offering a variety of à la carte dishes, plus two reasonably priced set menus.

La Pradelle Ambatoroka (southeast of the city). Tel: 326 51. English spoken, Malagasy and European food, highly recommended by readers and residents.

La Jonquille 7 Rue Rabezavana, Soarano. Tel 206 37. Good, imaginative menu. Especially recommended for seafood.

Restaurant Jasmin 8 Lalana Paul-Dussac. Tel: 342 96. Good Chinese food.

Restaurant Grand Orient 4 Kianja Ambiky, near the station. Tel: 202 88. Good food and fun – a pianist plays requests. Also, about 8 minutes' walk north, **Music**

Restaurant. Good Chinese food and – presumably – live music.

Au Bol Pékinois An excellent Chinese restaurant five minutes by taxi from the station.

La Palmeraie Out of town on the road to Antsirabe (Andoharanofotsy). Tel 460 42. Delicious food eaten in an elegant garden (or indoors). A popular Sunday lunch place for Malagasy and well worth the taxi ride.

Budget restaurants

Souimanga Near the Hotel l'Etape and Tsimbazaza, so popular with zoo personnel. Good value, food, and ambience, but closed on Sundays.

Restaurant Pati Down the road from Tsimbazaza. Very good and economically priced meals. Large portions. Try the Chinese soup.

Restaurant Indonesia Directly across from the zoo entrance. Surprisingly, this is the only Indonesian restaurant in Madagascar. Recommended.

Kashmir 5-7 Rue Dr Ranaivo (opposite Anjary Hotel). Muslim, very good and reasonably priced food.

Shalimar 5 Rue Mahafaka, Tsaralalana (two blocks from the station). Tel: 260 70. Good curries, and a selection of vegetarian dishes.

Hotel Bar Rivo Beyond the Hotel Lambert; turn right at the top of the stairs, and it's on your right. 'This is my favorite Tana cubby-hole for cheap beer and food.' (John Kupiec)

For a cheap meal, local style, try the smaller restaurants (*hotely gasy*) down Ave Andrianampoinimerina. Meals usually include Chinese soup which is filling and tasty. There are also plenty of good, cheap eateries on Ave Rabezavana. **Kimlung** (Chinese/ seafood), **La Tulipe** and **La Fuchsia** are recommended.

Snack bars

Le Buffet du Jardin Place de l'Indépendance (at the top of the steps). This fast food restaurant is *the* place for lunch, a beer or coffee, with pleasant outdoor tables. Ideal for people-watching, meeting other travellers or foreigners living in Madagascar. One tip: if you dislike being pestered by beggars and pedlars, choose a seat well away from the fence.

Croissant d'Or Lalana Indira Gandhi. Serves great breakfasts and is open at 07.30 all week and 08.00 on Sundays.

Ave de l'Indépendance has a growing number of eateries: **Tropique** (good pastries and ice-cream), **Honey** (very good for breakfast and ice-cream), **Solimar** for tamarind juice, and **le Croissanterie** near the *zoma* for fresh fruit juice. Also **Bouffe Rapide** and **La Potinerie** (near Air Mad). The **Glacier Hotel** bar is the best for people-watching and for *zoma* zombies.

In the Upper Town both the **Patisserie Suisse** (Lalana Rabehevitra) and the **Patisserie Colbert** do good pastries and teas. Patisserie Suisse serves a delicious range of cakes and tarts, but closes at midday for up to 3½ hours, so check it out early.

Do-it-yourself meals can be purchased anywhere. Yoghurt is a particularly good buy and is available even in small towns. Carry your own spoon. Even more convenient – and delicious – is the drinking yoghurt, 'Yaourt à boire'.

Sightseeing

As if to emphasise how different it is to other capitals, Tana has relatively little in the way of conventional sightseeing, and even less since the Queen's Palace (*Rova*) burned down (see box). At least it now has a tourist office, **La Maison du Tourisme de Madagascar** in Place de l'Indépendance. Tel: 325 29. They produce printed lists of hotels, tour operators, car-hire companies, etc. Open 09.30–11.30, 15.30–17.30; closed on Sunday.

Tsimbazaza

This comprises a museum (natural history and ethnology), botanical garden and zoo exhibiting – with a few exceptions – only Malagasy species.

Tsimbazaza (pronounced Tsimba<u>zaz</u>) is the centre for the Madagascar Fauna Group, an international consortium of zoos and universities working together to help conserve Madagascar's wildlife. The challenges of bringing such an internationally important zoo up to Western standards are immense: cultural differences, political instability and lack of money mean that even small changes take an inordinately long time, and visitors are often less than impressed.

A NATIONAL DISASTER

For over a century the Queen's Palace has dominated the Tana skyline. During the evening of November 7, 1995, every building in the complex was burned to the ground. Only the stone outer walls, built by the Scot, James Cameron, remain.

Although originally thought to have been caused by a random brush fire, the tragedy has since been attributed to arson. The reason for such an act of wanton destruction is still a mystery, although one suggestion is that it was to distract attention from a fire that broke out the same day at the Ministry of Finance which destroyed a number of documents. Tribal animosity is also a possibility since it was a site of particular importance to the Merina.

Eyewitnesses said that the grass started burning below the palace, then the fire crept up the hill and into the compound, spreading to the tombs, the residence and finally the palace itself. Other accounts say that fires started in all the main buildings simultaneously. One American eye-witness recalled what seemed like the whole of the capital's population standing in silence in the streets to watch the blaze. Tana has only two elderly emergency tenders, donated by the Russians, one of which was fighting another fire (deliberately set) on the opposite side of the city. Local people strove to save what they could of the priceless exhibits and succeeded in rescuing about 30% of them, including most of the paintings and photographs. One young man lost his life when a blazing roof collapsed on him. The fire started at about 6.45pm, and by 9pm little was left but smoking ruins.

The *Rova* was much more than a unique historic monument. It contained the sacred remains of all the kings and queens of Madagascar, the spiritual value of which is truly beyond our comprehension. The palace complex also housed a large collection of antiquities and royal memorabilia, including gold and silverware presented to King Radama by Queen Victoria. The French and British governments, and UNESCO, have offered financial and technical help, but an estimated US$20,000,000 will have to be raised to effect a complete restoration of the buildings. But for the Malagasy people there can be no compensation for the cultural and spiritual loss involved.

However, having first seen Tsimbazaza in 1976 and returned on each of my subsequent visits, I am full of admiration for what has already been achieved and excited about future plans.

Since the MFG was established the collection has grown to represent most of Madagascar's lemur species (except for the family Indridae which do not do well in captivity) and the animals are better housed. An admission fee has been introduced which draws much-needed income from tourists, the cages now bear illustrated signs with the names and distribution of the species shown, and signs abound in three languages stressing the conservation aspect. Such things are taken for granted in the West but required years of effort by the able and dedicated zoo director, Albert Randrianjafy, and Project Co-ordinator Dean Gibson from the USA, who left in 1996. The present Co-ordinator, Gabe Sigerson, is using his long experience of running zoos in Kenya and other developing countries, as well as his work in the USA, to set achievable goals.

A neat example of the difference between the American and the Malagasy view of animal management and life in general is the argument over a project to have a free-ranging group of lemurs in the park. There was no problem agreeing on the desirability and visitor appeal of this (there would be a supplementary feeding station but the animals are expected to forage for themselves); the conflict was about the components of the group. Gabe insists on single-sex lemurs ('One thing we do *not* want are babies when we have a surplus of lemurs') whilst the Malagasy are holding out for a proper family unit: mother, father and children, because that's what happiness is all about.

Among the animals on display in the zoo are four aye-ayes. Arrangements may be made to visit the aye-ayes after dark when they are active, for a fee of 25,000Fmg per person.

The vivarium has a collection of reptiles and small mammals, but needs a new building. A proper environment for these delicate animals is a high, but expensive, priority.

The botanical garden is spacious and well laid out, and its selection of Malagasy endemics is being improved with the help of advisers from Kew and the Missouri Botanical Garden. It provides a sanctuary for numerous birds including a huge colony of egrets. There are also some reproduction Sakalava graves.

It is the museum, however, that attracts the most interest, for its selection of skeletons of now extinct animals, including several species of giant lemur and the famous 'elephant bird' or *aepyornis* which may only have become extinct after the arrival of the first Europeans. It is displayed next to the skeleton of an ostrich, so its massive size can be appreciated. Another room displays stuffed animals, but the efforts of the taxidermist have left little to likeness and a lot to the imagination. It's worth taking a close look at the aye-aye, however, to study its remarkable hands. The museum has recently redesigned its ethnological section which is now very good.

Tsimbazaza is open every day from 09.00 to 17.00. For tourists the entrance fee is 20,000Fmg (5,000Fmg for children aged 6 to 12). This fee goes towards the upkeep of the park, so watch out that a used ticket is not reissued. Make sure your ticket comes out of a box not a drawer, check that the date is correct, and insist on keeping it when you leave the park.

Sundays are always very busy, so don't anticipate peace and quiet then. There is a souvenir shop with an excellent selection of good-quality T-shirts and postcards, but no restaurant or snack bar.

Tsimbazaza is about 4km from the city centre. There are buses from Avenue de l'Indépendance (number 15), but it is easier to take a taxi there and bus back.

Museum of Art and Archaeology
Recommended by J Buirski and L Meyer as being: 'Small, but interesting and well-kept. Entrance free! Look for a brass tree in the forecourt.' The museum is on a side street in Isoraka, near the Japanese Embassy and Galerie Yerden.

Cemetery
On the recommendation of reader Leone Badenhorst I am including this despite anxious visions of camera-toting tourists trampling on people's sensibilities as well as their tombs. Do show respect. 'Apart from the large variety of interesting tombs (Malagasy, French and Chinese – even a couple of English), some with extraordinary decorations and trimmings, this provides a peaceful break with superb views of the city.' Ask the taxi-driver for Cimetière Anjanahary.

Zoma (market)
Zoma means Friday and this is the day when the whole of Avenue de l'Indépendance erupts into a rash of white umbrellas. The market runs the length of the street and up the hillsides, filling every available space with an amazing variety of goods. There are stands selling nothing but bottles, or spare parts, or years-old French magazines; there are men who repair watches, or umbrellas or bicycles; there are flowers and fruit and animals (including cats) and herbal medicines and charms; and there are plenty of handicrafts although the artisans now have their own market (see below). This description by the missionary James Sibree, over 100 years ago, shows how little the market has changed:

> 'All the chief roads are thronged with people bringing in their goods for sale... and the hum of voices can be heard from a considerable distance. Here everything that is grown or manufactured in the interior province can be procured, and in no place can a better idea of the productions of the country or of the handicrafts skill of the Malagasy be obtained than in this great *zoma* market... it is certainly one of the most interesting sights in Tanarive.'

The *zoma* is, sadly, now too risky for serious shopping. Photographers should go with conspicuously empty pockets and with a companion to watch out for thieves. Providing you have nothing to steal – and nothing in your pockets or they will be slashed – the *zoma* is fascinating, and the warmth and concern of the stall-holders, who see their income disappearing with the tourists, a joy to experience.

TWO PERSPECTIVES ON TSIMBAZAZA

Like everything else in Madagascar, Tsimbazaza is at the mercy of political instability, fluctuating finances and a host of hidden variables. And like everything else, some visitors love it, some hate it.

These extracts from two unrelated letters, one from a South African visitor to Tsimbazaza (in 1995) and the other from Dean Gibson, formerly Project Co-ordinator of the Madagascar Fauna Group, highlight the contrast between appearance and fact. I have also incorporated some comments by the present co-ordinator, Gabe Sigerson.

Jeez! This place is the pits!! 20,000Fmg entrance fee and the only really nice thing was the lemurs on the little islands on the lake... (SAV)

The decision to increase entrance fees came after several discussions concerning the finances of the park. Due to devaluation of the Fmg, escalating expenses and decreases in the government's contribution, the zoo was simply not making ends meet... (DG)

The cages were filthy... (SAV)

This may be hard to believe, but the zoo can only afford the soap and labour to clean the cages once a week. Of course I know this is completely unacceptable... (GS)

I hope you warn tourists that this whole complex is only suitable for city-bred Malagasy schoolchildren and not for world-wise and educated people, eg tourists. (SAV)

My next project is to start a newsletter to encourage local interest. I feel that Malagasy children are as excited by animals as kids in the West. I want to nurture that enthusiasm... (GS)

If you want to support the work done by the MFG in improving the conditions at Tsimbazaza, do contact Gabe Sigerson on BP 8511, Antananarivo 101. He may also be reached by phone on 310 14 or 311 49. What is needed is money: US$100 would buy a year's supply of lemur biscuits, US$200 would provide the badly needed steel doors and replacement mesh for five cages. Larger projects held back for lack of money are quarantine facilities for the confiscated 'pets' which are often in appalling condition, a new vivarium, and housing and uniforms for the keepers to give them more pride in the job. As Gabe says, 'A zoo cannot function without properly paid, dedicated keepers'.

Although the *zoma* proper is on Fridays, there is always a market in Tana, always some white umbrellas shading fruit and vegetables opposite the stairs leading to the Upper Town, and some handicraft stalls down each side of the avenue towards the station.

Bargain if you want, or just enjoy the sights and sounds. A reader adds this observation: how do you know when you've paid too much at a fruit stall? When you get a free plastic bag, and when the other hawkers, not believing their companion's luck, follow you for several blocks trying to make a sale.

Shopping
The handicrafts market

The Marché Artisanal, which is best reached by taxi (unless you are staying at the Hotel Gregoire, from which it is a ten-minute walk), shows the enormous range and quality of Malagasy handicrafts. Most noteworthy is the embroidery and basketry, wood-carving, minerals, leatherwork (stiff cowhide, not soft leather) and the unique Antaimoro paper embedded with pressed flowers. The market is held in the Andravoahangy region of town. This is to the right of the station (as you face it) northeast on Lalana Me Albertini. Open 10.00–17.00, except Sunday.

This area is bad for crime, but Bill and Kathleen Love sent this recommendation: 'The Andravoahangy market has reformed prisoners working as guard/companions to tourists. This isn't quite as daunting as it sounds. They wear identity badges and are inconspicuous in the crowds. They don't charge for their services, but as they're likely to give you some protection from hustlers, pickpockets, beggars and over-enthusiastic vendors, they deserve a substantial tip.'

Avenue de l'Indépendance

Handicrafts are creeping back to Tana's main avenue, and reader Alistair Marshall claims that the selection is now just as good as at the Marché Artisanal and the area is safer. 'The quality of produce is exceptional, I have a house full of them...'

Serious shopping

The best quality goods are sold in specialist shops. One of the best is Galerie Le Bivouac, Antsofinondry – on the road to Ambohimanga – which sells beautiful painted silk items as well as other handicrafts of a high quality. Tel: 429 50. Nearby is the Atelier Jacaranda which specialises in batik. The quality here is excellent and the prices low. The Jacaranda workshop is next to Le Bivouac, but sales are made from the gallery 100m further down the road.

Nearer the centre of town, though still a taxi ride away, is Lisy Art Gallery on the Route de Mausolée opposite the Cercle Mess de la Police, and near the Hotel Panorama; tel: 277 33. It is also worth checking out La Galerie, in Ankadifotsy; tel: 354 50. One of the cheapest shops in Tana is Galerie Yerden on Rue du Dr. Thédore Villette, opposite the Japanese Embassy. Although the prices are slightly higher than the *zoma*, the peace and quiet, and wide range of arts and crafts, make a visit well worth while.

Alan Hickling (tel: 400 79) sells hand-painted T-shirts of Malagasy wild life and other good quality handicrafts.

For exquisite (and consequently expensive) weavings based on traditional *lamba* designs contact British resident Simon Peers. Tel: 29502; fax: 31956.

The best place in Tana to buy Antaimoro paper is at a small 'factory' on the way to the airport (it's a green building on the right) where an enterprising Malagasy, M Mahatsinjo, has a work-force which uses the traditional method of pressing the flowers into the paper pulp. This craft originated in Ambalavao (see page 183 for a detailed description of the paper and how it is made), but you can see all the stages just as easily here. The prices for the finished products are very reasonable, too.

For something a bit different, try the herbal beauty products made from Malagasy plants sold under the brand name Phytoline; they seem only to be available from the Hilton shop or in the airport departure lounge.

Finally, you can shop at the Centre Fihavanana (see page 126) in Mahamasina, near the stadium, which is run by the Sisters of the Good Shepherd. The centre is in a building set back from the road to the right of an orange-painted church. Ask the taxi driver to take you to the Église St Joseph. The women here work to an extremely high standard, producing beautiful embroidery, greetings cards, and sometimes soft toys of Malagasy wildlife. The centre is always in need of funds to continue their admirable work with the very poor, and a visit will warm the most resilient of hearts. For an appointment phone Sister Lucy on 299 81.

Supermarkets and the 'Chocolatery'

If you don't want handicrafts try some other locally-produced goodies such as chocolate and wine. Both are available from the Champion supermarket, formerly the Prisunic, on Lalana Printsy Ratsimamanga in the Upper Town. A cheaper supermarket is Magri, which is on the way to the airport.

Allow yourself to get hooked on the local chocolate, *Chocolat Robert*, then pay a visit to *La Chocolatière* where you can buy the stuff at wholesale prices. Address: 472 Bd Ratsimandrava (opposite Solima on the road to Antsirabe). Hours: 08.00–12.30, 14.00–17.30.

Maps

A large selection of maps can be bought at the Institut National de Géodésie et Cartographie (its long Malagasy name is shortened to FTM), Lalana Dama-Ntsoha RJB, Ambanidia (tel: 229 35). Hours 08.30–12.00, 14.00–18.00. They do a series of 12 maps, scale 1:500,000, covering each region of Madagascar. These are most inviting, but sadly no longer completely accurate, and some are now out of print. There are also excellent maps of Nosy Be and Île Sainte Marie. The staff are pleasant and helpful. The more popular maps can be bought in bookshops in the town centre.

The Hilton Hotel has a good map of Tana which depicts the many flights of stairs.

Bookshops

The best bookshop is Librairie de Madagascar, near the Hotel de France on Ave de l'Indépendance. Another, Tout pour l'École, on the left side of Rue de Nice, has a good selection of maps and town plans. Also recommended is Librairie Md Paoly, a small Catholic bookshop on the other side of Ave de l'Indépendance, opposite Sicam and the Banky Fampadrosoana. 'They've got

HIRA GASY

For a taste of genuine Malagasy folklore, try to attend the traditional entertainment of *hira gasy* which takes place every Sunday in Tana. It used to be held in an arena at Isotry, but now unfortunately happens in different locations. Taxi-drivers may know where: ask for 'hira gasy' (pronounced 'heera gash') and see what happens.

In the British magazine *Folk Roots* Jo Shinner describes *hira gasy*:

'It is a very strange, very exciting affair: a mixture of opera, dance and Speaker's Corner bound together with a sense of competition.

'The performance takes place between two competing troupes of singers and musicians on a central square stage. It's an all day event so the audience packs in early, tea and peanut vendors picking their way through the throng. Audience participation is an integral part – the best troupe is gauged by the crowd's response. Throughout the day performers come into the crowd to receive small coins offered in appreciation.

'The most immediate surprise is the costumes. The men enter wearing 19th-century French, red, military frock coats and the women are clad in evening dress from the same period. Traditional *lamba* are carefully arranged around their shoulders, and the men wear straw Malagasy hats.

'The musicians play French military drums, fanfare trumpets, flutes, violins and clarinets. The effect is bizarre rather than beautiful.'

'The *hira gasy* is in four parts. First there are the introductory speeches or *kabary*. Each troupe elects a speaker who is usually a respected elder. His skill is paramount to a troupe. He begins with a long, ferociously fast, convoluted speech excusing himself and his inadequacy, before the audience, ancestors, his troupe, his mother, God, his oxen, his rice fields and so on – and on! Then follows another speech glorifying God, and then a greeting largely made up of proverbs.

'The *hira gasy* pivots around a tale of everyday life, such as the dire consequences of laziness or excessive drinking, is packed with wit, morals and proverbs and offers advice, criticism and possible solutions.

'The performers align themselves along two sides of the square at a time to address different parts of the audience. They sing in harsh harmony, illustrating their words with fluttering hand movements and expressive gestures, egged on by the uproarious crowd's appreciation.

'Then it is the dancers' turn. The tempo increases and becomes more rhythmic as two young boys take to the floor with a synchronised display of acrobatic dancing that nowadays often takes its influence from karate.'

the most amazingly beautiful hand-painted greetings cards. The same cards are sold at the airport for almost double the price.' (J Buirski and L Meyer)

Entertainment

Traditional Malagasy music has become internationally famous in the last few years (see box on page 116). Look out for authentic performances in restaurants and bars. But for a truly Malagasy experience try to find a performance of *hira gasy* (see box) or keep an eye out for a poster announcing any entertainment which will allow you to join a Malagasy audience (see box on page 276).

Nightlife

A good nightclub is **Le Caveau** (4, Rue Jeneraly Rabehevitra, Antaninarenina; tel: 343 93) which has the **Kaleidoscope** disco on the same premises. Another disco is L'Amnesia (8 Rue Andriandafotsy, Ambondrono; tel: 273 41). The **Indra** nightclub is also recommended (taxi drivers know where it is). Located in Faravohitra (Lalana Andrianahifotsy) on the slope above the market, is **Cocktails et Rêves**, which has a darts board for homesick Brits.

The most popular nightspot is **Piano Bar Acapulco**, near Place de l'Indépendance (14, Rue Ratsimilaho; tel: 232 25), which features local bands, jazz and solo piano.

Miscellaneous
Fixers

A retired couple who felt they needed some help negotiating Madagascar independently wrote recommending Pierre (S Pierrot Patrick), Lot VT 62E, Ambohibato, Ambohipo, Antananarivo 101. Tel: 295 52. 'Each time we came upon a seemingly insuperable problem he came up with an idea which got us over that obstacle and on to the next – we could not have managed without him.' The Shannons communicated in French but Pierre seems to speak some English.

Monica D'Onofrio recommends a friendly and punctual taxi driver: Charles Razafintsialonina, tel: 238 61.

Newspapers and magazines

The main daily newspapers are the *Madagascar Tribune* (in French) which tends to follow the government line and is relatively up-market, and *Midi Madagasikara* (in French and Malagasy), the paper with the highest circulation and little international news. Both these newspapers are given out free on domestic flights. *Dans les Média Demain* is an independent weekly magazine, and *Revue de l'Océan Indien – Madagascar* appears monthly.

An informative and entertaining bilingual publication (French and English) is *Madactualités* which is published monthly and available in the better hotels.

Information and permits for nature reserves

ANGAP is the organisation responsible for the administration of almost all the protected areas of Madagascar. Permits for the national parks and reserves may be purchased here, although they are now usually available at the town serving the reserve. It is worth visiting the Tana office, however, for the latest information on the reserves that tourists are allowed to visit. It is in Antanimena, five minutes' walk from the Grand Orient restaurant. Tell the taxi-driver 'en face de Promodim'. Hours 08.00–12.00, 14.00–16.00. Tel: 319 94.

The Forestry Station of Ampijoroa is still administered by the Direction des Eaux et Forêts in Nanisana; although the permit is available in Mahajanga, it can be a complicated process so you may prefer to buy it in Tana. Bus number 3 from Ave de l'Indépendance stops outside the door. The hours are the same as ANGAP's.

The address for the World Wide Fund for Nature in Tana is BP 4373; tel: 2 25541.

Visa extension

A two-month extension can be obtained overnight from the Ministry of the Interior near the Hilton Hotel (see map).

Airline offices

Air Madagascar Ave de l'Indépendance. Hours: 07.30– 11.00; 14.30–17.00. Be there when it opens to avoid the crush.

Aeroflot Rue Mahafaka, between the restaurants Shalimar and Relais Normand.

Bank and emergency funds

The BTM bank next to the Champion supermarket will let you draw up to US$200 a day on American Express or MasterCard. Banking hours: 08.00– 15.00. Closed on Saturdays. The American Express office is in the Hilton Hotel.

Post office

The main post office is opposite the Hotel Colbert. There is a separate philately section where you can buy attractive stamps. The post office is open 24 hours a day for outgoing phone calls – useful in an emergency, and much cheaper than phoning from a hotel.

MALAGASY STAMPS

Like most things Malagasy, the choice of stamp design ranges from the sublime to the ridiculous. In the first category are the beautiful series on the fauna and flora: lemurs, birds, butterflies, orchids. However, their 1991 selection of competitive winter sports such as ski jumping (not a sport in which Madagascar has achieved international standing) was more surprising and we are now on to pedigree dogs. Again surprising since most dogs one sees in Madagascar seem to be made out of discarded string. Never mind, the stamps are mostly very attractive and can be purchased from the philately department of the main post office, and from street vendors outside the Colbert Hotel.

Women's hairdresser

The expatriates' favourite is Richard Coiffure, 15 Rue Patrice Lumumba. Tel: 226 50.

Medical clinic (private)

MM 24 X 24, Mpitsabo Mikambana, Route de l'Université, tel: 235 55. Inexpensive and very good. Of the government hospitals, the military hospital is better equipped than the civilian one.

Church services

Anglican (contact tel: 262 68): Cathedral St Laurent, Ambohimanoro; 9.00 service each Sunday. Roman Catholic (tel: 278 30): three churches have services in Malagasy, and three in French. Phone for details.

Golf course

There is a good golf course, the Club de Golf de Rova at Ambohidratrimo, 20km from town on the road to Mahajanga. It is open to visitors except at the weekend. Good meals are served at the club house and the Wednesday buffet is particularly recommended.

Embassies

British Embassy Immeuble Ny Havana, Cité des 67Ha, Antananarivo (BP 167). Tel: 277 49/273 70.

American Embassy Antsahavola (BP 620). Tel: 200 89/212 57. For visa/passport business it is open Mondays, Wednesdays and Fridays.

South African Embassy Lot IIJ 169 Ivandry (BP 4417). Tel: 424 94.

Italian Embassy Rue Pasteur Rabary, Ankadivato (BP 16). Tel: 212 17.

French Embassy Rue Jean Jaurès (BP 204). Tel: 237 00/200 08.

German Embassy Route Circulaire (BP 516). Tel: 238 02.

Transport out of Tana

Trains run east to Toamasina (Tamatave) and south to Antsirabe from the station at the end of Avenue de l'Indépendance. Most people, however, will be travelling by bus or taxi-brousse. The *gares routières* for these vehicles are on the outskirts of the city at the appropriate road junctions: Gare de l'Ouest, Anosibe (Lalana Pastora Rahajason on the far side of Lac Anosy) serving the south and west; Gare du Nord, at Lalana Doktor Raphael Raboto in the northeast of the city, serving the north and the east. Taxi drivers know where these places are.

Vehicle hire

Full details on hiring a car are given in *Chapter Six*. If you are dealing with a Tana travel agent they will also be able to arrange car hire. Recommended

THE MARTYR MEMORIAL CHURCHES

Dr G W Milledge

My grandfather, James Sibree, a civil engineer from Hull, was appointed by the London Missionary Society in 1863 to build four memorial churches to commemorate the Malagasy Christians put to death by order of Queen Ranavalona I during the period 1837 to her death in 1861. The sites, mainly within easy walking distance of the palace, were associated with the execution or imprisonment of the martyrs. Mr William Ellis of the London Mission had noted that the sites were suitable for church building, thought of the memorial churches and petitioned King Radama II for the sites to be reserved. This was granted. He also petitioned the mission board who agreed to raise funds in England.

Mention should be made of the difficulties and delays in starting to build large stone churches; quarry men, masons, carpenters all had to be trained. Stone was readily available but other materials were difficult to obtain. Workmen often departed for family functions, government work or military service, and work was held up for weeks. As the spire of Ambatonakangar rose to heights unknown in Malagasy buildings wives of his workmen pleaded with James Sibree not to ask their husbands to go up to such dangerous heights.

Ambatonakangar is situated at the meeting of five roads in an area given on the map as Ambohidahy. The first church in Madagascar was on this site: a low, dark, mud brick building in which Christians were imprisoned, often in chains before, in many cases, being led out to execution. The first printing press was also on this site and the first Malagasy bibles were printed here. The present church, opened in 1867, follows the Early English style, with 'Norman' arches. It was the first stone building in Madagascar.

Ambohipotsy is on a commanding site at the southern end of the ridge beyond the Queen's Palace. Its slender spire can be seen for miles around the surrounding plain. On this site the first martyr, a young woman called Rasalama, was speared to death in 1837. Later 11 other Christians suffered the same fate.

Faravohitra Church is on the northern side of the city ridge, built where four Christians of the nobility were burnt to death on March 28 1849. Though not as fine a site as Ambohipotsy, it also commands good views.

Ampamarinana Church is a short way below the Palace on the west side of the ridge on the summit of 'The Place of the Hurling' from where prisoners were thrown to their deaths. 14 Christians were killed here on the same day in 1849.

So the four churches stand on historic sites as a memorial to those brave martyrs for their faith, and witness to the interest and concern of Christians in Britain for their fellows in Madagascar.

Dr Milledge travelled to Madagascar at the age of 88 to visit the place where he was born. Throughout the trip he was honoured as a descendent of James Sibree, one of Madagascar's major benefactors and perhaps the greatest writer the island has inspired.

car-hire firms are Locaut (tel: 219 81), Rasseta (tel: 257 70), Aventour (tel: 317 61/217 78) and Eurorent (tel: 297 66). A full list is available from the Maison du Tourisme.

A reader recommends the following driver/guide as being 'cultured, well-travelled, immensely knowledgeable about Madagascar, and extremely considerate of our comfort'. Henri Serge Razafison, Logt 1384 Cité 67Ha, Antananarivo 101. Tel: 34190.

There is some good cycling around Tana (see box on page 159). Bicycles used to be available for hire in Tana, as in some other cities. Check with the Maison du Tourisme. If you are a keen cyclist, however, you should bring your own bike (see page 109).

'Some day, when I am old and worn and there is nothing new to see, I shall go back to the palm-fringed lagoons, the sun-drenched, rolling moors, the pink villages, and the purple peaks of Madagascar'.
E A Powell, Beyond the Utmost Purple Rim, *1925*

EXCURSIONS

EAST OF ANTANANARIVO
Ambohimanga

Lying 21km northeast of Antananarivo, Ambohimanga (pronounced Amboo̲imanga), meaning the 'blue hill', was for a long time forbidden to Europeans. From here began the line of kings and queens who were to unite Madagascar into one country, and it was here that they returned for rest and relaxation among the tree-covered slopes of this hill-top village. These days tourists find the same tranquillity and spirit of reverence and it is highly recommended as an easy day's trip, especially now its counterpart in Tana has been destroyed.

Ambohimanga has seven gates, though some are all but lost among the thick vegetation. One of the most spectacular gates, through which you enter the village, has an enormous stone disc which was formerly rolled in front of the gateway each night. Above the gateway is a thatched-roof sentry post and to the right is a bizarre Chinese pagoda (don't ask me what or why...). Climbing up the stairs towards the compound you pass some handicrafts stalls with a variety of unique and appealing souvenirs, and in the courtyard are two huge fig trees providing shade for a picnic.

Ambohimanga still retains its spiritual significance for the Malagasy people. On the slope to the left of the door to the compound (where you must pay your 10,000Fmg fee) is a sacrificial stone. Melted candle-wax and traces of blood show that it is still used for offerings, particularly in cases of infertility. Rituals involving the placing of seven small stones in the 'male' or 'female' hole will ensure the birth of a baby boy or girl.

Inside the compound the centre-piece is the wooden house of the great king Andrianampoinimerina (1787–1810). The simple one-roomed building is interesting for the insight it gives into everyday (royal) life of that era. There is a display of cooking utensils (and the stones that surrounded the cooking fire), and weapons, and the two beds – the top one for the king and the lower for one of his 12 wives. The roof is supported by a ten-metre rosewood pole. A visit here can be full of surprises: 'Remember this is not a museum, it is the King's palace: he is there. On all my visits there were always several people asking the King for favours. On one memorable occasion I entered his hut to find what seemed like a party in full flow. A man had been possessed by the spirit of a king from the south, and he had come to the palace to greet, and be greeted by, King Andrianampoinimerina. The man had gone into a trance and a group of mediums were assisting him. They had found an accordion player and the man was dancing to get the King's attention. We were spellbound by all this, but the Malagasy visitors totally ignored what was going on and continued to look round the hut as though nothing was happening!' (Alistair Marshall)

Andrianampoinimerina's son, Radama, with British help, went a long way to achieving his father's ambition to expand his kingdom to the sea. After

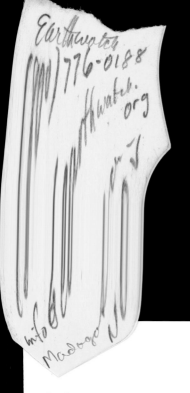

Radama came a number of queens and, although the capital had, by that time, been moved to Antananarivo, they built themselves elegant summer houses next to Andrianampoinimerina's simple royal home. These are currently closed for repairs, but when open you can see the strong influence of the British during those times, with several gifts sent to the monarchs by Queen Victoria. French influence is evident too: there are two cannons forged in Jean Laborde's Mantasoa iron foundry.

Also within the compound is a mundane-looking concrete pool (the concrete is a recent addition) which was used by the Queen for ritual bathing and had to be filled, so they say, by virgins, and a corral where zebu were sacrificed. An enclosing wall built in 1787, and faced with a rock-hard mixture of sand and egg, completes the tour.

Ambohimanga is reached on a good road by private taxi or bus/taxi-brousse from the Gare du Nord. The latter takes about 30 minutes and is inexpensive. To return to Tana, go to the square below the stone-disc entrance where the taxi-brousses wait for passengers.

The hours are 09.00–11.00, 14.00–17.00 (closed Mondays), and the entrance fee is 10,000Fmg.

Monica D'Onofrio, who was brought up in Madagascar, is now 18 and recently returned to see some of the places of her childhood. In her letter she described a visit to the house of an *ombiasy* in Ambohimanga. If you go to the restaurant next to the palace they can tell you where to find it. An old lady showed Monica the one-roomed house, which is between two others where the *ombiasy*'s two wives lived. Inside she found a shrine to Jesus Christ, and the man's tomb against the wall. He must have been a man of some talent, because as well as curing illnesses he prevented hailstorms. Monica says that if you go to the house wearing black shoes, they have to be taken off and left on the stairs.

MOUNTAIN BIKING IN THE HIGHLANDS

The following two itineraries are recommended by Derek Schuurman (Tana and Ankaratra area) and Bishop Brock (Tana to Tsiroanomandidy)

'After arriving in Tana, bike to Ambohimanga or Lac Mantasoa, where you can camp. From Mantasoa you ride on to Tsinjoarivo, the favourite summer retreat of Queen Ranavalona. There you'll find the remains of the old palace, a spectacular waterfall and some dense forest. After leaving Tsinjoarivo, you can bike on to Ambatolampy, which is near the Ankaratra mountains, and return to Tana or continue on to Antsirabe and Ranomafana.'

'I can heartily recommend the ride from Tana to Tsiroanomandidy: the surface is generally good, in some places excellent; during the dry season you are almost assured of tailwinds; there are nice side trips around Ampefy; formal accommodation is available in Miarinarivo, Ampefy, Babetville, and Tsiroanomandidy.'

Where to eat

Ambohimanga is an ideal place for a picnic, and there is a nice restaurant (tables in the garden) off the palace courtyard. Meals cost 18,000Fmg, and there is live music at weekends.

If you take a taxi-brousse back to Tana, Jeremy Buirski and Lindie Meyer recommend the following: 'Show "Sabotsy Namehana, tsena" to a taxi-driver and he will drop you off in front of the Hotel au Bon Coin, 10km outside the city. Next door is the Resto Romazava, a clean restaurant with ridiculously low prices. Just try their papaya juice. To continue your journey to Tana, wait on the veranda for the taxis that pass every few minutes, or walk to the taxi-brousse station about 100m towards Tana. You can also walk about 80m down a side street beside the restaurant to Batik Malagasy. This is a very small-scale manufacturer, the cheapest anywhere.'

Ambohimalaza

On the way to Mantasoa (see below) is a remarkable royal cemetery. Sir Mervyn Brown writes: 'Here there are scores of royal tombs going back several centuries and distinguished by small wooden houses built on top of the tombs which were the privilege of members of the royal family. Ask your driver/ guide to take you to La Nécropole Royale.'

Lake Mantasoa

Some 70km east of Antananarivo is Mantasoa (pronounced Manta_soo_) where in the 19th century Madagascar had its first taste of industrialisation. Indeed, historians now claim that industrial output was greater then than it ever was during the colonial period. It was thanks to Jean Laborde that a whole range of industries was started including an iron foundry which enabled Madagascar to become more or less self-sufficient in swords, guns and gunpowder, thereby increasing the power of the central government. Jean Laborde was soon highly influential at court and he built a country residence for the Queen at Mantasoa. Sadly most of the remains of the buildings have disappeared, drowned to make a reservoir. Not all, however, as Johan and Clare Hermans report: 'The chimney remains of the china factory beside the school playing field (the headmaster of the Lycée Moderne lives in Laborde's old house), the cannon factory still stands and part of it is lived in, and the large furnace of the foundry remains. All are signposted and fascinating to see and you realise the effort required to get them built. You also realise that if they were in Europe they would have been turned into a living museum and not left as crumbling relics in the school grounds.'

Jean Laborde is buried in the cemetery outside the village, along with 12 French soldiers; an imposing mausoleum surrounded by mature trees.

Mantasoa can be reached by taking a train to Manjakandriana and then a taxi or a taxi-brousse for the last 15km, or a taxi-brousse all the way from Tana.

THE TWO-MAN INDUSTRIAL REVOLUTION

Technology was largely introduced to Madagascar by two remarkable Europeans: James Cameron, a Scot, and Jean Laborde, a Frenchman.

James Cameron arrived in Madagascar in 1826 during the country's 'British' phase when the London Missionary Society (LMS) had attempted to set up local craftsmen to produce goods in wood, metal, leather and cotton. Cameron was only 26 when he came to Madagascar, but was already skilled as a carpenter and weaver, with wide knowledge of other subjects which he was later to put to use in his adopted land: physics, chemistry, mathematics, architecture and astronomy. Cameron seemed able to turn his hand to almost anything mechanical. Among his achievements were the successful installation and running of Madagascar's first printing press (by studying the manual – the printer sent out with the press had died with unseemly haste), a reservoir (now Lac Anosy) and aqueduct, and the production of bricks.

Cameron's success in making soap from local materials ensured his royal favour after King Radama died and the xenophobic Queen Ranavalona came to power. But when Christian practice and teaching were forbidden in 1835 Cameron left with the other missionaries and went to work in South Africa.

He returned in 1863 when the missionaries were once more welcome in Madagascar, to oversee the building of stone churches, a hospital, and the stone exterior to the *Rova* or Queen's palace in Antananarivo.

Jean Laborde was even more of a 'renaissance man'. The son of a blacksmith, Laborde was shipwrecked off the east coast of Madagascar in 1831. Queen Ranavalona, no doubt pleased to find a less godly European, asked him to manufacture muskets and gun-powder, and he soon filled the gap left by the departure of Cameron and the other artisan-missionaries. Laborde's initiative and inventiveness were amazing: in a huge industrial complex built by forced labour, he produced munitions and arms, bricks and tiles, pottery, glass and porcelain, silk, soap, candles, cement, dyes, sugar, rum ... in fact just about everything a thriving country in the nineteenth century needed. He ran a farm which experimented with suitable crops and animals, and a country estate for the Merina royalty and aristocracy to enjoy such novelties as firework displays. And he built the original Queen's palace in wood (in 1839), which was later enclosed in stone by Cameron.

So successful was Laborde in making Madagascar self-sufficient, that foreign trade was discontinued and foreigners – with the exception of Laborde – expelled. He remained in the Queen's favour until 1857 when he was expelled because of involvement in a plot to replace the Queen by her son. The 1,200 workmen who had laboured without pay in the foundries of Mantasoa rose up and destroyed everything – tools, machinery and buildings. The factories were never rebuilt, and Madagascar's Industrial Revolution came to an abrupt end.

He returned in 1861 and became French consul, dying in 1878. A dispute over his inheritance was one of the pretexts used by the French to justify the 1883-85 war.

Where to stay/eat

In the last edition I wrote: 'One of the fanciest hotels in Madagascar is located here, **Domaine de l'Ermitage** (BP 16, Manjakandriana; tel: 05).' The address/phone number is the same but conditions seem to have changed somewhat: 'Hotel completely empty except for us, bare wire light fittings and all wall paper showing damp stains. Staff friendly. Restaurant food good, set menu 37,000Fmg (about £6) but a little put off by the sight of a pair of large rats sauntering in through the missing restaurant window and through the room. This happened on both nights we were there, so perhaps they were trying to keep out of the rain and cold. The four resident dogs ignored the visitors, staying asleep on the porch. Signs in the rooms say "strictly no animals allowed in the hotel"! Mosquito coils are a must for the mosquitoes here and work on the cockroaches too.' (Clare and Johan Hermans)

Motel le Chalet BP 12, Mantasoa. Tel: 20. I have no recent reports on this but it used to be very efficiently run and consists of five bungalows and a restaurant serving superb food. Camping is usually permitted in the grounds.

Angavokely Station Forestière

The Hermans recommend this day trip from Tana. 'At Carion, 30km from Tana on the RN2, you follow the track to Angavokely which takes about 30 minutes down a rutted track that has once been cobbled. It ends at an extraordinary turreted barrier which will be opened after you have applied at the offices a ten-minute walk away. They are located in a large set of buildings amongst a defunct sawmill. A permit costs 20,000Fmg. Faded direction signs and a map indicate the way to the Arboretum with picnic tables and parasols, and you can camp. Mt Angavokely is a fair climb up past the eucalyptus plantation and takes about 30 minutes. Thoughtfully, steps with railings are built in the rock face so that you can enjoy the views from the top. A wide track leads back down through the Arboretum to the offices.'

Mandraka

This is usually visited en route to Périnet, but can also be done as a day trip from Tana. If you take RN2 towards Toamasina (Tamatave) the 'Nature Farm' is situated opposite the hydro-electric power plant, just west of Anjiro. It is owned by one of Madagascar's most respected naturalists, André Peyrieras.

The centre provides the opportunity to see and photograph some of Madagascar's most extraordinary reptiles and invertebrates, but at a price: the animals are kept in crowded conditions and handled roughly. Sometimes diseased or dead animals are seen in the cages. The main purpose of the centre is the breeding (for export) of comet moths and various butterflies, but the demand for reptiles for the pet trade is also satisfied, although, sadly, no breeding seems to be taking place.

The export of frogs and reptiles for the pet trade is a controversial subject which I have left to experts on both sides of the argument (see box on page 60-61).

Visitors pay about £2/US$3 to tour the collection, and may also be asked to pay extra for a guide. Make sure you bring fast film and a close-up lens to make the most of this unique opportunity to get pictures of species seldom seen in the wild.

Pizza Nino is a good, clean pizza restaurant on the left as you drive on RN2 towards Mandraka, near the village of Manjaka: a popular stop for resident *vazahas*.

WEST OF ANTANANARIVO
Antsahaointa

John Kupiec recommends a visit to this hilltop village which is a bus ride southwest of Tana. 'There are many royal tombs, a museum (small fee), wonderful views and a small house for visitors to sleep in. The guide speaks English.'

Lake Itasy

Off the road to Tsiroanomandidy (access town Analavory) this lake and its surrounding area are particularly beautiful and easily reached by taxi-brousse. The nearby village of **Ampefy** has accommodation: the Kavitaha, with very good food, and the humble Bungalows Administratifs. A better bet is the Village Touristique between the lakes: spacious but basic bungalows.

It is an 8km walk to Îlot de la Vièrge on Lac Itasy. West of the road are the Chutes de la Lily (waterfalls). 'It pays here to climb a hill – any hill – to get an overview of the lakes and volcanic countryside.' (H Snippe)

About 45 minutes' drive northwest of Ampefy are some hot springs with spectacular mineral deposits.

Tsiroanomandidy

Lying about 200km to the west of Tana, on a surfaced road (four hours), this town is worth visiting for its huge cattle market, held on Wednesdays and Thursdays. The tribe to the south, the Bara, drive huge herds of cattle through the Bongolava plateau to sell at the market.

There are two hotels. Bishop Brock recommends Chez Marcelline: 'Marcelline is a good hostess and a pretty good cook. A simple room costs 15,000–20,000Fmg (around £3/US$5). The hotel is north of the market, near the airport. Tsiroanomandidy is also a nice place to hang out: when viewed from a distance, with its twin-towered church against a backdrop of mountains, it reminded me of a town in Mexico!'

Tsiroanomandidy is linked to Maintirano and Majunga by Twin Otter, and also to Morondava. You can also travel west on river trips as far as the Manambolo gorges (see *Chapter Fourteen*).

NORTHWEST OF ANTANANARIVO
The forest of Ambohetantely

The name means 'Where honey is found' and is pronounced 'Ambweeton<u>tel</u>'. This is the last remnant of natural forest in the province of Ankazobe and there are hopes that it will shortly become a protected area. This report is by Dr Graham Noble and Sandra Baron of South Africa.

'It takes about 2½ hours to get to the forest which lies 150km northwest of Tana off the road to Mahajanga. The access village is Ararazana. The forest is 10km from the road and you do not see a tree until you reach the site. Estimates of its size vary from 1,400 to 3,000 hectares. It is surrounded by a barrier of burnt trees, but as you go two metres into the forest the leaf-litter is already 10–15cm deep. There is a network of paths through the forest. The University of Antananarivo has a right to a part of it as a study site and refers to that section as the Botanical Garden. The forestry director is very keen to receive tourists into the area for day walks and will also organise provisions for overnight stays. Good birding and lots of orchids.'

Derek Schuurman adds: 'This is actually a very beautiful little rainforest, with rufous mouse lemurs and common brown lemurs as well as common tenrecs. Birds found there include the Madagascar blue pigeon, long-billed greenbul, forest rock thrush, blue vanga and, en route, the Réunion harrier.'

Check with ANGAP on the current status of the forest, and make a further visit to the Direction des Eaux et Forêts in Ankazobe, 106km from Tana. Because of a problem with bandits in the area, you are advised to check with the Eaux et Forêts people about where to stay/camp, and always travel with a reliable guide.

Chapter Nine

The Highlands
South of Tana

INTRODUCTION

Now that Route Nationale 7 (RN7) has been improved, many visitors drive its
full length to Toliara, either by hired car or by public transport. It is a delightful
journey, providing an excellent overview of the *Hauts Plateaux* and Merina
and Betsileo culture, as well as spectacular scenery, especially around
Fianarantsoa.

FROM TANA TO ANTSIRABE

All along this stretch of road you will see Merina tombs, and can watch the
labour-intensive cultivation of rice paddies.

About 15km from Tana look out for a huge, white replica of the *rova* across
the paddy fields on the right. This was ex-president Ratsiraka's palace, funded
by North Korea, and stripped bare by the ex-president when he fled to France.
By the time you read this it may well be back in use – by the same president!

Ambatolampy

This small town lies some two hours from Tana and makes a convenient lunch
stop. The Albanian-owned Hotel au Rendezvous des Pecheurs serves fantastic
food and has nine clean, reasonably priced rooms with hot water. Tel: 207.

Some 2km south is the Manja Ranch owned by Doug Cook, an American,
and his Malagasy wife. If not booked up, Doug offers full board
accommodation, with horses or mountain bikes for hire. Try to phone first:
152 34. 'The reason most people visit the ranch is for the chance to horseback
ride. They have a stable with several horses and knowledgeable staff. The
food at the ranch was excellent. They always prepared a small portion of a
vegetarian dish for me as well as the main meal.' (Anne Axel)

About 15 minutes beyond Ambatolampy are some fine painted Merina tombs
(on both sides of the road, the most accessible on the right).

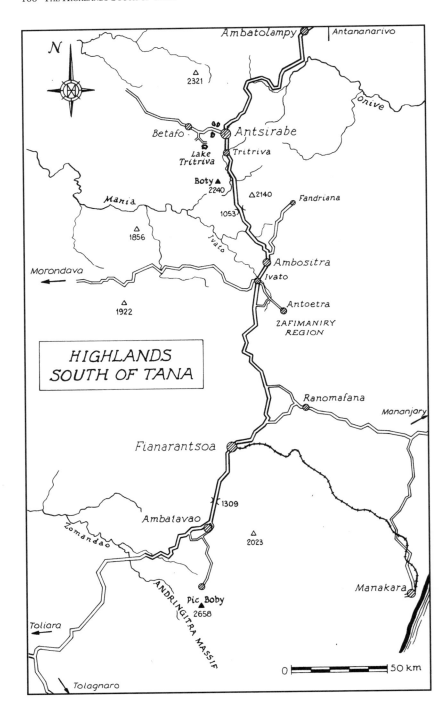

ANTSIRABE

Antsirabe lies 169km south of Antananarivo at 1,500m. It was founded in 1872 by Norwegian missionaries attracted by the cool climate and the healing properties of the thermal springs. The name means 'the place of much salt'.

This is an elegant city, and with its top class hotels and interesting excursions merits a stay of a few days. A broad avenue links the handsome station with the amazing Hotel des Thermes; at the station end is a monolith depicting Madagascar's 18 tribes.

Antsirabe is the agricultural and industrial centre of Madagascar; but don't worry, there are no Dark Satanic Mills here, it's mainly cotton goods, cigarettes, and – most important for the tourist – beer. You can smell the Star Brewery as you enter the town.

This is the *pousse-pousse* capital of Madagascar. There are hundreds, perhaps thousands of them. The drivers are insistent that you avail yourself of a ride, and why not? But be very firm about the price. Now that tourists come to Antsirabe in some numbers, the drivers have found they can make a dollar just by posing for pictures. To actually have to run somewhere, towing a large *vazaha*, for the same price must seem very unfair.

Saturday is market day in Antsirabe. The market resembles Tana's *zoma* in miniature but with an even greater cross-section of activities. It's also much better organised, and is enclosed in a walled area of the city on the hill before the road to Lake Tritriva. 'The entire back wall of the market is a row of open barber stalls. Each has a small mirror, a chair and a little peg for one's hat. There are a few local gambling places nearby, too. They're hard to find, and the stakes can get pretty high.' (Maggie Rush)

Antsirabe is famous for its minerals. The master stone-cutter of the town is said to be Monsieur Joseph. His studio is hard to find but someone will show you.

It is worth paying a visit to the thermal baths (*thermes*) although at the time of writing they are only open on Mondays. There is a wonderfully hot swimming pool full of laughing brown faces that laugh even harder at the sight of a foreigner. But it's friendly laughter. You can also take a private bath here (but there's a 20-minute limit) and have a massage.

On a promontory overlooking the baths stands the Hotel des Thermes: an amazing building in both size and architectural style. There is nothing else like it in Madagascar – it would not be out of place along the French Riviera and is set in equally elegant gardens (see *Where to stay*).

If you are travelling from May to September you will need a sweater in the evening. It gets quite cold.

Getting there

By rail The train now only runs spasmodically, the journey from Tana taking from four to ten (!) hours. When the schedule was regular there were three trains a week, leaving at 06.30 from Tana or Antsirabe. Don't lean out of the window, you might lose your head!

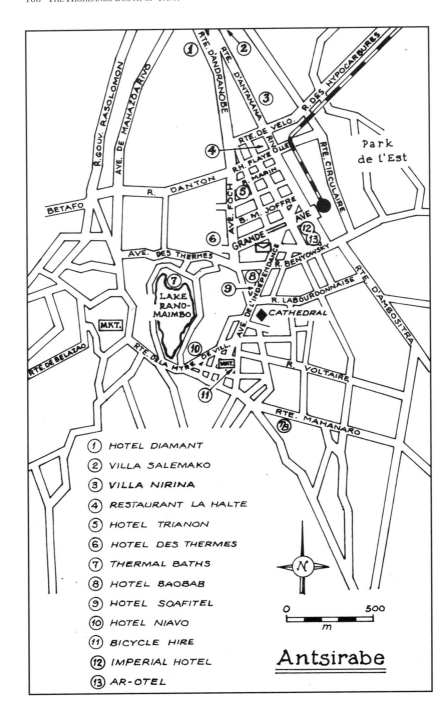

① HOTEL DIAMANT
② VILLA SALEMAKO
③ VILLA NIRINA
④ RESTAURANT LA HALTE
⑤ HOTEL TRIANON
⑥ HOTEL DES THERMES
⑦ THERMAL BATHS
⑧ HOTEL BAOBAB
⑨ HOTEL SOAFITEL
⑩ HOTEL NIAVO
⑪ BICYCLE HIRE
⑫ IMPERIAL HOTEL
⑬ AR-OTEL

Antsirabe

By road Antsirabe is generously served by buses and taxi-brousses. The journey takes about four hours.

Where to stay
Category A
Hotel des Thermes BP 72. Tel: 487 61/2. Fax 492 02. The interior does not match the exterior glamour, but there is a cosy bar and good food is served in the restaurant. In the warmer months the large garden and swimming pool make this a very pleasant place to relax. Room with two beds: 350Ff. Visa and MasterCard accepted.

Villa Nirina BP 245, 110 Antsirabe. Tel: 485 97 or 486 69. Owned by Mrs Zanoa Rasanjison, who speaks fluent English as well as French and German, this private home was cited in the last edition as possibly the best accommodation in Madagascar. However, recent reports are that, although this may well still be the case, it is almost impossible to get an advance booking, and payment must be in cash on arrival. The villa has four very modern bedrooms with private bath and Mrs Rasanjison's home cooking, which is excellent. It is just across the road from Diamant Restaurant.

Villa Salemako BP 14, 110 Antsirabe. Tel: 481 14. Another extraordinary private home with five rooms for visitors, run by Charles and Rosette Rakotonarivo. Beautiful garden, furniture and ambience. Double room with hot shower costs around 55,000Fmg, breakfast 8,000Fmg. The house is on the left just before the Y in the road on the approach to town. Look for the Malagasy motif on the chimney. Best to write or phone before you arrive.

Ar-Otel Rue Ralaimongo, Antsirabe 110. Tel: 04 481 20/485 73/485 74. Fax: 04 491 49. A well-situated, comfortable and posh new hotel. 400–460Ff (double rooms to a suite with four beds). Breakfast 15,000Fmg.

Category B
Imperial Hotel BP 74. Ave de la Gare, Antsirabe. Tel: 483 33. Chinese run. Comfortable. Double room 70,000Fmg (1995).

Hotel Diamant Route d'Andranobe. Tel: 488 40. A medium sized hotel with a good Chinese restaurant. 'Try the Chinese fondue, which is full of Madagascar's most exotic treats.' (Maggie Rush)

Hotel Manoro A newish hotel (1993) adjacent to the taxi-brousse station towards the south of the city. Rooms at 25,000–35,000Fmg, food only average. Reports from readers vary. One reckoned the room he stayed in hadn't been cleaned since the hotel opened, while another went out of his way to praise the hotel. So it goes...

Hotel Baobab Clean and friendly, with hot water in some rooms. Room with shower 15,000Fmg. There are cheaper rooms without hot water (and the *thermes* are only minutes away).

Hotel Soafitel Tel: 480 55. Four categories of rooms, all with hot water, from 23,800Fmg. Only the 'mini-apartment' at 70,000Fmg has an en-suite WC and shower. All other rooms have external showers, mostly communal. Rates include breakfast. Bicycles for hire.

Hotel Trianon Tel: 488 81. Since the former owner died this popular hotel seems to have deteriorated, and may even have closed. However, the French restaurant is highly recommended.

Category C

Hotel Coin d'Or Just off Ave de l'Indépendance in the centre of town. Clean but basic rooms for 10,000–15,000Fmg.

Hotel Niavo A family-run hotel with a garden on the far side of the lake. Popular, good food, but rather run-down. 10,000–15,000Fmg.

Hotel Fo Kri Fa Rooms from 8,000–10,000Fmg.

Where to eat

Restaurant à la Halte Tel: 489 94. In the last edition this was universally praised for the quality of the food at reasonable prices. A recent visitor, however, found some dishes to be considerably overcooked and others poorly presented.

Salon de Thé Moderne is a clean snack bar opposite the Pharmacie Mahosa.

Wheels and hoofs

In the first street (south) behind the daily market is a **bicycle hire** shop. Good mountain bikes for about 20,000Fmg per day. Bikes can also be hired from Soafitel. **Horses** may be hired near the Hotel des Thermes, the stables being near Parc d'Est.

Excursions from Antsirabe

It would be worth checking out a company called **Les Hautes Terres** who offer, among other things, tours by *calèche* (Malagasy stagecoach). I have their card but no further details. 30, Rue Maréchal Lyautes, Antsirabe. Tel: 480 97.

Lake Tritriva

There are actually two crater lakes; but the first, Lake Andraikiba, is unimpressive.

Tritriva is spectacular. The name comes from *tritry* – the Malagasy word for the ridge on the back of a chameleon (!) – and *iva*, deep. And this emerald-green crater lake is indeed deep – 80 metres, some say. It is reached by continuing past Lake Andraikiba for 12km on a rough, steep road past small villages of waving kids. Apart from the sheer beauty of the place (the best light for photography is in the morning), there are all sorts of interesting features. The water level *rises* in the dry season and debris thrown into the lake has reappeared down in the valley, supporting the theory of underground water channels.

Look across the lake and you'll see two thorn trees growing on a ledge above the water with intertwined branches. Legend says that these are two lovers, forbidden to marry by their parents, who drowned themselves in Tritriva. When the branches are cut, so they say, blood, not sap, oozes out.

The local people have not been slow to realise the financial potential of groups of *vazahas* corralled at the top of a hill. Don't think you will be alone at the lake.

You can get to Tritriva by taxi (45 mins each way) or by bus to Lake Andraikiba and then walk. The most enjoyable way is to rent a bike and make it a day trip. If you are self-sufficient you can stay in the village of Belazao, midway between the two lakes (no hotel), or camp at the lake.

Reader Maggie Rush went on excursions to Lake Tritriva three times in one year, between April and July. She found the road 'terrible' on each occasion. She reckons you can make it all the way with a good 4WD, or drive as far as possible then walk. She met many locals along the route, and describes it as 'a wonderful hike'. At the lake, the guardian will tell you its history; he will also tell you he expects a tip.

Betafo

About 22km west of Antsirabe, off the tarred road that goes as far as Morondava, lies Betafo, a town with typical Highlands red-brick churches and houses. Dotted among the houses are *vatolahy*, standing stones erected to commemorate warrior chieftains. A visit here is recommended. It is not on the normal tourist circuit, and gives you an excellent insight into Merina small-town activities. Monday is market day. There is no hotel in Betafo, but you should be able to find a room by asking around.

At one end of the town is the crater lake Tatamarina. From there it is a walk of about 3km to the Antafofo waterfalls among beautiful views of ricefields and volcanic hills. You will need to find someone to show you the way. 'It's very inviting for a swim but they told me there are ghosts in the pool under the falls. If you go swimming they will pull at your legs and pull you to the bottom.' (Luc Selleslagh)

On the outskirts of Betafo there are hot springs, where for a few francs you can have a hot bath with no time limit.

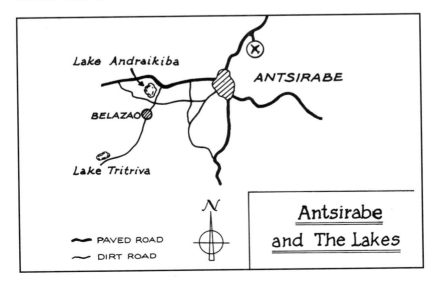

Lake Andraikiba

ANTSIRABE

BELAZAO

Lake Tritriva

N

PAVED ROAD
DIRT ROAD

Antsirabe
and The Lakes

CONTINUING SOUTH ON RN7

The next town of any consequence is Ambositra.

Leaving Antsirabe you continue to pass through typical Highland scenery of rice paddies and low hills. About 45 minutes beyond the town you'll cross a river and pass one of the nicest rural markets I've seen. There are strange fruit and vegetables, lots of peanuts, and fascinating grey balls that turn out to be soap made from the fat from zebu humps. At the back of the market is a makeshift barber-shop, and behind the men with the scissors are rolling green hills.

In about 2½ hours you reach Ambositra (pronounced 'Amb<u>oo</u>str') the centre of Madagascar's wood carving industry.

Ambositra

Wood carving is taken seriously here – even the houses have ornately carved wooden balconies and shutters. There is an abundant choice of carved figures and marquetry, in several shops, and the quality is improving although there are occasional lapses into pseudo-Africana. In an earlier edition I complained that I've yet to see a carved lemur. I've now seen some but sadly the carver obviously has yet to see a lemur...

For carvings of people, however, one artist stands out. 'Jean' carves exquisite scenes from Malagasy life, many in a fine-grained, creamy wood known locally as *fanazava*. Jean has now opened a shop on one of the minor roads that joins the RN7 just south of the town. Look for the signs 'Société Jean et Frère'.

RICE

The Malagasy have an almost mystical attachment to rice. King Andrianampoinimerina declared: 'Rice and I are one,' and loyalty to the Merina king was symbolised by industry in the rice paddies.

Today the Betsileo are masters of rice cultivation, and their neat terraces are a distinctive part of the scenery of the central highlands. However, rice is grown throughout the island, either in irrigated paddies or as 'hill rice' watered by the rain. Rice production is labour-intensive. First the ground must be prepared for the seeds. Often this is done by chasing zebu cattle round and round to break the clods and soften it – a muddy, sticky job, but evidently great fun for the boys who do it. Seeds are germinated in a small plot and replanted in the irrigated paddies when half-grown. In October and November you will see groups of women bent over in knee-deep water, performing this back-breaking work.

The Malagasy eat rice three times a day, the annual consumption being 135kg per person (about a pound of rice per day!). Rice marketing was nationalised in 1976, but this resulted in such a dramatic decline in the amount of rice reaching the open market that restrictions were lifted in 1984. Madagascar was once an exporter of rice; now half a million tons are imported each year. Most small farmers grow rice only for their own consumption but are forced to sell part of their crop for instant cash. Richer families in the community store this grain and sell it back at a profit later. To solve this small-scale exploitation, village co-operatives have been set up to buy rice and sell it back to the farmer at an agreed price, or at a profit to outsiders if any is left over.

If you are travelling south and returning by the same route, Jytte Arnfred Larson recommends a carver who will take orders and have them ready for you on your return: Rabekuto Robert, Lot II DIO Est-Vinany, Ambositra.

The excellent co-operative run by a French Catholic Mission and known as 'Arts Zafimaniry' has sadly collapsed, partly because of the illness of its founder, and partly because of the demand for high-quality carvings which were being bought by businessmen for resale in the boutiques of Tana. If you have time it would be worth checking out the monastery in case the problem has been rectified. In any case the buildings are worth a visit for the location and views. It is reached from the south side of town, up the hill towards the Grand Hotel, opposite the huge Catholic church.

Where to stay/eat

Grand Hotel This non-grand hotel has been around a long time and has a loyal clientele among frequent Mad travellers: 'Passport form rejected because I had left out some of my ancestors' biographical details. Rag-bag dog is called Bijoux. 45,000Fmg for deluxe rooms complete with bed bugs. Food cheap and reasonable.' (Clare Hermans)

Hotel Violette There are two hotels, the original Violette and its annexe. The old (and atmospheric) Violette is up the hill and to the left. The Annexe is on the south side of town about 200m past the Grand Hotel, and is a little more expensive. Friendly, good restaurant. Rooms are 25,000Fmg (1995).

Hotel Baby Near the southern taxi-brousse station. Friendly. 8,000Fmg.

Beyond the old Violette is a new eatery, the **Restaurant Tourisme Malagasy** A reader also recommends **Hotely ny Tanamasoandro**: 'Good, cheap, complete with punk waiter.'

Zafimaniry villages

The Zafimaniry people follow a traditional way of life in the forests southeast of Ambositra. This is not an area to attempt without an experienced guide, however. The danger is not so much in getting lost, but in the detrimental effects uncontrolled tourism has already had on the villagers nearest the road.

If you decide to go it alone, you should at least know that taxi-brousses only make the journey to Antoetra, the nearest Zafimaniry village to the road, on market days, Saturdays and Tuesdays. On other days, if you can't afford a taxi, you are stuck with a 23km hike from Ivato on RN7.

If you want to see the results of catastrophic deforestation this is as good an area as any. The impact is heightened by the beauty of the untouched forest and the simple way of life practised by the inhabitants of the more remote villages, where the picturesque houses show that wood carving is still the main industry.

Guided tours of the Zafimaniry country are advertised in hotels in Ambositra or Fianar (the Tsara Guest House, for instance). Dany and Sahondra, a French-Malagasy couple living in Tana, also do trekking trips there and are extremely knowledgeable. Write to them at BP 4313, Antananarivo; tel: 442 67.

SOUTH FROM AMBOSITRA ON RN7

From Ambositra, the scenery becomes increasingly spectacular. You now pass remnants of the western limit of the rainforest (being systematically destroyed). The road runs up and down steep hills, past neat Betsileo rice paddies interspersed with eucalyptus and pine groves. The steepest climb comes about two hours after Ambositra, when the vehicle labours up an endlessly curving road, through thick forests of introduced pine, and reaches the top where stalls selling oranges or baskets provide an excuse for a break. Then it's down through more forest, on a very poor stretch of road, to Ambohimahasoa. Leaving Ambohimahasoa you pass more forests, then open country, rice paddies and houses as you begin the approach to Fianarantsoa.

FIANARANTSOA

The name means 'Place of good learning'. Fianarantsoa (Fianar for short) was founded in 1830 as the administrative capital of Betsileo. It is one of the more attractive Malagasy towns, built on a hill like a small-scale Antananarivo.

There is a dramatic contrast between the charming Upper Town and the unutterably dreary Lower Town. Travellers making only a brief stop tend to see only the Lower Town, dominated by a huge concrete stadium and the stink of urine, and are not impressed. The Upper Town, with its narrow winding streets and plethora of churches, should be visited for the wonderful views, especially in the early morning when the mist is curling up from the valley. It's quite a way up: take bus number 3 or a taxi, and walk back.

'Fianarantsoa has a wonderful market, close to the Rue Verdun, which features a great variety of herbal medicines and dried fish brought up by train from Manakara. There is a path leading to the market from the Arinofy B&B. As well as the market, the town has its own version of Moulin Rouge, run by a Chinese, of course. If you like wine, there's the Domremy store, across the street from Le Panda. The store stocks a good selection of wines and aperitifs, and the French proprietors are very helpful.' (Maggie Rush)

Fianar is one of those cities that people either love or hate. A lone traveller, Anne Axel, said it was her least favourite place. She was hassled there by more men than anywhere else in Madagascar, and beggars seemed 'more pushy even than those in Tana'.

Getting there and away

Some travellers have complained about being hassled by touts at the taxi-brousse depot here, while others have nothing but praise for the people who helped find, and squeeze them into, a vehicle. For a tranquil journey the company KOFIAM, which runs between Fianar and Tana with a lunch stop in Ambositra, has been recommended. It even offers one seat per passenger!

In addition to access by road there are, in theory, several flights a week from Tana by Piper or Twin Otter aircraft.

Where to stay

Note: none of the hotels in Fianar accepts credit cards.

Category A

Hotel Soafia BP 1479. Tel/fax: 503 53. This is now one of the largest hotels in Madagascar, with 74 rooms and all sorts of unusual attractions. 'Looks like a cross between Disneyworld, a Chinese temple and a gigantic doll's house!' (J Hadfield). 'There's a swimming pool with its water analysis report from Tana's Pasteur Institute carefully affixed to the bedroom door, a sauna at 20,000Fmg but "Musculation" is free, as is "Gymn Tonic". Best breakfast bread and croissants in Madagascar.' (Clare Hermans) Double room 125Ff.

Radama Hotel Tel: 507 97/513 76. 14 rooms plus 18 studios. Hot water, TV, telephone. 200–210Ff.

Hotel Moderne du Betsileo BP 1161. Tel: 500 03. Near the station. Comfortable. Hot water. Only 12 rooms, so is often full. 144Ff.

Hotel Plazza Inn BP 1161. Tel: 515 72. Fax: 510 86. A new hotel with 30 rooms. Double room 150Ff. Worth checking out as an alternative to the flamboyant Soafia.

Tombontsoa Hotel Overlooks the football stadium near the Panda restaurant. Swimming pool and tennis court. Double room with hot shower and WC, 40,000Fmg. Friendly and clean. Good Malagasy meals.

Category B

Tsara Guest House BP 1373, Fianarantsoa 301 (Ambatolahikosoa, New Town). Tel: 502 06. For some years the Tsara has been the most popular *vazaha* place in Madagascar, universally praised by readers. It used to be conveniently placed near the taxi-brousse station but has now moved to an old house that began its life as a church, with a terrace from which you have a wonderful view of the town. The owners, Jim Heritsialonina and his Swiss wife Natalie, worked hard to ensure the unique success of the old place and deserve to build their custom back to former levels. His hallmark is the excellent meals eaten communally around a large table, and the treks and excursions he organises for his guests, making them feel part of a large family. Ideal for lone travellers.

Room prices range from 38,000Fmg (hot water but shared bathroom) to 52,000Fmg (double, ensuite bathroom).

Jim has put his profits to good use: 'We have used part of the money we won with the trekkings to build a small school for about 30 children in the rainforest. The village is called Andrambovato, 50km from Fianar by train.' That's just the sort of enterprise visitors should support.

Arinofy B&B BP 1426, Fianarantsoa 301. A clean and friendly place which reopened in 1995 in the former premises of the Tsara Guest House, a few hundred metres up the hill from the taxi-brousse depot. A twin-bedded room is 32,000Fmg, a four-bunk room is 15,000Fmg per person and breakfast is 7,000Fmg extra. Meals on request are from 12,000Fmg. You can eat in a communal dining room, and there is a laundry service. Excursions can be arranged.

Hotel Cotsoyannis BP 1229. Tel: 514 86. This hotel has had its ups and downs but with its new extension (it now has 30 rooms) it seems to be on the up. The rooms in

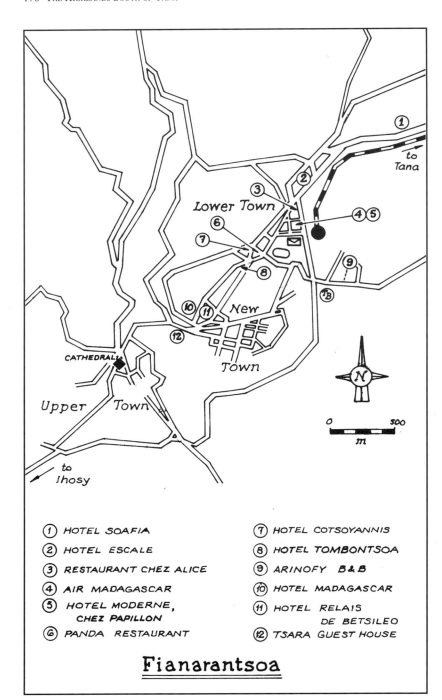

Fianarantsoa

the new block are very pleasant with good views (35,000–50,000Fmg) and the old rooms are reasonably good value at 25,000–30,000Fmg.

Category C

Hotel Relais du Betsileo Tel: 508 23. In the upper town, 37,000Fmg (1995). Reportedly friendly, though 'somewhat dirty' and in the prettier part of town.

Hotel Madagascar 7,200Fmg (1994) for a large double room and uncomfortable bed. Separate bathroom and WC.

Hotel Escale and **Ideal Hotel** may still exist – near the station.

Where to eat

Chez Papillon Tel: 500 03. Many people feel its reputation as the best restaurant in Madagascar is overrated, but the majority still praise the quality and wide choice of dishes, and the service, though snooty, is second to none. A meal for two with wine costs around 75,000Fmg. Breakfast (5,000Fmg) is highly recommended.

Le Panda Across the street from the Hotel Cotsoyannis. Chinese. Inexpensive. Good.

Resto Blue Very good, inexpensive food. Friendly.

Chez Alice Pizzeria A block away from the Papillon. Clean, pleasant, inexpensive.

Tiki dairy shop. Across from the train station. Great yoghurt and cheese.

Excellent bread is available from the bakery to the left of the Soafia Hotel.

Train to Manakara

If it's running, the train usually leaves for Manakara on Saturdays and Wednesdays. The schedule seems to be endlessly flexible, so you will need to check current whims at the station. It generally leaves at 07.00 and takes six to eight hours. The ticket office opens at 06.00. For more information on the trip see *Chapter Twelve* (page 278).

Escorted tours

There are many places of interest within a day's excursion from Fianar (see below). Jim, at the Tsara Guest House, can organise these, as can the owners of the Anofy B&B. Also recommended by (most) travellers is Stella Ravelomanantsoa. He (sic) can be found at the 'Regional Tourist Office', near the Papillon, opposite Lombardo. Tel: 506 67.

Excursions
Wine tasting

The Famoriana estate (Domaine Côtes de Famoriana) is one of the largest and best-known wine producers in Madagascar. Smaller ones, such as Maromby, also flourish. The vineyards are open to visitors. Famoriana is about 35km north-west of Fianar, beyond the small town of Isorana.

Tea estate

The Sahambavy Tea Estate is situated on one side of a very pretty valley beside Lake Sahambavy, 25km by road from Fianar, or by rail to the Sahambavy station on the way to Manakara. Although tea-growing was encouraged in Madagascar in pre-colonial times, this is a relatively new estate and is now managed by a Dutch company, HVA, and run by a Scot. The company employs 700 people and 75% of the tea produced must by law be exported.

Visitors are welcome at the estate which is a beautiful place for picnics. Camping is not encouraged because of the danger from cattle rustlers. The place is closed at weekends.

RANOMAFANA

Ranomafana itself is little more than a couple of hotels and the thermal baths, set by a river in the lush greenness of the eastern rainforest. The name Ranomafana means 'hot water' and it was the waters, not the lemurs, which drew visitors in the colonial days and financed the building of the elegant-looking Hotel Station Thermale de Ranomafana.

These days the baths (which are wonderful – and cheap) are often ignored by visitors anxious to visit the Ranomafana National Park which was created in 1991. This hitherto unprotected fragment of high-altitude rainforest first came to world attention with the discovery of the golden bamboo lemur in 1986 and is particularly rich in wildlife.

Ranomafana is not universally popular but I love it! First you have the marvellous drive down, with the dry highland vegetation giving way to greenery and flowers. Then there are the views of the tumbling waters of the Namorona river, and the relief when the hillsides become that lovely unbroken, knobbly green of virgin forest and you know you are near the reserve. Hidden in these trees are 12 species of lemur: diademed (Milne-Edwards) sifaka, red-bellied lemur, red-fronted lemur, ruffed lemur and three species of bamboo lemur. At night you can add mouse lemur, avahi, lepilemur, fat-tailed dwarf lemur, and even aye-aye. Then there are the birds: more than 100 species with 36 endemic. And the reptiles. And the butterflies and other insects. Even if you saw no wildlife, there is enough variety in the vegetation and scenery, and enough pleasure in walking the well-constructed trails, to make a visit worthwhile. And – I nearly forgot – in the warm summer months you can swim in the cold, clear water of the Namorona while a malachite kingfisher darts overhead. Some negative things: the trails are steep and arduous, accommodation is (so far) basic and often full, and the guides have yet to reach a good standard. It often rains, and there are leeches.

Getting there and away

In your own transport the journey is about three hours from Fianar and four hours from Ambositra. There are two roads leading there from RN7: an all-weather but potholed one which starts at Alakambohimana, about 26km north of Fianar, and a deeply rutted dry-season road starting about 53km north of Fianar.

Public transport is a problem since it is so often full. A taxi-brousse or *baché* (SONATRA is the best company) from Fianar should cost around £1/ $1.50, but desperate *vazahas* often end up paying nearly twice as much. It takes about five hours.

Coming from Manakara or Mananjary you should be at the taxi-brousse station as early as possible in the morning. When leaving Ranomafana you are safer to get a taxi-brousse to Fianar, rather than hope to get one going north to Antsirabe. These supposedly run only on Wednesdays and Saturdays.

Where to stay/eat

Hotel Domaine Nature A very nice new hotel by the river, halfway between the village and the park. At present there are only five bungalows, but another five are being built. 65,000Fmg. Food reportedly mediocre. Bookings (Tana) through Destinations Mada; tel: 31072, fax: 31067.

Station Thermale de Ranomafana BP 13, tel: 1 (!). This 'good' hotel is now so bad that some groups have been forced to give Ranomafana a miss. A 1995 traveller nominated it 'the worst value for money in Madagascar: I have never, anywhere, been in a more musty-smelling room'. Perhaps it will improve. Rooms cost about 30,000Fmg. Whatever the quality of the rooms the hotel is likely to be fully booked. The food is good/very good, so a compromise may be to eat at the restaurant but camp in the grounds.

Hotely Manja On the road to Ifanadiana (RN 26), five minutes' walk east along the river. 'Superb value at 35,000Fmg, and they'll bring you a bucket of hot water to use in your "shower" cubicle' (G and V Thomson). 'One of those places that made me consider tearing up my return airline ticket and staying forever!' says reader Bradley Rink. The hotely is a group of 10 bungalows, very high on the charm scale, although at present without electricity or running water. Bungalows 15,000Fmg (1994) per person. Long-drop toilets.

Hotely Ravenala Up the road from the Thermale towards the park entrance. Adequate, popular, and adding more rooms. No restaurant.

Hotelin Kavana This restaurant serves inexpensive, good food – the best, according to Gavin and Val Thomson (1995).

Camping

Camping at the new park entrance site is 5,000Fmg with your own tent, or you can rent a large one for 10,000Fmg a night (1995). There are six covered tent sites, with open-sided A-frame thatched shelters giving shade as well as protection from the rain. There's also a bungalow which has kitchen facilities and two rooms – a double for 20,000Fmg and an 8-bed dormitory for 10,000Fmg per bed. It shares long-drop toilets with the campsite, but there are no washing facilities apart from the kitchen sink. The villagers built the new compound so that they could benefit from tourists visiting the park, and to ensure this the village elders collect the money. Tents can be hired at the park entrance, where there is a campsite. Basic facilities including a long-drop toilet.

The campsite on a hill at Bellevue (within the park) may not now be open to

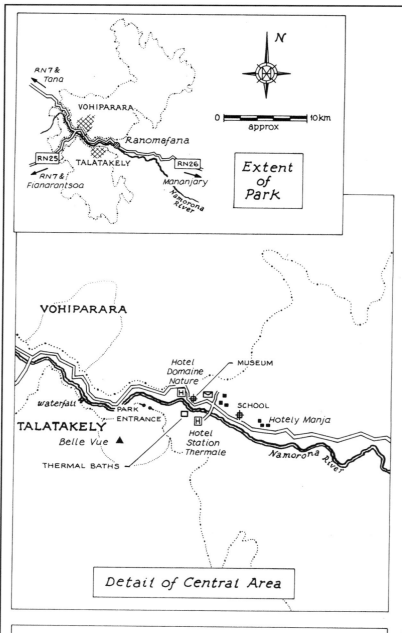

Extent of Park

Detail of Central Area

RANOMAFANA NATIONAL PARK

tourists (only to researchers). If you can camp here you will meet some charming furry inhabitants: ring-tailed mongoose (*Galidia elegans*) during the day and mouse-lemurs and the civet-like *Fossa fossana* at night. There is only room for three or four tents here and water must be carried up. By the time you read this another campsite may have been opened at a new site by the river with space for four tents. Both these are in the national park so you must be accompanied by a guide (although he/she does not have to stay the night there).

Visiting the national park
Permits and guides

Permits (20,000Fmg) are obtainable from the National Park Office near the hotel. You are not allowed into the park without a guide. Most only speak French, but they usually know the animals' names in English. More work needs to be done to ensure that the guides do not try to get extra money out of tourists and that they are skilled at their job – the best ones, such as Loret and his wife Eliane, tend to work for researchers. Some guides are very good – and honest – others are good but manipulative. Recommended guides for independent travellers are Edmond (Edmond le petit) and Roland. Fidi and his brother Jean-Cree are very knowledgable, but work more effectively with groups.

There have been problems in the past with guides trying to persuade visitors to part with extra money. The official fees are now posted at the park entrance: currently 20,000Fmg for a half-day for one to six people. Groups of more than six must have two guides. Nocturnal visits cost 30,000Fmg. Check the posted rate before hiring a guide, and confirm your intentions with him or her before you set out. You may always add a small tip on top of the standard fee if you feel your guide has been exceptional (and please write to me with his/her name for recommendation in the next edition).

In the forest

There are standard routes in the forest, mostly lasting a few hours. Your guide will assume that it is lemurs you have come to see; so, unless you stress that you are interested in other aspects such as botany, he will tend to concentrate on mammals and birds. You are most likely to see red-fronted brown lemurs (*Eulemur fulvus rufus*) and perhaps the rarer red-bellied lemur *Eulemur rubiventer*. The golden bamboo lemur is less easily seen. Gavin and Val Thomson spent six 'strenuous, sweaty hours' with a guide, but failed to find one. Nick Garbutt, on the other hand, saw one on a standard half-day tour, so you never know your luck. The most memorable of the easily found lemurs is a subspecies of the diademed sifaka, *Propithecus diadema edwardsi* – Milne-Edward's sifaka. Unlike the more familiar Verreaux's sifaka which is largely white, this is dark brown with cream-coloured sides. They wear snazzy coloured collars, much to the annoyance of tourists who want to take photos. These are radio collars and the colour identifies the troop. You should remember that these rare animals are being extensively studied. Be careful not to let your enthusiasm impede a researcher's work.

A delightful, if strenuous, walk is along the river to Cascade Riana. Allow at least two hours for the round trip plus time to swim in the pool at the base of the falls.

The entrance to the park is some 6km west of the hotel Station Thermale, on the main road. A bus is supposed to leave the museum at 07.00 to take visitors here but it is reportedly unreliable so you may be better to walk it and hope to get a lift.

Another trail system has been built on flatter ground at Vohiparara, near the boundary of the park 12km west of Ranomafana on the main road. It only takes about three hours to do all the trails here with a guide. 'Vohiparara is especially good for birders. Among many others you'll find the brown emutail, Madagascar snipe, Meller's duck and the extremely rare slenderbilled flufftail. The song of the cryptic warbler was first recorded here in 1987.' (Derek Schuurman)

Guides urge you to visit the park after dark to see the nocturnal animals. I am not convinced that this is worth it if you are not camping in the forest or taking a late afternoon tour, but it is a good chance to see mouse lemurs (which turn out obligingly to eat bananas) and the civet, *Fossa fossana*. The steep paths have been made safer in recent months, but even so negotiating them by torchlight can be risky.

Museum/gift shop

This is part of the Ranomafana National Park Project to improve visitor understanding of the area. The museum is still being added to (and often seems to be closed), but there is now quite a comprehensive collection labelled in English and Malagasy.

Thermal baths

These are close to the Station Thermale hotel: turn left out of the door, down the steps and follow the path. It only costs a few francs for a wonderful warm swimming pool or a hot shower or bath. Hours are 07.00–12.00, 14.00–17.00. Closed Fridays.

CONTINUING SOUTH ON RN7

Coming from Fianar the landscape is a fine blend of vineyards and terraced rice paddies (the Betsileo are acknowledged masters of rice cultivation), then after 20km a giant rock formation seems almost to hold the road in its grasp. Its name is, appropriately, Tanan'Andriamanitra, or Hand of God. From here to Ihosy is arguably the finest mountain scenery in Madagascar. Reader Bishop Brock who cycled the route writes: 'Those three days were the most rewarding of my career as a bicycle tourist. I pity people who only pass through that magnificent landscape jammed inside a taxi-brousse.'

It is worth noting that taxi-brousses from the north continue south in the afternoon. This may be the best time to get a place if you're pushed for time.

Ambalavao

Some 56km southwest of Fianarantsoa is my favourite town, Ambalavao. RN7 does not pass through the attractive part of town, and I strongly urge people to stop here for a few hours. 'Nowhere in Madagascar have I seen a town so resembling a medieval European village as here. Although the main street was not narrow, the wooden balconies with their handsomely carved railings leaned into the street, giving them that look of a fairy-tale book tilt. The roofs were tiled, and, lending that final touch of authenticity, pails of water were emptied on to people passing too near the gutter.' (Tim Cross)

This is where the famous Malagasy 'Antaimoro' paper is made. This papyrus-type paper impregnated with dried flowers is sold throughout the island as wall-hangings and lampshades. The people in this area are Betsileo, but paper-making in the area copies the coastal Antaimoro tradition which goes back to the Muslim immigrants who wrote verses from the Koran on this paper. This Arabic script was the only form of writing known in Madagascar before the LMS developed a written Malagasy language nearly five hundred years later using the Roman alphabet.

Antaimoro paper is traditionally made from the bark of the *avoha* tree from the eastern forests, but sisal paste is now sometimes used. After the bark is pounded and softened in water it is smoothed on to linen trays to dry in the sun. While still tacky, dried flowers are pressed into it and brushed over with a thin solution of the liquid bark to hold the flowers in place. The open-air 'factory' (more flowerbeds than buildings) where all this happens is to the left of the town (signposted) and is well worth a visit. It is fascinating to see the step-by-step process, and you get a good tour (in French with a smattering of English) from the manager. A shop sells the finished product at reasonable prices (although rolls of Antaimoro paper do not survive the average taxi-brousse trip).

Another attraction is the market which is held on Wednesdays. Or maybe Thursdays. Jill and Charlie Hadfield visited the cattle market (which is reached by walking off the road to the right of the taxi-brousse stop).

'This area of Madagascar is notorious for cattle-rustling: from Ambositra down to Tuléar is bandit country and for the Bara tribe cattle rustling is a test of manhood... What seems to have started out as a sporting activity is now a very dangerous pastime. From time to time the government makes a half-hearted attempt to put a stop to *dahalo* but it's doomed to failure. Most of the gendarmerie are in the pay of the bandits...

So we were very interested in the goings on at the cattle market which takes place on top of a hill, with a circular view for miles and miles of bare, rolling countryside, with flame trees and the granite-topped mountains in the distance. We got there early and for the next hour or so could see herds of zebu being driven in from all directions – some come from as far as Tuléar, two days' drive away. Betsileo farmers, wearing straw hats and with their blankets draped like ponchos, stood and chatted or strolled round eyeing up the cattle, and leather-jacketed smoothies strutted round importantly, prodding zebu with their sticks or pulling their tails. Calculations were done on pocket calculators.'

Getting there and away

Although Ambalavao is on RN7, southward-bound travellers may prefer to make it an excursion from Fianarantsoa, since vehicles heading to Ihosy and beyond will have filled up with passengers in Fianar.

Where to stay

Stop Hotel Five double rooms with communal WC and washing facilities. Basic but adequate. They expect you to eat at least one meal a day in the restaurant and to order it in advance.

CONTINUING SOUTH ON RN7

The scenery beyond Ambalavao is marvellous. Huge granite domes of rock dominate the grassy plains. The most striking one, with twin rock towers, is called Varavarana Ny Atsimo, the 'Door to the South' by the pass of the same name. Beyond is the 'Bonnet de l'Évêque' (Bishop's Hat), and a huge lump of granite shaped like an upturned boat, with its side gouged out into an amphitheatre; streams run into the lush vegetation at its foot. This dramatic landscape begs to be explored on foot, but keep away from the Bishop's Hat. It is a current and ancient burial site which the local people do not want disturbed; visitors would not be welcome.

You will notice that not only the scenery but the villages are different. These Bara houses are solidly constructed out of red earth (no elegant Merina pillars here) with small windows. Bunches of corn are often suspended from the roof to dry in the sun. Shortly after Ambalavao you start to see your first Bara tombs – some painted with scenes from the life of the deceased.

The next town of importance is Ihosy, described in *Chapter Ten*.

Andringitra and Pic Boby

South of Ambalavao lies the Andringitra massif, crowned by Madagascar's second highest mountain, Pic Boby (2,658m). The area constitutes the Réserve Naturelle Intégrale de l'Andringitra, which is one of the WWF's 'priority pilot zones'. Concerned as much with the communities surrounding the reserve as the protected area itself, the aim is to look at sustainable development which will include ecotourism. Although formerly a Strict Nature Reserve, visitors are now allowed here; contact ANGAP for the latest details.

Olivier Langrand, who made several research expeditions to the area in 1995, reports many exciting discoveries: all three species of bamboo lemur are found there, and a fourth one has just been found. An isolated population of ring-tailed lemurs live high up on the mountain and have adopted a completely different lifestyle and diet to their compatriots in the spiny forest. A new warbler species has been discovered there... and so it goes on. A chilly place (it quite often snows) but fascinating to the serious naturalist.

ANTANANARIVO
Above: *Queen's Palace* (Rova) *before it was destroyed by fire in 1996* (RH)
Left: *View from the steps leading to Place de l'Indépendance* (HB)
Right: *Carved balcony (French soldiers) near Ivato airport* (HB)

THE HIGHLANDS
Above: *After a death the deceased person's clothing is ritually washed in the nearest rive*
However, this scene may just show the family laundry! (HB)
Below: *Mineral deposits at the hot springs near Ampefy* (TC)

Typical houses and landscape of Imerina (HB)

THE SOUTH

Above: *Isalo National Park* (HB)

Below: *Pousse-pousses at Toliara* (HB)

Part Three

THE SOUTH

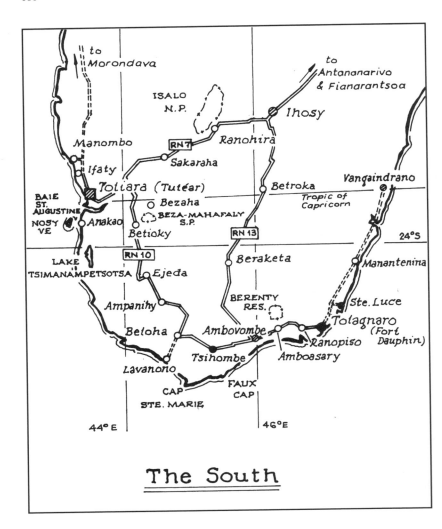

The South

EGG-VENTURE

In 1993 three children playing in sand-hills near a beach in Western Australia dug up a fossilised egg which appears to be that of Madagascar's *aepyomis* or elephant bird. How it got there is a mystery. Gondwanaland broke up before the evolution of birds, but this egg could have floated across the Indian Ocean. Or... your guess is as good as any.

Chapter Ten

The South

This is the most exotic and the most famous part of Madagascar, the region of 'spiny forest' or 'spiny desert' where weird cactus-like trees wave their thorny fingers in the sky, where pieces of 'elephant bird' shell may still be found, and where the Mahafaly tribe erect their intriguing and often entertaining *aloalo* stelae above the graves. Here also is the country's most popular nature reserve (Berenty), and one of the country's loveliest accessible beaches (Libanona). No wonder Tolagnaro (Fort Dauphin) features on almost all tour itineraries.

Europeans have been coming to this area for a long time. Perhaps the earliest were a group of 600 shipwrecked Portuguese sailors in 1527. Later, when sailors were deliberately landing in Madagascar during the days of the spice trade in the 16th and 17th centuries, St Augustine's Bay, south of the modern town of Toliara (Tuléar), became a favoured destination. They came for reprovisioning – Dutch and British – trading silver and beads for meat and fruit. One Englishman, Walter Hamond, was so overcome with the delights of Madagascar and the Malagasy, 'the happiest people in the world', that fired by his enthusiasm the British attempted to establish a colony at St Augustine's Bay. It was not a success. The original 140 settlers were soon whittled down to 60 through disease and murder by the local tribesmen who became less happy when they found their favourite beads were not available for trade and that these *vazahas* showed no sign of going away. The colonists left in 1646. Fifty years later St Augustine was a haven for pirates.

Several ethnic groups live in the south: the Vezo (fishermen) and Masikoro (pastoralists) are subclans of the Sakalava. The Mahafaly, Antanosy, Antandroy and Bara all have their regions in the interior. These southern Malagasy are tough, dark-skinned people, with African features, accustomed to the hardship of living in a region where rain seldom falls and finding water and grazing for their large herds of zebu is a constant challenge. In contrast to the highland people, who go in for second burial and whose tombs are the collective homes of ancestors, those in the south commemorate the recently dead. There is more opportunity to be remembered as an individual here, and a Mahafaly or Masikoro man who has lived eventfully, and died rich, will have the highlights of his life perpetuated in the form of wooden carvings (*aloalo*) and colourful paintings adorning his tomb. Formerly the *aloalo* were of more spiritual significance; but just as we, in our culture, have tended to bring an element of humour and realism into religion, so have the Malagasy. As John Mack says (in *Island of Ancestors*), 'Aloalo have become obituary announcements when formerly they were notices of rebirth'.

Antandroy tombs may be equally colourful. They are large and rectangular (the more important the person the bigger his tomb) and, like those of the Mahafaly, topped with zebu skulls left over from the funeral feast. A very rich man may have over 100 skulls on his grave. They usually have 'male and female' standing stones (or, in modern tombs, cement towers) at each side. Modern tombs may be brightly painted with geometric patterns on the sides. The Antanosy have upright stones, cement obelisks, or beautifully carved wooden memorials. These, however, are not over the graves themselves. This sacred and secret place will be elsewhere.

The spiny forest: an identification guide

The spiny forest (more correctly called 'thorn thicket') is typified by thorny, water-retaining trees and shrubs which are unique to Madagascar. They exist in a bewildering variety, but it adds interest to one's visit to be able to identify a few species.

First, the ones that look like cacti. There are four genera of Didiereaceae, but non-botanists are most interested in two: *Alluaudia* and *Didiera*. Some broad ground rules will help you tell the two apart. Look at the stems. In *Alluaudia* the spines and leaves are arranged in spirals, in *Didiera* they are in groups.

There are five species of *Alluaudia*. *A. ascendens* is tall and finger-like, with long thorns and short, heart-shaped leaves; *A. procera* has fewer and shorter thorns, long leaves arranged in spirals, and – in the spring – a clump of flowers at the end of each branch. The 'trunks' are woody and used for fencing and charcoal. Somewhat similar is *A. komosa* (tree-like branches, thick, oblong leaves), *A. dumosa* (no leaves and short, stubby thorns) and *A. humbertia* (shrub-like with long thorns and heart-shaped leaves).

There are four species of *Didiera*. Two that are easily identified are *D. trollii*, with anti-social branches trailing on the ground providing an impenetrable barrier, and *D. madagascariensis* which has the classic, many-fingered silhouette, and long, narrow leaves.

Now you've finished with the cactus-like jobs you can go on to the Euphorbiaceae, of which there are five families. Among the easily recognisable are *E. stenoclada*, which has characteristic spiky branches adapted for condensing sea mist, *E. oconclada* with long, droopy 'branches' like strings of sausages, *E. fiha*, similar but with peeling bark, and *E. enterophora*, tree-shaped with many green 'fingers'. Cut any euphorbia and white latex will ooze out of the wound.

Still on the quest for knowledge? Then turn your attention to the numerous Pachypodium species. Apart from the ones that really do resemble an elephant's foot crowned with yellow or pink flowers, there are a couple of taller species you may see in gardens which are particularly striking: *P. lamerii* is shaped like a slim bottle, very spiny, and has a burst of leaves at the top; and *P. geayi* is more like a standard bottle and topped with branches and white flowers. If your curiosity is still unsatiated, find Roger at Tolagnaro/Berenty from whom I learned most of this!

Getting around

Road travel in the south can be a challenging affair, but roads *are* being improved, and RN7 to Toliara (Tuléar) is now paved. Apart from this and the road between Tolagnaro (Fort Dauphin) and Ambovombe, the 'roads' that link other important towns are terrible, so most people prefer to fly. In addition to the regular flights to the main towns of Tolagnaro and Toliara there are occasional small planes to Ampanihy, Bekily, and Betioky as well as Ihosy. Check the current schedule with Air Mad.

Most overland travellers take a bus or taxi-brousse from Fianar to Ranohira, stopping here to visit Isalo National Park. Anne Axel took the KOFFI bus from Fianar; the trip took 13 hours and cost 20,000Fmg (1995): 'I was travelling with three South Africans. They said the ride was the worst travelling experience they'd had in Madagascar. I, on the other hand, felt it was one of the best, and I would recommend the company to other travellers.'

IHOSY

Pronounced 'Ee-oosh', this small town is the capital of the Bara people, who resisted Merina rule and were never really subdued until French colonial times. Cattle rustling is a time-honoured custom in this region – a Bara does not achieve manhood until he has stolen a few of his neighbour's cows (see also page 31). This is a medium-sized town which has, among other things, a BTM bank.

Ihosy is about five hours from Fianar by taxi-brousse, and lies at the junction for Toliara and Tolagnaro. The road to the former is good; to the latter, bad. A road also runs from Ihosy to Farafangana, on the east coast. This is still notorious for bandits, although it has become a popular route for overlanders. Drivers expecting to refuel at Ihosy, though, should be warned that they may be disappointed.

Where to stay/eat

Zaha Motel BP 67. Tel: 83. Pleasant, comfortable bungalows, cold water (hot if you ask them to turn on the gas heater); recent reports suggest declining standards. Bungalows 48,000Fmg, breakfast 8,000Fmg, dinner 20,000Fmg.

There is also the poor-value **Hotel Relais-Bara**; no hot water but a nice atmosphere. A better bet may be the **Hotel Ravaka**. For meals there is a nice little square of open-sided *hotelys* serving good Malagasy food. The **Hotely Dasimo** is recommended for its excellent *tsaramasy* (rice with beans and pork).

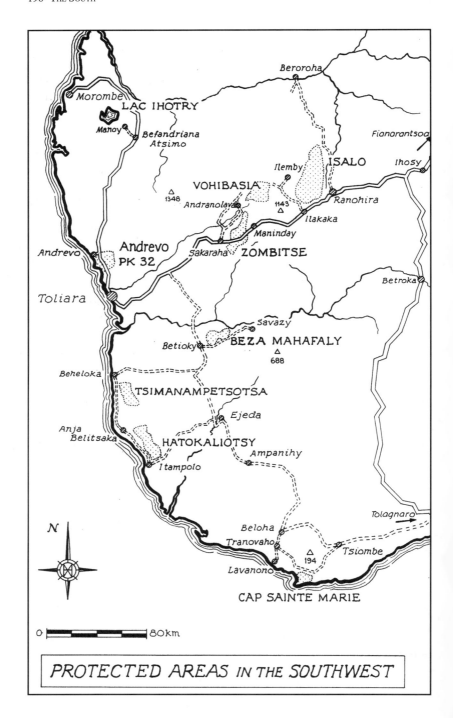

PROTECTED AREAS IN THE SOUTHWEST

FROM IHOSY TO TOLAGNARO (FORT DAUPHIN)

RN13 is in very poor condition. Adventurous travellers will enjoy the consequent lack of tourist development but don't underestimate the time it takes to travel even short distances.

The first town is **Betroka**, a friendly little place with a basic hotel and restaurant, Des Bons Amis, with a loo-shed outside. If you don't want to eat in the hotel there are plenty of hotelys. Next comes **Beraketa** which has the even more down-to-earth Herilaza Hotel. This seems to be the last accommodation (except in private houses) before Ambovombe and the paved road to Tolagnaro.

FROM IHOSY TO TOLIARA (TULÉAR)

After leaving Ihosy, RN7 takes you for two hours across the Horombe Plateau, grasslands dotted with termite hills and telegraph poles, each with its waiting kestrel (although Clare Hermans writes: 'The telegraph poles will soon become extinct as they are systematically being dug up and carted off for resale as lorry shafts, and what will happen to the kestrels then?').

As you approach Ranohira, *Medemia* palms enliven the monotonous scenery. Henk Beentje of Kew Gardens writes: 'The palms are properly called *Bismarckia*, but the French didn't like the most common palm in one of their colonies to be called after a German so changed the name, quite illegally according to the Code of Botanical Nomenclature!'

RANOHIRA AND ISALO NATIONAL PARK

The small town of Ranohira lies 97km south of Ihosy, and has sprung into prominence as the base for visiting the now popular Isalo National Park. Consequently it has several hotels and bars, and is generally tourist-friendly.

Getting there and away

Getting to Ranohira is usually no problem: about two hours from Ihosy by taxi-brousse. If leaving from Toliara note that the taxi-brousses and buses depart early in the morning; best to book your seat the night before. Leaving Ranohira can be a major problem. Most people wait many hours – sometimes days – and pay double the normal fare when they do find transport.

If time is short it's worth considering hiring a car and driver in Toliara.

Where to stay
Category A

Relais de la Reine This lovely French-run hotel is not in Ranohira but 9km further south, on the edge of the park. It has been thoughtfully designed to blend as much as possible into the surrounding landscape. There are blocks of six rooms grouped round a courtyard, and solar panels provide hot water. The water is drawn from their own stream. A twin-bedded room with bathroom costs 320Ff. Fans cool the rooms in the hot season and the Golombier family are reported to be superb hosts. Bookings must be made through Tana agencies, but the hotel reportedly sells meals (including breakfast) to non-residents anxious to take a look at what is probably Madagascar's best hotel.

Category B
Hotel Orchidée d'Isalo Highly praised as being a very friendly place with lovely rooms, excellent cooking and nice souvenirs. En suite double is currently 50,000Fmg, but this will go up if they install hot water.

Hotel les Joyeux Lemuriens The most popular backpacker hotel in Ranohira. Readers are full of praise for the hotel (which has 'marvellous hot *douches*'), the food, and its managers, Aujustin and Myriam Jaofera.

Category C
Hotel Berny In the centre of town, next to the ANGAP office. No running water but friendly, with 12 double rooms at 30,000Fmg (£5/$US7.50).

Isalo Ranch BP 3 313. A new group of eight bungalows 5km south of Ranohira. Basic facilities with communal (cold) showers, no electricity, but clean and comfortable, German-owned, and very good value at 30,000Fmg per bungalow. The meals are good too (18,000Fmg).

Chez R Thomas Clean, new, windowless rooms. Good value.

Isalo National Park
The combination of sandstone rocks (cut by deep canyons and eroded into weird shapes), rare endemic plants and dry weather (between June and August rain is almost unknown), makes this park particularly rewarding. For botanists there is *Pachypodium rosulatum* or elephant's foot – a bulbous rock-clinging plant – and a native species of aloe, *Aloe isaloensis*; and for lemur-lovers there may be sifakas, brown lemurs and ring-tails. 'Isalo is fantastic! It is not just the abstract sculpturing and colours of the eroded terrain or the sweeping panoramas which so impressed, but also the absolute and enveloping silence. No birds, insects or other animals, no wind, no rumbling of distant traffic and no other people.' (Peter Walbran). 'It's not just the curious sense of isolation... it's the sheer timelessness of it all, the fixed, almost prehistorical feel. Gazing from the top of cliffs over the valley I would have been genuinely unsurprised to have suddenly seen a line of hunter-gatherers in skins making its way across the bottom.' (G. Simpson)

Isalo is also sacred to the Bara tribe. For hundreds of years the Bara have used caves in the canyon walls as burial sites. There is one for a king in Canyon de Singes, high up in the cliff wall, but there are others scattered everywhere. Ask your guide about this but it is wise not to push the issue. Their beliefs and traditions need to be preserved. 'On several occasions our guide said it was *fady* to go to such a place. Insisting on going will only lead to a breakdown between the tourist and the local person.' (Maggie Rush)

Tourists who do not wish to hike (and this should not be undertaken lightly – it is *very* hot) or to pay the park fee have various options. Simply driving past the sandstone formations which can be seen from the road is exciting enough, and you can visit the **Oasis**, an idyllic palm-shaded grotto. The track leading here is about 10km south of Ranohira, on the left just before a 'milestone' ('Tulear 230 km'). There are *Pachypodium rosulatum* nearby, a waterfall and a pool.

Another popular visit – perhaps *too* popular at times – is to the **Fenêtre**, a natural rock formation providing a window to the setting sun. Walk behind the rocks for the proper Isalo feeling of space and tranquillity.

Permits and guides

For an excursion in the park you will need a permit (20,000Fmg) which must be purchased at the ANGAP office in Ranohira, next to Chez Berny. You must take an accredited guide with you, and sadly there is no-one I can presently recommend (I would welcome the names of guides who show the same knowledge and enthusiasm as those in Périnet). Charges are posted on the wall of the office, and vary according to the length of the excursion: currently 20,000Fmg to the Piscine Naturelle and 25,000Fmg to the Canyon des Singes, but likely to go up. Schematic maps of the park are available from ANGAP.

Hiking in the park

The two most popular hiking excursions are to the *Piscine Naturelle*, a natural swimming pool; and to the *Canyon des Singes*. With the help of a 4WD vehicle you can do both of these in one day, but a circular tour lasting three days is more rewarding.

Budget travellers with only a day in hand should opt for the *Piscine Naturelle*. It is a shorter distance to walk (6km/2hrs each way); and it provides the best viewpoints, *Pachypodium rosalatum* and *Aloe isaloensis*, and a wonderfully cool swim at the end. The increasing popularity of Isalo, however, means that you are unlikely to be alone in this idyllic spot. Starting from Ranohira (a guide is mandatory) it takes about two hours to walk to the pool. The first part is flat and relatively uninteresting, but once you reach the massif the views, colours, and botany are pure enchantment. 'The Piscine Naturelle is the essential Isalo. It appears to have been taken right out of the book of Genesis. The crystal clear water is a wonderful sight after all that walking and the swim makes the toil worthwhile.' (Will Pepper, 1994). 'The Piscine itself is more like a Pissoir, despite the WC sign.' (Clare Hermans, 1996)

Those with a 4WD vehicle can drive along a track (with one ford) from Ranohira for 30 minutes to the base of the rocks where the hiking trail starts. From there it is about 90 minutes to the pool. The Relais de la Reine makes vehicles available to guests, and they can sometimes be hired in Ranohira by approaching the drivers of suitable vehicles. In 1996 the charge was 90,000Fmg.

The Canyon des Singes can also be reached directly from Ranohira, either on foot (9km/3hrs each way) or part of the way by 4WD. In the dry season a vehicle can take you most of the way, in the rainy months it is more challenging:

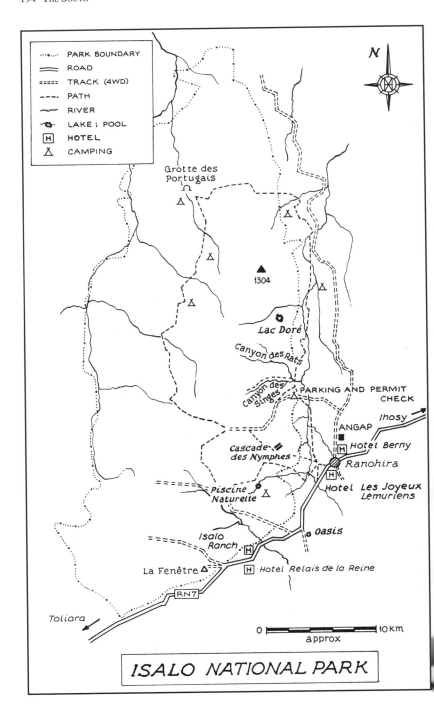

ISALO NATIONAL PARK

'A rutted track from the Horombe side of Ranohira took 45 mins, with some 90° hills. At the end there was a wade through the knee-deep river, then across paddy fields to a mango grove. There we found a campsite complete with officials to check your permit.' (Clare Hermans)

Hikers make the trek direct from the Ranohira church, striding across a flat plain with the Canyons des Singes and des Rats tantalisingly in view the whole time. The hot sun should be taken very seriously: carry two litres of water (and purifying tablets for the canyon water), wear a hat and apply liberal quantities of sun screen. The contrast between the space and yellowness of the plain and the ferny green of the canyon makes the effort well worth while; although when we arrived, sweat-soaked, at the first pool we were taken aback to find an elderly couple and their grandchild sitting in deckchairs at the water's edge. That was when I learned about vehicle access.

The canyon is lovely, although the lemurs that used to be seen there have apparently moved elsewhere. A path goes over rocks and along the edge of the tumbling river; and there are pools into which you can fling yourself at intervals, and, at the top, a small waterfall under which to have a shower. The sheer rocks hung with luxuriant ferns broaden out to provide views of the bare mountain behind, and trees and palms provide shade for a picnic.

For the real Isalo experience you should trek for a few days. The combined Piscine/Canyon des Singes circuit is the most popular and usually done in three days. The first day to the campsite at the swimming pool is only two or three hours, then five or six rugged hours the next day to the canyon. It is then a three-hour walk back to Ranohira.

The less visited parts of the park are even more rewarding. Bishop Brock took a five-day hike. 'The forest of Sakamolia... is one of the most beautiful places I have ever camped in, perhaps not in absolute beauty but in contrasts. In the middle of the dry, grassy plain, surrounded on two sides by massive rock walls, a small crystal-clear river runs over a clean, sandy bottom supporting a 20-metre-wide luxuriant green-belt. Paradise!'

YOUR PARK FEES AND THE LOCAL PEOPLE

Some visitors are sceptical about whether half of their entrance fee really does go to the local people. Here's what has been achieved at Isalo.

At the end of 1994 a management committee was set up to discuss the best use of the funds generated by the Isalo National Park fees. A proposal to divide the money between 12 *Fokotony* adjacent to the park was discarded since the amount per village would be inadequate. Instead the committee agreed to invest the money in improved health-care facilities in Ranohira. An accommodation unit has been built for the families of patients in the hospital, which has also gained some new beds and a new building to house patients with infectious diseases.

Within a year of the start of these projects, a change of attitude towards tourists was noticeable. Villagers who had refused to have tourists on their land made it clear that they now understood the benefits of tourism and asked for a Peace Corps volunteer to be placed in their village.

Warnings

Hiking Isalo is very hot work; bring a minimum of equipment (but remember it gets very cold at night from May to August) or hire porters. Bring plenty of drinking water, even in the rainy season. There have been reports of robberies from tents. This is a serious problem since it is impossible to protect yourself or your possessions. Discuss the matter with your guide and suggest he/she stays to guard the tent if camping in popular places.

The popularity of the park is bringing its own problems. Under every stone lurks a piece of toilet paper. Bring matches and burn yours.

CONTINUING SOUTH

The drive from Isalo to Toliara takes a minimum of four hours. The rugged mountains give way to grasslands, and following the rains there are many flowers – the large white *Crinum firmifolium* and the Madagascar periwinkle – but in the dry season it is quite monotonous. It is the people aspect that makes this final stretch so rewarding. First there are some charming villages – Bara, Mahafaly and Antandroy – and, once you pass Sakaraha, there are some wonderful tombs with *aloalo* near the road. As you get closer to Toliara you'll see your first baobabs and pass through a cotton-growing region. Look out for the enormous nests of hammerkop birds in roadside trees.

25km northeast of Sakaraha is **Zombitse Forest** which is popular with birders. See *Excursions*, page 201. About half an hour beyond **Sakaraha** (Hotel Eden – basic) you will pass the first Mahafaly tombs on your right. There are groups of tombs all the way into Toliara, and they merit several stops (the group nearest Toliara are described under *Excursions*).

About two hours beyond Sakaraha is the small village of **Andranovory** which has a colourful Sunday market. Another hour and Toliara's table mountain, *La Table*, comes into view on the right, and half an hour later you pass the airport and head for the town.

TOLIARA/TOLIARY (TULÉAR)

The pronunciation of the French, Tuléar, and the Malagasy names is the same: 'Toolee-ar'. Toliara's history is centred on St Augustine's Bay, described at the beginning of this chapter, although the name of the town is thought to derive from an encounter with one of those early sailors who asked a local inhabitant where he might moor his boat. The Malagasy replied: *Toly eroa*, 'Mooring down there'. The town itself is relatively modern – 1895 – and designed by an uninspired French architect. His tree-planting was more successfully aesthetic, and the shady tamarind trees, *kily*, give welcome respite from the blazing sun.

There are two good reasons to visit Toliara: the rich marine life with excellent snorkelling and diving, and the Mahafaly, Masikoro and Bara tombs (see *Excursions*).

The beaches north and south of the town have fine white sand, and this whole area is gradually opening up to tourism (fortunately the poor or non-existent roads are an effective deterrent to overdevelopment). Beyond the sandy beaches is an extensive coral reef but this is too far from shore to swim out to – a *pirogue* (for hire at the beach hotels) is necessary. Toliara itself, regrettably, has no beach, just mangroves and mud flats.

At present Toliara's coral reefs are not protected, but the WWF recognises the importance of these in developing ecotourism in the area and a conservation programme is under way, centred at the University of Toliara. The goal of the project is 'to ensure that the coral reefs and coastal zone are effectively conserved through the establishment of a multiple-use marine park and sustainable economic development'. Certainly there is potential for marine ecotourism. Those who spend some time snorkelling or diving here are sometimes disappointed, with pollution and damaged coral beginning to be a problem at Ifaty. Serious underwater buffs should head for Nosy Ve and Nosy Satrana, both of which have more pristine reefs.

Getting there and away

By road Readers of *Muddling through in Madagascar* by Dervla Murphy will be amazed at the beautiful condition of Route Nationale 7. These days quite comfortable vehicles make the journey from Tana, including a new 'luxury bus' which leaves Tana on Tuesdays, returning from Toliara on Thursdays. It is operated by Europe-Voyages in Behoririka in Tana (the office is opposite the Lac Hotel). Tel: 630 49/454 49 for further details and price. In Toliara contact Longo Voyages, tel: 412 68; fax: 417 68.

By air There are flights four days a week, and also a Twin Otter service. Flights are often fully booked, and in the high season the Air Mad office in Toliara is full of desperate *vazahas* trying to get back to Tana. To compound the problems the office is only open from 15.00 to 17.00 (at least in the hot season). Remember you must pay in hard currency. If you can pay in cash your chances of getting on may be better. It's always worth going to the airport whatever they say in the office.

Car hire

Joshua Calixte (tel: 427 47) has been recommended. Also Edgar's Car Tour, Villa Ashik, Andranomena. Tel: 423 19.

Where to stay

Most visitors spending any time in the Toliara area stay at the beach resort of Ifaty (see page 202) but there are some good-value hotels in or near the town.

Category A

Hotel Capricorne BP 158. Tel: 426 20. Fax: 413 20. 310Ff for a double room. About 2km from the town centre (Betania) on RN7. Considered the best of the Toliara hotels. It has a lovely garden, and is well run with excellent food and air-conditioning.

Hotel Plazza BP 486. Tel: 419 00-2. Fax: 419 03. Central, facing the ocean (or – to be more accurate – the mud flats). Hot water, air-conditioned. Good food. English spoken. 210-250Ff single/double room, breakfast 20Ff, dinner 45Ff. Visa credit cards accepted.

Category B

Chez Alain BP 89. Tel: 415 27. Fax: 423 79. One of the most popular *vazaha* hotels (bungalows) in Madagascar. About 55,000Fmg with hot water (cheaper ones available with cold water). Well run, friendly, good food. Mountain bikes available for hire.

Hotel Sud Place de la République. Reasonably priced double rooms (35,000Fmg in 1995) with a basin, shower, WC and hot water. Very good value.

Category C

L'Hotel Ambohimanga Tel: 415 47. Located on the outskirts of Toliara as you arrive on RN7 and recommended by Jim Bond: 'Very good value at 16,000Fmg per night. Comfortable. Very friendly family business, father and daughters speak good French, and some English (and German?). Good food but basic. No electricity, squat toilets and cold showers. Nice quiet setting out of town, cool under trees, but within easy walking distance. M Michou Eugene will run you into town for 5,000Fmg or to the airport for 10,000Fmg.'

Chez Micheline Rue no 18, Anketa. Tel: 415 86. Micheline is a warm, friendly woman (and a good cook) beloved by the *vazahas* who have written recommending her hotel. It is located five minutes' walk (north) from the centre of town, near the *gare routière* for Ifaty.

Hotel Central About 15,000Fmg (1994) and the only hotel in the centre of town. Noisy.

Le Corail Bungalows near the restaurant Étoile de Mer. Clean but very hot during the day (or cold at night, depending on the season) because of the tin roof. Good restaurant.

La Pirogue Tel: 415 37. Inexpensive, but very noisy and food reportedly poor.

Hotel Voamio Equally inexpensive primitive bungalows and – again – noisy (this is one of Toliara's main night clubs), but friendly.

Where to eat

An excellent meal (seafood) can be had in an unpretentious wooden building on the sea front, the **Étoile de Mer**, between the Plazza Hotel and the Voamio. Nearby is the **Club Za Za** (good fish) and **Corail** (pizza), both recommended. According to expatriates, the best food in town is at Chez Alain, located on the road to the airport, and Chez Micheline, but the Étoile de Mer has maintained its standards since I first visited Toliara in 1982.

Also recommended is Le Gourmet Restaurant, and the Chinese Dragon Rouge – 'which serves probably the best food in town at very reasonable prices. Nice, clean and friendly.' (Jytte Arnfred Larson)

Two good places for snacks are the rival **Salons des Thé** near the Hotel Central. They are in a constant battle to pull customers.

Nightlife

'The Za Za Club has a following across the world. You have not been to Tuléar unless you have been to Za Za!' (Hilana Steyn)

Medical clinic

The Clinique Saint-Luc is run by Dr Noel Rakotomavo who speaks excellent English. The profits from his paying beds go towards providing free treatment for the poor. Tel: (9) 421 76.

Warnings

In the cool season (May to October) the nights in Toliara are very cold. The cheaper hotels rarely supply enough blankets.

And in the hot season (November to April) everything closes for midday siesta between 13.00 and 15.00.

Sightseeing and half-day excursions

Toliara has more 'official' sightseeing than most Malagasy towns. Some places are worth the trip, others are not.

In town the most interesting place to visit is the little **museum** of the Sakalava and Mahafaly culture on Bd Philbert Tsiranana. There is a small entry fee. The exhibits are labelled in Malagasy and French, and include some Sakalava erotic tomb sculptures.

The **market** is lively, interesting, and easy to reach by pousse-pousse (bargain hard and have the agreed money ready. Change will not be given).

The most spectacular **tombs** within easy reach of the town are those of the Masikoro, a sub-division of the Sakalava. This small tribe is probably of African origin, and there is speculation that the name comes from *mashokora* which, in parts of Tanzania, means scrub forest. The tombs are off RN7 a little over an hour from Toliara, and are clearly visible on the right. There are several large, rectangular tombs, flamboyantly painted with scenes from the distinguished military life of the deceased, with a few mermaids and Rambos thrown in for good measure.

Another tomb on the outskirts of town, beyond the university, is **King Baba's**

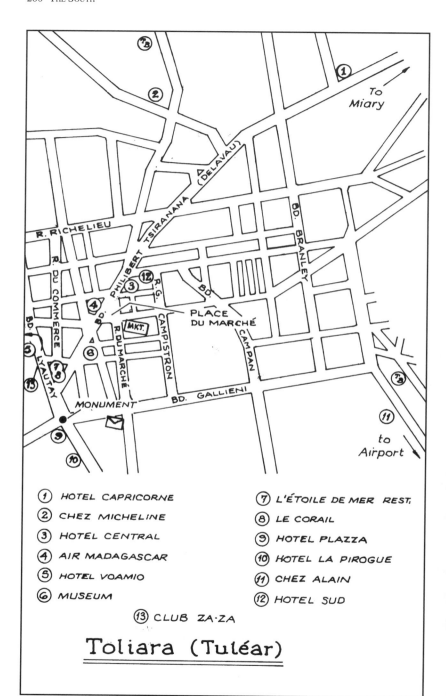

1. HOTEL CAPRICORNE
2. CHEZ MICHELINE
3. HOTEL CENTRAL
4. AIR MADAGASCAR
5. HOTEL VOAMIO
6. MUSEUM
7. L'ÉTOILE DE MER REST.
8. LE CORAIL
9. HOTEL PLAZZA
10. HOTEL LA PIROGUE
11. CHEZ ALAIN
12. HOTEL SUD
13. CLUB ZA·ZA

Toliara (Tuléar)

Tomb. This is set in a grove of Didiera trees and is interesting more for the somewhat bizarre funerary objects (an urn and a huge, cracked bell) displayed there and its spiritual significance to the local people (you may only approach barefoot) than for any aesthetic value. This King Baba, who seems to have died about 100 years ago, was presumably a descendant of one of the Masikoro Kings of Baba mentioned in British naval accounts of the 18th century. These kings used to trade with English ships calling at St Augustine's Bay and gave their family and courtiers English names such as the Prince of Wales and the Duke of Cumberland. On the way to King Baba's Tomb you may visit a little fenced-off park of **banyan trees**, all descending from one 'parent'. This is known as 'the sacred grove' and in theory would be a place for peaceful contemplation, but the hordes of tourist-aware children are a deterrent.

Day excursions from Toliara

Madagascar Airtours has an office in the grounds of the Plazza Hotel and runs some good tours, as do many of the hotels.

Arboretum d'Antsakay

Warmly recommended by Jim Bond is a visit to this collection of rare southwestern flora. It costs 10,000Fmg for a day visit and you can also stay here at the **Auberge de la Table**. The turn-off to the hotel/arboretum is on the right, just beyond the track to St Augustine on RN7. It is clearly signposted. A taxi here costs 18,000Fmg (£3/US$5). 'Hermann and Simone Pétignat are very hospitable. He is a Swiss-born botanist and passionate about conserving the area's rare plant species. Delicious food, with zebu in goat's cheese sauce highly recommended. Tranquil, relaxed setting. A good place to stay the night if you can arrange transport. 24,000Fmg per night.'

Zombitse Forest

This pocket of forest (21,500ha) straddling RN7 some 25km northeast of Sakaraha is of major importance to birdwatchers. Zombitse, and the neighbouring forest of Vohibasia, should by now be protected areas under Madagascar's Environmental Action Plan with a low-involvement programme based on community participation. The forests are an important example of a boundary zone between the Western and Southern Domains of vegetation and so have a high level of biodiversity. By 1996, however, the plans for Vohibasia had not been fulfilled, partly because of fears for the safety of tourists from bandits and cattle thieves.

Zombitse offers the chance to glimpse one of Madagascar's rarest endemics, Appert's greenbul, which is confined to this forest. Many other species may be seen. There are no official paths, only zebu trails, and tree felling in this vulnerable area is sadly evident. Nevertheless, a visit here is most rewarding. We were there at the worst possible time of day, noon, yet the forest was alive with birds and had we had more time I am sure we would have seen many species.

It takes two to three hours to reach Zombitse from Toliara, so serious birdwatchers should leave as early as possible in the morning. You should call in at the WWF office in Sakaraha to ask about permits and guides. A charming guide called Tena Soa accompanied us. He was an expert bird spotter, but unfortunately spoke only Malagasy.

Betioky and Mahafaly tombs

The first 70km are on a paved road, then it's a very dusty 70km or so on dirt road. The trip takes about five hours by private vehicle, six to nine hours by taxi- or truck-brousse (4,000Fmg). It is worth the effort for the chance to see the Mahafaly tombs for which the area is famous. The paintings on the tombs deteriorate quite quickly, while new tombs are always being built, so it is probably pointless to give specific details here. Just rely on your guide's knowledge or keep your eyes peeled. You should see both rectangular, painted tombs and the carved stelae, *aloalo*. Look out for the funeral/tomb 'invoice' which is often painted proudly on the side of the tombs. It is astounding to us Westerners how much money may be spent on these memorials.

In Betioky there is the basic but friendly Hotel Mahafaly. Meals are also available.

BEACH RESORTS NORTH OF TOLIARA

Ifaty has long been established as Toliara's main beach resort, but hotels are now being built further up the coast.

Ifaty

Ifaty offers sand, sea and snorkelling, and has several sets of beach bungalows. There is also some good bird-watching in the spiny forest nearby. The village lies only 26km north of Toliara, but the road is terrible so it can take as much as three hours by taxi-brousse. 'The villagers sometimes add to the difficulty by putting extra sand on the road, then "rescue" you and expect a tip – so they say.' (Clare Hermans)

Where to stay/eat

Mora Mora BP 41. Tel: 410 16. (*Category C*) The longest-established of Ifaty's beach resorts (and rather run down) but the least expensive, offering the same facilities as its neighbours. This is a good centre for birdwatchers since the best bird-finders for the area, Masindraka and his son Mosa, can be contacted via the hotel.

Hotel/Club Bamboo BP 47. Tel: 427 17. (*Category B*) Five minutes' walk north of Mora Mora. French run. A good diving club, run by Richard, a South African. For bookings and latest prices enquire at the Bamboo shop opposite the Hotel Central in town. Good-value accommodation, but meals and service have been reported as disappointing by some readers.

Deck's (*Category C*) Down the beach from the Bamboo Club. 'Reggae atmosphere for 10,000Fmg per room with mozzies.' (Jim Bond)

Dunes Hotel (*Category B*) BP 285. Tel: 428 85. A few kilometres south of Mora Mora, this is a set of concrete bungalows with two adjoining bedrooms: 62 rooms in all. Good restaurant, buffet and barbecue at weekends, and a tennis court. Recommended for water sports. 340Ff per bungalow. Transport from Toliara arranged. 'There are gas geysers in each room to provide hot water, but the water pressure was too low to activate the geysers.' (Joy Shannon). Waltraut Treilles found the same, and 'when I saw a three-inch cockroach on my bed sheet, I knew I was back in Madagascar.'

Hotel Lakana Vezo c/o Capricorne, Ifaty, BP 158. Tel: 462 20. (*Category A*) 10 bungalows. 310Ff per bungalow. One hour's walk south of the Dunes hotel. 'Peter Deswarte, the manager, goes out of his way to make your stay enjoyable, and Vincent the chef will prepare (at your request) calamari, octopus, crayfish...' (Hilana Steyn). The Club Nautique is run very professionally by Denis and Natalie Guillamot, with a wide variety of activities available, although snorkelling and scuba diving are favourites. The hotel also offers powerboat excursions to Nosy Ve and Anakao, as well as trips to the spiny forest. The boat excursion takes 1hr 30min, and is best started at early morning because the sea gets rough later.

If you are on a tight budget there are several alternative eateries in Ifaty. Local people will approach you on the beach to suggest their particular establishment.

Mandio Rano

Jim Bond recommends **Chez Bernard** at this village 35km north of Toliara.'Ideal for the discerning independent traveller – no tour groups. Five peaceful, comfortable bungalows near a quiet stretch of beach. Not far to walk to PK32 (the road). Excellent food, huge portions, 80,000Fmg incl. Rustic douche facilities. No phone, so pot luck off the taxi-brousse. Bernard Forgeau is a very pleasant and interesting Breton bush-hand and explorer. BP 283, Toliara 601.'

CONTINUING NORTH TO MOROMBE AND MORONDAVA

A sandy track runs from the Mora Mora (Ifaty) roadhead (inland) to Morombe. This road is used mostly by cotton trucks; the only time it may be impassable is after rain in February. A taxi-brousse to Morombe leaves Toliara or Ifaty twice a week and takes about 22 hours. If you want to continue to Morondava, there is a choice of sea (by pirogue, risky) or road. A vehicle known as the 'Bon Bon Caramel' leaves Toliara at 06.00 on Thursdays, spending the night at Manja (good food and bungalows) and arriving in Morondava Friday evening. For a full description of this glorious Mercedes truck and its crew, see the Morondava section in *Chapter Fourteen.*

An easier overland option is to take the transport offered by Lakana Veso to service their new bungalow complex in Morombe. More information – on the bungalows as well as the transport – from Peter at the Lakana Veso in Ifaty.

As an easy alternative to travelling overland there are flights between Toliara and Morondava via Morombe.

SOUTH OF TOLIARA

New beach hotels are opening up in the very attractive region south of Toliara, and it seems likely that these will soon become more popular than Ifaty.

St Augustine's Bay (Baie St Augustin)

Normally reached by *vedette* or *pirogue*, but also accessible by road, St Augustine has dramatic cliffs, a lovely beach and loads of history. It was the site of an ill-fated British colony, abandoned in 1646, and later frequented by pirates. St Augustine's Bay was mentioned by Daniel Defoe in *The King of Pirates*.

Where to stay

La Mangrove St Augustine's Bay, 8km from RN7 (the turn-off is signposted). A lovely French-run hotel (bungalows) on the north bank of the Onilahy, across the river from Anakao. Bungalows cost 50,000Fmg, and it has one of Madagascar's best restaurants. The diving instructor, Alan, is English and diving lessons including a *baptême* (first dive) plus excursion to Nosy Ve can be arranged here. This is a good centre for exploration. Near the hotel is a natural swimming pool at Grottes Sarodrano

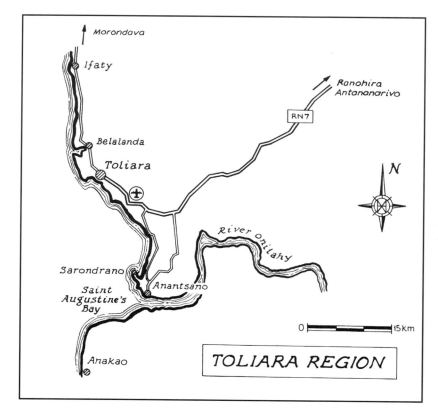

– cool, fresh water flows from the mountain into the pool and a layer of warm salt water flows on top of it from the sea. There are impressive sand-dunes to be visited, spectacular cliffs on the edge of the bay, and even hang gliding from the top of a nearby mountain. For naturalists a track leads up through spiny forest. There is a 'bizarre ensemble of reptiles which can be seen at night and local guides can show you where to find wild ring-tailed lemurs. If the hotel is full you can camp there and use the facilities.' (Derek Schuurman)

Anne Axel reports that some of the bikes for rent here are in poor condition, and a faulty bike in such hot, dehydrating conditions can be dangerous. If you hire one check it carefully, including saddle, brakes and gears.

Chez Andrea A new, Italian-owned hotel by the St Augustine sand dunes. Very friendly, excellent food and service. Excursions and transfers from Toliara.

Anakao

To reach Anakao you need either to take the package offered by Safari Vezo (see below) or Lakana Vezo or – if you are truly adventurous – to organise your own pirogue from the fishermen that gather near Rue Marius Jalep, 400m south of the Plazza Hotel in Toliara. 'We left at 2 o'clock in the morning when there was almost no wind. The fishermen said it would take almost three hours... in reality it took nine hours.' (Luc Selleslagh)

Where to stay/eat

Safari Vezo BP 427, Toliara 601. Tel: 413 81. This popular hotel, an unpretentious set of beach bungalows, is now run by Monique Vachoud, the Swiss lady previously at La Mangrove. Bungalows 120,000-160,000Fmg. Monique organises diving excursions, and the restaurant overlooking the sea is excellent. This hotel is a great favourite of visiting yachties from South Africa.

Boat transfers from Toliara cost 170Ff per person.

Nosy Ve and Nosy Satrana

Nosy Ve (the name means 'Is there an island?'!) lies 3km west of Anakao, and is a sacred site for the Vezo people who annually sacrifice zebu at its northern point. It has a long history of European domination: the first landing was by a Dutchman in 1595, and Nosy Ve was officially taken over by the French in 1888 before their conquest of the mainland although it is hard to see why: it is a flat, scrub-covered little island. What makes it special to modern-day invaders is the excellent snorkelling on its fringing reefs and the breeding colony of red-tailed tropic birds which are gradually increasing in number. As there are plans to create a marine reserve there, camping is no longer allowed. At present Vezo fishermen exploit part of the reef (although they, too, are not supposed to sleep on the island), but snorkellers still have plenty to delight them.

Nearby Nosy Satrana offers equally good snorkelling but no tropic birds.

Itampolo

The hotel expansion south continues with a new complex being built in this small town some 70km down the coast from Anakao. Details from Chez Alain in Toliara.

Lake Tsimanampetsotsa

This Strict Nature Reserve is a haven for waterfowl and other rare endemic birds, and as such is not accessible to tourists.

BEZA-MAHAFALY SPECIAL RESERVE

This reserve is the model for the WWF's integrated conservation and development efforts. It was established at the request of local people who volunteered to give up using part of the forest. In return they have been helped with a variety of social and agricultural projects, for example by the provision of a school and the building of irrigation channels.

The government has designated the reserve as its number one priority from ten sites in the Environmental Action Plan. Agroforestry is being developed under the guidance of Tana's School of Agronomy and the Direction des Eaux et Forêts, and many research projects take place there. The goal has always been to integrate conservation and rural development projects around the reserve, and to support the sustainable use of natural resources.

The reserve protects two distinct types of forest: spiny forest and gallery (riverine) forest. In this it mirrors Berenty, but there the comparison ends. Tourism is not discouraged, and there are plans for better facilities and information, but at present the Malagasy locals and researchers come first. This is an enormously rewarding place for the serious naturalist or the seriously interested. 'This was one of our best experiences with lemurs in the entire country. The reserve has a lot of ring-tails and sifakas, and some of the best spiny forest we saw. It makes an ideal two-day trip from Tuléar, the drive taking about five hours.' (David Bonderman)

Anne Axel's 1995 account of her visit to Beza-Mahafaly is so vivid that I've decided to include almost all of it. 'Getting to the reserve was half the fun! I took the "Betioky Bus" from Toliara to Betioky, where I stayed overnight at the Hotel Mahafaly. Meanwhile I tried to locate a zebu cart available for hire. I finally found one the next day for 25,000Fmg, with an additional charge of 10,000Fmg for a guide (mandatory).

'The zebu cart ride took six hours and was most unusual. Travelling at such a slow place on a trail, I was able to get a real feel for the area, but it certainly was rough on my body! I have to admit I was a bit nervous at first, venturing off into the bush alone with two strangers, but I checked with some women in town before I left, and they seemed to think it would be safe.

'We arrived at Beza-Mahafaly reserve by nightfall, and I pitched my tent in the small village at the park entrance. I stayed there for four nights (5,000Fmg/ night), mingling with researchers and some WWF employees. I spent each morning and most afternoons in the forest, being free to roam around as I pleased. The reserve is set up in a grid pattern, very like Ampijoroa, and a student gave me a rough drawing of the reserve, so I felt comfortable ambling around on my own. I accompanied students into the forest once, and we followed the same troop of ring-tailed lemurs for hours. Fascinating!

'I really enjoyed my stay at Beza. The researchers and staff made me feel welcome, and I often joined them for meals, contributing to the food kitty each time (approx. 500Fmg per meal). They have a well-stocked library of books in English including novels and scientific texts.

'The forest is a photographer's dream. Often the ring-tailed lemurs would come down to the forest floor to forage, making photography and observation much easier. There is a variety of wildlife, and without very heavy tree foliage it's relatively easy to see it all. It was so refreshing to be able to walk around without a guide. I could sit and watch one group of lemurs for hours without feeling as if I was boring somebody else.

'I was extremely fortunate to land a ride back to Toliara in a WWF Land Rover. We did the full trip in less than six hours, whereas it took more than 12 hours to do the same trip using public transportation. I have never ridden in such style!'

Practical information

Beza-Mahafaly is 30km from Betioky. To get there you need a 4WD vehicle, a zebu cart, a bicycle, or a strong pair of legs. The indefatigable John Kupiec walked from Betioky, despite warnings of bandits. 'Many times I was warned not to go somewhere alone. Whenever I did, I always found them to be the safest, most peaceful areas, including the walk to and from Beza Mahafaly.'

There is no accommodation, but a space for tents costs 5,000Fmg per night; you should bring your own food. Permits can be purchased at the reserve. Guides cost 3,000Fmg for a two-hour excursion and speak only Malagasy. If you want to go out with a guide all day you will need to negotiate the price.

THE ROAD TO TOLAGNARO (FORT DAUPHIN)

A taxi-brousse from Toliara to Tolagnaro takes three days. The fastest public vehicle is the Besalara truck, a Mercedes; the slowest is the Bienvenue. It's a shame to pass straight through such an exciting area, however. Much more interesting is to rent a vehicle and driver, or to do the trip by a combination of walking and whatever transport comes along. Luc Selleslagh took this option (in 1994) and provided the information that follows.

Betioky to Ampanihy

Betioky is a day's taxi-brousse ride from Toliara. The best hotel is now the Mamyrano Annexe, 25,000Fmg (1995) and pretty basic. There is also the popular Hotel Mahafaly.

Some 20km south of Betioky is the small village of **Ambatry**. The Mahafaly tombs near here are particularly interesting. Next comes **Ejeda**, about 2½ hours from Betioky on a reasonable dirt road. In the dry season you can watch the activity on the dry river bed. Holes are dug to reach the water: upstream for drinking, midstream for washing, and downsteam for clothes. The hotel here is 'good value for money: almost no value but also almost no money'.

About 10km south of Ejeda are a few big Mahafaly tombs, one with over 50 zebu horns. Look for them on the right, on a hill.

Ejeda to Ampanihy takes about five hours by truck on a very bad, rocky road.

Ampanihy

The name means 'the place of bats'; for a while it was the place of the mohair goats, but now that industry has collapsed it's just a town on the road south. But it's worth a couple of days. Luc recommends a visit to the WWF nursery for endemic plants, near the Protestant church. Walk 2km south to some good Mahafaly tombs.

Where to stay/eat

Motel Relais d'Ampanihy A touch of luxury in the desert. No hot water. Wonderful food. The owner, Luc Vital, can organise excursions to the forest adjoining the river Menarandra (lemurs), and to see baobabs and Mahafaly tombs.

Hotel Tahio About 300m from the big market. Very friendly, economically priced. Good meals. Showers. Highly recommended.

Ampanihy to Ambovombe

After Ampanihy you enter Antandroy country and will understand why they are called 'people of the thorns'. The road deteriorates (if you thought that possible) as you make your way to **Tranaroa** (about five hours). There's an interesting Antandroy tomb here crowned by an aeroplane which moves in the wind. Another five hours and you approach Beloha on an improving road (much favoured by tortoises, which thrive in the area since it is *fady* to eat them) and with tombs all around.

Beloha is probably the best place to spend the night on this leg of the journey. It has a basic hotel, Mon Plaisir, with a restaurant (10,000Fmg in 1995), and elsewhere there is a bar, Les Trois Frères, which serves ice-cold drinks. Luc recommends a visit to the new Catholic church with its beautiful stained glass, made by a local craftsman. Near Beloha is a good area of spiny forest.

Between Beloha and **Tsihombe** is the most interesting stretch of the entire journey. There are baobabs, tortoises (sadly it is not *fady* for the local Antanosoy to eat them) and some wonderful tombs. 'On one occasion it was like arriving at a journey-fair. A tomb with a life-size taxi-brousse, one with a big aeroplane, and another with an ocean steamer! There are also people to ask for money to see these attractions.' These tombs are about 33km before Tsihombe. 'If "be" means "big" then "Tsihom" must mean "cockroach"!' Luc describes his night with an army of huge, hissing cockroaches (actually one of my favourite Malagasy creatures, but I appreciate that I am in a minority), a generously-proportioned spider and a scorpion. 'This was not a hotel room but a terrarium!' Rupert Parker reports that in 1997 there is still no proper hotel but several *hotelys* have rooms.

After Tsihombe the road improves and it is a short journey to Ambovombe.

Ambovombe

With the end in sight, most travellers prefer to push on to Tolagnaro, but there are several hotels in Ambovombe: the **Relais des Androy** (no running water; good food, 23,000Fmg), the **Oasis** (running water, 25,000Fmg), and the **Fanantenana** (very basic, but only 10,000Fmg). Ambovombe has a good Monday market.

Amboasary to Tolagnaro
Amboasary

About 30km from Ambovombe is the village that marks the turn-off to Berenty. There is now simple accommodation here (it looks like a local initiative, so deserves support). The **Hotel-Restaurant Mandrare** is just after the village and is a series of Antanosy-style huts. You need your own sleeping bag etc, but food is provided.

If you decide to drop in to Berenty, thus saving the very high transfer fee from Tolagnaro (Fort Dauphin), bear in mind that a permit is needed (purchasable only in the Hotel Dauphin, Tolagnaro). It's better to go to Amboasary Sud instead!

Hotel Bon Coin is on the way to Lake Anony (see page 223). There is also a restaurant here.

From Amboasary to Tolagnaro is less than two hours on a paved road.

FAUX CAP AND CAP SAINTE MARIE

If you are in a four-wheel-drive vehicle, or are a good hiker, you should consider taking a side trip west to the southernmost point of Madagascar (see box). In the dry season an ordinary saloon car can probably make the trip.

Faux Cap is a lonely, beautiful spot, with wild breakers, enormous shifting sand-dunes, and a chance to find fragments of *aepyornis* eggs. In 1993 Luc Selleslagh walked the 30km from Tsihombe and was accommodated by the very friendly Président du Fokontany and his wife. Like many places in Madagascar, however, Faux Cap is being opened up to tourists and there are now beach bungalows and a small restaurant.

Where to stay/eat

Hotel Cactus About 18 basic bungalows for 30,000Fmg. No running water or electricity but beautifully located and run by the very friendly Marie Zela. Good food with huge portions for 10,500Fmg (fish) to 25,000Fmg (lobster). A great place to relax for a few days.

Cap Sainte Marie is an equally spectacular place with high sandstone cliffs and dwarf plants resembling a rock garden. It is also possible to get here without a vehicle. Andrew Cooke writes: 'I suppose the highlight for me was taking a taxi-brousse to Beloha and then taking a chavette to Lavanono (on the coast) and then walking to Cap Sainte Marie (the distance is 30km which took us two days). All the way we met great hospitality. Water is in very short

A CYCLONE AT THE END OF THE WORLD

This story by Rupert Parker arrived shortly before we went to press. Not many people make it to Faux Cap and not many experience a cyclone, so here is his (abbreviated) account.

We've been to all the obvious places in Madagascar and fancied a trip to the southernmost tip. Five gruelling hours in the back of a truck with 50 other people and assorted animals brought us from Fort Dauphin to Ambovombe, then with difficulty we found another truck to take us to Tsiombe. The helpful people at the hotely told us that there were occasional water trucks to Faux Cap, but otherwise we'd have to walk. We set off carrying the ever important supplies of Eau Vive, passing some interesting Mahafaly tombs, but with 30km ahead of us we couldn't afford too many diversions. After two hours' walking we were lucky – the local priest on his way to a funeral stopped for us. As he sped over the bumps in the road I remember thinking that if this was the sort of care he lavished on his flock, he wasn't going to have too many converts among the Antandroy.

When we arrived in Faux Cap excited children pointed us to the Hotel Cactus, a collection of wooden bungalows nestling on the edge of the sand dunes overlooking the sea. Marie Zela, the proprietor, produced that most welcome of sights in Madagascar, bottles of ice cold Three Horses beer. Marie is the local school teacher and her husband is the president of the local council; they have 14 children but she still manages to cook good meals.

The hotel is in a beautiful spot overlooking a deserted beach. Out to sea there is a coral reef which creates a natural lagoon, and is also home to lobsters which the local boys collect for hungry vazahas' suppers. There are spectacular sunsets, and it really does feel like the end of the world. That night there was a cyclone warning on the radio.

Next day we explored the huge sand dunes and searched for fragments of *Aepyornis* eggs. Around 4 o'clock it began to rain heavily, the wind picked up, and soon we were prisoners in our bungalow wondering whether everyone was going to be blown away. We physically had to hold the door shut against the howling wind. The rain by this time was horizontal. Marie Zela's house, the only structure made of durable materials, was directly opposite the door of our bungalow; and, as we watched through the crack in the door with mounting fear, we saw the corrugated iron roof began to lift, gently at first because it was held down by stones, but then – almost in slow motion – first one section and then the next suddenly were flying around, landing within inches of our door. I remembered that it wasn't cyclones themselves that caused fatalities, but flying materials which had the habit of decapitating people.

After it had disposed of the roof opposite, and also, as we found out later, of the roofs of the school and other buildings, the wind suddenly died down, the rain slowed to a mere drizzle, and everyone was emerging into the open to inspect the damage. Fortunately there was still about half an hour of daylight left, and Marie Zela and her family gathered up the missing parts of their roof, as though it were the most natural thing in the world, refixed them in position, weighed down by bags of sand, and proceeded to start cooking the dinner. As befits an Englishman after experiencing his first cyclone, I ordered a cup of tea.

supply.' Note that since Cap Sainte Marie is a reserve, a permit must be purchased, and this should be arranged in Tana. Visitors arriving without a permit have been turned away.

This is a good area to see humpback whales; between September and November they can be observed quite close to shore with their calves.

TOLAGNARO/TAOLAÑARO (FORT DAUPHIN)
History
The remains of two forts can still be seen in or near this town on the extreme southeast tip of Madagascar: Fort Flacourt built in 1643; and one that dates from 1504, so the oldest building in the country, which was erected by shipwrecked Portuguese sailors. This ill-fated group of 80 reluctant colonists stayed about 15 years before falling foul of the local tribes. The survivors of the massacre fled to the surrounding countryside where disease and hostile natives finished them off.

1642 saw a French expedition, organised by the Société Française de l'Orient and led by Sieur Pronis with instructions to 'found colonies and commerce in Madagascar and to take possession of it in the name of His Most Christian Majesty'. An early settlement at the Bay of Sainte Luce was soon abandoned in favour of a healthier peninsula to the south, and a fort was built and named after the Dauphin (later Louis XIV) in 1643. At first the Antanosy were quite keen on the commerce part of the deal but were less enthusiastic about losing their land. The heavily defended fort only survived by use of force and with many casualties from both sides. The French finally abandoned the place in 1674, but their 30-year occupation formed one of the foundations of the later claim to the island as a French colony. During this period the first published work on Madagascar was written by Pronis's successor, Étienne de Flacourt. His *Histoire de la Grande Île de Madagascar* brought the island's amazing flora and fauna to the attention of European naturalists, and is still used as a valuable historical source book.

Tolagnaro/Fort Dauphin today
The town itself is unattractive, but it is the most beautifully located of all popular destinations in Madagascar. Built on a small peninsula, the town is bordered on three sides by beaches and breakers and backed by high green mountains which dwindle into spiny forest to the west. More geared to tourism than any other Malagasy mainland town, Tolagnaro offers a variety of exceptionally interesting excursions (Berenty, the spiny forest, the Portuguese Fort, the Bay of Sainte Luce) and some fine beaches.

Most people (myself included) still use the French name, Fort Dauphin, but to be consistent with the rest of the book I shall stick to Tolagnaro in the text.

Warnings Tolagnaro is buffeted by almost continuous strong winds in September and much of October. Muggings have been reported on the beach below the Hotel Dauphin.

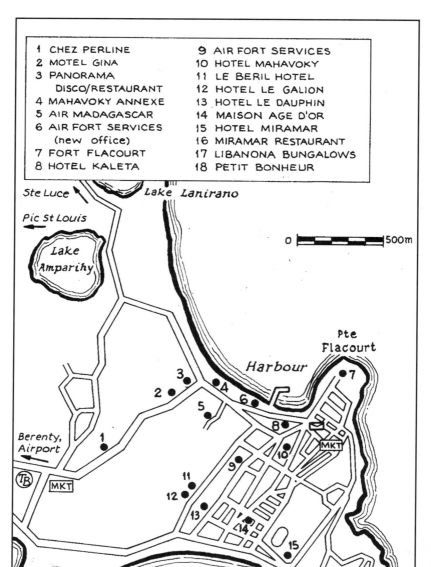

1	CHEZ PERLINE	9	AIR FORT SERVICES
2	MOTEL GINA	10	HOTEL MAHAVOKY
3	PANORAMA DISCO/RESTAURANT	11	LE BERIL HOTEL
4	MAHAVOKY ANNEXE	12	HOTEL LE GALION
5	AIR MADAGASCAR	13	HOTEL LE DAUPHIN
6	AIR FORT SERVICES (new office)	14	MAISON AGE D'OR
7	FORT FLACOURT	15	HOTEL MIRAMAR
8	HOTEL KALETA	16	MIRAMAR RESTAURANT
		17	LIBANONA BUNGALOWS
		18	PETIT BONHEUR

Ste Luce

Pic St Louis

Lake Laniarano

Lake Amparihy

0 — 500m

Pte Flacourt

Harbour

Berenty, Airport

MKT

MKT

Lake D'Ambinanikely

TOLAGNARO (FORT DAUPHIN)

Getting there and away

By road The overland route from Tana is reportedly best done with the companies SONATRA or TATA which operate from the taxi-brousse station on the far side of Lake Anosy. They go via Ihosy, Betroka and Ambovombe. You should book your seat as far in advance as possible.

By air There are flights to Tolagnaro four days a week (check the latest Air Mad schedule). Sit on the right for the best views of Tolagnaro's mountains and bays. Flights are usually heavily booked.

Where to stay

Most of Tolagnaro belongs to M Jean de Heaulme, the owner of Berenty reserve. His hotels are the Dauphin, the Galion, and the Miramar. You are expected to stay in one of these if you want to visit Berenty, but it is not compulsory.

Category A

Hotels **Le Dauphin** and **Le Galion** PO Box 54. Tel: 210 48. The Dauphin is the main hotel and Galion its annexe. Meals (excellent) are taken in the Dauphin which has a lovely garden. Prices are about 300Ff single and 330Ff double. The manager, Saymoi, is very friendly and helpful and speaks good English.

Le Beril Hotel New, opposite Le Dauphin, rooms for 100,000Fmg.

Hotel Miramar The most beautifully situated hotel and best restaurant in Tolagnaro. On a promontory overlooking Libanona beach, which is excellent for swimming, sunbathing and tide-pooling. There is a limited number of rooms costing the same as the Dauphin, through which bookings must be made. The restaurant is about 50 metres from the hotel itself, with a superb view overlooking Libanona beach: a rough walk in the dark (bring a torch). Meals cost about 25,000Fmg.

Category B

Libanona Beach BP 70. Tel: 213 78; fax: 213 84. Its location vies with the Miramar as the best in Tolagnaro, but the bungalows vary in quality: 55,000Fmg. Breakfast 10,000Fmg, dinner 25,000Fmg.

Petit Bonheur BP 210. Tel: 211 56. Another very friendly hotel on Libanona beach. Single/double rooms with a shared shower are 50,000Fmg (or 65,000Fmg if by the sea) and bungalows are 60,000Fmg.

Hotel Kaleta BP 70. Tel: 212 87; fax: 213 84. Under the same management as Libanona Beach (both are government-owned). A 32-room hotel in the centre of town offering a good alternative for those looking for comfort and lemurs but unable to afford the De Heaulme/Berenty prices. Run by a husband and wife team, Armand and Janette Rivert. Rooms 65,000–80,000Fmg (the more expensive ones have a view over the sea). Breakfast 10,000Fmg, dinner 25,000Fmg.

Motel Gina BP 107. Tel/fax: 212 66. Pleasant thatched or brick bungalows located on the outskirts of town, ranging from 40,000Fmg to 100,000Fmg. There's an excellent – though quite expensive – restaurant. 'What impressed me was the care taken to reconfirm my flight, to send baggage ahead to the airport, and obtain a boarding card so I did not have to wait too long.' (Jay Heale) The Gina has another advantage: unlike the other hotels it accepts Visa credit cards. An annexe has opened across the road. 65,000Fmg.

Hotel Casino A little further out of town and similar in quality to the Gina.

Category C
Hotel Mahavoky Town centre opposite the Catholic cathedral. 30,000Fmg for rooms with communal (outside) shower and WC. Occupies an old missionary school which gives added interest. There's a helpful, English-speaking manager and excellent restaurant. The old hotel is becoming run down, but there is now a new **annexe** with good rooms overlooking the sea for 45,000Fmg.

Maison Age d'Or Readers' praise has been heaped on this establishment and its hugely hospitable host, Krishna Hasimboto, known universally as Monsieur Maison Age d'Or. He and his family speak only French, but if you can communicate in this language you will learn a great deal about Madagascar. Jim Bond reports in 1996 that M Hasimboto lacks clients because of uncooperative taxi-drivers (he refuses to pay them a backhander). Do support this enterprising man. 'Good food if you give him notice, especially if he can get you lobster.'

Chez Anita 50m from the Age d'Or and similarly priced and recommended.

Where to eat
In Tolagnaro eating is taken seriously. All the Category A hotels serve very good food with an emphasis on 'fruits de la mer', and the Gina's restaurant is also recommended. Favourites with expatriates are the **Mahavoky Annexe**, across from the BTM bank. 'An excellent little restaurant. The name means "to make satisfied with food!"' and **Chez Perline**: 'A great small resto near the markets. Wonderful food but expect to wait at least an hour to get it!' This continues to be a hotely with attitude (1995), so it's lucky the food's still good as the service seems to be worse! **Chez Anita** serves delicious *Sambos* and zebu brochettes, while providing entertainment with a television that alternates between French-dubbed action movies and Malagasy pop-stars singing favourite tunes. The sound and picture quality is so bad it's impossible to know what's going on, but everyone sits glued to the tube anyway! There are other small restaurants in the market area, some of which serve great food. Making your own discoveries is part of the fun.

Other recommendations include the **Panorama** (renowned for its disco; see *Nightlife*) and La Détente in the same building as Air Fort Services, with a fine view overlooking the bay. On the road to the airport is **Relax Mini Resto**, which has a good selection of meals at very reasonable prices. 'An excellent place to stop for a rest on your return from climbing Pic St Louis.'

Nightlife
'The Panorama disco is an institution for locals. Open every night except Mondays, this is rated by everyone who has been there as Madagascar's best

disco. Much of its appeal is in its location, perched on the edge of the bay. When you get too hot and sweaty from dancing you can take a stroll outside to cool off in the ocean breeze and watch the waves roll in. Especially great at full moon.' (R Mulder)

Vehicle hire/tour operator

Air Fort Services is a tour operator which hires out bicycles, vehicles (from cars to buses) and even small planes, as well as offering a variety of tours. They are located on Ave Gallieni. Postal address: BP 159. Tel: 212 34 or 212 64; fax: 212 24 or 261 9. There is another Air Fort Services office in the town centre.

Excursions around town

Apart from its lively market, Tolagnaro offers a choice of beach and mountain.

The beach is **Libanona**, with excellent swimming and superb tide-pools. Admirers of the weird and wonderful can spend many hours poking around at low tide. The pools to the right of the beach seem the best. Look out for a bizarre, frilly nudibranch or sea-hare, anemones, and other extraordinary invertebrates. There is another beach below the Hotel Dauphin, but this is dirty (turdy) and there have been muggings here.

Pic Louis, the mountain that dominates the town, is quite an easy climb up a good path and offers nice views. The trail starts opposite SIFOR, the sisal factory about 3km along the road to Lanirano. Alternatively you can take a taxi to the RC mission near the airport; the trail goes up past the statue of the Virgin Mary. Allow at least a half day to get up there and back – or better still take a picnic. It is a strenuous climb in the midday sun. If you're unsure about doing it on your own several hotels/tour operators run trips up there.

Another arm of the De Heaulme empire is the **Botanical Gardens** situated

---

THE LIBANONA ECOLOGY CENTRE

Madagascar suffers from a great shortage of trained Malagasy conservationists. The Libanona Ecology Centre was set up in Tolagnaro (Fort Dauphin) in August 1995, to help address this problem. It is currently managed by Mark Fenn of the World Wide Fund for Nature, together with a team of Malagasy professors. Classrooms and a library were built using funds from the Andrew Lees Memorial Trust, started after the tragic death of Friends of the Earth's Campaigns Director in Madagascar in 1995.

Various research and teaching programmes are being developed which cover a broad range of biological disciplines and also sociology and resource economics. Malagasy conservationists trained at the Centre teach in the surrounding villages and work with local people to find more sustainable ways of farming, timber-cropping, and fishing. The Centre also trains local tourist guides and runs various training programmes and summer schools for visiting scientists and students from abroad.

For further information, please contact Dr Christine Orengo in London: 0171 419 3284 or email orengo@biochemistry.ucl.ac.uk

MINING IN THE SOUTH: AN ENVIRONMENTAL AND SOCIOLOGICAL DILEMMA

The dry south of Madagascar has large deposits of titanium dioxide. Among other things this mineral is used as a base for paint. The Canadian company, Qit-Fer et Titane Inc (owned by RTZ), in partnership with the Malagasy government, want to start mining for this mineral. Their plan is for the mine to be active for 40 or 50 years. It would be the largest such venture in Madagascar and would involve the building of a US$260-million factory, with a further US$90 million required to create a new harbour.

The project could bring 500 new jobs to a severely depressed area of the country. Jobs would create prosperity which would reduce the pressure on the environment caused by *tavy* and the felling of trees for charcoal. The project would involve clearing some coastal littoral forest with its endemic flora and fauna.

An RTZ representative writes: 'RTZ I&T and our Malagasy partner are well aware of the unique natural environment of Madagascar and the worldwide concern that it should be preserved and protected. That is why, in 1987, a comprehensive environmental study program which covered the range of physical, biological and community environments was initiated. An international team of specialists, each recognized in their respective fields, was drawn from Madagascar, Canada, the United States, Britain, Australia and France. A key issue identified by the report is the special botanical interest of the littoral forest that occupies some of the area to be mined. Their studies concluded that with the appropriate conservation and rehabilitation programs, the mining could proceed with virtually total conservation of fauna values and protection of most floral endemic species including all types of representative forest. A proposed conservation program seeks to protect significant parcels of littoral forests which are on or adjacent to the deposit. Therefore only about 2,200ha of littoral forest area would be subject to mining and rehabilitation practices.

'Additional environmental studies are required prior to an environmental review process by the government of Madagascar. After that, feasibility studies must be completed along with financing before an investment decision can be considered.'

Friends of the Earth respond: 'While Madagascar is keen for foreign investment, large multinational companies will not necessarily provide the answer. Exploitative activities, such as those proposed by RTZ for the unique southeastern coastal region, will provide quick and relatively short-lived earnings which will largely be spent on paying off the country's debts at the expense of some of the Earth's most unique and precious habitats. Friends of the Earth believes that the international community should encourage the Malagasy government to develop small-scale sustainable economic activity from which both the local people and the natural environment can benefit. FOE also believes that large-scale debt cancellation is necessary for the country's development.'

about 16km out of town towards Sainte Luce.

You can also stroll around the fort. Jay Heale had an unexpected experience here: 'Suddenly I realised that, from my perch on one of the crumbling turrets, I was overlooking the yard of the local prison. The inmates waved, I waved back, the guards grinned. In Africa I had been arrested and interrogated because, unwittingly, I had carried a camera within sight of a prison. I preferred the Madagascar experience!'

Further afield

Apart from Berenty, which is described later, there are numerous places to visit in this beautiful part of Madagascar. If you haven't a car you will probably need to join an organised trip. Many hotels run excursions and Air Fort Services go to most places.

Portuguese Fort (Île aux Portuguais)

The tour to the old fort, built in 1504, involves a pirogue ride up the river Vinanibe, about 6km from Tolagnaro, and then a short walk to the sturdy-looking stone fortress (the walls are one metre thick) set in zebu-grazed parkland.

Baie Sainte Luce

About 65km northeast of Tolagnaro is the beautiful and historically interesting bay where the French colonists of 1638 first landed. This tour is universally praised by all who've done it.

Lokaro

Another popular excursion which begins at Lake Lanirano, just north of Tolagnaro, then passes through various waterways. The trip culminates in a 1½ hour walk to the final destination, a beach resort. The cost includes meals.

BERENTY RESERVE

This is the key destination of most package tours and I've never known a visitor who hasn't loved Berenty (well, there was one...). The combination of tame lemurs, comfortable accommodation and the tranquillity of the forest trails makes this *the* Madagascar memory for many people. The danger is that Berenty is already becoming overcrowded, and too many groups bring problems. Fortunately there is only a limited amount of accommodation, so if you can arrange to spend a night or two you can still have the reserve to yourself in the magic hours of dawn and dusk.

Visits to the reserve must be organised through the Hotel Dauphin (or the Capricorne in Toliara) and are expensive: 950Ff for one to three people for transport (350Ff per extra person) and 350Ff per double bungalow in the reserve. If you use your own transport you must buy a permit at the Hotel Dauphin. This costs 100,000Fmg.

The road to Berenty

The reserve lies some 80km to the west of Tolagnaro, amid a vast sisal plantation, and the drive there is part of the experience. For the first half of the journey the skyline is composed of rugged green mountains often backed by menacing grey clouds or obscured by rain. Travellers' trees (*ravenala*) dot the landscape, and near Ranopiso is a grove of the very rare three-cornered palm, *Neodypsis decary*. To see an example close to, wait until you arrive in Berenty where there is one near the entrance gate.

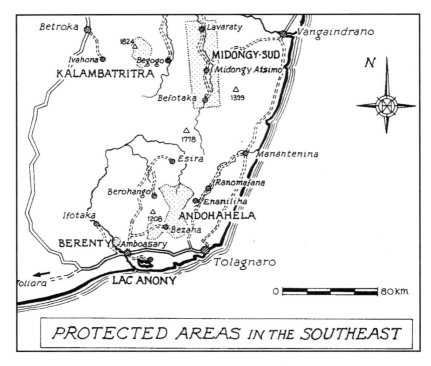

PROTECTED AREAS IN THE SOUTHEAST

Your first stop is to visit some pitcher plants – *Nepenthes madagascariensis* – whose nearest relatives are in Asia. The yellow 'flowers' (actually modified leaves) lure insects into their sticky depths where they are digested, probably for their nitrogen content.

The next (optional) stop before reaching the spiny forest is at an Antanosy 'tomb' (actually the dead are buried elsewhere) known as the tomb of Ranonda. It was carved by the renowned sculptor Fiasia. The artistry of this unpainted wooden memorial is of a very high standard although the carvings are deteriorating in the frequently wet weather. There's a girl carrying the Christian emblems of bible and cross; someone losing a leg to a crocodile; and the most famous piece, a boatload of people who are said to have died in a pirogue accident. On the far side there used to be a charming herd of zebu, portrayed with unusual liveliness (a cow turns her head to lick her suckling calf). In 1990 the cow and her calf were ripped away by thieves. To add to the poignancy, a row of cattle skulls indicate the zebu that had to be sacrificed to counteract this sacrilege. One hopes the revenge of the Ancestors was terrible.

The very reasonable response by the villagers to this desecration has been to fence the tombs and charge tourists an admission fee.

In the area are other memorials, but without carvings. These cenotaphs commemorate those buried in a communal tomb or where the body could not be recovered, and look like clusters of missiles lurking in the forest.

Shortly after Ranopiso there is a dramatic change in the scenery: within a few kilometres the hills flatten and disappear, the clouds clear, and the bizarre fingers of Didiera and Alluaudia appear on the skyline interspersed with the bulky trunks of baobabs. You are entering the spiny forest, making the transition from the Eastern Domain to the Southern Domain. If you are on a Berenty tour your guide will identify some of the flora. If on your own turn to page 188.

The exhilaration of driving through the spiny forest is dampened by the sight of all the charcoal sellers waiting by their sacks of ex-Alluaudia. These marvellous trees are being cut down at an alarming rate by people who have no other means of support. While condemning the practice give uneasy thought to the fact that your sumptuous meals in Berenty will be cooked on stoves fuelled with locally-produced charcoal.

Amboasary (for accommodation see page 209) is the last town before the bridge across the river Mandrare and the turn-off to Berenty. The rutted red road takes you past acres of sisal and some lonely-looking baobabs, to the entrance of the reserve.

The reserve

The name means 'big eel' but Berenty is famous for its population of ring-tailed lemurs and sifakas. Henri de Heaulme and now his son Jean have made this one of the best-studied 260 hectares of forest in Madagascar. Although in the arid south, its location along the river Mandrare ensures a well-watered habitat (gallery or riverine forest) for the large variety of animals that live there. In previous years the forest itself was threatened by the rampant spread of the cactus-like 'rubber vine', *Cissus quadrangularis*, but this is being vigorously tackled.

The following species of lemur are sure to be seen: brown lemur, ring-tailed lemur and sifaka. The lemurs here are well-used to people and the ring-tails will jump on your shoulders to eat proffered bananas. *Lemur catta* have an air of swaggering arrogance, are as at home on the ground as in trees, and are highly photogenic with their black and white markings and waving striped tails. These fluffy tails play an important part in communication and act as benign weapons against neighbouring troops which might have designs on their territory. Ring-tailed lemurs indulge in 'stink fights' when they scent their tails with the musk secreted from wrist and anal glands and wave them in their neighbours' faces; that is usually enough to make a potential intruder retreat. They also rub their anal glands on the trunks of trees and score the bark with their wrist-spur to scent-mark their territory. There are approximately 350 ring-tailed lemurs in Berenty, and the population has stayed remarkably stable considering that only about a quarter of the babies survive to adulthood. The females, which like most lemurs are dominant over the males, are receptive to mating for only a week or so in April/May, so there is plenty of competition amongst the males for this once-a-year treat. The young are born in September and at first cling to their mother's belly, later climbing on to her back and

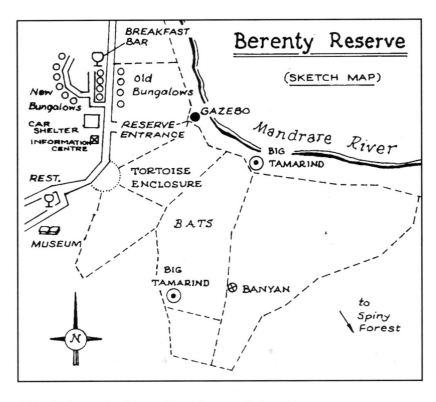

riding jockey-style. Ring-tails eat flowers, fruit and insects.

Attractive though the ring-tails are, no lemur can compete with the Verreaux's sifaka for soft-toy cuddliness, with its creamy white fur, brown cap, and black face. Sifaka belong to the same sub-family of lemur as the indri (seen in Périnet). The species here is *Propithecus verreauxi verreauxi* and there are about 300 of them in the reserve. Unlike the ring-tails, they rarely come down to the ground but when they do the length of their legs in comparison with their short arms necessitates a comical form of locomotion: they stand upright and jump with their feet together like competitors in a sack race. The best places to see them do this are on the trail to the left at the river and across the road by the aeroplane hangar near the restaurant and museum. Sifaka troop boundaries do not change, so your guide will know where to find the animals. The young are born in July. Like the ring-tails, sifaka make a speciality of sunbathing – spreading their arms to the morning rays from the top of their trees. They feed primarily on leaves and tamarind fruit so are not interested in tourist-proffered bananas.

The brown lemurs of Berenty were introduced from the west and are now well established and almost as tame as the ring-tails. There are two subspecies, the red-fronted brown lemur (*Eulemur fulvus rufus*) and the collared lemur

(*Eulemur fulvus collaris*). See box.

There are other lemurs which, being nocturnal, are harder to spot although the lepilemur (white-footed sportive lemur) can be seen peering out of its hollow tree nest during the day. Mouse lemurs may be glimpsed in the beam of a flashlight, especially in the area of spiny forest near the reserve, a popular destination for night walks.

Apart from lemurs there are other striking mammals. Fruit bats or flying foxes live in noisy groups on 'bat trees' in one part of the forest; with their wingspan of over a metre they are an impressive sight.

Birdwatching is rewarding in Berenty, and even better in Bealoka ('Place of much shade') beyond the sisal factory. Nearly 100 species have been recorded. You are likely to see several families unique to Madagascar, including the hook-billed vanga, and two handsome species of couas – the crested coua and the giant coua with its dramatic blue face-markings. The cuckoo-like coucal is common, as are grey-headed lovebirds and the beautiful paradise flycatcher with its long tail feathers (a subspecies of the genus that occurs in east Africa). These birds come in two colour phases: chestnut brown and black and white. Two-thirds of the Berenty paradise flycatchers are black and white. Look out for the nest which is built three to four feet from the ground.

If you visit from mid-October to May you will see a variety of migrant birds from southeast Africa: broad-billed roller, Malagasy lesser cuckoo and lots of waders (sanderlings, greenshank, sandpiper, white-throated plover).

The joy of Berenty is the selection of broad forest trails that allow safe wandering on your own, including nocturnal jaunts (remember, many creatures are only active at night and are easy to spot with a torch/flashight); also the

BROWN LEMURS AT BERENTY

John Buchan

Two subspecies of brown lemur, *Eulemur fulvus*, have been introduced to Berenty from other parts of the island.

The most numerous are the red-fronted lemurs, *Eulemur fulvus rufus*. There are two races in Madagascar, one of which comes from the southwest, near Toliara, and the other from the northeast. Colours are similar in both races: males are grey to grey-brown, with a black muzzle, pale patches above the eyes, and a fluffy orange cap; females lack the orange cap, have light grey cheeks as well as patches above the eyes, and are more of a rufous brown colour.

Note how these lemurs carry their young. Whereas a ring-tail baby clings to the mother's belly for the first couple of weeks and then transfers to her back, the red-fronted lemurs carry their young ventrally.

The other brown lemur is *E. f. collaris* which was introduced from the rainforest near Tolagnaro where it is endangered. The males have black faces, ears and crown of head, set off by bushy orange cheeks which extend to the neck forming a collar, hence the name. The females have greyish faces but the same orange cheeks/neck, although not as prominently as the male's. Both sexes are darkish brown to grey, with a stripe down the spine.

The two subspecies are interbreeding, so you may see hybrids in Berenty. This would not happen in their normal habitat where the ranges do not overlap.

eyes of moths and spiders shine red, and all sorts of other arthropods and reptiles can be easily seen. By getting up at dawn you can do your best bird-watching, see the sifakas opening their arms to the sun, and enjoy the coolness of the forest before going in to breakfast.

Berenty has been welcoming tourists longer than any other place in Madagascar, and all who fall in love with it will want to do what they can to preserve it and its inhabitants. Cutting down on lemur feeding is one way. Voluntary restraints of this sort will avoid a 'Galapagisation' of Berenty, where strict rules will have to be imposed on tourists to protect the wildlife.

An Information Centre will shortly open, the museum has been enlarged, and there is a library available for students. An outdoor museum of Antandroy culture helps us to know the human inhabitants of the region as well as the animals.

Excursions from Berenty include an area (within the reserve) of spiny forest, and a visit to the sisal factory, which sounds boring but is, in fact, fascinating.

Although you are free to explore the reserve on your own, a tour with the excellent English-speaking guides Andreas or Olivier will greatly increase your knowledge and understanding.

Their fee is paid by the reserve but a tip is appropriate.

SISAL

This crop was introduced to Madagascar in the inter-war years, with the first exports taking place in 1922 when 42 tons were sent to France. By 1938 2,537 tons were exported and 3,500 hectares of sisal were planted in the Tuléar and Fort Dauphin region. By 1950 production reached 3,080 tons. In 1952 a synthetic substitute was developed in the US and the market dropped. The French government stepped in with subsidies and bought 10,000 tons.

The Tuléar plantations were closed in 1958 leaving only the De Heaulme plantations. In 1960 these covered 16,000 hectares, and by 1993 30,000 hectares of endemic spiny forest had been cleared to make way for the crop.

KALETA PARK (AMBOASARY-SUD)

The management of the Kaleta, Libanona and Gina hotels have gone into competition with Berenty by starting their own lemur reserve, just south of the Berenty turn-off. This is considerably cheaper than its rival, and most (but not all) visitors speak highly of it. It is degraded forest (ie not in its natural state) and has been browsed by domestic animals, but is said to be as good for naturalists as Berenty.

The reserve is run by Rolande Laha, who for many years worked in Berenty and makes guests feel really special; it is geared to independent travellers rather than groups, and for day trips. Camping is allowed, for a fee, and the price for a day's visit includes lunch and a visit to a sisal factory.

One of the attractions here is the sifakas which are more approachable than in Berenty and even accept food from visitors. Whether this is a Good Thing I'm not sure, but it is certainly a marvellous experience.

The usual Berenty extras along the road to Ambovombe – tombs and pitcher plants – are also visited.

LAC ANONY

About 12km south of Amboasary is a brackish lagoon, Lac Anony. There are flamingoes here and a large number of other wading birds in a lunar landscape. There is a village, Antsovelo, and accommodation and food are available.

ANDOHAHELA

At present this is a Strict Nature Reserve, and so closed to tourists. Plans are afoot, however, to reclassify parts of the reserve as a National Park, thus allowing visitors access to one of Madagascar's most diverse and exciting regions.

The reserve spans rainforest and spiny forest, and thus is of major importance and interest. A third component is the east/west transition forest which is the last place the triangulated palm (*Neodypsis decaryi*) can be found. These three distinct zones make Andohahela unique in its biodiversity.

At the time of writing ecological monitoring is under way (financed by USAID and two American foundations) before a decision about if or when reclassification can take place. It is widely recognised that tourist revenue will do much to help this economically depressed region, and access to this wonderful reserve will certainly make for happy tourist-naturalists! For an update on the situation contact ANGAP in Antananarivo.

224

COMMERSON

Joseph Philibert Commerson has provided the best-known quote on Madagascar:

'C'est à Madagascar que je puis annoncer aux naturalistes qu'est la véritable terre promise pour eux. C'est là que la nature semble s'être retirée dans un sanctuaire particulier pour y travailler sur d'autres modèles que ceux auxquels elle s'est asservie ailleurs. Les formes les plus insolites et les plus merveilleuses s'y rencontrent à chaque pas.'

'Of Madagascar I can say to naturalists that it is truly their promised land. There nature seems to have retreated into a private sanctuary to work on models other than those she has created elsewhere. At every step one encounters the most strange and marvellous forms.'

Commerson was a doctor who travelled with Bougainville on a world expedition in 1766, arriving at Mauritius in 1768. He studied the natural history of that island, then in 1770 journeyed on to Madagascar where he stayed for three or four months in the Fort Dauphin region. His famous description of 'nature's sanctuary' was in a 1771 letter to his old tutor in Paris.

Part Four

THE EAST

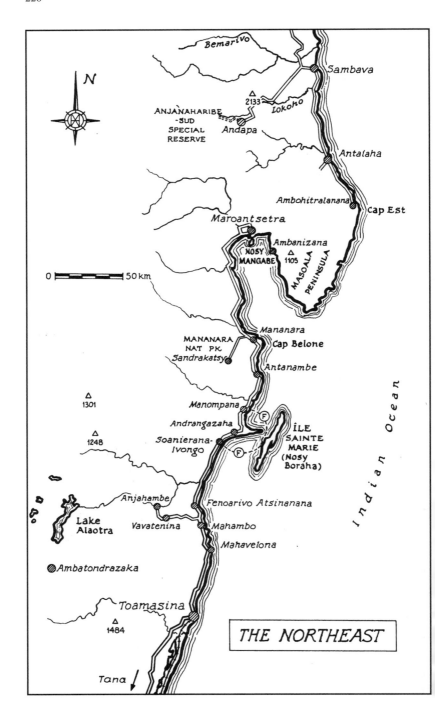

THE NORTHEAST

Chapter Eleven

Toamasina (Tamatave) and the Northeast

Punished by its weather (rain, cyclones), the east coast is notoriously challenging to travellers. In July 1817 James Hastie wrote in his diary: 'If this is the good season for travelling this country, I assert it is impossible to proceed in the bad.' With this in mind you should avoid the wettest months of February and March, and remember that June to August can be very damp as well. The driest months are September to November, with December and January worth the risk. April and May are fairly safe apart from the possibility of cyclones.

The east coast has another problem: sharks (see box, page 232) and dangerous currents. So although there are beautiful beaches, swimming is safe only in protected areas. Despite this, there is plenty to draw the adventurous traveller. Much of Madagascar's unique flora and fauna is concentrated in the eastern rainforests and any serious naturalist will want to pay a visit. So should others for the rugged mountain scenery with rivers tumbling down to the Indian Ocean, the friendly people, abundant fruit and seafood, and the lovely island of Nosy Boraha (Sainte Marie).

The chief products of the east are coffee, vanilla, bananas, coconuts and cloves.

This region has an interesting history dominated by European pirates and slave traders. While powerful kingdoms were being forged in other parts of the country, the east coast remained divided among numerous small clans. It was not until the 18th century that one ruler, Ratsimilaho, unified the region. The half-caste son of Thomas White, an English pirate, and briefly educated in Britain, Ratsimilaho responded to the attempt by Chief Ramanano to take over all the east coast ports. His successful revolt was furthered by his judiciously marrying an important princess; by his death in 1754 he ruled an area stretching from the Masoala Peninsula to Mananjary.

The result of this liaison of various tribes was the Betsimisaraka, now the second largest ethnic group in Madagascar. Some (in the area of Maroantsetra) practise second burial, although with less ritual than the Merina and Betsileo.

Maggie Rush gives a sharp little picture of how she saw the region: 'Ah, to the east coast! This is really different again from the rest of the country. I immediately noticed that the dialect along the coast seemed to be much more

Asian and sing-songish than the dialects of the west coast and inland... There is a lot to see. I would recommend Mananjary or Sambava if you only have time to visit a few places.' I agree.

Getting around

Although the map shows roads of some sort running almost the full length of the east coast, this is deceptive. Rain and cyclones regularly destroy bridges so it is impossible to know in advance whether a selected route will be usable, even in the 'dry' season. The rain-saturated forests drain into the Indian Ocean in numerous rivers, many of which can only be crossed by ferry. And there is not enough traffic to ensure a regular service. For those with limited time, therefore, the only practical way to get to the less accessible towns is by air: there are regular planes to Nosy Boraha (Île Sainte Marie), and usually flights between Toamasina (Tamatave) and Antsiranana (Diego Suarez). There are flights several days a week from Toamasina to Maroantsetra, Antalaha and Mananara, and to Sambava.

For the truly adventurous it *is* possible to work your way down (or up) the coast providing you have plenty of time and don't mind walking.

TOAMASINA (TAMATAVE)
History

As in all the east coast ports, Toamasina (pronounced 'Tourmasin') began as a pirate community. In the late 18th century its harbour attracted the French, who already had a foothold in Île Sainte Marie, and Napoleon I sent his agent Sylvain Roux to establish a trading post there. In 1811, Sir Robert Farquhar, governor of the newly British island of Mauritius, sent a small naval squadron to take the port of Toamasina. This was not simply an extension of the usual British/French antagonism, but an effort to stamp out slavery at its source, Madagascar being the main supplier to the Indian Ocean. The slave trade had been abolished by the British Parliament in 1807. The attack was successful, Sylvain Roux was exiled, and a small British garrison remained. During subsequent years, trade between Mauritius and Madagascar built Toamasina into a major port. In 1845, after a royal edict subjecting European traders to the harsh Malagasy laws, French and British warships bombarded Toamasina, but a landing was repelled leaving 20 dead. During the 1883-85 war the French occupied Toamasina but Malagasy troops successfully defended the fort of Farafaty just outside the town.

Theories on the origin of the name Toamasina vary, but one is that King Radama I tasted the sea-water here and remarked 'Toa masina' – 'It's salty'.

Toamasina today

Cyclone Geralda, which struck on February 2 1994 with winds of 230mph, destroyed more than 360,000 buildings. However, the people of this port are used to rebuilding their city, and that's what they have done.

Toamasina has always had an air of shabby elegance with some fine palm-lined boulevards and once-impressive colonial houses. Now it's just a bit shabbier, but still bustling, with a good variety of bars, snackbars and restaurants.

Getting there

By road Route Nationale 2 is arguably the country's best road. And so it should be: they've been constructing it for 20 years. First the Chinese completed their version in 1985. This deteriorated almost immediately and a highly competent Swedish company was brought in and by 1993 RN2 was the most heavily used road in the country. In April 1994, following cyclone Geralda, a traveller counted over 300 landslips; but the road is too important to be neglected, and this is now the best way of reaching Toamasina.

The fastest and most comfortable road transport is the Fitato Bus, run like an airline, with hostesses who even speak some English. There's an on-board video, complete with the usual 95% sound distortion. Book your seat at the back, as far away from it as possible. The ticket office in Toamasina is about 2km beyond the taxi-brousse station. Be sure to reserve your seat a day in advance. The SODIAT bus offers an equally good service and runs overnight, leaving Tana at 18.30 and arriving in Toamasina at 05.00, dropping you at the hotel of your choice.

There are also plenty of taxi-brousses which leave throughout the day; the journey takes from six to eight hours. It's best just to go along to the taxi-brousse departure point in the east of the city.

Warning: Even if you've never suffered from motion sickness, take precautions on this trip. The macho drivers and winding road are a challenge to any stomach.

By air There are daily flights between Tana and Toamasina.

Note: The luggage retrieval area in Toamasina is in a separate room to the right of Arrivals.

By train This used to be the most popular transport for tourists. The service had deteriorated long before the cyclone, however. During the political upheavals of 1991/2 the line was repeatedly sabotaged, and the management seemed to lose heart. First-class carriages were removed, and the service reduced to three times a week. The line was cut by landslides in the cyclone, and now operates only irregularly. Trains are always a tourist attraction, however, and this is a spectacular line, so it is worth enquiring about current schedules at the station in Tana.

When Anne Axel used the line in December 1994 the train only went as far as Moramanga, and it was an exciting ride. 'In some places I felt like I was riding on a roller coaster. The train would labour up a hill and then go barrelling down the other side.'

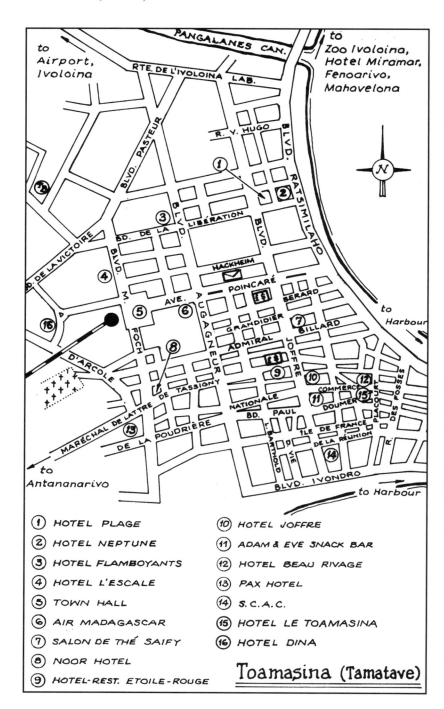

Toamasina (Tamatave)

1. HOTEL PLAGE
2. HOTEL NEPTUNE
3. HOTEL FLAMBOYANTS
4. HOTEL L'ESCALE
5. TOWN HALL
6. AIR MADAGASCAR
7. SALON DE THÉ SAIFY
8. NOOR HOTEL
9. HOTEL-REST. ETOILE-ROUGE
10. HOTEL JOFFRE
11. ADAM & EVE SNACK BAR
12. HOTEL BEAU RIVAGE
13. PAX HOTEL
14. S.C.A.C.
15. HOTEL LE TOAMASINA
16. HOTEL DINA

Where to stay
Category A

Neptune 35 Boulevard Ratsimilaho (on the seafront). Tel: 336 30; fax: 324 26. The poshest hotel in town. About 440Ff double. Swimming pool, excellent food, good bar. Credit cards accepted.

Noor Hotel Tel: 338 45. At intersection of Bd Mal Foch and Rue de Mal de Lattre de Tassigny (north side). About 300Ff (air-conditioned), 200Ff (with fan). No restaurant. Credit cards accepted.

Hotel Joffre 30, Bd Joffre. Tel: 323 90. An atmospheric old hotel with all facilities, rooms in the 250Ff range. Credit cards accepted.

Hotel les Flamboyants Av de la Libération. Tel: 323 50. Air-conditioned room with WC and shower. 'Best value in town.' Credit cards accepted.

Hotel Le Toamasina Rue Reine Betty. Tucked away on a puddled side street, round the corner from the Beau Rivage. Tel: 335 49; fax: 336 12. Comfortable and efficient. Reasonable food. Visa cards accepted.

Hotel Generation 129, Bd Joffre. Tel: 321 05/328 34. A new hotel. Recommended.

Hotel Miramar Tel: 328 70. This beautiful seaside hotel was destroyed in cyclone Geralda, but has since been fully rebuilt. Chalets are from 65,000Fmg, with hot and cold water, and it's all extremely civilised. The pool is open to the public, and the hotel is very convenient for the airport. Excellent food, too. 'The brochette of prawns and fish is unmissable, and the service was outstanding.' (Gavin and Val Thomson). MasterCard accepted.

Category B

Capricorn New hotel. 'Very nice double room with en suite bath, hot shower, air conditioning and balcony.' (Stringer Guaba, 1995)

Hotel Etoile-Rouge 13 Rue de Lattre de Tassigny. Tel: 322 90. 32,000Fmg for a room with twin beds. Rather dingy, with poor restaurant and service.

Hotel Beau Rivage (Better known by the name of its very good Italian restaurant, La Paillotte). Rue de Commerce (near the Adam and Eve Snack Bar). Tel: 330 35. Twelve clean rooms. Noisy (all-night disco) but good value at 25,000Fmg (1995).

Hotel Eden Appropriately situated near the Adam and Eve restaurant on Bd Joffre. Hot water. About 25,000Fmg (1995).

Category C

Hotel Plage Tel: 320 90. Boulevard de la Libération (round the corner from the Neptune). Rooms from 20,000Fmg (1995). Quite clean and comfortable, but the disco is murder and appears to go on seven nights a week.

Hotel Capucine Near the station (off Bd Poincaré, opposite the Hotel de Ville). Clean, friendly. Double with outside WC (soft paper), cold shower: 25,000Fmg (1995). 'All very clean; neat garden still being trimmed after dark; restaurant had good food and was excellent value. No complaints at all.' (Jeremy Buirski and Lindie Meyer)

Hotel Dina Formerly the Hotel Niavo. Basic, with cold water and smelly loos. 'Stand facing the railway station, go down the road to the right past some snack shops, before the road bends to the right there is a forked left turn which runs alongside the tracks. Go down this road, take the first road to the right, and the building on the corner is the Hotel Dina.'

Where to eat

The Hotel **Neptune** has the best restaurant; especially recommended is its all-you-can-eat Sunday buffet (lunch). The **Joffre** and **Flamboyants** are almost as good.

Jade Next door to the Noor Hotel. This is an upmarket Chinese restaurant with good food but quite expensive.

La Pacifique Rue de la Batterie. A popular and good-value Chinese restaurant.

La Récrea. 'A trendy new place on the beach, north side. A bit pricey but a beautiful view.'

Queens Club (Round the corner from the Hotel Plage). Recommended.

Adam & Eve Snack Bar 13 Rue Nationale. Tel: 334 56 (near Hotel Joffre). 'Best cuppa in Madagascar.' Other star features are good prices, strong, hot coffee and delicious samosas called *sambos*.

Shopping

'Mme Noeline, Brodeuse', Rue de l'Ova, BP 557, sells all kinds of embroidered goods, from handkerchiefs to tablecloths. M Fauris and his staff preside over their amazing range of stock with patience and good humour. Visa and MasterCard accepted. Recommended. (Jeremy Buirski and Lindie Meyer)

The *Librairie* near the market is very good and sells CDs of Malagasy music as well as books and nice postcards.

UNDER WATER

South African diver and spearfisher Jeremy Buirski says that his first view of the east coast at Toamasina was a revelation. It confirmed his belief that the reason the area is notorious for shark attacks is the dirty water. All the way up the coast as far as Pointe Larée the water had been turned a muddy brown by the run-off from numerous rivers – he wasn't at all surprised that people got bitten there. At Sainte Marie, where the water varied from clear to moderately dirty (three metres visibility), he never saw a shark.

Before venturing into the ocean in Madagascar ask local opinion on the safety. The French word for shark is *requin* and in Malagasy it's *antsantsa*. Bear in mind, however, that drowning, not shark attacks, is responsible for most sea deaths, and that there is often a formidable undertow on the east coast.

In addition to keeping a wary eye on sharks, Jeremy warns prospective snorkellers to avoid coming into bodily contact with underwater plants, as there are several types that sting. He also saw at least one stonefish, and urges caution when peering into holes, because lionfish are common and spend most of the daylight hours hidden away.

Car hire
Aventour has an office here: Rue Bir Hakeim. Tel: 322 43.

Day excursion from Toamasina
Zoo Ivoloina
This began life in 1898 as a rather grand Botanical Garden, but is now an animal rehabilitation centre funded mainly by Duke University (North Carolina) and restored with great dedication by Charles Welch and Andrea Katz. Radiated tortoises live in ample enclosures, as well as a troop of white-fronted brown lemurs; and there is also an education pavilion and a library. The black and white ruffed lemurs (*Varecia variegata variegata*) are unique in Madagascar in that they were brought here from America (where they were born) to form the nucleus of a population that will eventually be returned to the wild. There are plans to breed other highly endangered lemur species such as diademed sifaka.

Various other lemurs at Ivoloina are being carefully prepared for rehabilitation; many of them have been confiscated at the airport or rescued from being kept as pets. There is also a trio of grey bamboo lemurs, living in a small patch of bamboo out in the open – great for close-up photographs.

Ivoloina is 12km north of town, and is open daily from 09.00 to 17.00; entrance fee is 10,000Fmg. Drinks (no food) are available at a kiosk next to the lake (where you used to be able to take a pirogue trip, although these may no longer be running).

THE ROUTE NORTH

The road is passable – mostly – as far as Maroantsetra and the Masoala Peninsula. Then you have to take to the air or journey on foot across the neck of this roadfree peninsula.

Travelling north by taxi-brousse is always eventful: 'Left at 09.00 instead of 08.00 in Mazda minibus with 22 people on board. Tape playing South African reggae flat out. Road very bad in places, but more straight sections than on the whole route to Tana. Very rural and scenic. Took an hour and a half to leave Fénérive because driver was looking for petrol and more passengers. Exhaust broke off at the manifold 30km before destination and had to be repaired.' (Jeremy Buirski and Lindie Meyer)

If you want a more reliable ride, try to find 'Monsieur Cocos' who makes the run between Toamasina and Manompana on Tuesdays or Wednesdays. He may be easier to find in Soanierana-Ivongo.

Mahavelona (Foulpointe)
The town of Mahavelona is unremarkable, but nearby is an interesting old circular fortress with mighty walls faced with an iron-hard mixture of sand, shells and eggs. There are some old British cannons marked GR. This fortress was built in the early 19th century by the Merina governor of the town,

Rafaralahy, shortly after the Merina conquest of the east coast. There may now be a charge to visit the fortress.

Where to stay/eat
Before reaching the town you will pass the very smart **Manda Beach** hotel and the smaller **Au Gentil Pêcheur** next door. Both offer bungalows, safe swimming, and the Gentil Pêcheur is known for its excellent food. Manda Beach may be booked in Tana (tel: 317 61) as well as locally (322 43). It accepts credit cards.

Mahambo
A beach resort with safe swimming and some beach chalets. The best is **Le Dola**, Spanish run, with good food, mosquito nets, and endless beaches. Alternatives are **Le Récif** or **Zanatany** (bungalows at 23,000Fmg). Beware of sandfleas on the beach. Also: 'I spent two nights on the beach where the biggest problem was tiny caterpillars with nasty chilling bites that fell on me from the trees.' (John Kupiec)

Between Mahambo and Fenoarivo Atsinanana is a road leading inland to **Vavatenina**, where there is basic accommodation in bungalows, and on to **Anjahambe**. This town marks the beginning (or end) of the Smugglers' Path to Lake Alaotra (see page 274).

Fenoarivo Atsinanana (Fénérive)
Beyond Mahambo is the former capital of the Betsimisaraka empire. There are several basic hotels, including **Belle Rose** bungalows on the road leading to the hospital. Dolphins can be seen swimming off shore.

Soanierana-Ivongo
Known more familiarly as 'Sierra Ivongo', this little town is one of the starting-points for the boat ride to Sainte Marie (see page 251). It is also the end of the tarred road.

Hotel Zanatany (if still open) is a friendly, family-owned place. **The Bon Hotel**, say Jeremy Buirski and Lindie Meyer, is anything but – 'an absolute dump: 15,000Fmg for a bungalow in the back, no electricity, no bath, communal hole-in-the-ground, make your own food and watch the fireflies.'

If you are continuing north, try to find 'Monsieur Cocos'. Go to the Bureau of Forestry at the S-Ivongo barge jetty (opposite the police station). The Chef de Forêt usually knows when M Cocos is expected. 'If Cocos is not due for a day or two ignore the Sainte Marie touts and ask for Ben and his pirogue. Ben will take you 16km along the inland waterways: a truly enchanting experience – birds, flowers, forest. A hidden corner of Madagascar.' (Paul and Sarah McBride)

CONTINUING NORTH (IF YOU DARE)

From Soanierana-Ivongo the road is unreliable, to say the least. As fast as bridges are repaired they wash away again. You may have a fairly smooth taxi-brousse ride with ferries taking you across the rivers, or you may end up walking for hours and wading rivers or finding a pirogue to take you across. You should get local advice before setting out, especially if you have a lot of luggage to carry or are on a tight schedule. John Kupiec gives a flavour of the experience in his 1996 report: 'I took a *camion* north. We came to a river where we found a broken-down barge that would have to be removed so another could be put in its place. A *camion* towed the wrecked barge out of the way, driving in the water parallel to the shore. Then he got stuck. Another *camion* backed down to the water's edge to tow him out. He got stuck. Finally our truck pulled that one out, leaving the original one in the water. The whole affair lasted 24 hours. At any time I could have walked across the low part of the river but I wanted to experience this. From the truck's destination, Marorisy, I began a 165km walk to Maroantsetra.'

Andrangazaha

There is just one reason to stop at this little place mid-way between S-Ivongo and Manompana: Madame Zakia. 'Madame runs the best place north of Tamatave. All vehicles going north stop there to eat. Why? Because Madame feeds the drivers for free, passengers pay. Her food is excellent, bungalows clean with mozzie nets, 8,000Fmg per night, away from the noise and bustle of town in the bush where you can wait for a lift in quiet comfort.' (Paul and Sarah McBride)

Manompana

For many years this village, pronounced 'Manompe', was *the* departure point for Nosy Boraha/Sainte Marie. Despite the competition from Soanierana-Ivongo, there are still boats to the island. See page 253.

Much of the information in this section was supplied by Paul and Sarah McBride, who live in Manompana. Paul and Sarah will welcome any tourist who wants to drop in at their boat shed on RN5 for up-to-date advice and a hot English cuppa with home-made bread and jam or (gasp!) Marmite.

Around Manompana there is good surfing and swimming, 'the occasional shark, but by southern hemisphere standards no problem. Diving on the reefs is safe. There are three cascades in the rainforest nearby, all magnificent. A day's walk there and back but not overly tiring.'

Where to stay/eat

Chez Lou Lou Central. Six beachfront A-frame bungalows, very clean, good toilets, good seafood. 15,000Fmg per bungalow, 10,000Fmg per meal.

Chez Vankies Far end of town. Five beachfront bungalows. Secluded, 10,000Fmg per bungalow, no mozzie nets. Meals around 2,500Fmg.

Mahle Hotel On Mahle Point, 1km from the village. French owned. It usually takes only prearranged package bookings from Réunion. 'Very beautiful place, oceanfront, good diving on 4km of reef, untouched forest, will allow campers, price varies depending on day and mood.'

Medical clinic

Manompana has a new, French-built first aid post with eight beds and two resident doctors as well as an ample supply of medicines, but it's closed on weekends and holidays.

MANOMPANA TO MAROANTSETRA

Paul and Sarah McBride tell me that Hotel Chez Lou Lou will arrange for a 4WD taxi-brousse to take visitors from the town to Mananara-Nord 'sort of weekly' at 15,000Fmg per head.

Antanambe

Some 35km north of Manompana, on the edge of the UNESCO biosphere project, is this pretty little town and a French-owned hotel (bungalows) which has everything: gas cooking, filtered running water, pressure showers and flushing toilets with soft paper, comfortable beds with mozzie nets; all this plus a superb restaurant with Creole and French cooking and fresh fish daily! Not surprisingly, it's already very popular, and being expanded. Alain and Céline Grandian arrange tours in the Mananara biosphere reserve, and diving and fishing excursions to a vast reef 1km from the hotel.

John Kupiec was also enchanted by Antanambe. 'The setting is beautiful, with the bay curving round, but I wanted to keep on walking. The road leading out of town from the Biosphere was almost a boulevard with classic palm trees. Here I found a *hotely*. I was brought fish and rice (more than I could eat). It was delicious and the price was only 3,500Fmg. I ended up camping on the beach before walking for two days to reach Mananara, living mainly on coconuts and bananas.'

Cap Belone

Don't go there! The hotel just south of the Cape, Belle View, closed suddenly when the owner left for Europe with no forwarding address. The McBrides warn: 'It is hard to get there, there's nowhere to sleep, and the next hotel north is 25km away on a very poor stretch of road. The local village is not friendly, there is no food, no help.'

Mananara-Nord

Mananara, 185km north of Soanierana-Ivongo at the entrance to the Bay of Antongil, is the only place in Madagascar where one can be pretty much assured of seeing an aye-aye in the wild, on Aye-Aye Island. The hotel of choice is **Hotel Aye-Aye** on the beachfront next to the airport. They offer island tours, motor-bike rental, and very good food. The former owner, Dieter, who featured in earlier editions of this guide, has sadly died but his Malagasy widow maintains the same German standards. The manager, Madame Mio, is also known as Madame Emu (real name Edeline Kolobe!), and the hotel organises 'wonderful excursions with guides, chefs and porters into the rainforests and reef areas'. They also arrange trips to Antanambe, where the whale-watching is as good as around Sainte Marie. (Derek Schuurman)

Other hotels include the once recommended **Chez Roger**, which has reportedly gone downhill and is poor value for money, and full of prostitutes. A better bet is the **Ton-ton Galet**, a friendly, modest set of bungalows located near the hospital. Good value for 10,000Fmg (1996).

Aye-Aye Island

Visitors who imagine Aye-Aye Island to be a chunk of pristine forest are in for a shock: 'Sharing the island with the aye-ayes are the warden and his family, dogs, chickens, pigs and a pet lemur. But seeing an aye-aye is almost guaranteed. On the night we visited we saw a mother and her baby. The warden was very entertaining and obviously very fond of, and proud of, his aye-ayes. It was a wonderful experience.' (R Harris and G Jackson)

Visits to the island are organised by Roger (Chez Roger) or the Aye-Aye Hotel. The cost is around 30,000Fmg.

Mananara National Park and Biosphere Reserve

This example of eastern rainforest has been described by John Dransfield of Kew Gardens as 'The Biosphere's Botanical Paradise'. To visit it you need to obtain a permit from the Biosphere office in Mananara-Nord. A recommended 'interpreter' (not necessarily a guide) is Billy Graham. The most interesting part of the park is inland. You drive to **Sandrakatsy** by taxi-brousse (the first one leaves at 08.00 and the journey takes about two hours) and then walk for 1½ hours to **Ivavary** where there is accommodation for park (Biosphere) visitors. From here to the park is a further 1½ hours. 'We ended up with two Biosphere workers to show us the place. This was the real rainforest that I had imagined: thick brush with no trails, almost closed canopy, plants for which the medicinal value was explained, and a woolly lemur... Also leeches.' (John Kupiec)

If all this sounds too much like hard work, you can arrange an organised visit to the park through the Hotel Aye-Aye or – further south – the French-run hotel in Antanambe.

Mananara to Maroantsetra

To continue the journey north is an adventure, and at least two readers have risen to the challenge.

The intrepid Luc Selleslagh set out in a small boat: 'On the way the sea got rougher and rougher, the waves twice as high as the boat... I thought we were going to end between the sharks. The five other passengers were all sick. I was too afraid to be sick. Finally the captain decided to return!' After that Luc set out on foot. The bridges across the rivers sounded almost as dangerous as the sea but at least he was master of his fate. After two days and one lift he reached **Rantobe** from where there is at least a vehicle a day heading for Maroantsetra. Luc warns that even in ideal conditions it takes at least eight hours to go the 110km.

John Kupiec also set out on foot. 'The walk was all level, with the perfect setting of sea to my right and rainforest to my left.' Several rivers had to be crossed by pirogue before John reached Maroantsetra.

MAROANTSETRA AND THE MASOALA PENINSULA

Despite difficulty of access and dodgy weather, this has long been a sought-after destination for intrepid wildlife enthusiasts because of the nearby island reserve of Nosy Mangabe (aye-ayes, ruffed lemurs, plus *uroplatus* and other exciting fauna) and the Masoala Peninsula with its primary rainforest. Now that there is a first class hotel, Maroantsetra seems likely to become a regular stop on the ecotourist circuit.

Maroantsetra

Maroantsetra is a sizable town with plenty of well-stocked shops and a nice lively market.

Getting there and away

By air Most people will fly. Consequently flights tend to be booked for months in advance. Check latest schedules/availability with Air Mad.

The airport is 8km from town.

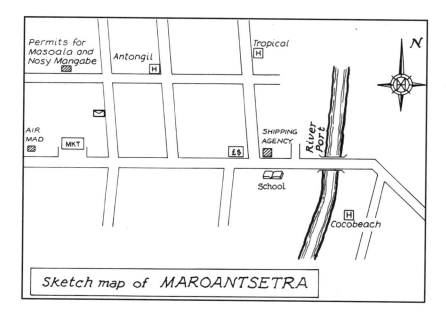

Sketch map of *MAROANTSETRA*

By land and sea Of course Real Travellers wouldn't dream of flying when there's the option of walking in from the south or – better – a leech-infested trail to Antalaha (see page 243) or the shark-infested sea.

Where to stay/eat

Relais du Masoala Spanking new and tastefully luxurious. Ten spacious, palm-thatched bungalows are set in 7ha of coconut groves overlooking the Bay of Antongil. Described proudly as 'Malagasy huts with American bathrooms', the rooms contain beds which are extra long to accommodate large *vazahas*, the showers work, and the covered verandas overlook the bay. Price: US$50 per bungalow per day, plus US$10 for meals and US$5 for an American breakfast. Bookings through Cortez Travel in California or Tana (see advert on page 70).

The Relais runs tours to Nosy Mangabe (with optional camping overnight), birdwatching in the Iaraka area of the Masoala Peninsula, pirogue excursions up river, whale-watching, and many other trips.

Motel Coco Beach BP 1. Tel: 18. Bungalows on the outskirts of town. Those with a shower and a WC cost 25,000Fmg, those without a WC are 20,000Fmg (1995). Meals in the spacious dining room are 'uneven', despite an extensive menu. Permits for Nosy Mangabe used to be obtainable from the hotel but this was stopped after financial irregularities came to light. The manager, Fidel, can arrange boat hire from Ramil (Pierre Ramilison). One attraction of Coco Beach is the striped tenrecs running about in the garden at night.

Hotel Vatsy New bungalows for 15,000Fmg and rooms for 10,000Fmg (1996), and small restaurant. Recommended.

Hotel du Centre Across from the market offering rooms and bungalows.

La Tropicale Bungalows, cold water but hot water is brought to you in a bucket for washing. 'The toilet is a privy in the yard and consists of a raised shed with a seat on it. On the ground below is an oil drum so you need to aim carefully!' (Frances Kerridge)

John Kupiec recommends the following restaurant: '**Le Pagode de Chine** across from the gas station serves wonderful seafood. Once I discovered it I ate nowhere else.'

Excursions

Andranofotsy and Navana This very worthwhile tour is a pirogue trip up the Andranofotsy river to the village of the same name. The vegetation and river life viewed on the way are fascinating, and the unspoilt (so far) village, with its inquisitive inhabitants, is peaceful and endearing.

Equally worthwhile is a visit to Navana. Follow the coast east along a beach backed by thickets, through waterways clogged with flowering water-hyacinth and past plenty of forest. You need to cross a lot of water on a pirogue, a regular local service. It takes an hour through little canals and costs very little. There is a hotel in Navana and you can also get there by boat from Maroantsetra.

Nosy Mangabe
Getting there and away

To visit the island you must have a permit. They are available for 20,000Fmg from the Projet Masoala office near the market in Maroantsetra. A guide is mandatory and costs 25,000Fmg (day) and 35,000Fmg (night). Information on boat hire can be had from the Motel Coco Beach; the usual price is 90,000Fmg. However, there is also the option (risky) of going by pirogue. All boats leave early in the morning when the Bay of Antongil is calm. It takes 45 minutes (by motorised launch) to Nosy Mangabe.

Don't forget to bring sunscreen and drinking water. If you're intending to camp, bring biodegradable soap or a similar product, to avoid polluting the brook at the site. There is a camping place on the island with a natural cold shower – a waterfall. Camping is 5,000Fmg per tent per night.

Exploring the island: what to look for

In fine weather Nosy Mangabe is superb. It has beautiful sandy coves, marvellous trees with huge buttress roots and also strangler figs. And it's

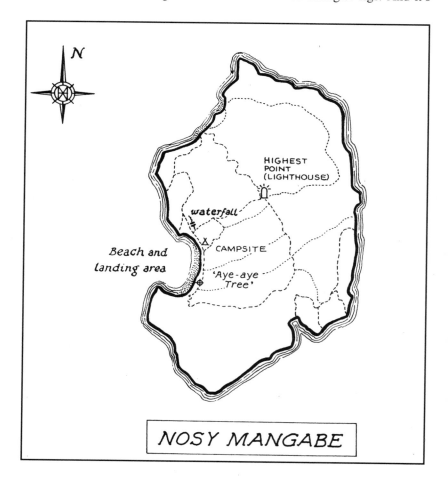

NOSY MANGABE

bursting with wildlife including, of course, its famous aye-ayes which were released here in the 1960s to prevent what was then thought to be their imminent extinction.

Aye-ayes are secretive and nocturnal but are becoming somewhat habituated so are more often seen these days. The best time to see them is between June and September, when they come right down to the trees by the shore to feed. There is a wealth of other creatures: black and white ruffed lemurs – these are wild and quite difficult to see – bright red frogs, and reptiles such as the marvellous leaf-tailed lizard, *Uroplatus fimbriatus*, chameleons, and snakes.

To complete your experience of Nosy Mangabe climb the hill to the lighthouse. The views here are superb and en route you will have a chance to see all sorts of reptiles, invertebrates, and other sights and sounds and smells. It's a magical island. In rain, though, it's slippery and pretty unpleasant. And it rains often.

As you leave Nosy Mangabe the boatman will often take you to see some old (15th century) inscriptions carved on some rocks on the shore. Fascinating!

The Masoala Peninsula

The peninsula (pronounced 'Mash<u>wahl</u>') is one of the largest and most diverse areas of virgin rainforest in Madagascar, and probably harbours the greatest number of unclassified species. Any scientific expedition here hits the jackpot – for example a Harvard biologist identified 100 species of ant in Masoala alone, many of them new to science.

The peninsula's importance was recognised by the French back in 1927 when they gave it reserve status, but independent Madagascar was swift to degazette it in 1964. However, the story has a happy ending – we hope. On June 5 1996 210,000ha of the Masoala Peninsula were declared a National Park, and this is only one fifth of the area recommended for protection. A lot of thought has gone into getting it right this time. The US-based agency, CARE International, which is in charge of the project, has been involving the local people in all stages of the development of the plan, trying to find sustainable sources of income through tourism or other schemes which are not alien to the local traditions. In conflict with these admirable aims are the disturbing reports that logging concessions have been granted to a Japanese company within the park. Rumour has it that one million hectares will be made available, and that high-ranking government officials are involved. It remains to be seen where the truth lies and what will happen to this wonderful piece of our planet. Experience it while you can.

How to visit Masoala National Park

As always, the easiest way is to join a tour. Both the Coco Beach Hotel and Relais du Masoala run comprehensive trips here with all arrangements taken care of. Independent travellers have a more exciting time, starting with the knowledge that one of the local boat owners hires the town dwarf to sit in the boat with his foot plugging the hole at the bottom to prevent the water coming in.

The area of the park currently visited by ecotourists is the part being studied by naturalists from the Missouri Botanical Gardens and the Peregrine Fund. The access village is **Ambanizana** which can only be reached by boat (2½ hours from Maroantsetra). Talk to Fidel at the Coco Beach for details of boat availability and price. Pack your gear in plastic bags to protect it from rain, and bring sunscreen to protect yourself from sunburn.

Located near Ambanizana at one time was The Modeste Settlement. Georges and Malene Modeste took care of the research centre and any tourists who turned up, but according to a 1996 report they have since left for Tana. Boats will still take you to the landing point, but you now have to camp on your own or with the advice of a guide. Well-trained guides can be arranged at the Coco Beach or Relais du Masoala hotels.

One of the most significant recent finds at Masoala is the red owl. In 1995 the Peregrine Fund located some owls and radio-tagged the adult female and one of her young. Victor Baba, a local technician who lives at Modeste, has tracking equipment and can take birders to see the owls at roost. In return, the visitor is asked for a donation which goes towards buying equipment for the recently opened village primary school, which had previously been shut for six years. 'The Peregrine Fund buys materials for the school (as requested by the teacher) who tells the pupils and thus their parents that the gifts come from tourists wishing to see the special birds which are dependent on the local forest. The forest's existence depends on the parents...a neat and very simple ecotourism project.' (Gavin and Val Thomson)

When planning a visit to Masoala, those wishing to see the red owl and the equally rare Madagascar serpent-eagle (a strenuous day trip to the research station at Andranobe, 7km down the coast) should first contact Rick Watson of the Peregrine Fund in Tana (tel: 257 72).

Most visitors will content themselves with hiking the trails and examining the wonderful natural world around them. You need to be quite fit to do these hikes – the lower semi-cultivated slopes are very hot, and where it is cooler and wetter there are leeches – but the rewards are limitless, especially for birders. Species recorded here include helmet and Bernier's vanga, red-breasted coua and scaly groundroller. There is also a good chance of seeing red ruffed lemurs. 'We descended the mountain just before dusk. It was for me unquestionably the most incredible part of Madagascar I have experienced. I kept thinking "This is how Madagascar *should* be" because there are still (1996) 300,000 hectares of primary rainforest left.' (Derek Schuurman)

There is not just the forest to delight you. The village of Ambanizana is a peaceful collection of bamboo and palm-thatched huts and shyly curious people. There are no cars, no discarded rubbish (because there is nothing to discard) and no hassle. If visitors follow the principles of 'minimum impact' (which is what ecotourism should be all about) and do nothing that will alter this (and remember, one sweet or pen given to one child will cause immediate and irreversible change) then Masoala will have registered a significant success.

There are snorkelling possibilities around the coral reefs off Masoala but never go into the water without checking on safe areas with your guide; the Bay of Antongil is notorious for sharks. It is safe to swim off the beach at Ambanizana (but there is no coral).

Walking from Maroantsetra to Antalaha

Luc Selleslagh walked (of course) across the Masoala Peninsula. It took him five days to cover the 152km. Normally this trip is done with a guide but Luc points out this is not really necessary. The path is well used by Malagasy and if you become confused just wait for someone to come. Abandon any idea of keeping your feet dry. A tent is useful in emergencies (and a mosquito net, or at least mosquito coils, essential) but there are houses you can stay in and meals will be cooked for you for a reasonable charge. The villagers may expect presents. They may also expect medicines. Be cautious of introducing – or perpetuating – expectations here.

If possible get hold of the relevant FTM map. If you don't manage to buy this in Tana there is one in the Hotel Coco Beach which you can trace.

There are alternatives to the shortest route detailed below. One trail runs from Ampokafo to Ambohitralalana (Cap Est), the most easterly point of Madagascar. This goes through largely untouched forests and villages are few and far between. A guide is advised. It may be easier to walk *from* Ambohitralalana; see below.

Day 1 Maroantsetra to Mahalenana. Mahalenana is the village beyond Navana, described under *Excursions*. A pleasant 5km walk.

Day 2 Mahalenana to Ankovona. The track climbs into the mountains and there are rivers to cross.

Day 3 Ankovona to Ampokafo. A long trek to Ampokafo which marks the halfway point. Very hilly and very beautiful, with lots of streams and orchids. The village has a small shop.

Day 4 Ampokafo to Analampontsy. Less wild, but still orchids along the way. Most villages en route have shops.

Day 5 Analampontsy to Antalaha. You emerge on to the road at the village of Marfinar, about 30km from Antalaha. From here you can get a taxi-brousse to Antalaha.

Another route across Masoala

An alternative route starts from Antalaha, providing a more exciting (but expensive) option of crossing through primary forest on a three-to-four-day trek organised by the South-African run **La Résidence du Cap** located near Cap Est, the most easterly point in Madagascar. Contact BP 122, Antalaha, tel: 813 65. To stay here costs 50,000Fmg for a bungalow. There is a generator for electricity but no hot water.

The trip can be done on your own providing you are equipped for walking and camping. The village at the cape is **Ambohitralanana**, reached by a rough track (occasional vehicles). Here you can find a pirogue to take you further

VANILLA IN MADAGASCAR

Clare and Johan Hermans

Vanilla is the major foreign currency earner for Madagascar, which together with Réunion and the Comoros grows 80% of the world's crop.Its cultivation in Madagascar is centred along the eastern coastal region, the main production centres being Andapa, Antalaha and Sambava.

The climbing plants are normally grown supported on 1.5m high moisture retaining trunks and under ideal conditions take three years to mature. When the plants bloom, during the drier months, the vines are checked on alternate days for open flowers to hand-pollinate. The pod then takes nine months to develop; each 15–20cm pod will contain tens of thousands of tiny seeds.

The pods are taken to a vanilla processing plant to begin the long process of preparing them for the commercial market. First they are plunged into a cauldron of hot water (70°C) for two minutes, and are then kept hot for two days. During this time the pods change colour from green to chestnut brown. At this stage they are exposed to the sun (mornings only to avoid over-cooking) for three to four weeks.

After maturing, the pods are sorted by size; the workers sit in front of a large rack with 'pigeonholes' for the different lengths. The bundles of sorted pods, approximately 30 to a bunch, are tied with raffia. They are checked for quality by sniffing and bending before being packed into wooden crates with 90% of the product going to the USA for use in the ice-cream industry.

The vanilla used in cultivation in Madagascar is *Vanilla planifolia* which originates from Mexico. It was brought to Madagascar by the French once the secret of hand pollination had been discovered – the flower has no natural pollinator in its foreign home. The culinary and pharmaceutical use of vanilla dates back to pre-Aztec times when it was used as a drink or as an ingredient of a lotion against fatigue for those holding public office. Similarly a native Malagasy vanilla stem can be found for sale in the *zoma* in Tana as a male invigorator.

Four different species of vanilla orchid occur naturally in Madagascar, most of them totally leafless. One species can be seen on the roadside between Sambava and Antahala resembling lengths of red-green tubing festooned over the scrub, another is to be found in the spiny forest near Berenty in the south. Most of the native species contain sap that burns the skin and their fruits contain too little vanillin to make cultivation economic.

Uses for vanilla pods

Although conventionally used for cooking, vanilla is also an insect repellent (see page 97) or the wonderful-smelling pods can be put in drawers instead of the traditional pomander to scent clothing or linen.

When cooking with vanilla you can reuse the pods for as long as you remember to retrieve them – wash and dry them after each use. Vanilla does wonders to tea or coffee (just add a pod to the teapot or coffee filter, or grind a dried pod with the coffee beans) and can be boiled with milk to make a yummy hot drink (add a dash of brandy!) or custard. If you take sugar in tea or coffee put some beans in your sugar tin and the flavour will be absorbed. Vanilla adds a subtle flavour to chicken or duck, rice or... whatever you fancy.

SAMBAVA AND ANDAPA 245

south to Ampanavoana. From here back to Ambohitralanana is a two-day trek through rainforest via the village of Ratsianarana. Alternatively from Ambohitralanana you can head due west and hope to end up at Ampokafo from where you walk to Maroantsetra (see page 238). Good luck!

ANTALAHA AND BEYOND
Antalaha
A prosperous, vanilla-financed town with large houses and broad boulevards. There are several hotels:

Hotel Florida Tel: 813 30. The best hotel, with air-conditioning and hot water.

Hotel du Centre Tel: 811 67. In the centre of town, European run, comfortable with good meals. About 17,000Fmg.

Hotel Ocean Plage Tel:812 05. Rooms for about 25,000Fmg.

Hotel Le Cocotier Tel: 811 77. Bungalows for about 25,000Fmg.

The road to Sambava is fairly good, about three hours by taxi-brousse.

SAMBAVA AND ANDAPA
Sambava
The centre of the vanilla and coconut growing region, and an important area for cloves and coffee production, Sambava merits a stay of a few days. The town has a definite charm, the people are friendly and easy-going, and there is plenty to see and do. 'Sambava was one of our best memories: a sublime bay; to the south some beautiful and deserted beaches; to the north lovely countryside with high mountains on the horizon. At the end of the world, but no worse for that!' (P Weber and L Durand)

Excursions can be made on your own or with the help of the local tour operator, Sambava-Voyages, or arranged by your hotel.

The airport is not far from town: you can even walk it if you are a backpacker.

Getting there and away
Sambava has quite good air-connections with Toamasina and Antsiranana, and is accessible by road from Vohemar (seven hours approximately).

Where to stay/eat
Category A
Hotel Carrefour BP 53. Tel: 60. Situated near the beach, with all mod cons (hot water, air conditioning). From 45,000 to 80,000Fmg. Good food.

Le Club Plage (bungalows). BP 33. Tel: 44. A posh hotel overlooking the sea with a swimming pool. Two-person bungalows for about 70,000Fmg; bungalow de luxe 85,000Fmg. Also **Hotel Le Club** with conventional rooms at 50,000Fmg.

Hotel Le Club offers a choice of several tours, including trekking; and transfer to and from the airport, 4WD vehicles with driver, and mountain bikes.

Las Palmas BP 120. Tel: 87. Nicely situated by the beach, well-run with conscientious and friendly staff. Hot water but poor water pressure. Good food. Air-conditioned rooms 125Ff/75,000Fmg, bungalows 70,000Fmg (1996). The hotel offers a variety of excursions, such as the Bemarivo river for 90,000Fmg.

Category B

Hotel Esmeralda BP 113. Tel: 128. This was formerly the very popular Orchidea Beach, but changed its name and ownership after the Italian proprietor was murdered. The new manageress is Russian. This is the backpackers' favourite Sambava hotel, pleasantly located with bungalows overlooking the ocean. Cold water, and a waitress who has developed apathy into an art form, but very good food. About 25,000Fmg (1996).

Hotel Cantonnais Tel: 124. A hotel rather than beach bungalows, but in a quiet part of town and most rooms have balconies. There are five rooms with toilets; hot water (with good pressure). Good value at 35,000–40,000Fmg (1996). The Chinese owner also sells precious stones.

Nouvel Hotel 20,000–40,000Fmg. In town. Recommended for its good food.

Category C

Hotel Pacifique Tel: 124. Three rooms at about 25,000Fmg. Also bungalows.

Hotel Calypso BP 40. Tel: 108. An unassuming hotel in town. 30,000–50,000Fmg.

La Romance North of the taxi-brousse station. Basic romance costs 10,000Fmg.

All the restaurants at the above hotels serve good meals. Specialist restaurants include Cantonnais and Mandarin (Chinese) and the Étoile Rouge.

Things to do
In and around town

Sambava itself is one long main street with parallel dirt roads, so you won't get lost. There is a good **market** which is known as *Bazaar Kely*, not because it's small (it isn't – and certainly not on Tuesdays, market day) but because there used to be two markets and no one thought of changing the name when they amalgamated them.

As this is one of the main vanilla-producing areas in Madagascar, a tour of the **vanilla factory**, Lopat, is interesting and teaches you a lot about the laborious process of preparing Madagascar's main export. Likewise a visit to the **coconut plantation** *(germoir pépinière)* some 3km south of the airport, is more rewarding than it sounds. You need a permit and a guide so it's easiest to go on an organised tour arranged by one of the hotels.

The highlight for us, however, was a visit to CLUE, the Center for Learning and Understanding English. This lively place is overseen by two dynamic Peace Corps women, Karen and Paige, who welcome visits from tourists to help the (adult) students practise their spoken English and understanding of a variety of accents. For the visitors it's an excellent chance to learn from the people of the east coast. CLUE is on the main street (you can't miss it) and you should look for Patrice, the Malagasy English teacher.

North of Sambava is a beautiful beach with safe swimming, and marvellous *Nephila* spiders on their golden webs between the branches of the shady trees.

Excursions further afield

Independent travellers will make their own arrangements, but if you want help the very efficient Sambava-Voyages (BP 28a. Tel: 110) will sort you out. The manageress, Mme Seramila, speaks some English.

The nearby **River Bemarivo** has plenty of possibilities. Boats go to the village of Amboahangibe (where there is at least one basic hotel) to transport coffee. You may be fortunate enough to get a lift (though you will still have to pay), or arrange your own pirogue. Cargo boats leave from Nosiarina on the main road northwest of Sambava. There is a small *hotely* in Nosiarina. John Kupiec took a cargo boat to Amboahangibe and walked back – a pleasant hike with some interesting above-ground coffins on the way and groves of shady giant bamboos.

Bear in mind that river trips in large boats cannot be made when the river is low at the end of the dry season – for instance October is often too early.

There is a very beautiful lake and **fishing village** about 9km south of the airport.

Andapa

Andapa lies in a fertile and beautiful region, 108km west of Sambava, where much of Madagascar's rice is grown. This is also a major coffee-producing area and it was to facilitate the export of coffee that the EEC provided funding for the building of an all-weather road in the 1960s (see box). The journey up this road to Andapa is most beautiful, with the jagged peaks of the massif of Marojejy (a Strict Nature Reserve to which tourists are not admitted) to the right, and bamboo and palm-thatch villages by the roadside. The journey takes about three hours by taxi-brousse.

A new road is being built linking Andapa with Beamalona, near Anjanaharibe-Sud.

Where to stay/eat

Hotel Vatosoa (pronounced 'Vats'). Comfortable but rather noisy rooms with hot water cost 37,000Fmg to 50,000Fmg (1996). The food is excellent and the hotel has all sorts of pluses. There is a large detailed map on the wall of the lounge which shows footpaths and tracks in the area. For hikers this is invaluable for planning (see *Excursions*). There are also two pet fosas in a cage in the yard. Much as I disapprove of Madagascar's endangered fauna being kept as pets, I was won over by the good condition and charm of these animals which were bottle-reared when a woodcutter found them in a tree he had just felled. It is a rare opportunity to see one of the country's most elusive animals at close quarters.

The Chinese owner, Mr Tam Hyok, is Mr Andapa. This dynamic man likes to take a personal interest in his guests and their plans, and will accompany those whom he

FOREIGN AID IN ANDAPA

Before 1963, Andapa's only link with the rest of the island was through Air Madagascar's flights to Sambava and Antalaha. This made the export of its cash crops, vanilla and Robusta coffee, prohibitively expensive. The newly-independent government, under President Tsiranana whose tribal roots (Tsimihety) were the same as those of the people of Andapa, applied to the EEC for funding to build a road to the coast. Also at the request of the government, a European team carried out a thorough agronomic survey and census of the region in the early 1960s; which led to 20 years of agricultural development overseen by a Belgian agency.

The initial achievements were considerable. Traditional hill rice (dependent on rain so with low productivity) gave way to irrigated rice paddies, served by a pumping station and irrigation channels. Thus 3,000ha of land were brought under cultivation. The hand-plough was replaced by more efficient zebu-hauled ploughs, and fertilisers and improved seeds were introduced. The same expertise was put into improving coffee production, and after ten years the previous yield of 300-450kg per hectare had risen to over 2,000kg/hectare for some farmers.

In the mid 1990s Andapa has retained some of this prosperity, but the high yields have fallen victim of Madagascar's malaise: deforestation. The once-verdant forests that encircled the Andapa Basin have been depleted and smoke rises from the new areas of *tavy* hacked out by land-hungry peasants. Topsoil has poured into the rivers which feed the pumping station, clogging the machinery and causing the closure of the station. Less rice means more poverty which means more deforestation. The story of Madagascar.

feels will most benefit from his attentions.

Chez Tam Hyok About 15 minutes' drive towards Sambava is Mr Tam Hyok's *pièce de résistance*: his own house and some bungalows overlooking arguably the most beautiful mountain view in Madagascar. Free-range lemurs (white-fronted and crowned lemurs) leap around the trees, and flowering shrubs blaze against the dark green of the Marojejy massif.

Bureaucratic problems have slowed down the work on these bungalows and at the time of writing only two are finished so just four people can be accommodated. For information enquire at the Hotel Vatosoa in town.

Hotel du Centre Chez Simonette Bungalows cost 16,000Fmg.

Hotel Nouveau At least one bungalow, 10,000Fmg. 'I loved the fact that the filthy WC was right in a filthy pig pen.' (John Kupiec)

Excursions

This is a wonderful area for wandering. At every step you see something interesting from the people or wildlife perspective (in the latter category butterflies, snakes and chameleons) and the scenery is consistently beautiful.

Mr Tam Hyok will have suggestions for more organised sightseeing, including the local **cemetery** where the dead are interred in coffins above the ground or in the trees.

Hiking

By using the map in the Hotel Vatosoa you can plan a variety of day hikes. The one we did was recommended by a Swiss couple (thank you!) and was the highlight of my 1996 visit to Madagascar. After a tussle with my conscience I have decided not to include details: it would take just one thoughtless visitor to threaten the integrity of those communities, changing their behaviour towards *vazahas* from shy curiosity to avarice or hostility. And anyway, the area abounds in tracks which would be equally rewarding.

Here are some of the highlights: chameleons in the bushes, coffee laid out to dry on the ground, an entire school of shrieking kids surging up the hill towards us, a village elder matching his stride with ours in order to converse in French, little girls fishing with basket-nets in the irrigation channels, home-made musical instruments, smiles, laughter and stares. It helped that we had our local guide with us who could interpret the village activities. In one place we experienced the power of Malagasy oratory (*kabary*) at full throttle. The theme was communal work. The 20 or so men of the village listened respectfully as the Président du Fokontany exhorted them to contribute their labour towards the building of a new fence. Some young men demurred: they would rather pay the let-out fee of 2,500Fmg. The Président discussed the issue with them, explaining the importance of the community working together. By the end of the discussion the young men had started stripping the leaves of a raffia palm to bind up the bamboo poles and begin fence-making.

Anjanaharibe-Sud Reserve

The Anjanaharabe-Sud Special Reserve/Befingitra Forest region, some 20km southwest of Andapa, is the closest tourists can get to Marojejy, which is rated one of Madagascar's richest area in terms of biodiversity. Anjanaharabe-Sud can be equally rewarding for naturalists with sufficient time to seek out the shy wildlife. This is the most northerly range of the indri which here occurs in a very dark form – almost black. The silky sifaka is also found here, but you are more likely to see the troops of white-fronted brown lemurs. Birders will be on the lookout for four species of ground roller.

Even without seeing any mammals it is a most rewarding visit, with an easy-to-follow (though rugged) trail through primary forest to some hot springs. The reserve is also a vital element in the prosperity of the area. The Lokoho River, which rises in Anjanaharibe-Sud, is the *only* source of water for the largest irrigated rice producer in the country.

Visiting the reserve

Mr Tam Hyok can arrange a day visit to the Anjanaharabe-Sud, but it is possible and rewarding to visit it on your own. Camping is permitted and would allow you to get the most out of your stay.

You need a permit from the WWF office in Andapa, but a guide is not mandatory.

If you are camping you may prefer to arrange a transfer with Mr Tam Hyok since private vehicles can get to the trailhead. Otherwise taxi-brousses only go to the barrier some way before the village of Befingitra where you can pick up a guide. From the barrier it is a two-hour walk up the road to the trailhead, clearly signposted with a WWF board: 'Piste Touristique de Ranomafana Source Thermal, a 4260m.' It gives the time needed for a there-and-back trip as five hours which is roughly accurate although it does not allow much time for examining, watching and listening. Or photography.

The path is clearly marked (the trees are tagged with orange tape) and worn enough that a careful walker would not need a guide. It follows an up-and-down route, slippery at times, but full of interest. On our rather fast day trip we saw no mammals, but campers should see brown lemurs and perhaps indri. John Kupiec reports: 'When you get to the river area it is hard to find the springs without someone to show you. There are three: one is too hot to keep your feet in; another is shallow but it meets a stream which makes it easier to take; the third is a pool to swim in which also merged with stream water.'

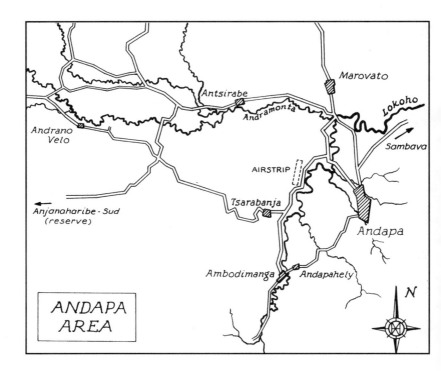

NOSY BORAHA (ÎLE SAINTE MARIE)
History
The origin of the Malagasy name is obscure. It means either 'Island of Abraham' or 'Island of Ibrahim', with probable reference to an early Semitic culture. Most people still call it Île Sainte Marie, the name given by European sailors when the island became the major hide-out of pirates in the Indian Ocean. From the 1680s to around 1720 these pirates dominated the seas around Africa. There was a Welshman (David Williams), Englishmen (Thomas White, John Every and William Kidd) and an American (Thomas Tew) among a Madagascar pirate population which in its heyday numbered nearly one thousand.

Later a Frenchman, Jean-Onésime Filet ('La Bigorne'), was shipwrecked on Sainte Marie while escaping the wrath of a jealous husband in Réunion. La Bigorne turned his amorous attentions with remarkable success to Princess Bety, the daughter of King Ratsimilaho. On their marriage the happy couple received Nosy Boraha as a gift from the king, and the island was in turn presented to the mother country by La Bigorne (or rather, put under the protection of France by Princess Bety). Thus France gained its first piece of Madagascar in 1750.

Île Sainte Marie today
Here is a cliché of a tropical island with endless deserted beaches overhung by coconut palms, bays protected from sharks by coral reefs, hills covered with luxuriant vegetation, and a relative absence of unsightly tourist development – although this is changing fast. Most travellers still love it: 'Nosy Be is for people who want A Good Time, Sainte Marie is for those looking for tranquillity and beauty.'

Sainte Marie unfortunately – or perhaps fortunately, given the dangers of overdevelopment – has a far less settled weather pattern than its more sophisticated island rival, Nosy Be. Cyclones strike regularly and you can expect several days of rain and wind all year round, but interspersed with calm sunny weather. The best months for a visit seem to be June and mid-August to November, although a reader tells me she twice had perfect weather in January, and another reports that in July most days were sunny and hot, but with frequent light rain overnight or in the morning, and fairly strong winds from the south.

Sainte Marie is 50km long and 7km at its widest point. The only real town is Ambodifotatra (pronounced 'Amboodifootatr'). Other small villages comprise bamboo and palm huts.

Getting there and away
By air Air Madagascar flies to Sainte Marie most days (check the latest schedule) from Tana or Toamasina. All flights are heavily booked, especially in July and August, and you should try to make your reservations well in

Nosy Boraha (Île Sainte Marie)

advance. Reconfirm your return flight at the Air Mad office in the north part of Ambodifotatra. The office is closed when the personnel are needed at the airport because a flight is coming in, but there is a café next door in which you can wait. However adamant the Air Mad people are that the flight is full, it is worth going stand-by.

By fast motor launch An (expensive) boat service now runs between Soanierana-Ivongo, at the end of the surfaced road north of Toamasina, and Ambodifotatra. Polymar is run by French expats and in 1995 cost 160,000Fmg one way. The trip takes 1½ hours.

By basic boat *Le Dugong* may still be running from Soanierana-Ivongo. Enquire at the restaurant Le Barachois in Ambodifotatra, Sainte Marie, or in Soanierana-Ivongo. This boat waits to fill up with passengers, so the schedule is erratic.

If you are a masochist you can take the *Rapiko*, which leaves Toamasina on Wednesdays at 20.00 and takes at least 10 murderous hours. Tickets are available from SCAC in Toamasina (see map) or in Sainte Marie from Roso's, next to Le Barachois.

'Due to bad weather, the boat didn't leave until the next day... We started out at 8pm, and the sea was very rough. Fortunately the boat wasn't crowded and we could all lie down. Once we hit open sea, the seas got even more rough... Water poured in the windows and people began passing round the can, since many were seasick... At 10pm we turned around and headed back for Tamatave... I stayed on board and slept as best I could. We started off again at 8am, and while the seas were still rough, it was an easier ride... The trip itself took just over 12 hours and was otherwise uneventful.' (Anne Axel)

A number of boats run regularly from Manompana (see page 235). Manompana is not always accessible from the south – it depends on the state of bridges and ferries crossing the several rivers up the east coast. The *Monia* costs around 30,000Fmg per head (1995) and takes four hours. 'It's a dirty old motor cruiser, leaks constantly and has no safety equipment, but it somehow always makes it over and back. The *Maria II* is a lovely, well-built 1956 sailing schooner with no motor, four sails, and two grinning crew. The trip costs 20,000Fmg (1995), but for 40,000Fmg it will take you across, wait for 24 hours and bring you back. Sailing time each way is about seven hours. If you're in a hurry, you can use *Ming* a 9-metre outboard-powered sailing boat. It's clean, quick and expensive – 60,000Fmg, but this changes according to how much of a hurry you're in.' (Paul and Sarah McBride)

'On the crossing you're quite likely to see plenty of flying fish, dolphins which attempt to surf in the bow waves, bonito and lots of very visible plankton particularly a luminescent blue variety. In August and September you may see whales.' (W Pepper)

By pirogue Rick Partridge sent this report: 'We took a taxi-brousse from

Tamatave to Soanierana-Ivongo. Next morning we negotiated a fee to travel by dug-out canoe along the inland waters for about 15km to a small ferry-point village where there are bungalows. Then next morning we had to walk at least 15km to the headland (*pointe*), where there is a village called Andragazana, from where we took a larger dug-out sailing boat to Île Sainte Marie. The crossing took 1½ hours. An unmissable experience! Arriving at Bon Coin on Sainte Marie made us feel like Christopher Columbus.' There may now be a 4WD vehicle to take passengers to Andragazana.

In 1995 Jeremy Buirski and Lindie Meyer made a similar crossing. 'The sailing pirogue cost 50,000Fmg for the two of us. It looked incredibly unseaworthy, full of water and with the sails held together with string. The crew rowed us along various river paths and out of the mouth of a small river well northwest of the *pointe*, where they hoisted the three sails and sat back. Going to Sainte Marie this way is a must, and I recommend it to anyone who is even remotely adventurous. For most of the trip over the wind was 10-12 knots, later increasing to 15-20 knots. The only water that came inboard was the occasional splash from the paddles as the crew rowed to stop the keel-less pirogue being blown too far northward. We saw lots of tuna jumping, and many fishermen. We reached Sainte Marie about 1km north of La Crique then stowed the sails and rowed up the coast to Loukintsy.'

Where to stay

Almost all Île Sainte Marie's hotels are ranged along the west coast of the island. A few others are in the east or on Île aux Nattes in the south.

Note: There are no taxis on the island, but most hotels have their own vehicles and meet the incoming planes. Check with the 'courtesy vehicles' if there is room at their hotel before climbing aboard.

West coast hotels

These hotels are listed in geographical order, from south to north. Their price/ quality category is given in brackets.

Chez Vavate (*Category C*). Six rooms/bungalows, from 20,000Fmg; 11,000Fmg for a three-course meal. On first appearance an unprepossessing collection of local huts built on a ridge overlooking the airstrip. Don't be taken in by first impressions, the food here is wonderful (and the *punch coco* ensures that you spend your evenings in a convivial haze) and the relaxed family atmosphere makes this a very popular place with young travellers. The only catch is you must walk 1½km from the airport. There is no road, and the 'courtesy vehicle' is a man with a wheelbarrow! If you miss him take the wide grassy track which runs parallel to the airstrip then veers to the left up a steep hill, but be warned – if Chez Vavate is full you will have missed the vehicles going to the other places.

Bungalows Vohilava French-owned self-catering bungalows (a first for Madagascar) about 3km from the airport. From 200Ff (two people) to 700Ff (eight people) per day. Fully equipped kitchens; suppliers come daily to sell fresh food.

Stany's Bungalows/Bungalows Mayer (*Category C*). About 10km south of Ambodifotatra, 20 minutes up the road from the airport. Adequate bungalows. Nice view looking out to sea. Bush showers and toilet. Very helpful and friendly owner.

Soanambo BP 20. Tel: 40. Manageress: Agnes Fayd'Herbe. (*Category A*). 3km from airport, 10km from Ambodifotatra. The most expensive hotel on the island. 325Ff per bungalow. Meals 95Ff. Very comfortable with a lovely garden with *Angraecum* orchids. Bicycles available for hire. Credit cards accepted.

Lakana (*Category B*). BP 2. Six simple but very comfortable wooden bungalows, 5km from the airport, and including four perched along the jetty. From 78Ff (with shared shower) to 90Ff (en suite bathroom). Breakfast 13Ff, airport transfer 10Ff. Mountain bikes for hire. Visa cards accepted.

Hotel La Baleine (*Category C*). Owned by Albert Lanton, this set of bungalows receives rave reviews. It is one of the few hotels on the island that are Malagasy-owned. With the proceeds of the hotel Albert sponsors a youth football club and other local projects. There are eight rustic bungalows with mosquito nets and the minimum of furniture, about 7km from the airport. Communal bathroom with cold water. 'The food is absolutely superb! I spent 10 days here and never had rice cooked the same way twice.' (Luc Selleslagh). The only negative point is that the beach is not particularly nice here... but who cares?

Bungalows Orchidée Tel: 54. (*Category A*). Located 3km south of Ambodifotatra, and trying, unsuccessfully, to outsmart Soanambo. David Sayers writes: 'the cabins badly need decorating, food is unimaginative and very expensive, and I do not like chickens feeding off the breakfast tables.' Single 250Ff; double 300Ff. Ten bungalows, four double rooms. Hot water, air-conditioning, water sports, excursions. Bookings may be made in Tana, tel: 237 62/270 15; fax: 269 86. Also in Tamatave: tel: 333 51/337 66. Credit cards accepted.

Hotel Zinnia (*Category C*). Right by the harbour wall at Ambodifotatra. Bungalows (six) at 25,000Fmg for a double, with hot water, fans and outside flushing toilet. Good, neat and pleasant restaurant with excellent food and 'the best coffee on Sainte Marie'. Mountain bikes for hire at 25,000Fmg a day.

La Falafa This restaurant in Ambodifotatra (good food) also has a few inexpensive rooms (*Category C*). 'The walls were paper thin and I heard everything within a one block radius, including the disco across the street. Additionally, I heard rats scurrying around all night.' (Anne Axel)

Hotel Drakkar (*Category C*). 1km north of Ambodifotatra. Simple bamboo bungalows with cold shower. Rooms from 15,000Fmg. The main building is an old colonial house with lovely decor and a sitting/dining room on the water's edge. Excellent food.

Hotel Bety Plage 6km north of Ambodifotatra. When I first visited Île Sainte Marie in 1976 this was the only hotel on the island. It was destroyed by a cyclone a few years later and is only now being rebuilt. It is in a good location with a nice sandy beach. No details available at the time of going to press.

Hotel Bambou (*Category C*). Between Ambodifotatra and Loukintsy. Inexpensive beach huts, with a superb view of the sunset over a pristine sandy bay – and friendly. Recommended.

Atafana BP 14. (*Category C*). About 4km south of La Crique, run by the Noel family. Described by some as having the best location, on a private bay, with good food. Rooms with cold-water shower and washbasin are about 25,000Fmg. Communal flushing toilets. Easy to get into the sea for swimming or snorkelling. Power comes from a generator. Residents can rent two mountain bikes and a rowing pirogue. Warm hospitality. 'We finally made it to paradise', says Maggie Rush. 'The family that runs it is wonderful, and I like the idea of supporting a Malagasy enterprise rather than a foreign one.'

Hotel Voania (*Category C*). Roughly 200m from the Atafana. On a clean beach, raked every morning to get rid of rocks and flotsam. 12,500Fmg for a basic double bungalow, 15,000Fmg with shower, 25,000Fmg for double with shower. Next to the local village, but the newest part is very private and secluded. No electricity, but equipped with powerful pressure lanterns. The reef in front of the beach is very shallow, the restaurant slightly cheaper than the Atafana's. The delicious large prawn 'crevettes' are recommended, but must be ordered in advance.

Hotel Bon Coin (*Category C*). This hotel at Loukintsy, with rooms at 10,000Fmg, is described as 'OK' by Rick Partridge. It's 1km before La Crique, and the last place easily reached by road going north. The only minus point is 'an unhygienic beach'.

La Crique BP 1. (*Category B*). Deservedly the most popular of all hotels, in one of the prettiest locations, 1km north of Loukintsy, with a wonderful ambience and good food. In September you can watch humpbacked whales cavorting off shore. Bungalows with shared facilities 86Ff/65,000Fmg; bungalows with en-suite bathrooms 145Ff/110,000Fmg. Breakfast 12,000Fmg, dinner 35,000Fmg. Often full, so try to book ahead. Transport to/from the airport costs 25,000Fmg, and there is a regular minibus to town.

Hotel Antsara (*Category B*). 300m north of La Crique. Five beach bungalows, plus eight more on a slope further from the sea. Rooms from about 15,000Fmg, with or without WC or bathroom. Excellent Réunionnaise-French hosts. Snorkelling gear available. Has a noisy disco, but only at weekends.

La Cocoteraie Robert BP 29. (*Category A*). In the extreme north of the island, described by one who knows as 'the most beautiful beach in the world', and has recently added 40 more bungalows. Transport from the airport is expensive, but a boat goes there from Soanambo (it's run by the same French family). It even has its own airstrip. 280-310Ff double (depending on the season), 350-390Ff for a four-bedded bungalow. Breakfast 18,000, dinner 35,000Fmg.

East Sainte Marie

Restaurant Bungalows Paradis d'Ampanihy (*Category C*). On the river close to Anafiafy, opposite the Forêt d'Ampanihy. Owned and run by an expatriate Swiss called Pablo. A basic bungalow is 20,000Fmg, with shower 30,000Fmg. Nice, clean, solidly-made bungalows. Four-course meals from 15,000Fmg to 40,000Fmg. 'Really beautiful dining room with outside tables and several tame lemurs. A pirogue trip across the river to the Forêt d'Ampanihy and back is only 4,000Fmg per person.' Ten minutes' walk to the sea.

Chez Famindra (*Category C*). This is not really a hotel (I've made up the name) but a family enterprise run by a friend of Madophile Rick Partridge. 'Clébert Famindra is a tourist guide (he speaks only French) who lives near Anafiafy on the other side of Sainte Marie in a really peaceful location by the Bay of Ampanihy. I would suggest staying with him and his family for a few days; it's an excellent way to get to know Malagasy people. His prices are inexpensive and negotiable. M Famindra has extra accommodation in the form of two beach-hut type houses a few hundred metres from the sea and river. Conditions are hygienic but not developed (eg earth privy). He is gradually developing a hotel/restaurant business in addition to his tourist guide activities. In the spring of 1997 a small catamaran will be available, built using traditional methods, which he hopes to use for whale-watching, among other activities.'

Hotel Lagon Bleu On the east coast, near Marofilao, 7km from Anafiafy (*Category C*). A smallish cosy site, but clean and peaceful. Complimentary daily *punch coco*.

Accommodation on Île Aux Nattes (Nosy Nato)

In recent years this island has been taken over by the tourist industry. I don't know how the local people feel, but it's hard to complain: it is a wonderful place. 'Our idea of what a tropical island should look like. Lovely bungalows, some with verandas, on lawns under palm trees next to a shiny white beach. The water was clear as glass all the way back to Sainte Marie.' (Jeremy Buirski and Lindie Meyer)

Chez Napoléon Napoléon was a charismatic character who 'ruled' – in various guises – this little island and enjoyed entertaining *vazahas*. He died in 1986, but his name lives on in a hotel which would amaze him: bungalows here (with hot water) are between 30,000 and 50,000Fmg. There's a restaurant, where Napoléon's famous *poulet au coco* is still served to appreciative diners, even if taped pop music has replaced the sound of wind in the palm trees. You can camp on the grass for 5,000Fmg per person.

Hotel Pandanus (*Category B*). A double bungalow is 25,000Fmg. The communal toilets have soft paper and are very clean. Food prices are reasonable.

Les Bungalows Vohilava (*Category C*). Five bungalows, 28 beds, fans and showers.

It is well worth taking a tour around this little island. There is much to see during a short walking tour, including the island's unique – and amazing – orchid *Eulophiella roempleriana*, known popularly as L'orchidée rose. It is two metres high with deep pink flowers.

Where to eat

If you are not staying on Île Aux Nattes, take a day trip there to enjoy lunch **Chez Napoléon**.

Restaurant **La Jardine**, Ambodifotatra, serves good, inexpensive food. Recommended for breakfast. Home-made hot croissants with hot chocolate, and friendly people. **The Hotel Antsara** is recommended for its set dinner for 12,000Fmg. **Bar-Restaurant Le Barachois** is across the road from the harbour, next to the ferry booking office, and has 'the most comprehensive menu encountered anywhere'. Quite inexpensive, and the tables on the porch are fine for people-watching.

In the north of the island at Anafiafy, visit the **Restaurant Bar Bleu**. People rave about its menu!

Sightseeing

There are some interesting sights around Ambodifotatra and the Baie des Forbans which are an easy cycle ride from most of the hotels. In the town itself there is an interesting **church** built in 1837, so shortly after the arrival of the Welsh missionaries from the London Missionary Society. There is also a **war monument** to a French-British skirmish in 1845.

The **Pirates' Cemetery** is just before the bay bridge to the town (when coming from the south). A track leads to the cemetery, 20 minutes away. You don't need a guide, and some of them are unscrupulous. The turning is clearly signposted, and small bridges have been built so that you can visit the cemetery at any state of the tide. This is quite an impressive place, with gravestones dating from the 1830s, one with a classic skull and crossbones carved on it, but not many graves. There is now a 1,000Fmg charge to visit the cemetery.

The **town cemetery** is worth a visit, although it lacks the story-book drama of the pirates' final resting place. The graveyard is about 6km north of Ambodifotatra, at Bety Plage on the right side of the road.

Excursions around Sainte Marie

Rick Partridge writes: 'Visitors are recommended not just to stay in the seductive south. There's plenty to see further up the island, where life is even more tranquil. The road isn't bad to Hotels Atafana or La Crique (good for swimming) or to Hotel Antsara (good for disco fun, nestling in the foothills). From these sites an interesting day's outing is to hike over the hills to the Indian Ocean side. The walk takes about two hours, not arduous in dry weather but a bit of a scramble in places – good shoes recommended.'

Jeremy Buirski and Lindie Meyer walked across the island from **Atafana to Anafiafy** with a guide. They strongly recommend this hike because it has beautiful and dramatic scenery, with 'some Tarzan-type jungle' in places. It can get quite muddy, as the dense forest canopy ensures that the ground stays wet for several days after heavy rain. They walked through huge growths of ferns, and saw lychee, coffee, vanilla and cinnamon growing.

About one hour's walk from La Cocoteraie Robert is a beautiful and impressive **piscine naturelle**, with a big pool and enormous basalt rocks. It is *fady* to urinate in the pool, according to Waltraut Treilles, who was most impressed by her visit there.

The **Forêt d'Ampanihy**, in the west, was visited by Jeremy Buirski and Lindie Meyer: 'A quite dramatic pirogue trip along the river, as the trees met overhead to form a tunnel. The pirogue will take you to an inlet where the peninsula is at its narrowest, and it's a five-minute walk to the sea on the other side. The coral reef is several hundred metres offshore, so you need another pirogue to dive there – diving from the shore is too dangerous because of the tidal flow. Absolutely deserted, with huge trees on the shore and here and there a lone fisherman.'

Cycling around the island

Bikes can be hired from many of the hotels but are cheaper at Ambodifotatra. You can see quite a lot of the island this way, but don't reckon on covering much ground – the roads are very rough and most bikes in poor condition (check the brakes!).

If you are staying at Ambodifotatra you will have time to explore the north of the island, which is more dramatic scenically than the south. There is quite a good stretch of tarred road between the town and La Crique.

You can hire motorbikes opposite the Hotel Soanambo and mopeds are also available in Ambodifotatra.

In 1995 Anne Axel had her own bike with her on Sainte Marie. 'My favourite cycling adventure came next. I'd heard there was a beautiful beach on the east coast, and that maybe there was a place to stay the night, so I set off on a road that crossed the island from west to east. The road travelled over rolling terrain until I finally reached the ocean, and then I started south on a level road coated with sand. A small sign on the road pointed the way to **Bar Bleu**, a small hotel in the village of Anafiafy. It's run by a European expatriate who has built a bungalow for himself and three others for guests. There's a small restaurant with excellent food at a good price, especially considering how far removed they are from everything.

I hired a villager to take me by pirogue across the bay to the beach on the peninsula. The beach was the most beautiful one I have ever seen. The colour of the water was a mixture of deep blue and emerald green. There weren't any other tourists – in fact I saw only three other people, fishermen, the whole time I was there. I ate a leisurely lunch then walked along the beach for miles. I would hate to see this place spoiled by tourism – it's so pristine!'

Warning If you carry food, or virtually anything else remotely edible, keep it in heavy-gauge plastic zip-up bags inside your backpack. Sainte Marie cockroaches are enormous, have gargantuan appetites and always come out after dark. They can easily chew through an exposed plastic bag overnight.

Snorkelling and diving

The shallows around Sainte Marie are ideal for snorkelling and diving, although the island's inshore waters are horrendously overfished by local Malagasy, who set fine-mesh gill nets everywhere – watch out for them. These nets catch small, inedible fish as well as larger ones, and this must have an adverse effect on stocks, which can only prove disastrous in the long term. Crayfish are very much in evidence in and around the reefs, of which there are many, six to ten metres down in clear water and close to Atafana and La Crique. There are also several huge coral 'tables', some nearly two metres wide, but unfortunately a number have been broken off by fish traps.

Balenottero Dive Centre Tel: 48 (Ambodifotatra) or 450 17 (Tana). Italian owned. Very good equipment, organised dive trips to wrecks of Sainte Marie as well as the coral reefs. Whale-watching. 4WD vehicles for overland trips too.

Whale-watching

July to September seems to be the best time to see humpbacked whales; you can watch them from the beach at La Crique or Atafana, or take a boat excursion (offered by some of the hotels or the Centre Nautique). Several hotels offer whale-watching trips, with or without a beach barbecue. The cost ranges from 200 to 400Ff.

HAINTENY

The *dingadingana* has borne fruit without coming into leaf,
 the *hazotokana* has borne fruit without coming into flower,
and the fishing has been uncertain this year.
Why have these changes occurred, my elder brother?
- Have you forgotten, perhaps, the sayings of our ancestors?
Consider, children, the conditions here on earth:
the trees grow, but not unceasingly,
for if they grew unceasingly, they would reach the sky.
Not only this,
but there is a time for their growing,
a time for their becoming old,
and a time for their breaking.
So it is, too, for man: there is a time for youth,
a time for old age,
a time for good,
a time for evil,
and a time for death.

Chapter Twelve

South and West of Toamasina

This section incorporates the increasingly visited Pangalanes lake resorts to the south of Toamasina and the most popular reserve in Madagascar, Analamazoatra (still known by most people as Périnet), and Lake Alaotra. Good roads and the Pangalanes waterway mean that getting around is no major problem. Also included is the coastal area around Manakara and Mananjary, popular with independent travellers, and the road south to Tolagnaro (Fort Dauphin).

PANGALANES

This series of lakes was linked by artificial canals in French Colonial times for commercial use, a quiet inland water being preferable to an often stormy sea. Over the years the canals became choked with vegetation and no longer passable, but plans are now being made to rehabilitate them and re-establish the unbroken waterway which stretched from Toamasina to Vangaindrano.

The quiet waters of the canal and lakes are much used by local fishermen for transporting their goods in pirogues and for fishing. With only 100 metres or so of land separating the canal from the ocean, sea and lake-side villages are in easy reach of each other.

In recent years Pangalanes has been developed for tourism, with lake-side bungalows and private nature reserves competing with the traditional ocean resorts for custom. There's even a new shallow-draught canal cruiser, the *M/V Mpanjakamena*, which has six double cabins, sundeck, dining saloon and cocktail bar. The cruiser is operated by Softline, 25 Boulevard Joffre, BP532 Toamasina (tel: 329 75). They have a contact in Tana, too (tel: 341 75). Although Softline's brochure implies that all 420km of the Pangalanes are navigable, this shouldn't be accepted as fact.

The centre for Pangalanes tourism is Lake Ampitabe, which has broad beaches of dazzlingly white sand, clean water for swimming (and only a few crocs), and a private nature reserve with several introduced species of lemur. The three hotels are in a small village called Ankanin'ny Nofy, which means 'House of Dreams'. Lake Ampitabe is 25km by boat from the village of

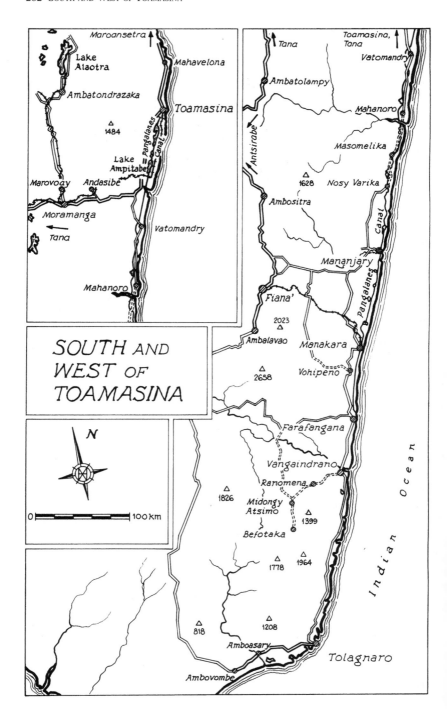

Maroansetra

Lake Alaotra

Mahavelona

Ambatondrazaka

Toamasina

△ 1484

Pangalanes Canal

Lake Ampitabe

Marovoay Andasibe

Moramanga

Tana

Vatomandry

Mahanoro

Tana

Toamasina, Tana

Vatomandry

Ambatolampy

Mahanoro

Masomelika

Antsirabe

△ 1628

Nosy Varika

Ambositra

Mananjary

Fiana'

Pangalanes Canal

△ 2023

Ambalavao

Manakara

△ 2658

Vohipeno

Farafangana

Vangaindrano

Ranomena

△ 1826

Midongy Atsimo

△ 1399

Befotaka

△ 1778 △ 1964

Indian Ocean

△ 818

△ 1208

Amboasary

Tolagnaro

Ambovombe

SOUTH AND WEST OF TOAMASINA

N

0 [====] 100 Km

Manambato on RN2, or there is a 35km track (negotiable by 4WD vehicles) linking the lake and RN2.

Getting there and away

Each hotel provides its own transport for booked-in guests. Reaching the lodges on Lake Ampitabe (Akanin'ny Nofy) from RN2 involves a drive to Manambato, at the edge of Lake Rasoabe, 7km south of Vohibinany (Brickaville), followed by a 45-minute boat journey along Pangalanes. You can also take a motor launch from Port Fluvial (Toamasina harbour). The ride takes 1½ hours and is most enjoyable, giving a good flavour of the lakes and connecting canal, and the activities of the local people.

Independent travellers can take a taxi-brousse to Manambato where there is a hotel, and the possibility of hiring a boat or pirogue to take them further.

If you've made a last-minute decision to stay at Ankanin'ny Nofy and are coming by train, get off at Andranokoditra (Brickaville), one stop after Ambila-Lemaitso (60km south of Toamasina). Someone from one of the hotels may be meeting the train and you could hitch a ride, or you can take a pirogue from behind the station and walk along a clear track, 15 minutes to the Pangalanes Hotel and 45 minutes to Bush House. Obviously, though, it is more convenient for everyone if you make a reservation.

An alternative for rail travellers is to get off at Ambila-Lemaitso where there are hotels and water transport to other Pangalanes areas.

Where to stay/eat
Ambila-Lemaitso

Hotel Relais Malaky 48,000Fmg, shared facilities. Reasonable food, and good situation close to the station.

Hotel les Cocotiers 65,000Fmg for self-contained bungalows. Good, but about a mile from the station and a bit cut off.

Lakeside hotels

There are three sets of beach bungalows at Ankanin'ny Nofy (Lake Ampitabe). The cost for these is approximately £10/US$15 for a double bungalow, plus transfers and meals. Phone the agencies in Tana or Toamasina for latest prices and availability.

For those wanting a cheaper look at the Pangalanes, there is an additional lodge at Lake Raoabe, near RN2.

Village Atafana Lake Ampitabe. 2/3-person bungalows on a lovely stretch of beach; excellent meals and excursions. Reservations in Tana through the agency MTB, 20 Rue Ratsimilaho (Isoraka, near the Colbert). Tel: 223 64. Postal address: BP 121.

Hotel des Pangalanes Lake Ampitabe. Seven 2-person bungalows, meals and excursions. Bookings: BP 112, Toamasina. Tel: 334 03 or 321 77.

Bush House Lake Ampitabe. German run, very comfortable, and in a beautiful situation.

Only five rooms so a pleasant family atmosphere. Book through Boogie Pilgrim, 40 Ave de L'Indépendance, Tana. Tel: 331 85 or 204 54; email bopi@bow.dts.mg.

Hotel Rasoa Beach Lake Raoabe, near Manambato. A friendly hotel offering a good taste of the Pangalanes without the expensive transfers. In 1996, 2-person bungalows cost 50,000Fmg, 4-person 70,000 and a 'Tarzan' hut on stilts 30,000Fmg. Good food. For bookings phone 252 35 in Tana.

Bush House Reserve

Bush House owns a small private reserve a 30-minute stroll away along the beach. This is well worth the 5,000Fmg entrance fee. Although it's more a zoo than a real reserve in that most of the lemurs have been introduced, they are free-ranging but tame enough to make photographing normally rare species easy and rewarding. There are crowned lemurs, red-bellied lemurs (and a fascinating hybrid of the two), ring-tailed lemurs, black and white ruffed lemurs, and Coquerel's sifaka. There is also a rather desperately affectionate red-fronted brown lemur.

In a separate area you'll see chameleons and radiated tortoises, and there is a well-tended garden of succulents.

Independent travel down the Pangalanes waterways

Difficult! Mark Hughes tried in 1995, making exhaustive enquiries. There would be no problem having a tour operator put together an expensive package for you, but for shoestring travellers there are not enough cargo boats to make hitching an easy option. There are pirogues, however, so my hunch is that you should either do it in short hops by pirogue, taking pot luck in finding a place to stay each night (bring your own mozzie net), or make an expedition of it with your own boat. I'd love to hear from anyone who tries either of these two options.

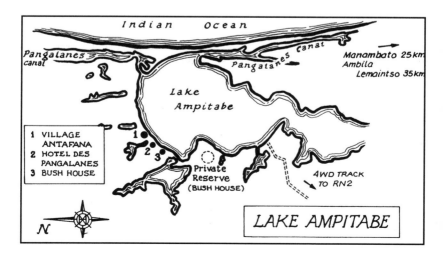

ANDASIBE (PÉRINET)

This famous reserve is currently undergoing something of an identity crisis. Formerly known as Périnet (and formally as Special Reserve, Périnet-Analamazoatra) the latest brochure calls it Andasibe National Park. This incorporates two protected areas: Mantadia National Park (which, unlike other national parks, is not generally open to tourists) and Special Reserve Analamazoatra, still called Périnet by most people, which is open to everyone. Then there's an additional area of primary forest, Maromizaha, which receives no formal protection. Confused? No matter, this block of moist montane forest (altitude: 930–1,049m) is extremely rich in fauna and flora, including – some experts say – a higher number of frog species than any comparable rainforest on earth. It is also the reserve closest to Tana and consequently the most popular in Madagascar. Andasibe is the name of the nearby town and railway station.

Getting there and away

When running, the train from Tana to Andasibe leaves at 06.00 three days a week; Toamasina to Andasibe leaves at 06.00 and costs a little more; from either direction it takes about six hours.

Taxi-brousses are much faster and those used on this route tend to be quite comfortable. You will pay less from Tana if you take a taxi-brousse to Moramanga (a regular stop) and a local taxi-be to the Andasibe turn-off from RN2.

Where to stay/eat

Hotel Vakona BP 750, Antananarivo. Tel: 213 94; fax: 230 70. This is the luxury hotel upmarket visitors have been wishing for. Its location near the graphite mine (same ownership) is not idyllic, and it is too far from the reserve, but the hotel itself works to perfection. The main building has been thoughtfully designed as an octagonal reception area, bar and lounge-dining room with a huge log-fire in the middle. When completed the upper storey will house a library and information centre. The 14 bungalows are quiet and comfortable and there will be a swimming pool. The manager, Yann, is energetic and charming, and the food delicious. The price per room (1996) is 260Fr (about £30/US$50) or 80,000Fmg.

To reach Vakona from Andasibe, cross the bridge into the village, and take the left fork. After a few kilometres you arrive at the entrance to the graphite mine on your left. Pass through the mine to the hotel.

Hotel Feon' Ny Ala The name means 'Window of the Forest' or 'Voice of the Forest'. This well-recommended place is on the right side of the road that runs from RN2 to Andasibe. There are six bungalows (in 1996, 35,000Fmg for shared outside bathroom/WC, 60,000Fmg with adjoining bathroom) and a flat, grassy area for camping. The Chinese owners, M and Mme Sum Chuk Lan, are very helpful and eager to please, and the food is ample and excellent (20,000Fmg for dinner). There is a beautiful orchid garden on the river bank. You are close enough to the reserve to hear the indri call: 'they make the most amazing racket before sundown.' Gavin and Val Thomson

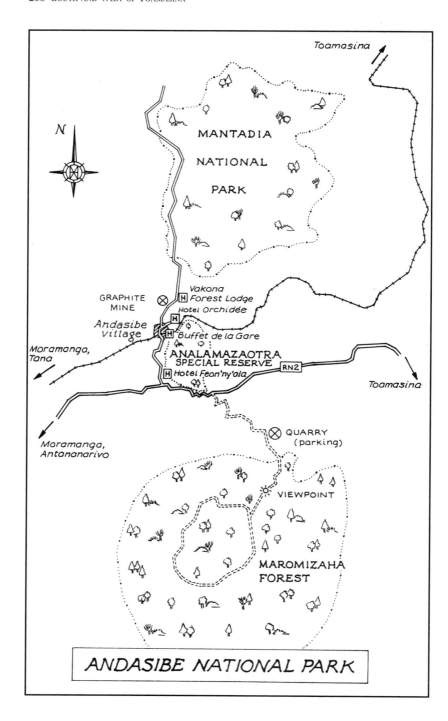

ANDASIBE NATIONAL PARK

add that the Feon' Ny Ala must be the best-run hotel in Madagascar – and there's every chance of sighting indri at the edge of the forest and the Madagascar little grebe on the small lake. The only problem is that it is usually full.

The Feon' ny Ala is the farthest hotel from the town of Andasibe (a 40-minute walk), so you should plan to eat your meals in the restaurant, or bring food with you from Tana if you're camping at the hotel.

Hotel Buffet de la Gare Until 1993 this was the only place to stay in Andasibe, and its list of distinguished guests included Prince Philip, Gerald Durrell and David Attenborough. Built in 1938 it must once have been appropriate for its role of housing the Great and the Good who wished to visit Périnet, but not within my memory. For the last two decades it has been a typical Category C hotel, with saggy beds, a non-functioning loo, and a certain amount of non-endemic wildlife in the bedrooms (one distinguished guest suffered a rat bite). A great social leveller.

Now, alas, there are good, well-run hotels in Andasibe and the Buffet will lose its mix of backpackers and posh visitors. I am very fond of this place and of its courteous owner, Monsieur Joseph. The dining room is truly elegant – fresh flowers on the tables and a marvellous rosewood bar. There are nice little features such as the resident dog called Bijou which looks as though it might be used to mop the floor, and a *phelsuma* gecko which stuck to the new paintwork near the door; the enthusiastic workman simply applied another coat of paint over the little body and there it remains. I like the food; others don't.

This is still the hotel nearest to the reserve and fine for budget travellers who don't want to miss a moment of nature-watching. There are eight basic rooms, and seven chalet-bungalows. A further series of bungalows have been built in a more attractive area even nearer the reserve. These have three beds, fireplaces and hot water. Here you are surrounded by wildlife including, if you're lucky, lemurs.

Maison des Orchidées A wooden hotel right in the village of Andasibe, so noisy. Comfortable, Malagasy-run, hot water. Rooms for around 30,000Fmg (1995).

Permits and guides

You can get your permit from ANGAP in Tana, or at the park entrance. Though not compulsory, you are strongly urged to take a guide since the ones here are the best in Madagascar and an example to the rest of the country for knowledge, enthusiasm, and an awareness of what tourists want. The Association des Guides Andasibe (AGA) ensures that standards are maintained. All the guides know where to find indri and other lemurs. Those that I can particularly recommend are Desiré, Maurice and his brother Patrice (the latter is an expert on birds), Lala and Marie, Eugene, Nirina and Zac; but there are other rising stars. The fee is now (1996) set at 20,000Fmg for two hours during the day (three people). A night tour (18.30 to 20.00) is 40,000Fmg. A guide here can make as much in one day as a Malagasy worker earns in a month. I wish I were more confident that some of the financial benefits of ecotourism were reaching the villagers of Andasibe.

Périnet (Analamazoatra) Special Reserve

This 810ha reserve protects the largest of the lemur family, *Indri indri*. Standing about three feet high, with a barely visible tail, black and white markings and a surprised teddy-bear face, the indri looks more like a gone-wrong panda than a lemur. The long back legs are immensely powerful, and an indri can propel itself backwards 30 feet, execute a turn in mid-air, and land face-forward

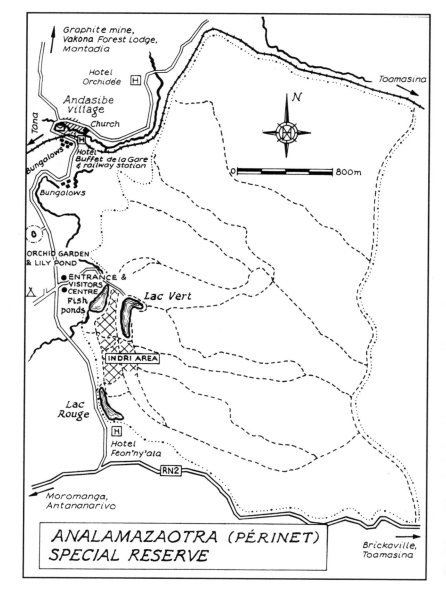

ANALAMAZAOTRA (PÉRINET) SPECIAL RESERVE

to gaze down benevolently at its observers. And you will be an observer: everyone now sees indris in Périnet, and most also hear them. For it is the voice that makes this lemur extra special: whilst other lemurs grunt or swear, the indri sings. It is an eerie, wailing sound somewhere between the song of a whale and a police-siren, and it carries for up to two miles as troops call to each other across the forest. The indris are fairly punctual with their song: if you are in the reserve between one and two hours after daybreak and shortly before dusk you should hear them. There's little point in looking for indri at other times; they spend much of the day dozing in the tops of trees. Indri live in small family groups of up to five animals, and give birth in June. Births usually occur every two years. At the last count there were 280 indris in Périnet.

In Malagasy the indri is called *Babakoto* which means 'Father of Man'. It is *fady* to kill an indri, and there are various legends explaining why. One links the indri with the origin of man (thus supporting modern evolutionary thought) and another tells of a man who climbed a forest tree to gather wild honey, and was severely stung by the bees. Losing his hold, he fell, but was caught by a huge indri which carried him on its back to safety.

There are nine species of lemur altogether in Périnet (including aye-aye), although you will not see them all. You may find the troop of grey bamboo lemurs (*Hapelemur griseus*) which are diurnal and sometimes feed on the bamboo near the warden's house (although I have not seen them recently), brown lemurs, and perhaps a sleeping avahi (woolly lemur) curled up in the fork of a tree. It is worth going on a nocturnal lemur hunt (the guides are experts at this) to look for mouse lemurs, and the greater dwarf lemur (*Cheirogaleus major*) which hibernates during the cold season.

Lemurs are only a few of the creatures to be found in Périnet. There are tenrecs, beautiful and varied insects and spiders, and lots of reptiles. One of Madagascar's biggest chameleons lives here: *Chameleon parsonii*, which is bright green, about two feet long and has twin horns at the end of its snout, and the smallest, *Chameleon nasutus*. The guides keep a selection of chameleons near the entrance for tourists to photograph. Boas are quite common and placid. This is also a great place for birdwatching.

Botanists will not be disappointed. In French colonial days an orchid garden was started by the lily pond to the right of the road to the reserve, and a variety of species flourishes here although most flower in the warm wet season.

Leeches can be an unpleasant aspect of Périnet if you've pushed through vegetation and it's been raining recently. Tuck your trousers into your socks and apply insect repellent.

Where to go in Périnet

At the Périnet gate is 'the most beautiful toilet in all Madagascar'. Trimmed with tiles cut from Malagasy stone, it was built with the aid of a Japanese donation. It will cost you 200Fmg to use it, and is almost worth a visit on its own.

Maromizaha

This 10,000ha area of mainly primary forest offers a great day's hiking for enthusiastic and fit visitors. An 18km trail runs from a stone quarry area to the town of Andasibe. It is slippery when wet and requires a full day (bring a picnic) but gives hikers the chance to see some additional species such as – if you are really lucky – the *simpona* or diademed sifaka, and black and white ruffed lemur. It is also the best place I know for finding some of Madagascar's 1,000 or so bizarre and colourful weevils! If you have only a half day available, it is still worth walking along the trail to the main viewpoint.

Maromizaha (pronouned Marom<u>ee</u>z) is about 7km from Andasibe in the direction of Toamasina, off RN2. The track leading to Maromizaha (closed by a barrier) is on the right, about 4km from the Andasibe turning. Walk – or get permission to drive – up the track to the stone quarry. The trail starts to the left of the flat area above the workers' houses (as you face back to the road). Since this is not a protected area you can camp here.

Mantady (Mantadia) National Park

This newly created national park is 25km to the north of Périnet. It lies at a higher altitude than the more popular reserve and consequently harbours different species in its untouched primary forest. However, at the time of writing (1996) it was not officially open to tourists though interested visitors can usually get permission to visit it. Ask one of the experienced guides at Périnet to do this for you – and to accompany you. Once there, Mantady is a naturalist's goldmine, with many seldom-seen species of mammals, reptiles and birds. To do justice to Mantady you should spend a couple of days there, camping. There are no supplies and you should be completely self-sufficient and prepared for some muddy, rugged hiking.

To reach Mantady, follow the signs to the Vakona hotel, but continue along the road from the mine rather than taking the turning to the right that leads to the hotel. The park entrance is at the '14km' sign.

OTHER PLACES OF INTEREST ON RN2
Antsampanana
If you are driving up RN2 from Toamasina this is a popular place to stop to buy fruit. The little town is bursting with stalls offering all sorts of goodies. Nice for photography, too. If you want to dally longer there is the basic Hotel Espérance and some restaurants. From here it is about 1½ hours' drive to Andasibe.

Moramanga
This formerly sleepy town is about a half-hour's drive from Andasibe. It gained a new lease of life with the completion of the Chinese road (there is a memorial here to the Chinese workers) and, during the 1980s and early '90s, from the absence of comfortable hotels in Andasibe. Some groups preferred to stay here than to suffer the privations of Périnet. Moramanga is still a popular lunch stop when driving to Andasibe from Tana.

Where to stay/eat
Grand Hotel Tel: 620 16. Helpful, friendly; hot water.

Emeraude Tel: 621 57. Hot showers. Good value.

Mirasoa A new hotel on RN2 about 1km from the centre on the Tana side of town. Basic but clean. 15,000Fmg (1995).

Other basic hotels include the **Restau-Hotel Maitso an'Ala**, the **Hotel Fivami**, and **Hotel au Poisson**.

The Chinese restaurant **Guangzou** serves good food and is popular with groups so reservations may be necessary in the high season. Tel: 04 62089. Almost as popular is the **Au Coq d'Or**. Tel: 62045.

Mandraka (nature farm)
Described in *Chapter Eight*, page 162.

Marovoay
This is the first stop on the railway line north towards Lake Alaotra, and the name means 'Many Crocodiles'. Appropriately, a commercial crocodile farm has been started here which is open to visitors. There are over a thousand *Crocodylus niloticus*, some over two and a half metres in length, living in semi-wild conditions. The best season to visit is January, when the eggs are hatching. For a visit write to: Reptel Madagascar, 50 Ave Grandidier, BP 563, Isoraka, Antananarivo. Tel: 348 86, fax: 206 48.

LAKE ALAOTRA

This is the largest lake in Madagascar and looks wonderful on the map: one imagines it surrounded by overhanging forest. Sadly, forest has made way for rice, and this is one of the most abused and degraded areas in Madagascar. Deforestation has silted up the lake so that its maximum dry-season depth is only 60cm. Introduction of exotic fish has done further damage. The area has been designated a Site of Special Biological Interest by the WWF because of its endemic waterfowl, although it is too late to save Delacour's grebe (Alaotra little grebe , *Tachybaptus rufolavatus*) which is now extinct. The Madagascar pochard (*Aythy innonata*) may have gone the same way. Lemurs are faring better. Some Alaotran grey bamboo lemur, *Hapalemur griseus alaotrensis*, are breeding happily in their new home at Jersey Zoo (having been brought there by Gerald Durrell); and Tsimbazaza also has a successful captive breeding programme, although whether there will be any habitat to release their descendants into is debatable.

Getting there and away

By rail A spur of the railway runs from Moramanga, with trains leaving Tana early in the morning, and ends at Ambatondrazaka near the southeast side of the lake.

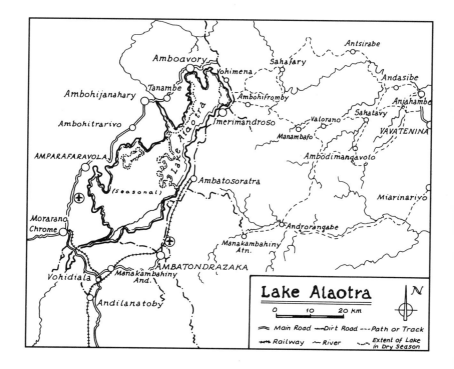

By road The dirt road (RN44) from Moramanga is being improved, bridges are being built, and it may soon be the easiest way to reach the lake.

Bishop Brock, who cycled this route in 1996, writes: 'It's a good dirt road, nice scenery, sparsely populated. If you happen to be going that way I can recommend a stop at the Hotely Mahandry in **Amboasary-Gara**, about 60km north of Moramanga. This may be the prettiest *hotely* in Madagascar. The owner grows orchids, is very friendly, and rents a single room for 15,000Fmg.'

Ambatondrazaka

The main town of the area, and a good centre for excursions, with a couple of *Category B* or *C* hotels.

Where to stay/eat

Hotel Voahirana BP 65, Côte Postale 503. Good value, at 20,000Fmg (1995) and room price included breakfast. Quite a walk from the station. Next door is the restaurant **Cantonnais**; very good value.

Hotel Max Near the station. 14 rooms. The restaurant **Fanantenana** is next door.

Excursions

Probably the best reason to come to Lake Alaotra is to meet the guide Jean-Baptiste Randrianomanana and join him for one of his excursions. 'He speaks excellent English, studied sociology and philosophy and is extremely knowledgeable about all aspects of Madagascar. His wife is a geographer. He will take you on a tour of the lake which involves a taxi drive to a traditional village on the shores of the lake, a night with a local family at Imerimandroso, a pirogue crossing on the lake to another village called Vohitsara to meet the medicine man and the school teacher etc, and a taxi-ride back to Ambatondrazaka.' (J. and R. McFarlaine). Jean-Baptiste may be able to invite you to a *famadihana* and can give you detailed information for hiking the Smugglers' Path to the coast – a four or five day hike (see below). He usually meets the train and keeps an eye out for *vazahas* or he can be contacted through the Hotel Voahirana.

Imerimandroso

A small town near the lake; half an hour's walk to the south is a village from where you can take a pirogue.

There is one basic hotel, the **Bellevue**.

Note: There are no hotels in Ambatosoatra, midway up the east side of Lake Alaotra.

The Smugglers' Path

John Kupiec – an exceptionally adventurous and independent traveller – decided to do this trail on his own. He writes: 'From the following story you will see what happens when an out-of-the-way path in Madagascar gets touristed.' It is quite a long story. The core of it is that John's contact with the local people was almost entirely negative (in sharp contrast to his experiences elsewhere), he was cheated out of money at almost every stage (despite speaking some Malagasy), and the uncertainty of what would happen each day spoiled the walk anyway.

John's conclusion is that even with the FTM map it is not possible to follow this path without a guide, and that it would be better to seek out the services of Jean-Baptiste.

For the record, John's journey took him from the train station at **Vohidiala** then by taxi-brousse to **Tanambe** where there is a basic hotel. Next day he walked to **Vohitsara** and took a pirogue across the lake to **Andromba** where the Smugglers' Path begins. In **Ambohitromby** he picked up one of a series of guides to take him to **Manambato**. Three days and several villages later he reached the end of the trail at **Anjahambe**. From there it was a short taxi-brousse ride to **Vavatenina**, where he stayed in some hotel-bungalows, and thence to the east coast road.

THE SOUTHEAST

For most people this area begins with Mananjary, which is linked to the Highlands by both air and road. Adventurous souls, however, can slowly make their way south, leaving RN2 after Brickaville.

Cyclone Gretelle hit the southeast of Madagascar in January 1997, killing approximately 100 villagers and rendering some 30,000 people homeless. The worst hit towns were Manakara, Vohipeno and Farafangana.

The rough route south

The following report is from Helena Drysdale. The journey she describes formed the basis of her book *Dancing with the Dead* (see *Further Reading*).

'We travelled from Tamatave to Mananjary over two weeks. Generally people assured us it was impossible, that there were no roads, that all the bridges were down in the cyclone, and the ferries were *en panne* (that familiar phrase). But with luck and ingenuity we made it. One taxi-brousse per week from Tamatave to Mahanoro (two days), otherwise river boats available at Tamatave's river port for hitching (we went on boats travelling south to a graphite mine in Vatomandry – a very uncomfortable three days).

'In **Vatomandry** we stayed in the Hotel Fotsy; thatched bungalows. Good food here and some Chinese restaurants in town. From there to **Mahanoro**, one day by taxi-brousse, two by boat. Hotel Pangalanes, full of ladies of the night and noisy revellers but a nice atmosphere. Boat from Mahanoro to **Masomelika** one day; very simple hotel but friendly people (I asked for the toilet and was pointed to a bucket. This was the shower – the toilet was in the bushes). From Masomelika to **Nosy Varika** took half a day hitchhiking. There's a relatively expensive Chinese hotel here. Then on to Mananjary, one night by boat.'

The Chinese-owned hotel described by Helena is **Hotel Petite Oasis**, which 'serves excellent food, is clean and light and has rooms as well as little bungalows at the back' (Maggie Rush). Another nearby is the **Hotel de la Saraleona**.

HAINTENY

It is through his subjects that the sovereign reigns,
It is the rocks that cause the stream to sing.
It is its feathers that make the chicken large.
The palm-trees are the feet of the water.
The winds are the feet of the fire.
The beloved is the tree of life.

MANANJARY AND MANAKARA

These two pleasant seaside towns have good communications with the rest of Madagascar and are gaining in popularity among discerning travellers.

Getting there and away

Mananjary is usually reached by road from Ranomafana, and Manakara is the end (or beginning) of the railway journey from Fianarantsoa (see page 177). The road between the two towns is surfaced, but badly potholed. Even so, the journey by taxi-brousse takes only four hours.

Mananjary is linked by air (HS 748 and Twin Otter) to Tana or Tolagnaro.

Mananjary

A very nice small town accessible by good road and taxi-brousse (lovely scenery) from Ranomafana, and famous for its circumcision ceremony which

---

THE MAGIC SHOW

Chris Ballance

We saw a poster in Manakara for a Magic Show so bought tickets. The magician was quite good in a relaxed way. The audience were brilliant. About 120 people in a dingy youth centre hall without lights. He began with a couple of simple disappearing tricks that drew rounds of applause. It was the lesser tricks that were applauded; the better ones left the audience too spell-bound to think of clapping. His magic wand was a flute-sized rod which he empowered by touching a plastic skull with a red robe hanging from it. He used few other props – two or three magic boxes, a few packs of cards and a glass. He filled this with flour, wrapped it in a 'magicked' newspaper and turned it into a glass of bon-bons which he threw into the audience. From this moment the audience were his, body and soul. There was no 'willing suspension of disbelief'. These people had eaten the proof of his powers.

He repeated the trick later, turning coffee powder into cigarettes. He put one of the cigarettes into a guillotine and cut it. Then he put a volunteer boy's finger into the guillotine. Another boy had to hold a hat to catch the finger. Down came the guillotine, the hand was hidden in the hat and then magicked better. As the boy left the stage he was mobbed. All we could see was a heap of every child in the audience. Suddenly a finger shot up from the centre of the heap, triumphantly showing everyone it was attached to its hand. And when the conjurer got a girl in the audience to lay an egg, everyone – but *everyone* – had to see it, touch it, and marvel at it.

The show ended with a draw in which names were put into a hat (we prayed we wouldn't win). There were prizes of 1,000, 5,000 and 10,000Fmg notes. Each winner was given the note to put into an envelope which was put into a magic box, magicked, and then given back. We suspected they got a message to the effect of 'You've been had'. The girl next to me goggled – that's the only word – at the sight of the money. *'Cinq mille francs!'* she kept repeating over and over in an ecstasy of hope. The sight of the 10,000Fmg note shut her up entirely.

Next day we changed £40 to last us for three days. We received 138,000Fmg. The obscenity of international finance, beside that girl, shamed us.

takes place every seven years. The next one will be in the year 2000.

There is a long beach with terrific breakers (dangerous swimming – and there are sharks) and the Pangalanes Canal, and all the attractions of people-watching. 'The men go out early (4am) in a tremendous surf and row or sail back into the river. Shrimps are sold to wholesalers. Other fish (some very pretty ones) are eaten. Some fishermen *fadys*: Wives are not allowed to look at another man until 12pm or something will happen to the husband at sea; a man who eats pork cannot go to sea.' (C and J Hermans). Maggie Rush adds: 'Mananjary seems to be the hideaway for foreigners who live in Madagascar. The town itself is small, but the market is colourful and lively, full of woven goods and all kinds of fish and spices.'

Where to stay/eat
Jardin de la Mer This hotel was badly damaged by the cyclone and may still be closed. If open it is the hotel of choice in Mananjary: a very pleasant set of beach bungalows serving good food.

Solimotel Bd Maritime. The best hotel if Jardin de la Mer is closed. Good, but rather expensive food.

Hotel aux Bons Amis Rooms about 15,000Fmg (1995). Proprietor friendly and accommodating.

Snack Central, near the market, has a modest menu with modest prices, good food, and is willing to serve meals mid-afternoon.

Manakara
Manakara was severely damaged by Cyclone Gretelle in January 1997, so some of the recommended hotels may not be operating.

The old part of town is recommended by Andrea Jarman. 'The *Allée des Filaos* running between ex-colonial buildings and the ocean makes the waterfront a very attractive part of town. The beach, with its crashing waves, is the favourite place for gymnasts and martial arts enthusiasts to train. The new town and station are across the river bridge and of no interest. Pousse-pousses provide the best local transport.'

You should not swim in Manakara because of dangerous currents and sharks.

Where to stay/eat
Two hotels under the same ownership (Alex Andriamifidy and his wife) are **Hotel Sidi**, and **Hotel Eden Sidi** situated 13km north of Manakara on the coast. BP 80, Ambinagny. Tel: 212 02/212 03. In 1995 the price of rooms was 40,000Fmg, and the food reportedly excellent.

Parthenay Club Tel: 211 60. This used to be a posh tennis club for the locals, with a swimming pool, with some tourist bungalows on the side. It was severely damaged in the cyclone so may take a while to pick up. Bungalows cost 20,000 (1995). It's located a bit south of the Hotel Manakara. No regular restaurant but you can order food in advance.

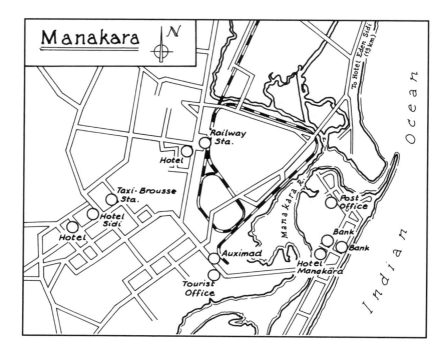

Hotel Manakara A friendly, once-pretty hotel popular with travellers (and ants), in town but near the ocean. 16,000–40,000Fmg (1995). 'The hotel waiter approached us over breakfast. "Excuse me. You had a small bottle of beer yesterday evening and I'm afraid we charged you for a large one. Here is your change." Can you imagine that happening in Britain?' (Chris Ballance).

Le Chalet Suisse BP 31 Manakara (316) Tel: 213 89. An excellent place to eat 'grillades, Swiss specialities including raclette and macaroni à la crème, and a variety of other well-prepared dishes. It is easy to spot its large red and white sign on the right side of the road to the airport, on the edge of town a short distance after you pass the railway station. The owners are Mme Voahangy, the gracious Malgache hostess, and Claude Bays, a Swiss architect who designed and built this real chalet in 1994. Both friendly and well informed about the Manakara area.' (Mark Ward)

Manakara to Fianar by train

With the Tana-Toamasina line in disrepair, this now offers the most interesting – and beautiful – train ride in Madagascar. The track is cyclone-damaged and the locomotives ancient, so it is an exciting ride. Mark Hughes took it in 1995: 'We couldn't book seats but were told to board the parked train with a porter and point out which ones we wanted. The following morning the porter took our luggage as soon as we arrived, and when we eventually boarded our luggage and the porter were waiting at our selected seats! The train ride is a story in itself. The views were great and the stops were interesting. Each station seemed to have a speciality – all the vendors sold bananas, or eggs, or fried things. Things got exciting as the train went uphill. It became a real "Little Train that Could" ('I think I can, I think I can...'). The engine was really straining and we weren't going anywhere. Three times the train started rolling backwards despite the squealing brakes and the engine's best efforts.'

The train is running on an erratic schedule. You will have to check at the station and see when it is likely to feel strong enough to make the journey. When it does, the cost (1995) is 22,000Fmg first class. Without breakdowns it takes about seven hours to reach Fianar from Manakara, but 20 hours is not unknown. For the best views sit on the right hand side.

ZEBU

The hump-backed cattle, zebu, which nearly outnumber the country's human population, produce a relatively low yield in milk and meat. These animals are near-sacred and generally are not eaten by the Malagasy, other than at ceremonies of social or religious significance. Zebu are said to have originated from northeast India, eventually spreading as far as Egypt and then down to Ethiopia and other parts of East Africa. It is not known how they were introduced to Madagascar but they are a symbol of wealth and status as well as being used for burden.

Zebu come in a variety of colours, the most sought-after being the *omby volavita*, which is chestnut with a white spot on the head. There are 80 words in the Malagasy language to describe the physical attributes of zebu, in particular the colour, horns and hump.

In the south, zebu meat is always served at funerals and among certain southern tribes the cattle are used as marriage settlements, as is done in Africa. Whenever there is a traditional ritual or ceremony, zebu are sacrificed, the heads being given to the highest ranking members of the community. Blood is smeared on participants as it is believed to have purification properties, and the fat from the hump of the cattle is used as an ingredient for incense.

While zebu theft in the past was considered an act of bravery, it is now confined mainly to the Bara. The traditional penalty for cattle-rustling was the *dina* whereby the culprit and his family were reduced to slavery. Among the Antandroy and Mahafaly a fine of ten zebu would have to be paid by the thief: five for the family from whom the cattle were stolen and five for the king.

To the rural Malagasy a herd of zebu is as symbolic of prosperity as is a new car in our culture. Government aid programmes must take this into account; for instance improved rice yields will indirectly lead to more environmental degradation by providing more money to buy more zebu.

The French colonial government thought they had an answer: they introduced a tax on each animal. However, local politicians were quick to point out that since Malagasy women had always been exempt from taxation, the same rule should apply to cows!

CONTINUING SOUTH

Note: Both Vohipeno and Farafangana were badly damaged by Cyclone Gretelle in January 1997.

Vohipeno

Situated some 45km south of Manakara, this small town is the centre of the Antaimoro tribe who came from Arabia about 600 years ago, bringing the first script to Madagascar. Their Islamic history is shown by their clothing (turban and fez, as well as Arab-style robes). They are the inheritors of the 'great writings', *sorabe*, written in Malagasy but in Arabic script. *Sorabe* continue to be written, still in Arabic, still on 'Antaimoro paper'. The scribes who practise this art are known as *katibo* and the writing and their knowledge of it give them a special power. The writing itself ranges from accounts of historical events to astrology, and the books are considered sacred.

Farafangana

Accessible by taxi-brousse from Manakara, this is a pleasant and comfortable town to hang around in for a while.

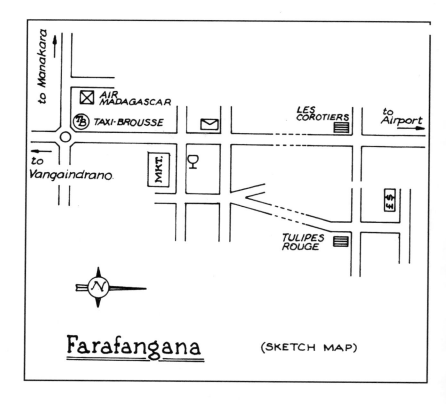

THE EAST
Above: *Beach near Sambava* (HB)
Below left: *Walking in the reserve of Anjanaharibe-Sud, near Andapa* (HB)
Below right: *Schoolchildren near Andapa* (HB)

THE NORTH
An adventurous chameleon on the beach at Nosy Komba (NG)

THE WEST

Above: *On the* tsingy *of Ankarana* (HB)

Below: *The Avenue of the Baobabs, Morondava* (NG)

Taxi-brousse (RH)

Where to stay/eat
Hotel Les Cocotiers A newish up-market hotel near the post office.

Hotel Les Tulipes Rouges Rooms are all called after different shades of red! Clean, good food and safe parking.

There are several small *hotelys* with low-priced rooms. The **Salon de Thé Dahlia** is recommended for a snack.

To the south or west
The road from Farafangana to Ihosy has long been infamous for bandits, but has reportedly been improved, allowing a Highlands/East Coast circuit of great interest. You should check locally, however, about conditions and safety.

Those with time, a 4WD vehicle or mountain bike, or a light backpack and lots of energy, can continue south. The following notes are from two readers who travelled the area in 1992. Conditions are likely to have got better, rather than worse.

'**Vangaindrano** has the feel of a frontier town and the bridge which crosses the Manañara river just before you get there is only about ten years old. There is a BTM bank and four basic hotels: the Ny Antsika (a yellow-fronted shop,

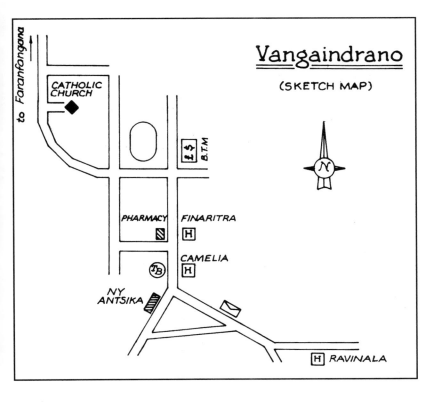

with the best rooms of the four), and the Finaritra, Camelia and Ravinala. The latter is the best of the budget hotels and is situated some 200m east of the market on the way to Tolagnaro.'

Vangaindrano is the end of the road for most people, but you can continue further: 'There is a road southwest to **Midongy Atsimo** (no regular TB service, occasional bashie) which is maintained reasonably well because of a new coffee project. Muddy in places. 4WD advisable but not essential. 95km, 5-6 hours, with one excellent ferry. Food on the road in La Rose du Sud in **Ranomena**, oodles of *couleur locale*. No hotel in Midongy, but we rented a nice house with three beds, outside toilet, and tub of water for 4,000Fmg. All this, plus meals, was obtained from the Épicerie on the Befotaka road (south end of town). The road to **Befotaka** (40km) was impassable most of the time, very skiddy, but has some very good forest at 20-25km south of Midongy.'

'Maps show that you can follow the gloriously named RN12 to Fort Dauphin. Only those prepared to suffer some privations should attempt to do this. Transport in the area is erratic and unpredictable, the roads are very bad. Be prepared to travel over rickety bridges in overladen lorries, walk long distances, and cross rivers in what may appear to be very unstable dug-out canoes (without a counter-balance). Of the latter the secret is to get your centre of gravity as low as possible, so for *vazaha* this invariably means kneeling down in the bottom of the canoe and remaining still. It is also advisable to remove footwear for a crossing. You may only fear losing your luggage if the canoe capsizes, but remember that most people here cannot swim well and that luggage is not what they fear losing, but their lives.'

☏

'The breast-leaper... It is a small animal which attaches itself to the bark of trees and being of a greenish hue is not easily perceived; there it remains with its throat open to receive the flies, spiders and other insects that approach it, which it devours. This animal is described as having attached to the back, tail, legs, neck, and the extremity of the chin, little paws or hooks like those at the end of a bat's wing with which it adheres to whatever it attaches itself in such a manner as if it were really glued. If a native happens to approach the tree where it hangs, it instantly leaps upon his naked breast, and sticks so firmly that in order to remove it, they are obliged, with a razor, to cut away the skin also'.
Samuel Copland, History of the Island of Madagascar, *1822*

Part Five

THE NORTH AND WEST

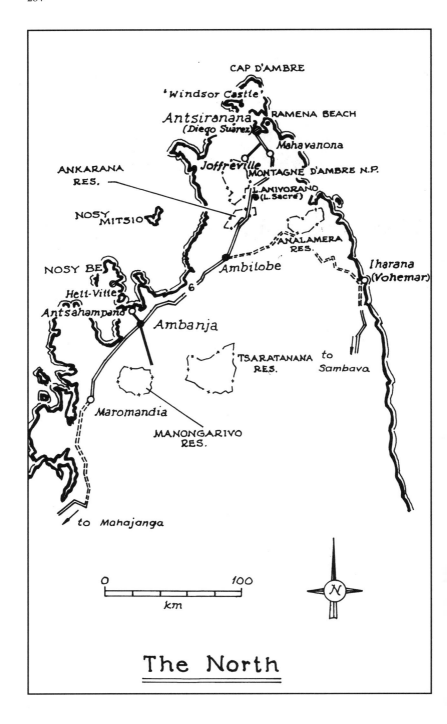

The North

Chapter Thirteen

The North

The northern part of Madagascar is the domain of the Antankarana people. Cut off by rugged mountains, the Antankarana were left to their own devices until the mid-1700s when they were conquered by the Sakalava; they in turn submitted to the Merina king Radama I, aided by his military adviser James Hastie, in 1823.

The north is characterised by its variety. With the Tsaratanana massif (which includes Madagascar's highest peak, Maromokotro, 2,876m) bringing more rain to the Nosy Be area than is normal on the west coast, and the pocket of dry climate around Antsiranana (Diego Suarez) which has seven months of dry weather with 90% of the 900mm of rain falling between December and April, the weather can alter dramatically within short distances. With changes of weather go changes of vegetation and its accompanying fauna, making this region particularly interesting for botanists and other naturalists.

Getting around

Roads in the area are being improved and Antsiranana is losing its isolation. Distances are long, however, so most people prefer to fly.

ANTSIRANANA (DIEGO SUAREZ)

History

Forgivingly named after a Portuguese captain, Diego Suarez, who arrived in 1543 and proceeded to murder and rape the inhabitants and sell them into slavery, this large town has had an eventful history with truth blending into fiction. An often-told story, originated by Daniel Defoe, is that pirates in the 17th century founded the Republic of Libertalia here. Not true, say modern historians.

Most people still call the town Diego. The Malagasy name simply means 'Port' and its strategic importance as a deep-water harbour has long been recognised. The French installed a military base here in 1885, and the town played an important role in the Second World War when Madagascar was under the control of the Vichy French (see box). To prevent the island falling into Japanese hands, Britain and the allies captured and occupied Diego Suarez in 1942. There is a British Cemetery in the town honouring those killed at this time.

MADAGASCAR OPERATIONS IN WORLD WAR II

Peter La Niece (who was there)

After the fall of Singapore in 1942 a Japanese Strike Force bombed Colombo and sank three major British warships in the vicinity. At the time Madagascar was in the hands of the Vichy French sympathetic to the Axis Powers. Churchill and the War Cabinet feared that if Japan or Germany were afforded facilities in Madagascar the vital supply routes round the Cape through the Mozambique Channel to Egypt and India could be threatened and cut off. The capture of the strategic harbour of Diego Suarez was ordered.

The assault took place on May 5 1942 on three beaches on the northwest corner of Madagascar. There was some opposition but the advance towards Diego Suarez proceeded satisfactorily until it reached the outskirts of the town where it was halted with fairly heavy casualties at a fixed defence line. It was decided to break the stalemate by despatching the ship's detachment of 50 Royal Marines from the battleship *Ramillies* to take the French defences from the rear. They were embarked in the destroyer *Anthony* which proceeded at 30 knots through the night round the northern tip of Madagascar and succeeded in entering Diego Suarez harbour undetected, landing the very seasick Royal Marines. All they had in the way of maps was a page torn from a 15-year-old tourist guide. They set off in the dark and soon came to a large barracks building. Inside they found all the French soldiers asleep and their firearms piled neatly in the entrance to their dormitories. The French were called upon to surrender which they did. The Royal Marines then set off again towards their objective. Very soon they arrived at the telephone exchange where an enterprising French-speaking Royal Marine officer phoned the Commander of the French defences, informed him that his colleagues in the barracks had surrendered and requested him to do the same. He complied and Diego Suarez was in British hands.

The following month a Japanese submarine dropped two human torpedoes off the entrance to Diego Suarez and succeeded in sinking a tanker and heavily damaging the *Ramillies*. There were also indications that the town of Majunga on the west coast of Madagascar was being used as a base by Vichy French and probably German U-boats. It was therefore decided to launch two further operations and occupy Madagascar completely.

The second assault took place at Majunga on September 10 1942 which, after incurring some casualties, was successful. Elements of an East African brigade started their march on the capital. The assault force was re-embarked and all ships went round and anchored in Diego Suarez Bay to finalise plans for the third operation.

On September 18 the whole force appeared off the east coast town of Tamatave. An ultimatum was signalled to the French Commander to the effect that unless he surrendered, his positions would be bombarded by the *Warspite* and her escorting cruisers as well as air strikes from the carrier *Illustrious*. He capitulated and the landings were unopposed. Troops of the East African brigade set off immediately for Tananarive which fell on September 23. The Governor General escaped southwards with 700 troops but was overtaken later in October which ended the campaign.

Antsiranana (Diego) today

This is Madagascar's fifth largest town (population about 80,000) and of increasing interest to visitors for its diverse attractions. Traditionally rated second in beauty after Rio de Janeiro (presumably by people who had never seen Brazil) the harbour is encircled by hills, with a conical 'sugar loaf' plonked in one of the bays to the east of the town. From the air or the top of Montagne des Français, Antsiranana's superb position can be appreciated but the city itself is in the usual state of decay, though with a particular charm. The port's isolation behind its mountain barrier and its long association with non-Malagasy races have given it an unusually cosmopolitan population and lots of colour: there are Arabs, Creoles (descendants of Europeans), Indians, Chinese, and Comorans.

It's a town you either love or hate; generally speaking, independent travellers love it (good food, beach, atmosphere) whilst groups hate it because of the lack of a decent hotel.

The name Joffre seems to be everywhere in and around the town. General Joseph Joffre was the military commander of the town in 1897 and later became Maréchal de France. In 1911 he took over the supreme command of the French armies, and was the victor of the Battle of the Marne in 1914.

Antsiranana is a pleasant town for wandering; take a look at the market, poke around the harbour, and investigate a few souvenir shops. The best is probably Bijouterie Chez Babou, at 10 Rue de Colbert.

There's a standard taxi tariff for journeys within the town. In 1996 it was 1000Fmg, doubling after 8pm.

Getting there and away

There are flights from Tana (returning the same day) via Mahajanga on most days. You can also fly via the east coast towns of Toamasina and Sambava, and from Nosy Be. For the overland route to Sambava see page 301; to Nosy Be see 302.

Where to stay
Category A
None!

Category B

Hotel Escale On the road to the airport. Tel: 223 82. From 90,000Fmg to 115,000Fmg for a double bungalow. I have no reports on its quality but it's worth checking out.

Hotel Paradis du Nord Rue Villaret Joyeuse, across from the market. Tel: 214 05. This is probably the best value in town since everything works – air-conditioning, hot water... The rooms themselves (45,000Fmg) are cell-like except for No 1 which is marvellously spacious and overlooks the colourful market. There is a pleasant balcony dining room (with good food), a laundry service, and a secure garage if you are driving (you can rent cars from here, including 4WD). There's a Chinese restaurant at the hotel, but the noisy night club has (thank goodness) closed down.

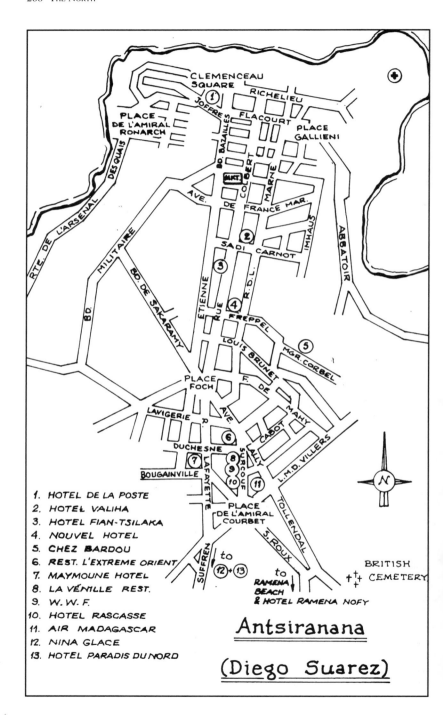

1. HOTEL DE LA POSTE
2. HOTEL VALIHA
3. HOTEL FIAN-TSILAKA
4. NOUVEL HOTEL
5. CHEZ BARDOU
6. REST. L'EXTREME ORIENT
7. MAYMOUNE HOTEL
8. LA VÉNILLE REST.
9. W. W. F.
10. HOTEL RASCASSE
11. AIR MADAGASCAR
12. NINA GLACE
13. HOTEL PARADIS DU NORD

Antsiranana

(Diego Suarez)

Hotel Ramena Nofy BPC, Antsiranana 201. Tel: 228 62/294 15, fax: (261 8) 294 13. 18km from town (near Ramena beach), 45 mins from the airport (transfers cost about £10/$15). When first built this seemed to offer the good hotel that Diego needed: 15 chalets with modern bathrooms, hot water, mosquito nets, a large restaurant with a terrace. Also excursions to Ankarana and deep-sea fishing. However, recent reports indicate that it has deteriorated rapidly. It is now under new management so worth checking out. Bungalows (with breakfast) currently cost about £15/US$22.50.

Hotel de la Poste BP 121. Tel: 214 53. Near Clémenceau Square, overlooking the bay. Officially the best in town, but so casually managed that it cannot be recommended. There's an annexe where the air-conditioning and hot water sometimes work and a wonderful view; rooms from 80,000Fmg. At least the caged lemurs have gone. 'Poor value; pretty girls but lousy service.' (Bjorn Donnis)

Hotel Maymoune 7 Rue Bougainville. Around 45,000Fmg. Recently refurbished and upgraded, but still good value; rooms have fan, bidet, shower and sink. Balcony with view. Very helpful owner/manager. 'Attached to the hotel is the **Le Jonquil** Vietnamese restaurant which actually has one of the hotel rooms in its dining room!'(JK)

Hotel Valiha 41 Rue Colbert. BP 270. Tel: 215 31. Popular, with helpful staff. About 60,000Fmg for rooms with air-conditioning and hot water. But there are cheaper ones.

Hotel Orchidée Rue Surcouf. Tel: 210 65. Friendly, helpful, Chinese-run hotel with a small restaurant and a few rooms for 40,000Fmg with fan, 50,000Fmg with air-conditioning.

Hotel la Rascasse Rue Surcouf, opposite Air Mad. Tel: 223 64. Rooms from 42,000Fmg. 'The restaurant and the terrace are mostly occupied by lonely men and easy-going girls.' (Clare Hermans)

Category C
Hotel Royale Rue Suffren, around the corner from the Paradis du Nord. 25,000Fmg. 'Friendly, some English spoken, hand laundry, closet with lock in each room. I think this was my best find in Diego.' (John Kupiec)

Hotel Fian-tsilaka 13 Bd Etienne. Tel: 223 48. 37,000Fmg. Good restaurant.

Hotel Diamant Rue Mozambique, around the corner from the Royale. 26,000Fmg.

Nouvel Hotel 75, Rue Colbert. Tel: 222 62. Double rooms with all facilities, 15,000Fmg, but noisy with an all-night disco, which is, nevertheless, recommended, as is the restaurant.

L'Auberge l'Ankarana Rue de l'Ankarana. 30,000Fmg. Creole restaurant.

Where to eat
Balafomanga A French-run, expensive new restaurant, with very good food but French-sized (nouvelle cuisine) portions.

La Venilla This used to be the best food in town (but I have had no recent reports). The restaurant, run by two Malagasy brothers, is up the road from the Hotel Rascasse and next to the WWF office.

La Candela Formerly the famous Yachy, this is now an Italian/pizza place. It is north of La Venilla (next to the Alliance Française). 'Nice view from the terrace of some of Diego's most characteristic buildings.' But the best pizza is at...

Nouvel Hotel John Kupiec says 'I had a large seafood pizza for 10,000Fmg. If you eat a pizza here you won't need anything else. There's a lot of filling.'

Restaurant Libertalia Next to the Candela. Offers a few good, low-priced meals on the first floor. 'On the second floor is the same menu for more money plus a few different dishes.'

L'Extreme Orient A popular restaurant near Air Mad; inexpensive, good food.

Snacks and fast food are easy to find. The **Hortensia**, near the post office, does fast food at all times of the day. If your hotel does not serve breakfast, go to the **Boulangerie Amicale**, between the Rascasse and the cinema. Excellent hot rolls and *pain au chocolat*. **Glace Gourmande** probably serves the best ice-cream in town.

Sightseeing and half-day excursions
The British Cemetery
On the outskirts of town on the road that leads to the airport, the British Cemetery is on a side road opposite the main Malagasy cemetery. It is well signposted. Here is a sad insight into Anglo-Malagasy history: rows of graves of the British troops killed in the battle for Diego in 1942, and the larger numbers, mainly East African and Indian soldiers serving in the British army, who died from disease during the occupation of the port. Impeccably maintained by the Commonwealth War Graves Commission, this is a peaceful and moving place.

Ramena Beach
This is a nice sandy beach about 20km from the town centre. Get there by taxi-brousse or by private taxi. It's a beautiful drive around the curve of the bay, with some fine baobabs en route.

By the beach is the **Hotel Badamera**, with good food and a relaxed atmosphere. And a few rooms.

Montagne des Français (French Mountain)
The mountain gets its name from the memorial to the French and Malagasy killed during the allied invasion in 1942. Another sad reminder of a war about which the locals can have had little understanding. There are several crosses but the main one was laboriously carried up in 1956 to emulate Jesus's journey to Calvary.

It is a hot but rewarding climb up to this high point with splendid views and some nearby caves. Take a taxi 8km along the coast road towards Ramena beach, to the start of the old road up the mountain. The track winds upwards, with obvious short cuts; the big cross is reached in about an hour. It's best to go very early in the morning (good birdwatching) or in the evening. The mountain supports unusual vegetation: baobabs, aloes, and until recently pachypodium, but these have evidently all been dug up.

The cross is not the highest point. Sven Oudgenoeg (from the Netherlands) writes: 'After the seventh cross there is a small path running up to the top of the mountain. Here there are ruins, with at least three buildings and a long, ruined, circular wall. These ruins are well preserved and very interesting. For instance, one can still distinguish what used to be a toilet and there is a small staircase betraying that there used to be a second floor.

'From this height you have an even better view of Diego Suarez and its bay. You can get on this path the following way: after the seventh cross take a path across an open field and then into the forest where the path becomes more distinct. Follow it until a junction with a smaller path off to the right. Follow this little path into dense bushes. After about five minutes you go through a tunnel and then come to a junction. A good path goes to the left. Do not take it! The path you want continues straight on and after about three minutes there is a path to the right which leads to the ruins and the top. Leave the first set of ruins (two buildings) on your right and continue higher to more ruins, the circular wall, and the splendid view.'

EXCURSIONS FROM ANTSIRANANA
Getting organised
Tour operators
Nature et Océan 5 Rue Cabot, BP 436, Antsiranana. They run 4WD vehicles to places of interest such as Montagne d'Ambre, Ankarana, Antanavo, Windsor Castle, Courriers Bay, and Ambilobe. They also run sea trips and fishing expeditions. Madagascar Airtours also has an office here.

Le King de la Piste Bd Bazeilles (near Hotel de la Poste), Antsiranana. Tel/fax: (261 8) 225 99. This agency, run by Jorge Pareik (German), is recommended as the best in town for trips by 4WD (minimum two people) to hard-to-reach places such as Windsor Castle, Cap d'Ambre and Analamera. Jorge and his Malagasy wife also organise excursions by motorbike or mountain bike. Prices range from 60Ff per day for a mountain bike to 350Ff for a 4WD with driver.

Many of Diego's hotels can organise tours so it is worth shopping around.

Car and bike hire
The most economical place to hire a car is probably the Hotel Paradis du Nord. Bikes are available from The Blue Marine, 67 Colbert (near the Nouvel Hotel).

Windsor Castle and Courriers Bay
A half-day drive (4WD) or full-day bike excursion takes you to the fantastic rock known as Windsor Castle. This monolith (visible from Antsiranana and – better – if you arrive by ship) is steep-sided and flat-topped, so made a perfect look-out point during times of war. The views from there are superb. It was fortified by the French, occupied by the Vichy forces, and liberated by the British. A ruined staircase still runs to the top (if you can find it). There is

some *tsingy* here, and many endemic water-retaining plants including a local species of pachypodium, *Pachypodium windsorii*.

To get there take the road that runs west towards Ampasindava, where you turn right (north) along a rocky road, then left towards Windsor Castle. The road continuing north is the very rough one to Cap d'Ambre.

The stone staircase to the top of Windsor Castle is not easy to find, and alternative routes sometimes bring you to dense forest or an impassable rock face. Sven Oudgenoeg, who also initially failed to find the staircase, enlisted the help of a local fisherman who acted as a guide and showed him the path. He gives these precise instructions: 'Drive exactly 28.2km from Diego Suarez towards Cap d'Ambre; here you come to a fork in the road. The 'main' road (once metalled, now potholed) continues towards Cap d'Ambre, the left branch goes to Windsor Castle. After 4.2km the road passes through a clump of mango trees where it divides into two paths. Take the one to the left which leads along a steep ridge to the foot of the ruined staircase. The way up the staircase is not always clear, so you have to apply a little logic, but it can be done, and takes about an hour to the top.'

This is a hot, dry climb. Take plenty of water and allow yourself enough time.

Courriers Bay, half an hour beyond Windsor Castle, is an exceptionally fine beach.

Cap d'Ambre
To reach the northernmost tip of Madagascar you need a 4WD vehicle or motor-bike and nerves of steel. Or a mountain bike and plenty of time. If you can carry enough water this area merits exploration; it is seldom visited and is particularly interesting for its flora. I have yet to hear of a traveller who has reached the Cape, however. Even John Kupiec had to give up because of sickness.

Lac Antanavo (Lac Sacré)
The sacred lake is about 75km south of Antsiranana, near the small town of Anivorano. It attracts visitors more for its legends than for the reality of a not particularly scenic lake and the possibility of seeing a crocodile. The story is that once upon a time Anivorano was situated amid semi-desert and a thirsty traveller arrived at the village and asked for a drink. When his request was refused he warned the villagers that they would soon have more water than they could cope with. No sooner had he left than the earth opened, water gushed out, and the mean-minded villagers and their houses were inundated. The crocodiles which now inhabit the lake are considered to be ancestors (and to wear jewellery belonging to their previous selves. So they say).

The crocodiles are sometimes fed by the villagers, so you may do best to book a tour in Diego; the tour operator should know when croc feeding day is.

There are two smaller lakes nearby which the locals fish cautiously – often from the branches of a tree to avoid a surprise crocodile attack.

THE NORTHERN RESERVES
Montagne d'Ambre (Amber Mountain) National Park

This 18,500ha national park was created in 1958, the French colonial government recognising the unique nature of the volcanic massif and its forest. The park is now part of the Montagne d'Ambre Reserves Complex which also includes the Special Reserves of Ankarana, Analamera, and Forêt d'Ambre. The project, initiated in 1989, is funded by USAID, the Malagasy government and the WWF; and was the first to involve local people in all stages of planning and management. The aims were conservation, rural development, and education. These have largely been achieved. Ecotourism has been encouraged successfully with good information and facilities now available.

Montagne d'Ambre National Park is a splendid example of upland moist forest, or montane rainforest. The massif ranges in altitude from 850m to 1,475m and has its own micro-climate with rainfall equal to the eastern region. It is arguably the most visitor-friendly of all the protected areas of Madagascar, with broad trails, fascinating flora and fauna, a comfortable climate, and readily available information. In the dry season vehicles can drive right up to the main picnic area, giving a unique opportunity (in Madagascar) for elderly or disabled visitors to see the rainforest and its inhabitants. Hikers can range as far as they wish, and there is no compulsion to use a guide.

The name comes not from deposits of precious amber, but from the amber-coloured resin which oozes from some of its trees and is used medicinally by the local people.

Warning: Antsiranana is now firmly on the itinerary of cruise ships, with Montagne d'Ambre the focus of the day's excursion. This means that upward of 100 passengers will pour into the park. Independent travellers may wish to visit the port to check if a ship is due before planning their visit.

Getting/staying there

The entrance to the park is 27km south of Antsiranana, 4km from the town of Ambohitra, or Joffreville as almost everyone still calls it. Although it can be visited in one day through a tour operator, Montagne d'Ambre is really too nice a place to hurry. Camping is permitted in the park and there will eventually be accommodation for visitors.

The road from Antsiranana to **Joffreville** is tarred. Taxi-brousses leave Diego at 07.00 for Joffreville, and return at 14.00. The journey takes about an hour, and costs around 3,000Fmg. A decade ago Joffreville was a rather glorious symbol of post-colonial decay, with its Grand Avenue (a two-lane boulevard) sprouting weeds and rubbish. Now it has been given a face-lift, flowers have been planted, and the town may be restored to something near its former splendour. It would be a worthwhile endeavour. Meanwhile, it has a few new shops and a small restaurant. A few rooms are available at Chez Henriette.

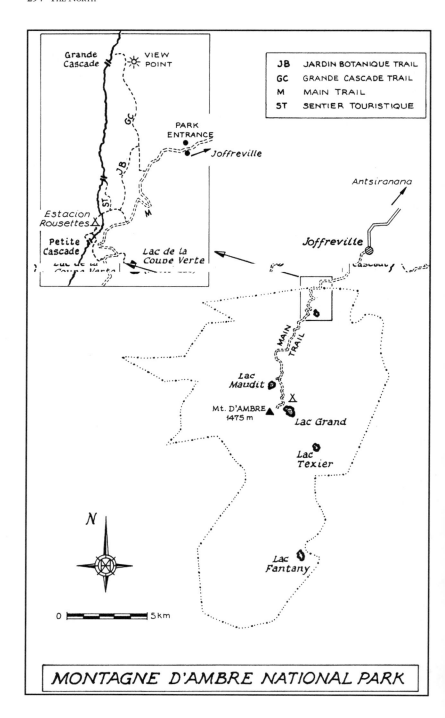

MONTAGNE D'AMBRE NATIONAL PARK

There is a campsite (often crowded) at the car park/picnic area (known as Estacion Rousettes) where a visitor centre is being built.

Permits and information

Permits and a very good information booklet are available in Antsiranana from the WWF office on Rue Surcouf, opposite Air Mad (the entrance is on a side street). Permits are also available at the park entrance. They cost the usual 20,000Fmg.

A new ANGAP office is opening diagonally across from the west taxi-brousse station, on Rue Suffren. In due course this office will probably replace the WWF one.

Guides

Although a guide is not essential, you will see more and understand more if accompanied by one. Angeluc and Angelin have been recommended, although they are often working with scientists so unavailable.

Weather

The rainy season (and cyclone season) is from December through April. The dry season is May through August, but there is a strong wind, *varatraza*, almost every day, and it can feel very cold. The most rewarding time to visit is during the warm season: September through November. There will be some rain, but most animals are active and visible, and the lemurs have babies.

The temperature in the park is, on average, 10ºF cooler than in Diego, and it is often wet and muddy. There may also be leeches. Be wary of wearing shorts and sandals. Bring rain gear, insect repellent, and a light sweater, however hot you are at sea-level.

Flora and fauna of the national park

Montagne d'Ambre is as exciting for its plants as for its animals. A very informative booklet available from the WWF or ANGAP offices gives details and illustrations of the species most commonly seen. All visitors are impressed by the tree ferns (*Cyathea* spp) and the huge, epiphytic bird's-nest ferns (*Asplenium nidus*) which grow on trees. The distinctive *Pandanus* is also common, and you can see Madagascar's endemic cycad, *Cycas thouarsii*. Huge strangler figs (*Ficus* spp) add to the spectacle.

Most visitors want to see lemurs and, as the two diurnal species become habituated, this is becoming easier. The park is home to a subspecies of brown lemur, Sanfords brown lemur (*Eulemur fulvus sanfordi*) and the larger crowned lemur (*Eulemur coronatus*). Sanfords lemur is mainly brown, the males having splendid white/beige ear-tufts and side-whiskers surrounding black faces, whilst the females are of a more uniform colour with no whiskers and a grey face. Crowned lemurs get their names from the triangle of black between the ears of the male; the rest of the animal is reddish brown, with a light-coloured face and ears. Females are mainly grey, with a little red tiara across the forehead.

Both sexes have a lighter-coloured belly; in the female this is almost white. Young are born from September to November.

Other mammals occasionally seen are the ring-tailed mongoose (*Galidia elegans*) and – if you are really lucky – the fosa. And there are five species of nocturnal lemur.

Take time to look carefully at the forest floor; this is the place to find the leaf-mimic *Brookesia tuberculata* chameleon, no more than an inch long, pill millipedes rolled into a perfect ball, frogs, lizards, butterflies, mysterious fungi and a whole host of other living things. At eye-level you may spot chameleons – although the drive up from Antsiranana is a better hunting ground for these reptiles.

Even non-birders will be fascinated by the numerous species here: the Madagascar crested ibis is striking enough to impress anybody, as is the paradise flycatcher with its long, trailing tail feathers. The forest rock thrush is tame and ubiquitous, and the black and white magpie robin is often seen. The jackpot, however, is Madagascar's most beautiful bird: the pitta-like ground roller.

Trails, waterfalls and lakes

The park has, in theory, 30km of paths, but many of these are overgrown although they are gradually being cleared. The best, and most heavily used, trails lead to the Petit Lac, the Jardin Botanique, and two waterfalls, Grande Cascade and Petite Cascade. There is also a Sentier Touristique with another lovely waterfall at the end.

The three waterfalls provide the focal points for day visitors. If time is short and you want to watch wildlife rather than walk far, go to the Petite Cascade. This is only about 100m along the track beyond the picnic area (Estacion Rousettes) and on the way you should see lemurs, orchids, and birds galore. Take a small path on your left to the river for a possible glimpse of the white-throated rail, and the pygmy (malachite) kingfisher. The Petite Cascade is an idyllic fern-fringed grotto with waterfalls splashing into a pool. In the hot season there is a colony of little bats (I don't know the species) twittering in the overhang to the right of the pool. John Kupiec writes: 'I arrived here at dusk and had my most enjoyable experience. The bats were leaving the area for their nightly jaunt. They flew right at my face, but when they were about an inch away they would veer off to the left. I liked challenging myself to see if I would flinch or not.'

The Sentier Touristique is also easy and starts near the Estacion Rousettes (walk back towards the entrance, cross the bridge and turn left). The path terminates at a viewpoint above a waterfall: a highly photogenic spot and a good place to find the forest rock thrush and other birds.

The walk to the Grande Cascade is tougher, with some up and down stretches, and a steep descent to the waterfall. There is some excellent birdwatching here, some lovely tree ferns, and a good chance of seeing lemurs – especially if you bring a picnic which includes bananas... On your way back you'll pass a path on the right (left as you go towards the waterfall) marked 'Jardin Botanique'; don't be misled into thinking this will lead you to the rose-garden. It's a tough roller-coaster of a walk, but very rewarding, and eventually joins the main track.

Another easy walk from Estacion Rousettes is the viewpoint above the crater lake, Lac de la Coupe Verte.

A full day's walk beyond Estacion Rousettes takes you to a crater lake known as Lac Maudit, or *Matsabory Fantany*, then on for another hour to Lac Grand. Beyond that is the highest point in the park, Montagne D'Ambre (1,475m) itself. Unless you are a fit, fast walker it would be best to take two days on this trek and camp by Lac Grand. That way you can wait for weather conditions to allow the spectacular view. John Kupiec made it up to the summit (in cloud). He reports: 'The trailhead from the lake is difficult to find. On arriving at the lake you must look for the trail on your right. I only found it after many false starts...'

Analamera Special Reserve

This 34,700ha reserve is in remote and virtually unexplored deciduous forest some 20km southeast of Montagne d'Ambre, and is the last refuge of the very rare Perrier's black sifaka (*Propithecus diadema perrieri*) which very few people have been fortunate enough to see. The reserve is now open to visitors and, for the enthusiast, easily merits between two and four nights' camping. There are no facilities of any kind, so visitors must be totally self-sufficient.

To reach the reserve from Diego you drive 50km south on a good road, and are then faced with a further 11km on a dreadful stretch which is impassable in the rainy season. Guides and porters can be organised in the nearby village of Menagisy, but it is more sensible to arrange the visit through an operator in Antsiranana. In addition to the black sifaka, you may also see the white-breasted mesite and Van Dam's vanga, which are also seriously threatened species. Nick Garbutt sent this report after his visit in December 1996: 'I hired a 4WD from Le King de la Piste and along with my driver-guide, Ali Baba (fortunately the 40 thieves had the day off), we set off on our four-day trip. After Menagisy, where we picked up a local guide, the track became almost non-existent. On the edge of Analamera we set up base camp, then walked for around 12km south, following the dry river bed of the Bobakindro river. The two main blocks of dry deciduous forest are on the hills either side of the river, but thin corridors follow the river like green ribbons. In November the mango trees are in fruit and the sifaka sometimes come down to these areas to feed. At first we found only crowned and Sanfords lemurs gorging themselves on the fruit. We walked up and down the dry river bed several times. No sifakas. Next morning we were up before dawn and almost immediately heard agitated "tsisk tsisk tsisk" alarm calls from the trees. And there they were! A group of four black sifaka gazing down indignantly through piercing ruby red eyes.'

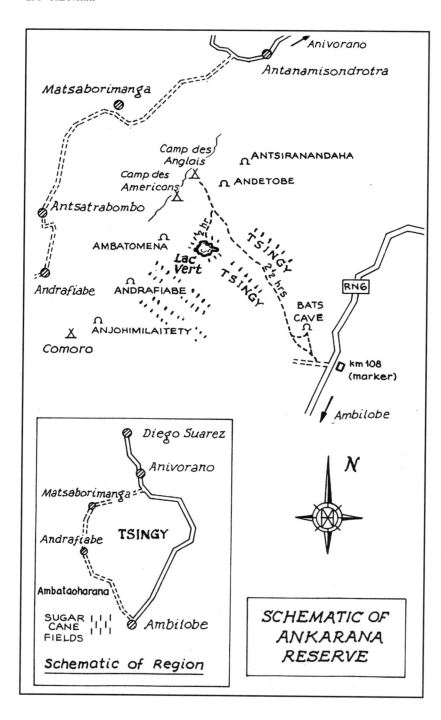

SCHEMATIC OF
ANKARANA
RESERVE

Schematic of Region

Ankarara Special Reserve

About 108km south of Antsiranana is a small limestone massif, Ankarana. An 'island' of *tsingy* (limestone karst pinnacles) and forest, the massif is penetrated by numerous caves and canyons. Some of the largest caves have collapsed, forming isolated pockets of river-fed forest with their own perfectly protected flora and fauna. Dry deciduous forest grows around the periphery of the forest and into the wider canyons. The caves and their rivers are also home to crocodiles, some reportedly six metres long. The reserve is known for its many lemur species, including crowned and Sanfords brown lemur, but it is marvellous for birds, reptiles and insects as well. Indeed, the 'Wow!' factor is as high here as anywhere I have visited.

After a preliminary look in 1981, an expedition led by Dr Jane Wilson (Bradt's very own medical consultant) spent several months in 1986 exploring and studying the area. Their findings excited considerable scientific interest, a TV film and a book (see *Further Reading*).

Ankarana is a Special Reserve (18,220ha) which is included in the WWF's Montagne d'Ambre Reserves Complex. It is rightly becoming the western reserve most people want to visit, although at present it is a hiking and camping trip only.

Getting there and away

With a 4WD vehicle you can usually drive all the way to the Camp des Anglais in the dry season. There are two access towns off the main Antsiranana-Ambanja road, Anivorano and Ambilobe. Most drivers approach from the north, turning off at Anivorano and heading for the village of Matsaborimanga. Allow five hours from Antsiranana.

By far the best way to get there is to hike in from RN6 which runs between Ambanja and Antsiranana. Coming from Ambanja, this is a good, metalled road, and the journey should take about three hours. The trail starts exactly opposite the 108km sign on the road, and is – I think – 11km to the Camp des Anglais (I'm vague about the distance since our guide said 15km but was bargained down to 7km. It took 2½ hours of fast walking). It's a super walk. The first part is down a wide track, then, after about 20 minutes, you turn right down a gully and cross a river. Shortly after that the trail levels out, enters some beautiful forest (you are now in one of the wide canyons) and you can keep walking until you reach the camp.

On the way back, if you use the same route, your guide will take you along an alternative trail to visit the bat caves – a tough scramble, but well worth it.

Camping

The main campsite is known as 'Camp des Anglais' (following the Crocodile Caves Expedition). There are three separate areas, so although it tends to get crowded you can usually escape from other travellers. Note that the camp offers considerably more shade than its American counterpart, as well as a chance to bathe in the river running through the cave. However, as the reserve becomes more popular, so does the likelihood of finding this campsite fully occupied. The water supply is a good 30 minutes' walk away down a slippery slope.

Other campsites are Camp des Américains, Camp des Africains, and Camp de Fleur. Camp des Africains is near the caves, some four hours' walk from Camp des Anglais. Camp de Fleur is about two hours from Camp des Anglais and is a good base for visiting Lac Vert and some of the best *tsingy*.

Permits and guides
A permit for Ankarana should be purchased from the WWF (or ANGAP) in Antsiranana or from ANGAP in Tana.

It would be dangerous to go into the reserve without a guide. Not only do they know the paths and the most interesting areas, but they know where the campsites are located and where scarce water is to be found. Most guides live in Matsaborimanga, but it can be arranged for them to meet you on RN6. Recommended guides include Christo and Felix. We had Angélique, who was superb: very knowledgeable and courteous. Not all so-called guides know the area.

Organised tours
Given the difficulty in getting to Ankarana, and the challenge of finding your way once there, it makes sense to let a tour operator organise the trip for you. Many hotels in Diego offer this tour, as do the two tour operators.

Recommended is the package organised by the Palma Rosa in Ambanja. Unless you pre-book you will need to stay a night or two in the hotel so they can make the arrangements.

What to bring
You'll need strong shoes or boots, a rucksack, food for the duration of your stay and food for your guide (rice can be bought in Matsaborimanga), a 2-litre water bottle, insect repellent, torch (flashlight) for the caves plus batteries. Plus, of course, a tent unless you are on a package tour. A light sleeping bag or sheet plus blanket is enough for the hot season. Oh, and bring earplugs. The lepilemurs of Ankarana are highly vocal!

What to see
Ankarana reminds me of J-P Commerson's famous quote: 'There one meets the most strange and marvellous forms at every step!' Everything is strange and marvellous: the animals, the birds, the plants, the landscape. It was at Ankarana that Anne Axel saw her first lemur: 'My heart raced, and I stared wide-eyed up in the trees, straining for another glimpse of the magnificent creature. I was filled with emotion, and I think it was at that moment that I realised I was finally in Madagascar. Little did I know that later that afternoon I would be treated to an appearance of several crowned lemurs who regularly forage for food in the camp. While I enjoyed seeing them up close and personal,

nothing will top that magical feeling of seeing them for the first time high in the treetops.'

The best *tsingy* is about two hours away, over very rugged terrain, just beyond the beautiful crater lake, Lac Vert. This is a very hot, all-day trip (bring a picnic and plenty of water) and is absolutely magnificent. You can walk (carefully) on the *tsingy*, admiring the strange succulents such as pachypodium which seem to grow right out of the limestone. Lac Vert is as green as its name, and if you are crazy enough you can hike down a steep, slippery slope to the water's edge.

OVERLAND FROM ANTSIRANANA TO SAMBAVA

In 1993 a French correspondent defined this trip as 'Ambiance "Camel Trophy" garantie'. However, the road and transport have improved and providing you have time for the odd break-down or delay you will reach your destination. The following information is from John Kupiec (1996).

A taxi-brousse from Antsiranana (Diego) to Ambilobe (on RN6) takes about three hours and costs around £2/US$3.50. Then you head east, on a poor road, to the coastal town of Vohemar.

Ambilobe
Where to stay/eat
John lists the following hotels: Hotel Golden Night (25,000Fmg), Hotel Mahavavy (15,000Fmg), and (bungalows) Rêve d'Or (12,500Fmg). Then, near the market, there's the Hotel Bagdad (15,000Fmg), the Hazar and the Amical which is near the taxi-brousse station.

Excursion
'I took a TB to **Sirama** where there is a sugar-cane factory. I was given a complete one-hour tour (they seldom see tourists) seeing – and tasting – the whole process of making cane into sugar. There is also a distillery there and I had a couple of different tastes of rum. Wonderful!' (JK)

Expect to take about 12 hours (£5/US$7.50) to reach Iharana (Vohemar) by taxi-brousse from Antsiranana on a rough, dirt road.

Iharana (Vohemar)
A pleasant town with a reasonable selection of places to stay if you need to recover from travelling. There are regular flights to/from here. The Air Mad office is hard to find; it's tucked away in the Star Breweries yard!

'I walked to Lac Vert/Andranotsara, taking the road/path, and walked back along the coast.' (JK)

Where to stay/eat
Sol y Mar Excellent bungalows in a beautiful setting by the shore with shower and WC (cold water). 35,000Fmg. Good, reasonably priced food. 'Best punch coco I had in Madagascar!' (JK)

Poisson d'Or 10,000Fmg with a good restaurant.

Railouvy Across from the Poisson: 10,000Fmg.

Apart from the hotels, there seems to be one restaurant, **La Cigogne**.

A taxi-brousse on to Sambava (see *Chapter Eleven*) is about seven hours, 5,000Fmg.

OVERLAND FROM ANTSIRANANA TO AMBANJA AND NOSY BE

RN6 has recently been improved, and this route is popular with travellers heading for Nosy Be but there is plenty to see in the area so it is a shame to rush through. The journey from Antsiranana to Ambanja at present takes about five hours.

The first place to break your journey is **Ambilobe** (see page 301). Then on to Ambanja (two hours), which merits a stay of a few days. The information below is (mostly) from – you guessed it – John Kupiec.

Ambanja
Where to stay/eat
Hotel Palma Rosa Tel: 42. This hotel has a good restaurant, nice rooms and bungalows, and the owners, Olga Razafindramboa and Pierre Rakotoseheno (who previously worked for the WWF), organise tours to Ankarana. They are also the Air Mad agent in Ambanja. Recommended (*Category A*).

Hotel Patricia Shared WC, no running water. Popular with travellers.

Hotel Riviera Room with a shower and WC, 15,000Fmg.

Hotel Belle Rose 12,000Fmg.

Excursion
'I took a nice walk along the river Sambirano. The path goes up and down/to and from the river, and at one high point there's a good view of the bridge in Ambanja. I saw lemurs high up in bamboo trees.' (JK)

Ankify
This is a beautiful beach 25km south of Ambanja with some newly built double bungalows at **Le Baobab**. Run by Mr and Mrs Tabagh, this is described by Derek Schuurman as 'a great place'.

Tsaratanana
Adventurous travellers look at a map of Madagascar and long to climb its highest mountain. However, Tsaratanana is not open to tourists and those who have tried to penetrate it for scientific research have had a rough time. In a long and entertaining report Kenneth Emberton, of the Molluscan Biodiversity Institute in New Jersey, described the problems of collecting endemic snails

in the region. There *are* guides (APNs) for Tsaratanana, but they live in the village of Bemaneviky, not in Ambanja. 'Vehicles can only go as far as the river in Antsirasira; there we have to cross by pirogue, then perhaps hire an ox-cart for 10+ kilometres, then it's all on foot.' And so it was, for a couple of weeks. For several days they followed the Sambirano River up the mountain but, disappointingly, most of the hillsides had been denuded of forests, and the villagers encountered en route were reluctant to work as porters. Water (lack of) was often a problem, and pushing through the grasslands in blazing sun was exhausting. In short, the expedition was successful in terms of snail collecting but not sufficiently rewarding as a trek to make the difficulties and dangers worthwhile.

If you also have your eye on the **Bora Reserve**, forget it. According to Olivier Langrand it is now 'completely deforested'.

✍

'When this island was first inhabited the ground was all cleared by means of fire. It would, however, have been prudent to leave rows of trees here and there at certain distances. Those rains, which in warm countries are so necessary to render the earth fertile, seldom fall on ground after it has been cleared; for it is the forests that attract the clouds and draw moisture from them... cultivation without measure, and without method, has sometimes done much more hurt than good'.

Abbe Rochon, A Voyage to Madagascar and the East Indies, *1792*

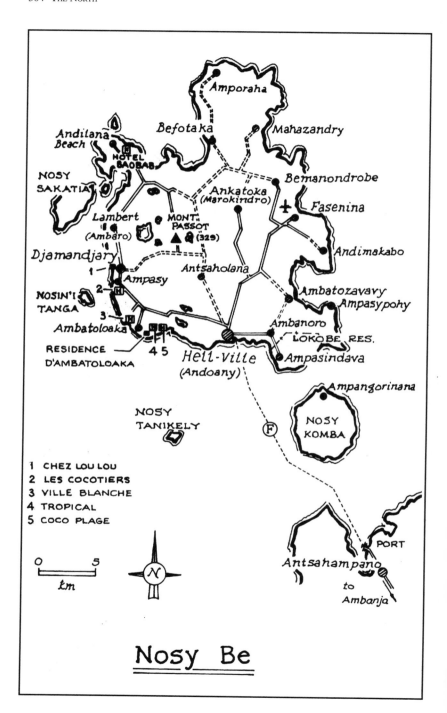

Nosy Be

NOSY BE

History

Nosy Be's charms were recognised as long ago as 1649 when the British colonel, Robert Hunt, wrote: 'I do believe, by God's blessing, that not any part of the world is more advantageous for a plantation, being every way as well for pleasure as well as profit, in my estimation.' Hunt was attempting to set up an English colony on the island, at that time known as Assada, but failed because of hostile natives and disease.

Future immigrants, both accidental and intentional, contributed to Nosy Be's racial variety. Shipwrecked Indians built a magnificent settlement several centuries ago in the southeast of the island, where the ruins can still be seen. The crew of a Russian ship that arrived during the Russo-Japanese war of 1904-5 with orders to attack any passing Japanese vessel, and were then forgotten, are buried in the Hell-Ville cemetery. Other arrivals were Arabs, Comorans, and – more recently – Europeans flocking to Madagascar's foremost holiday resort.

When King Radama I was completing his wars of conquest, the Boina kings took refuge in Nosy Be. First they sought protection from the Sultan of Zanzibar, who sent a warship in 1838, then two years later they requested help from Commander Passot, who had docked his ship at Nosy Be. The Frenchman was only too happy to oblige, and asked Admiral de Hell, the governor of Bourbon Island (now La Réunion), to place Nosy Be under the protection of France. The island was formally annexed in 1841.

Nosy Be today

The name means 'Big Island' and is usually pronounced 'Nossy Bay' although 'Noos Bay' is nearer the Malagasy pronunciation. This is very much a holiday island, which comes as a bit of a shock after the rest of Madagascar. Those who have become happily accustomed to the unstructured nature of travel in the mainland find Nosy Be unbearably touristy; those who have barely survived the effort breathe a sigh of relief.

Blessed with an almost perfect climate (sunshine with brief showers), fertile and prosperous, with sugar, pepper, and vanilla grown for export, and the heady scent of *ylang-ylang* blossoms giving it the tourist-brochure name of 'Perfumed Isle', this is the place to come for a rest – providing you can afford it. Compared with the rest of Madagascar Nosy Be is very expensive.

Most of the easily accessible beaches on Nosy Be have been taken over by hotels, but adventurous visitors can find a few completely unspoilt places. The FTM map of Nosy Be (scale 1:80,000) which is readily available in Tana is very detailed and marks beaches.

Nosy Be even has some good roads (money from sugar and tourism has helped here). Transport around the island is by taxi-be or private taxi (of which there are plenty). Taxis are much more expensive than on the mainland. Bicycles are the best option.

Getting there and away

By air There are regular flights from Tana, Mahajanga and Antsiranana. The airline TAM now operates between La Réunion and Nosy Be, providing an international link.

A taxi from the airport to Hell-Ville will cost around 90,000Fmg.

By boat from Mahajanga Two days and two nights of acute discomfort. See page 325.

By road and ferry The nearest town of any size is Ambanja. The overland route here is described earlier in this chapter, and in *Chapter Fourteen*.

Times of boats to Nosy Be are posted on a board in the Hotel Patricia. Taxis leave from outside the Hotel de Ville for Antsahampano, the departure point for the ferry. There are two ferries a day; the sailing times depend on the tide, and the trip takes two hours. You have the alternative of going by small steam boat (*vedette*). Being smaller, they are less tied to the tides, and often call first at Nosy Komba. However, you are likely to be overcharged.

If you are taking the ferry back from Nosy Be to Antsahampano, check the board outside the ferry office in Hell-Ville (A M Hassanaly et fils) a few doors up from Air Madagascar.

Hell-Ville (Andoany)

The name comes from Admiral de Hell rather than an evocation of the state of the town. Hell-Ville is quite a smart little place, its main street lined with boutiques and tourist shops. There is a market selling fresh fruit and vegetables (which may also be purchased from roadside stalls), and an interesting cemetery neatly arranged according to nationality.

Where to stay/eat in Hell-Ville

Hotel de la Mer Bd du Docteur Manceau. Tel: 61 353. This once infamous hotel (known popularly as Hotel de Merde) is now a respectable and pleasant place to stay in town. Prices range from 15,000 to 55,000Fmg for a spacious room in the annexe. There's a great view from the restaurant.

Blue Fish Lodge By the harbour. Six clean rooms, good food, about 280FF per night. If you stay two nights you get a free trip to Nosy Komba and Tanikely. Deep-sea fishing trips.

Chez Papillon A relatively expensive but highly recommended Italian restaurant located on the right, just before the harbour. 'Best meal for me in the whole of Madagascar. Try the fried cheese! They have a good pizza if you have a craving. And the chocolate mousse cake is unusually rich.'

Most visitors prefer to stay in beach hotels, of which there are many and more going up every year. These are listed according to region. The prices are for high season (mid-July to mid-September, and over the Christmas holiday). Low-season rates are more reasonable.

Car, bike and motorcycle hire

A car (five passengers), plus driver, costs about £50/US$75. Aly Amiry from Dzamandzar is recommended. Ask for him at one of the Dzamandzar hotels.

The daily rate for a Honda 125cc motorbike is around £25/US$37.50 and a Suzuki 50cc goes for £15/US$22.50; mountain bikes cost £5/US$7.50 per day. All these can be hired from Location Jeunesse in Ambataloaka. Villa Blanche (Dzamandzar) has a Vespa Piaggio for around £20/US$35 per day.

Cruising

Several operators run sailing boats or small cabin cruisers to take visitors to the outlying islands. **Nosy Be Croisières** in Hell-Ville has five sailing boats of various sizes, the **Blue Fish Lodge** has a 12m boat, and **Priscilla** offers a Boston Whaler which takes six passengers. Contact Pascal at the Hotel Ylang Ylang. Jean-François Py at Soleil et Découverte in Ambataloaka has several boats and offers a good service. Daniel also runs trips to the main islands. **Albatros** has two boats and camping equipment. A new (to me) operator worth checking out is **Alefa** who has a pirogue with sails and outriggers. Nicholas Quehen, in Madirokely/Ambataloaka (BP 89), organises snorkelling and camping trips with this vessel.

This is just a selection of boat-owners; there will be others that I don't know about.

Diving

Nosy Be is Madagascar's main centre for diving; May to October are the recommended months for this.

Madagascar Dive Club Behind the Marlin Club Hotel. Member of PADI International Resort Association. First class equipment.

Ocean's Dream BP 173, Hell-Ville 207. In addition to the usual diving place they offer dive trips to Radamas, Sakatia, and the Comoros. Run by Laurent Duriez, this is probably the best diving centre on Nosy Be.

Sakatia Dive Inn BP 186, Hell-Ville. Tel: (8) 61091; fax: 613 97. See *Nosy Sakatia* (page 313).

The north

The north part of Nosy Be is the most beautiful, so it is with mixed feelings – no, let's be honest, delight – that I have to report that the hideous Andilana Beach Hotel has closed down. Whether a new hotel will be built in this lovely bay remains to be seen. Meanwhile it may be possible to get away from it all here. Andilana is 45 minutes' drive from town.

Where to stay

Le Baobab BP 45. Fax (Tana): 31 280. A new and very good hotel (bungalows) set on a beautiful beach near the ex-Andilana. Superb seafood in the restaurant.

Djamandjary area

Djamandjary is an ugly small town with some strange igloo-shaped cement structures which, long ago, were provided by a relief organisation as cyclone-proof housing. They are, indeed, indestructible, and have mostly been abandoned by the villagers who have got tired of waiting for them to fall down in the time-honoured Malagasy way. Opposite the town is a sugar-cane and rum processing factory. Worth a visit. Bring your own bottle!

Although the beach here is uninspiring (it shelves too gradually for good swimming) it is shaded by coconut palms, and a chain of hotels stretches down the coast. Each hotel rakes away the dead seaweed that the high tide deposits daily on the beach.

Where to stay

Chez Lou Lou Approximately 4km up the coast from Djamandjary. 'Very nice bungalow, with proper bathroom, barbecue, etc. on the terrace. Room with shared facilities 35,000Fmg, bungalow 60,000Fmg.'

Case Depart Adjacent to Chez Lou Lou. Owned by a French family with noisy children, this has tiny rooms with shared facilities opening on to a terrace. No electricity or running water, but the surfboards and snorkelling gear are provided free of charge.

Les Cocotiers BP 191. Tel: 613 14. 16 very pleasant bungalows in full working order. Very good food. High season: about 500Ff per person (double) half board. Almost half that price low season.

Villa Blanche Tel (in Tana): 228 54. Single with breakfast 215Ff, double 320Ff. Airport transfer, 50Ff.

The service and rooms have been criticised, but the brochure is wonderful! Among the delights they offer are 'transfert by car or motor-bat' and an excursion to Nosy Iranja, 'A beautiful island... with its thin and white beaches. And the lunch served by Villa Blanche is also thin and fine.' If you are still undecided they give further encouragement: 'You are not ready to die, but let profi of some this tropical heaven... You surely will be enjoyed by beauties, fragrances and cooking.' And to dispel the last shadow of doubt they assure you that they 'agree paying Master-Cad'. Yes, so I've heard...

Mont Passot excursion

While in the area, take a trip to the island's highest point, Mont Passot. There are marvellous views of a series of deep-blue crater lakes, which are said to contain crocodiles (though I have never seen one) and to be sacred as the home of the spirits of the Sakalava and Antakarana princes. It is *fady* to fish there, or to smoke, wear trousers or any garment put on over the feet, or a hat, while on the lakes' shores. It is, in any case, difficult to get down to the water since the crater sides are very steep.

The road to the peak runs from Djamandjary, and can be hiked or cycled. Tour groups come to Mont Passot to see the sunset, but in the clear air of Nosy Be this is generally less than spectacular, so it is better to make a day excursion of it and take a picnic. Souvenir sellers have discovered the joys of having captive *vazahas* waiting for the sun to dip, and have set up tables for their wares. This is not a hill of solitude.

Ambatoloaka

This is a charming little fishing village with the best options for inexpensive places to stay. Several private houses rent out the odd room, so ask around. The established places are listed below.

Where to stay

Résidence Ambatoloaka BP 130. Tel: 613 68. This popular place is inconsistent in its service and food, but at its best is very good, with pleasant air-conditioned en suite rooms and a good terrace/lounge.

Hotel Tropical Newish bungalows with shower and WC.

Hotel Coco Plage 1km from the Résidence Ambatoloaka (away from town). About 30,000Fmg per person with breakfast. Very nice beach bungalows with bathrooms.

Hotel Ylang Ylang The best hotel from the lower range. Nice rooms, not such pleasant surroundings.

Hotel Soleil et Découverte A few rooms and restaurant run by Jean-François Py (see *Cruising*).

Gérard et Francine Nine rooms, low price, reportedly always full but it's worth trying!

Chez Aly Clean, friendly atmosphere, no running water. 35,000Fmg.

There are several **restaurants** at Ambatoloaka. Highly recommended are **Chez Madame Tabagh** and the **Karibo**. Longest established is the modest but highly acclaimed **Chez Angeline** which does a superb set meal of sea food and *poulet au coco*. Book it in advance. Competition for Chez Angeline is provided by a Malagasy woman in a food-stall opposite. 'Cooking on an open fire she turns out the best food in the village. We had grilled fish, crab, salad, and rice all for 4,000Fmg.' Opposite the entrance to La Résidence is a bar selling 'possibly the cheapest beers in the country'.

Lokobe

Nosy Be's only protected area, Lokobe, is a Strict Reserve and as such is not currently open to visitors (although there are plans for it to become a National Park). However, it is possible to visit the buffer zone on the northeast side of the peninsula where permits are not required. The two little villages here, Ambatozavavy and Ampasypohy, now have simple hotels which allow visitors a chance to get a proper look at this lovely, unspoiled area. Ambatozavavy means 'Woman stone', a reference to the nearby sacred rock which is said to represent women's genitalia, and to bestow fertility on those who visit it.

For years an excursion to Lokobe was the preserve of Jean-Robert who runs day-trips from the main Nosy Be hotels to Ampasipohy, 45 minutes by pirogue from Ambatozavavy. This trip is still a good option for those who cannot spend the night (see *Where to stay*). During the course of the day you are served a traditional lunch by his wife and taken on a tour of the forest where Jean-Robert, who speaks excellent English and is a natural showman, explains the traditional uses of various plants and points out a variety of animals. You are bound to see a lepilemur, *Lepilemur dorsalis*, which, unlike the species in Berenty, spends its day dozing in the fork of a favourite tree rather than in a hole. You should see black lemurs (shyer than those on Nosy Komba) and with luck a boa and chameleons. The chameleons here are the *pardalis* species and in the breeding season (November to May) the male is bright green and the female a pinkish colour. The villagers grow vanilla and peppers, so you will observe the non-destructive combination of crops and forest. You may also be treated to a unique rendition of 'Old Macdonald had a Farm'.

Jean-Robert meets most planes, but if you miss him your hotel will know where he is. His 1996 price was 100,000Fmg.

Lokobe is the centre for the Black Lemur Forest Project (see page 130). Visit the new Community Centre in Ambanaro for more information.

Where to stay

Eco-village Fihavanana BP 203, Ambatozavavy. Designed for ecotourists rather than beach fanatics, this Swiss-managed lodge consists of nine clean and spacious palm-thatched bungalows with hot showers and solar-powered electricity. 1996 rates are 290,000Fmg (double) full board, or 120,000Fmg (single) for B&B with a three-course meal costing 35,000Fmg. Transfer from Hell-Ville costs 25,000Fmg for two people. The manager can organise trips with local fisherman, but they also have their own Zodiac. An excellent feature is the Lokobe Nature Trail, which can be walked at night so is of particular interest to those devoted to reptiles and nocturnal fauna of all kinds.

Jungle village BP 208, Hell-Ville. Six bungalows in Ampasypohy, run by Marc Dehlinger. Beautifully located, and excellent value for money. 70,000–90,000Fmg per bungalow, or 500,000Fmg for the main house (5–6 people). Dinner 35,000Fmg.

Nosy Komba (Nosy Ambariovato)

Once upon a time Nosy Komba was an isolated island with an occasional boat service, a tiny, self-sufficient village, and a troop of semi-tame black lemurs which were held to be sacred so never hunted. Now all that has changed. Tourists arrive in boat-loads from Nosy Be and from passing cruise ships which can land over 100 people.

'Komba' means 'Lemur' (interestingly it is the Swahili word for bush-baby which of course is the African relative of the lemur) and it is the lemurs that bring in the visitors. During the 1980s the villagers made nothing out of these visits apart from the sale of clay animals which they glazed with the acid of spent batteries. Then they instigated a modest fee for seeing the animals and increased the variety of handicrafts. Now that Nosy Komba is on some cruise-ship itineraries they have taken on the works: 'tribal dancing', face decoration, escorted walk... anything that will earn a dollar or two.

With all the demands on your purse, it sometimes takes a bit of mental effort to see the underlying charm of the village, but it is nevertheless a typical

Malagasy community living largely on fishing and *tavy* farming (witness the horrendous deforestation of their little island; when I first visited in 1976, it was completely covered with luxuriant trees).

It is the black lemurs that provide the financial support (and probably prevent further degradation of their environment). The ancestor who initiated the hunting *fady* must be pleased with himself. If you want the lemurs-on-your-shoulders experience and the chance to see these engaging animals at close quarters you should definitely come here. Only the male *Eulemur macaco* is black; the females, which give birth in September, are chestnut brown with white ear-tufts.

Nosy Komba also provides an excellent opportunity for observing lemur behaviour. Note the bossiness of the females, who make sure that they get the bananas first, and the way the males rub their bottoms on branches to scent-mark them and gain some authority. Take a look at a lemur's hands: you will see the four flat primate fingernails (such wonderfully human hands!) and the single claw which is used for grooming.

A small fee (2,500Fmg) is charged to see the lemurs, and en route to their 'compound' everyone in the village will try to sell you something. Since you are buying direct from the grower/maker, this is the best place to get vanilla and handicrafts (carved pirogues, clay animals, and unusual and attractive 'lace' table-cloths and curtains).

One of the former glories of Nosy Komba, its coral, has sadly almost completely disappeared so snorkelling is no longer rewarding. The sea and beach near the village are polluted with human waste, but there is a good swimming beach round to the left (as you face the sea).

All the Nosy Be hotels do excursions to Nosy Komba which is usually combined with Nosy Tanikely. Much cheaper is to go by pirogue. Late afternoon is the best time. Increasingly visitors are choosing to stay on the island for a few days; the simple backpacker hotels of yesteryear are being joined by more upmarket establishments.

Where to stay

Les Floralies New, French-run bungalows on the beach, with bar and restaurant. BP 107, Nosy Be, fax: 613 67 for bookings.

Chez Bernie Mrs Bernie and Remo, who run Albatros (see *Cruising*), have four luxury bungalows. 450Ff full board (which includes unlimited boat hire). They also organise hiking trips across Nosy Komba and can provide camping equipment. Recommended.

Hotel Lemuriens Backpacker bungalows run by Martin (German) and Henriette (Malagasy), 30,000–40,000Fmg. Meals 25,000–45,000Fmg. For bookings write to BP 185, Nosy Be.

Hotel Karibu Run by an Italian and his Malagasy wife. Reasonably priced.

Hotel Madio BP 207. Previously run with flair by Toto, who is apparently no longer there. Mrs Madio shares some of her guests with her neighbouring cousin Mrs Yvonne, an excellent cook (5,000Fmg a day, using your own food) with a two-room bungalow at 7,000Fmg. Several other bungalows in the village have similar arrangements. The 'proper' Madio charges about 15,000Fmg for a bungalow with shared facilities.

Other islands in the Nosy Be archipelago
Nosy Tanikely

Although now much-visited, this is still pretty close to Paradise. Nosy Tanikely is a tiny island inhabited only by the lighthouse keeper and his family (I think... there seem to be quite a lot of them these days!) and largely unspoiled by tourism. The island is a marine reserve and it is for the snorkelling that most people visit it. And the snorkelling is excellent (even if too many ships dropping too many anchors are beginning to take their toll on the coral). In clear water you can see an amazing variety of marine life – coral, starfish, anemones, every colour and shape of fish, turtles, lobsters...

With this new world beneath your gaze there is a real danger of forgetting the passing of time and becoming seriously sunburnt. Even the most carefully applied sunblock tends to miss some areas, so wear a T-shirt and shorts.

Don't think you have finished with Nosy Tanikely when you come out of the water; at low tide it is possible to walk right round the island. During your circumambulation you will see (if you go anticlockwise): a broad beach of white sand covered in shells and bleached pieces of coral, a couple of trees full of flying foxes (*Pteropus rufus*), and – in the spring – graceful white tropic birds (*Phaethon lepturus lepturus*) flying in and out of their nests in the high cliffs. At your feet will be rock pools and some scrambling, but nothing too challenging.

Then there is the climb up to the top of the island for the view and perhaps a tour (tip expected) of the antique and beautifully maintained lighthouse.

Sadly, Nosy Tanikely has started to suffer a litter problem. Mostly it is the boat crews who prepare the sumptuous lunches on the picnic tables under the trees that are careless in this respect, but a responsible visitor will offer them an extra tip if they clear up meticulously. And if every reader brought a large plastic bag and did their bit to clear it up, the island would once again be spotless. As would be your conscience.

Most hotels arrange trips to Nosy Tanikely, usually combined with Nosy Komba although I think this is a bit rushed. To do justice to Nosy Tanikely you really need a full day – and a small boat. Instead of an organised trip you can hire a pirogue to take you there.

Nosy Mitsio
Charlotte de la Bedoyère

If you are something of a desert island/snorkelling addict, and have been to Nosy Tanikely, try to visit the archipelago of Nosy Mitsio. This handful of islands lies some 60-70km from Nosy Be and about the same distance from the mainland. The largest is La Grande Mitsio, but the one I visited was the uninhabited Tsara Banjina ('Beautiful Beaches'). This island sprang to fame in 1994 when Joanna Lumley was 'stranded' there for a few days; the TV programme and accompanying book *Girl Friday* were the result. Tsara Banjina is a tiny jewel. The red, grey and black volcanic rocks, rising quite high at its centre, have a mass of lush, green vegetation clinging to them, from full-grown trees to tiny rockery plants. But its real glory is the pure white beaches of coarse sand, along which laps a crystal-clear green/indigo sea. Every rock, however small, sparkles with an abundance of coral and marine life. Turtles and stingrays loll near the beaches.

In a small boat it takes 6-8 hours to reach Nosy Mitsio, depending on the winds, so you must reckon on a minimum of 2-3 days or you will have no time to experience its peace and purity. Almost any of the major hotels on Nosy Be will organise a trip, which costs about £50/US$75 per day per person for a group of three to five, all meals (but no drinks) included.

The long journey is also rewarding. We saw dolphins and fished tuna and carangue. The latter was made into a superb dinner by the crew. I spent the night in a very adequate tent, sleeping on the groundsheet, so if you want something softer than sand, bring it with you.

Nosy Iranja

The classic palm-fringed island (actually two islands connected by a sandy causeway) with clear water for swimming and snorkelling, and a small village of fisherfolk at one end. This is a breeding area for sea-turtles. To be worthwhile you need to make this a three-day excursion (with tents). Prices are comparable with Mitsio.

Nosy Sakatia

Off the west side of Nosy Be, Sakatia is a diver's paradise and its two hotels reflect this.

Sakatia Passions Run by fishing specialist Jacques Toussaint and Jean-Claude Clement. It has accommodation for 24 people in 12 bungalows, and features windsurfing, kayaks, hiking on the island and boat excursions. Book through tour operators in Tana.

Sakatia Dive Inn is strictly for divers only. Owned by Christian Solterer, it has six bungalows (for contact details see *Diving*).

∅

'There are some birds the size of a large turkeycock which have the head made like a cat and the rest of the body like a griffin; these birds hide themselves in the thick woods, and when anyone passes under the tree where they are they let themselves fall so heavily on the head of the passengers that they stun them, and in the moment they pierce their heads with their talons, then they eat them'.
Sieur de Bois, 1669

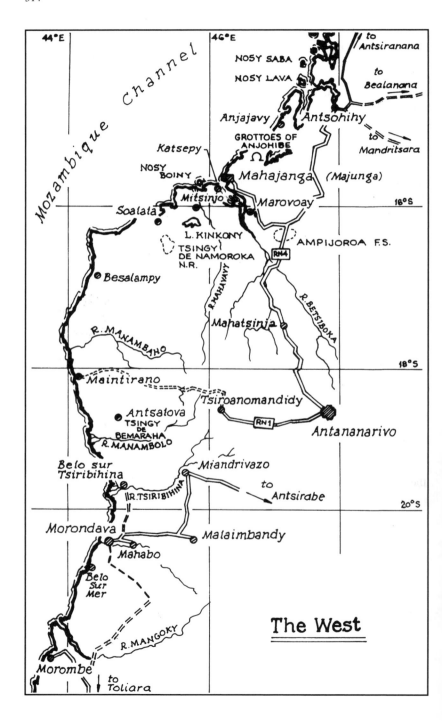

The West

Chapter Fourteen

The West

The west of Madagascar offers a dry climate, deciduous forest (with two excellent reserves to protect it), endless sandy beaches with little danger from sharks – although the sea can be very rough – and fewer tourists than many parts of the country. The lack of roads is one of its attractions; this is the ideal area for mountain bikers or walkers. Adventurous travellers will have no trouble finding a warm welcome in un-touristed villages, their own deserted beach and some spectacular landscapes.

This is the region to see one of Madagascar's extraordinary natural wonders: the *tsingy*. Pronounced 'zing' this is exactly the sound made when one of the limestone pinnacles is struck by a small stone (they can be played like a xylophone!). Limestone karst is not unique to Madagascar, but it is rare to see such dramatic forms, such an impenetrable forest of spikes and spires. The endemic succulents that struggle for a foothold in this waterless environment add to the unworldly feeling of a *tsingy* landscape.

Opposite major rivers the sea water along the west coast is a brick red colour: 'like swimming in soup', as one traveller puts it. This is the laterite washed into the rivers from the eroded hillsides of the highlands and discharged into the sea: Madagascar's bleeding wounds.

The Sakalava

The west of Madagascar is the home of the Sakalava people. For a while in Malagasy history this was the largest and most powerful tribe, ruled by their own kings and queens. The Sakalava kingdom was founded by the Volamena branch of the Maroserana dynasty which emerged in the southwest during the 16th century. Early in the 17th century a Volamena prince, Andriamisara, reached the Sakalava river and gave its name to his new kingdom. His son, Andriandahifotsy (which means 'white man'), succeeded him around 1650 and, with the aid of firearms acquired from European traders, conquered the southwestern area between the two rivers, Onilahy and Manambolo. This region became known as the Menabe. Later kings conquered first the Boina, the area from the Manambolo to north of present-day Mahajanga, and then the northwest coast as far as Antsiranana.

By the 18th century the Sakalava empire occupied a huge area in the west, but was divided into the Menabe in the south and the Boina in the north. The two rulers fell out, unity was abandoned, and in the 19th century the area came under the control of the Merina. The Sakalava did not take kindly to domination and sporadic guerrilla warfare continued in the Menabe area until French colonial times.

The Sakalava kingdom bore the brunt of the first serious efforts by the French to colonise the island. For some years France had laid claims (based on treaties made with local princes) on parts of the north and northwest, and in 1883 two fortresses in this region were bombarded. An attack on Mahajanga followed. This was the beginning of the end of Madagascar as an independent kingdom.

The modern Sakalava have relatively dark skins. The west of Madagascar received a number of African immigrants from across the Mozambique Channel and their influence shows not only in the racial characteristics of the people, but in their language and customs. There are a number of Bantu words in their dialect, and their belief in *tromba* (possession by spirits) and *dady* (royal relics cult) is of African origin.

The Sakalava do not practise second burial. The quality of their funerary art (in one small area) rivals that of the Mahafaly: birds and naked figures are a feature of Sakalava tombs, the latter frequently in erotic positions. Concepts

---

KING RADAMA II

The son of the 'Wicked Queen' Ranavalona, King Radama II was a gentle ruler who abhorred bloodshed. He was pro-European, interested in Christianity (although never formally a Christian) and a friend of William Ellis, missionary and chronicler of 19th-century Madagascar. After Radama's death, Ellis wrote: 'I have never said that Radama was an able ruler, or a man of large views, for these he was not; but a more humane ruler never wore a crown.' With missionaries of all denominations invited back into Madagascar, intense rivalry sprang up between the Protestants sent by Britain, and the Jesuits who arrived from France. Resentment at the influence of these foreigners over the young king and disgust at the often rash changes he instigated boiled over in 1863, and after only eight months on the throne he was assassinated, strangled with a silken sash so that the *fady* against shedding royal blood was not infringed.

The French-British rivalry was fuelled by the violent death of the king, even to the extent that Ellis was accused of being party to the assassination. But was Radama really dead? Both Ellis and Jean Laborde believed that he had survived the strangling and had been allowed to escape by the courtiers bearing him to the countryside for burial. Uprisings, supposedly organised by the 'dead' king, supported this rumour. In a biography of King Radama II, the French historian Raymond Delval makes a strong case that the ex-monarch eventually retreated to the area of Lake Kinkony and lived out the rest of his life in this Sakalava region.

The Malagasy publication *Madactualités* puts it succinctly: 'Delval assures that Radama 2 took refuge in the region when he was thrown away of its thrown and would-be assassinated.'

of sexuality and rebirth are implied here. The female figures are often disproportionately large, perhaps recognising the importance of women in the Sakalava culture.

Sakalava royalty does not require an elaborate tomb since kings are considered to continue their spiritual existence through a medium with healing powers, and in royal relics.

Getting around

Roads in the west are being improved, but driving from town to town in the west is still challenging and in much of the area the roads simply aren't there. There are regular flights to the large towns and a Twin Otter serves many of the smaller ones.

MAHAJANGA (MAJUNGA)
History

Ideally located for trade with east Africa, Arabia and western Asia, Mahajanga has been a major commercial port since 1745, when the Boina capital was moved here from Marovoay. One ruler of the Boina was Queen Ravahiny, a very able monarch who maintained the unity of the Boina which was threatened by rebellions in both the north and the south. It was Mahajanga which provided her with her imported riches and caught the admiration of visiting foreigners. Madagascar was at that time a major supplier of slaves to Arab traders and in return received jewels and rich fabrics. Indian merchants were active then, as today, with a variety of exotic goods. Some of these traders from the east stayed on, the Indians remaining a separate community and running small businesses. More Indians arrived during colonial times.

In the 1883-85 war Mahajanga was occupied by the French. In 1895 it served as the base for the military expedition to Antananarivo which established a French Protectorate. Shortly thereafter the French set about enlarging Mahajanga and reclaiming swampland from the Bombetoka river delta. Much of today's extensive town is on reclaimed land.

Mahajanga today

A hot but breezy town with a large Indian population and enough interesting excursions to make a visit of a few days well worthwhile. Besides, you can eat one of the best meals in Madagascar here (Chez Chabaud)!

The town has two 'centres', the town hall (Hotel de Ville) and statue of Tsiranana (the commercial centre), and the streets near the famous baobab. Some offices, including Air Madagascar, are here. It is quite a long walk between the two – take a pousse-pousse, of which there are many. There are also some smart new buses, and taxis which operate on a fixed tariff.

A wide boulevard follows the sea along the west part of town, terminating by a lighthouse. At its elbow is the **Mahajanga baobab**, said to be at least 700 years old with a circumference of 14 metres.

Getting there and away

Mahajanga is 560km from Tana by fairly good road. There is a regular air service. And a luxury ferry service to the Comoros!

By road If coming from Tana, the most comfortable transport seems to be the Mazda bus run by Transtour. It even has head-rests! Their office in Tana is on the road that leads from the station to the Marché Artisanal. Seats are bookable in advance. There are also regular taxi-brousses which leave around 08.00, taking 15 to 18 hours. It's a lovely trip (at least until it gets dark) taking you through typical *Hauts Plateaux* landscape of craggy, grassy hills, rice paddies, and characteristic Merina houses with steep eaves supported by thin brick or wood pillars.

The taxi-brousse station in Mahajanga is on Ave Philbert Tsiranana.

By air There is a twice weekly service from Tana to Mahajanga (which goes on to Nosy Be so is likely to be crowded). Flights on other days are by Twin Otter.

By sea The *M/S Sam-Son* is a motor vessel belonging to the JAG Group, which owns several hotels in this part of Madagascar, which takes passengers from Mahajanga to the Comoro Islands. Prices: Mahajanga–Mayotte 450Ff/£53/US$80 per person (economy), 640Ff (first class). Mahajanga–Anjouan–Moroni 515Ff/£60/US$90 (economy), 700Ff (first class). Rates include all meals and non-alcoholic drinks.

A very different sea experience is provided by the cargo boat to Nosy Be (see page 325).

Where to stay

Category A

Le Tropicana This incorporates the **Hotel Gatinière** and the Restaurant Oasis. Tel: 220 69. This fine hotel-restaurant is up the hill from the Don Bosco school behind the cathedral, in a 1930s French colonial house. Ten rooms, hot water, swimming pool, excursions to the Anjohibe caves etc. French and Malagasy cuisine. 'The dining is superb. Even on an oppressively hot day you can escape from the dust of urban Mahajanga and sit on the terrace with friends over lunch... telling stories of exotic places and pretending you are Joseph Conrad.' (Mark Ward)

Kanto Hotel Tel: 229 78. Overlooking the sea about 2km north of the town. A variety of rooms are available at a range of prices. Good food.

The Kanto has an annexe near the central market: corner of Ave de la Républic and Rue Henri Palu. Good value.

New Hotel Rue Henri Palu. Tel: 221 10; fax: 293 91. For a while this was the best hotel in town, but recent reports suggest that it may have deteriorated. At its best it has clean, air-conditioned rooms with bathrooms en suite, hot and cold running water, and a very good restaurant. It is also the only Mahajanga hotel at the time of writing that accepts credit cards (Visa and MasterCard).

Hotel de France Rue Maréchal Joffre. BP 45. Tel: 237 81. In late 1996 this was being renovated, so chances are that by mid-1997 it will be the best in town – at least for a while.

Zaha Motel Tel: 23 24. At Amborovy beach (not far from the airport, and 8km from Mahajanga). Beach bungalows. Recently bought by SOFITRANS and now managed by Madagascar Air Tours. Rooms 250Ff (£30/US$45), bungalows 390Ff (£46/US$69). Nice beach with blue, not red, sea.

Category B

Hotel Les Roches Rouges Bd La Corniche. Tel: 238 71. A rather sterile big hotel, with air-conditioning. Rooms 65,000–70,000Fmg. The two following quotes (1996) show the bad and the good side of the hotel: 'Rooms in a dilapidated state. Many large rats scuttling about in the restaurant – not endemic rats either.' (Derek Schuurman). 'Restaurant very good (try the Crabe Farci) and better service than at the hotel.' (Bjorn Donnis)

Hotel de la Plage, Chez Karon. BP 149. Tel: 226 94. A beach hotel 2km from the town centre, with some air-conditioned rooms. Organises tours for hunting groups (Mahajanga is Madagascar's centre for duck shooting).

Boina Beach Tel: 238 09. New hotel/restaurant located on Bd La Corniche, by the beach 2km from the town and opposite Les Roches Rouges. Nine air-conditioned rooms but badly built and noisy. Service reputedly poor.

New Continental Ave de la République. Tel: 225 70. Town centre hotel, which replaced the Old Continental, a favourite with backpackers in the '80s. Newly built, with 15 air-conditioned rooms priced up to 75,000Fmg (1996). Indian-owned. Recommended.

Hotel Kizmat Ave de la République. Newly renovated air-conditioned rooms at 72,000Fmg. Clean, recommended; as is the restaurant which has good curry and samosas. It is Muslim, so no alcohol. Take-away food is sold here, too.

Hotel Voanio Tel: 238 78. In a quiet part of town; clean and friendly.

Hotel Ravinala Quai Orsini. Tel: 229 68. 50,000Fmg (1996) with toilet, bathroom, and air-conditioning. Good value.

Category C

Hotel Tropic Tel: 236 10. Near the port. 35,000Fmg for nice rooms and a modern bathroom.

Hotel Boina Tel: 224 69. 40,000Fmg (1996) with shower.

Yaar Hotel Tel: 230 12. Near the New Hotel. 26,000Fmg (1996).

Hotel des Voyageurs Tel: 231 90. A basic hotel near the market.

Chez Chabaud (see *Katsepy*) Tel: 233 27. Mme Chabaud's daughter runs a basic hotel near the Hotel de Ville. Rooms 20,000Fmg (1996). The restaurant opposite is run by another daughter, Christiane. All the family speaks excellent English.

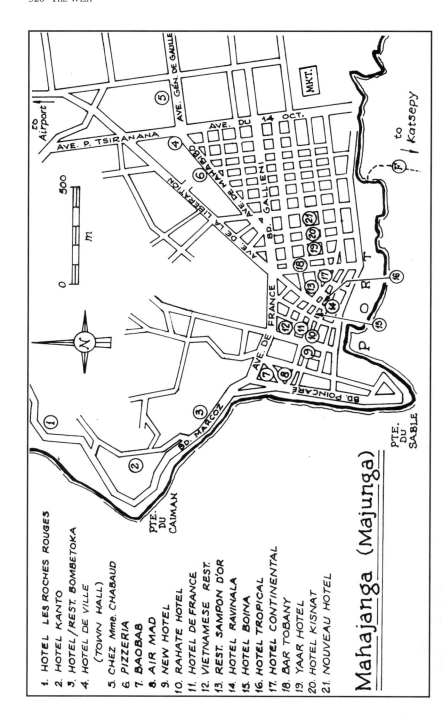

Mahajanga (Majunga)

1. HOTEL LES ROCHES ROUGES
2. HOTEL KANTO
3. HOTEL / REST. BOMBETOKA
4. HOTEL DE VILLE (TOWN HALL)
5. CHEZ Mme. CHABAUD
6. PIZZERIA
7. BAOBAB
8. AIR MAD
9. NEW HOTEL
10. RAHATE HOTEL
11. HOTEL DE FRANCE
12. VIETNAMESE REST.
13. REST. SAMPON D'OR
14. HOTEL RAVINALA
15. HOTEL BOINA
16. HOTEL TROPICAL
17. HOTEL CONTINENTAL
18. BAR TOBANY
19. YAAR HOTEL
20. HOTEL KISNAT
21. NOUVEAU HOTEL

Where to eat

John Kupiec 'found Mahajanga to be the best all-round place for ice-cream, milk shakes and natural juice.'

The restaurant at the **New Hotel** is recommended for its very good, if expensive, food. Likewise see the description of dining at **Restaurant L'Oasis** at Le Tropicana.

Le Sampan d'Or, a Chinese-owned restaurant, but not serving Chinese cuisine, is recommended. Round the corner is a wonderful bakery.

Vietnamese restaurant Name unknown (but possibly Chez Thilan Doan Van Bien, on Ave P Tsiranana); near the post office, with very good food and friendly staff.

Kohinoor Restaurant Indian restaurant with good food and kitsch decor.

Pizza restaurant On Ave de Mahabibo. A Swedish reader recommends this place 'runned by a Belch. Strange, but good pizzas...'

Pakiza Ave de la République, near the New Continental. A great variety of ice-creams and milk shakes, also good for breakfast.

Bar Tabany A popular meeting place in the west part of town, near the market.

Salon de Thé Saify Near the post office and cathedral. A perennial favourite for breakfast and snacks.

Parad'Ice Next to the Air Madagascar office off Bd Poincaré. 'The best ice-cream in Madagascar.'

Maps

The Librairie de Madagascar (on Avenues de Mahabido and Gallieni) reportedly has a good selection of maps including the FTM one of the Mahajanga region.

Sightseeing

Thanks to Project Madagascar (Gotland College of Higher Education), which sponsors a programme to improve the places of cultural interest around Mahajanga, there are now several sightseeing possibilities near to town.

Mozea Akiba is situated about 2km from the centre of town, near the Plage Touristique. It now houses a history of the region, as well as an exhibition of paleontology and ethnology. With the aid it is receiving from Sweden it is hoped that it will become a not-to-be-missed museum. Hours: 09.00–11.00, 15.00–17.00.

Fort Rova was built on the highest point in Mahajanga in 1824 by King Radama I. The entrance to the fort has now been restored, and it is well worth a visit.

Excursions
Cirque Rouge

About 12km from Mahajanga and 2km from the airport (as the crow flies) is a canyon ending in an amphitheatre of red, beige and lilac-coloured rock eroded into strange shapes – peaks, spires, and castles. The canyon has a broad, sandy bottom decorated with chunks of lilac-coloured clay. It is a beautiful and dramatic spot and, with its stream of fresh water running to the nearby beach, makes an idyllic camping place. The area, Amborovy, is popular with Mahajangans who have holiday beach bungalows there so if you decide to camp you can probably hitch a ride back to town, particularly at weekends. Bring your own food.

As a day trip a taxi will take you from Mahajanga and back, but a cheaper alternative is to take a taxi-brousse from the street west of Chez Chabaud (opposite a BTM bank). This will take you to the intersection of the Zaha Motel and airport, from where you can walk the final 6km. Give yourself at least one hour to look around. Late afternoon is best, when the sun sets the reds and mauves alight.

Anjajavy

About 140km north of Mahajanga are some of the most impressive mangrove forests to be found in Madagascar (according to Derek Schuurman). There are also a number of peculiar rock formations set among the trees. Although not true *tsingy*, they are nevertheless quite spectacular, the remarkably eroded rocks towering above the forest canopy.

The Anjajavy beach itself is exquisite, with coconut palms, white sand and incredibly blue water – surely one of the most attractive places along the Malagasy coastline.

Jackie's Lodge, at Anjajavy, is neatly built of wood and thatch, and tastefully furnished using natural materials. There are hammocks everywhere, even in the bar/lounge, which looks out to sea. But perhaps the strangest thing about this beautiful place is that the beach has not only palm trees but baobabs and very dense deciduous forest, as well as several more very odd rock outcrops. Anjajavy also has its own airstrip, which can handle aircraft carrying between six and ten people. Contact Jackie Cauvin, Villa Faritany, Bd Marcos, Mahajanga. Closed December to April.

Anjohibe caves

The *Grottes de Anjohibe* are 82km northeast of Mahajanga and accessible only by 4WD vehicle, and then only in the dry season. There are two places to visit, the caves themselves and a natural swimming pool above a waterfall. The caves are full of stalactites and stalagmites (and bats), and have 2km of passages.

To reach the caves turn left at the village of Antanamarina, from where it is another 5km. Then, to cool off, return to the village and take the road straight ahead to the waterfall and pools. There is a troop of sifaka here, and natural pools both above and below the waterfall. To add to the excitement there may be crocodiles in the lower pool.

Dan Carlsson of Project Madagascar (Sweden) excavated these caves in 1996. 'It seems as though the caves have been used for normal living but also as a place of sacrifice. We found...pottery with ash, charcoal and animal bones...

also several hippopotamus bones believed to be some million years old.'

The best person to organise a tour here is probably Patrice Kerloc. His phone number is 236 62 (address: BP 376, Mahajanga). He can also arrange trips to Nosy Boiny.

Nosy Boiny (Nosy Antsoheribory)

This is a small island, about a kilometre long, in Boina Bay, with some fascinating ruins of an Arab settlement established around 1580 after a Portuguese raid on the mainland. The settlement thrived until 1750, when the Sakalava conquered the area. In its heyday the town, known as Masselage, probably supported a population of about 7,000. The ruins include several cemeteries, houses and mosques, and the 'surface of the island is scattered with pottery. There are also many baobabs'. (Dan Carlsson)

To reach the island start from Katsepy and continue by road to the village of Boeny-Ampasy on the west side of the bay. There are some bungalows here. A 1½-hour boat journey brings you to Nosy Boiny. Patrice (see above) is the best person to organise this trip.

Katsepy

No visit to Mahajanga is complete without a meal **Chez Madame Chabaud**. She runs a small beach hotel at Katsepy (pronounced 'Katsep'), a tiny fishing village across the bay from Mahajanga. Trained as a cook in France (Nice) she returned to her home town to practise her art for weekend visitors and now an increasing number of tourists. Since my delicious meal in 1984 I have had nothing but praise from readers. Katsepy is 45 minutes' journey by ferry, the *Avotra*, which runs three times a day. It takes about an hour. Be prepared for a 'wet landing' if you arrive at low tide. An alternative is to hire a pirogue at the river mouth to take you across – it's cheaper and more pleasant than the ferry.

On arrival there are rows of stalls selling basic food and coconut milk if you don't want to splash out at the restaurant, and also souvenirs. Do try to buy something from these local traders who gain little profit from tourist visits. Chez Chabaud is signposted. There are ten simple bungalows, with mosquito nets, shower and WC, and three beautifully presented meals a day. A splendid bonus is the troop of extremely rare crowned sifaka which hang around in the garden.

In between eating you can lounge around, walk on the beach, watch mud-hoppers (tree-climbing fish!) skipping around the mangroves, and swim in the murky-red sea.

It is best to make a reservation in advance through Madame Chabaud's daughter in Mahajanga. Madame Chabaud will also arrange for a local guide to go with you on a day walk to the lighthouse. There are some good beaches on this walk, and you'll see white Decken's sifaka and numerous birds.

Warning: Sadly, the beach at Katsepy is sometimes used by thieves on the look-out for tourists. John Kupiec slept on the beach and was attacked at night. He survived with a few cuts and all his possessions intact, but it was a frightening experience.

KATSEPY TO MITSINJO, LAKE KINKONY AND SOUTHWARD

Taxi-brousses sometimes meet the ferry at Katsepy for the onward journey to **Mitsinjo** (and vehicles taking the ferry are almost certainly bound for that town). The journey takes about three hours. 'Mitsinjo is a lovely town with a wide main street, trees with semi-tame sifakas, a general store that has a few rooms available, and Hotely Salama which serves wonderful food and even has a fridge [actually, a cooler] so cold beer!' (Petra Jenkins)

Not far from Mitsinjo is **Lake Kinkony** (a protected area). Petra reports: 'About once a week in the dry season the fishermen of Lac Kinkony do a supply run to Mitsinjo and you may be able to get a lift. The lake is wonderful. It boasts fish eagles, flamingoes, sacred ibis ... need I say more? It is free from bilharzia but the northeast end is a bit silty for swimming. Cadge a lift by pirogue and you've got paradise! Crocodiles are friendly and don't bother swimmers (!).'

John Kupiec enjoyed a pirogue and walking trip with Patrick, the English-speaking son of the owner of Hotely Salama. They stayed away for five days and saw plenty of wildlife as well as the lovely lake-side scenery. On the southern part of the lake is the little village of **Antseza** which has a Thursday market where you may be able to reprovision if you are camping. In the lake is a small island, Mandrave. The legend is that this island rose up in the lake after the boats of the invading Merina had been sunk by the Sakalava. It is a sacred island with many *fady*s: you may not wear gold jewellery on the lake and if you have gold teeth you must not speak while on the lake! No-one can live on the island, nor urinate there, nor approach too close to the sacred tamarind tree that grows there (although prayers may be offered to it). A Sakalava king is buried beneath the tree.

From Mitsinjo you may be able to make your way to **Soalala** although there is no longer any road transport there. Joanna Durbin, working on the Project Angonoka, reports: 'You may be able to catch a motor vedette from Mahajanga. These go (irregularly) to Soalala to collect prawns, crabs and fish. There is no hotel in Soalala, but you can camp on the beach and the local Hotely serves excellent fish in coconut sauce – *filao voanio*. You should also try the coconut cakes *godrogodro* and *firafira* which are specialities of the region. The APN (Agents pour la Protection de la Nature) based at the Eaux et Forêts office should be able to find you a guide to take you to **Sada**, the most accessible Angonoka tortoise location, which is visible from Soalala on the peninsula on the east side of Baly Bay. It is a long walk and a short sail in a pirogue, or if you are lucky with the wind you can sail all the way. Angonoka are hard to find, especially in the dry season, but there is usually a family of Decken's sifaka, *Propithecus verreauxi deckeni* – the all-white sifaka – living in the village of Antsira, near Sada. They are protected from hunting by a *fady*.'

There is an air service (Twin Otter, once a week) out of Soalala, or you can go on to **Besalampy** (which is also served by Air Mad). Then you can continue to make your way down the coast, taking cars, pirogues or whatever transport presents itself. This route is only practical in the dry season and for rugged and self-sufficient travellers. You can fly out of Maintirano, Antsalova, or Belo sur Tsiribihina (and other towns – check the Air Mad timetable). Good luck!

FROM MAHAJANGA TO NOSY BE

By cargo boat If you're determined to go to Nosy Be the uncomfortable way, there are occasional cargo boats from Mahajanga. Their office, Ramzana Aly, is at Armement Tawakal, around the corner from the Sampan d'Or restaurant. Boats leave once a week (currently Tuesdays) and in theory take 48 hours. Bring your own food and water and be prepared for a miserable trip of three days or more.

By road Most of RN6 is now paved, making the journey between Mahajanga and Ambanja, gateway to Nosy Be, reasonably easy. The countryside en route is lovely.

Marovoay

This is the first town of any importance after Mahajanga on RN4 (6,000Fmg by taxi-brousse). Formerly the residence of the Boina kings, the town's name means 'many crocodiles'. When the French attacked the Malagasy forces assembled in Marovoay in 1895, in their successful drive to conquer Madagascar, it is reported that hundreds of crocodiles emerged from the river to devour the dead and dying. Malagasy hunters have since got their revenge, and you would be lucky to see a croc these days. Since this town is on the river Betsiboka it should be possible to find someone to take you to Mahajanga by pirogue. So far, however, no traveller has succeeded (as far as I know).

From Marovoay to Antsohihy

After Marovoay you pass through the reserve of **Ampijoroa** (see page 328) to meet RN6, the road to Antsiranana. Heading north you can spend the night at **Mampikony**. The Hotel Les Cocotiers is adequate. **Port Bergé** (Boriziny) is a pleasant town with at least two hotels, the Zinnia and Le Monde. Henk Beentje recommends the restaurant Chez Joli Pain, on the big square, with fast service and good food. Try the *tsaramasa henan' kisoa*.

The road improves after Port Bergé and is quite good to Antsohihy.

Antsohihy

Pronounced 'Antsoo<u>ee</u>' this town is a good centre for exploration; there is a Solima petrol station here so you can be sure of finding transport. Like many towns in Madagascar it is built on two levels.

Where to stay/eat

There are several hotels: **Hotel Tsara Talio**, near the port, basic but very cheap; **Hotel de France** (15,000Fmg); **Hotel La Plaisance** and **Hotel Central** in the Upper Town; **Hotel Diego**, near the taxi-brousse station.

Getting there and away

A taxi-brousse to/from Mahajanga takes about 15 hours and costs around 60,000Fmg. You can reach Ambanja in 10 hours by taxi-brousse (about 40,000Fmg).

Excursions from Antsohihy

Antsohihy is situated on a fjord-like arm of the sea which becomes the River Loza. There is a regular boat service (20,000Fmg) to **Ananalava**, an isolated village accessible in the dry season by taxi-brousse (20,000Fmg) but otherwise only by boat or plane (Twin Otter). The **Paradise Hotel** costs (1996) 10,000Fmg. The owner of the *épicerie* across the road from the Paradise has a few rooms to let (for the same price) in a building further down the main street.

John Kupiec writes: 'I loved the maze of paths on both sides of the village. There is a *fady* in effect on one stretch of the river. At one time this area was ruled by a queen and many trees may not be cut down and there are other taboos. In the boat everyone removed their hats when we passed.

There is still a powerful queen in the area who occasionally grants an audience. In her presence you must ask your question to the guard who repeats it to the queen. Her answer is made the same way.'

Nosy Saba

From Ananalava you may be lucky enough to find a sturdy boat to take you to this almost perfect island for a few days. I have been here twice and doubt if any island comes closer to paradise. There is fresh water, a few fishermen's huts (abandoned in the rainy season), coconut palms, curving coves of yellow sand, a densely forested section with clouds of fruit-bats, coral, chameleons...

Warning: The large island of **Nosy Lava** lies temptingly off Ananalava. Why not go there? It's a penal colony with an interesting recent history of murder and mayhem.

From Antsohihy into the interior

Two roads run from Antsohihy in an easterly direction into the lush and mountainous interior: a lovely area for the adventurous to explore, although a word of warning from Bishop Brock: 'My original plan was to cycle from Tana to Diego up the middle of the country, using the *piste* that links Andilamena (north of Lake Alaotra) with Mandritsara. I received nothing but discouragement, however, including "The area is full of bandits" and "The people in this area hate *vazahas*".' Whether the latter pertains to Mandritsara

I don't know, but it might be safer not to explore alone.

From Antsohihy a paved road runs southeast to Mandritsara, a small town set in beautiful mountainous scenery. Taxi-brousses leave every morning, passing through **Befandriana Nord** where there is a hotel, the Rose de Chine.

Mandritsara

The name means peaceful (literally 'lies down well'), and was reportedly bestowed on it by King Radama I during his campaigns. There are several hotels here including **Hotel Pattes**, a nice little place with excellent food. In 1996 this cost 30,000Fmg for a double room with fan, or 25,000Fmg without a fan. Meals are 4,000Fmg to 12,000Fmg.

Mandritsara is linked with the outside world by Twin Otter.

Bealanana

An alternative road from Antsohihy runs northeast to Bealanana, also served by Air Mad (the office is in a convent and run by a nun!). The road is paved, and probably, by now, has a taxi-brousse service. If you have your own transport this is a worthwhile trip. The town is quite high, and the temperate climate with ample rainfall allows the cultivation of potatoes and a great variety of fruit. There is (was?) no electricity in Bealanana. **Hotel La Crête** has double rooms with basin and shower, but cold water (and remember, this is a cold place). Good food. Friendly.

AMPIJOROA FORESTRY STATION

This is part of the Réserve Naturelle Intégrale d'Ankarafantsika. Ampijoroa (pronounced Ampijeroo) is one of the few areas of protected western vegetation, and is run by Conservation International, with funding from the German organisation KfW.

This is a super reserve. It is easy to get to, thrilling to visit, with an abundance of wildlife of all kinds, and with many clear, level paths which make hiking a pleasure. 'What a great reserve! I camped there for five days. There were only a few other visitors camping each night, and only once did a tour group come through. The forest trails are set up in a large grid pattern, with paths leading north/south and east/west. Wildlife viewing was excellent. I arose each morning and climbed into the forest and always located several lemur troops and various species of birds.' (Anne Axel)

Ampijoroa straddles RN4 from Mahajanga. The main part of the reserve is on the southern side of the road (on your right coming from Mahajanga), with Lake Ravelobe to the north.

Getting/staying there

The reserve is 120km from Mahajanga; it takes a little over two hours to make the journey by car on a good road. It is worth stopping at Lac Amboromalandy, a reservoir on the way to Ampijoroa. This is an excellent place to see waterfowl.

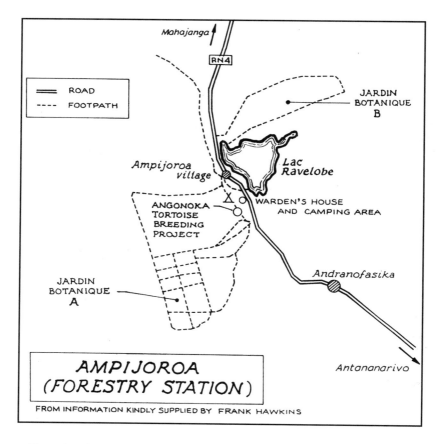

ROAD
FOOTPATH

Mahajanga

RN4

JARDIN
BOTANIQUE
B

Ampijoroa
village

Lac
Ravelobe

ANGONOKA
TORTOISE
BREEDING
PROJECT

WARDEN'S HOUSE
AND CAMPING AREA

Andranofasika

JARDIN
BOTANIQUE
A

AMPIJOROA
(FORESTRY STATION)

Antananarivo

FROM INFORMATION KINDLY SUPPLIED BY FRANK HAWKINS

If coming from Tana, note that Ampijoroa is just north of Andranofasika. There is a taxi-brousse run by KOFMAD which takes about 16 hours.

There is no accommodation in Ampijoroa. The few bungalows there are reserved for research students. If at all possible you should camp at the reserve (with your own tent), or go very early in the morning from Mahajanga (the Hotel Les Roches Rouges runs a pre-dawn trip for birders) or you can arrange to stay until nightfall. The wildlife is far less active in the heat of midday. To be on the safe side bring your own food, but usually the warden's wife will cook a very good and inexpensive meal. There is also a tiny 'shop' with a freezer, so you can buy cold beers and other basic necessities.

Permits and guides

Unlike other reserves, permits for Ampijoroa must be obtained from the Direction des Eaux et Forêts in Mahajanga (near the Ravinala Hotel) or Tana. Paula Harwood found that it was quite a hassle to buy the permit in Mahajanga; she was only allowed to pay with a postal order.

The best guide is undoubtedly Jackie – highly praised by several readers. 'Better than ever,' according to Gavin and Val Thomson (1995), 'finding us all the special birds, including Schlegel's asity. The best thing about him is that he still gets excited about seeing special things.' Other recommended guides are Charles and Roman.

Flora and fauna of Ampijoroa

This is typical dry, deciduous forest with sparse understorey and lots of lianas. In the dry winter season many of the trees will have shed their leaves, but in the wet months the forest is a sea of bright greens.

Wildlife viewing in Ampijoroa starts as soon as you arrive. Right beside the warden's house is a tree that Coquerel's sifaka, *Propithecus verreauxi coquereli*, use as a dormitory. They are extremely handsome animals with the usual silky white fur but with chestnut-brown arms and thighs. Other lemurs to be seen in the forest are brown lemurs, *Lemur fulvus fulvus*, *Lemur mongoz* (if you're very lucky), woolly lemur and *Lepilemur edwardsi* if the guide shows you its tree. This is a birder's paradise. 'Within minutes we found sicklebill, Chabert's and hookbilled vangas all nesting round the campsite... and then the highlight: white-breasted mesites which walk just like clockwork toys.' (Derek Schuurman).

After seeing the main reserve you should cross the road to the lake. A path runs right round the lake, providing excellent birding; lots of waterfowl and the very rare fish eagle. 'The lake, Ravelobe, is sacred. Each New Year's Day a zebu is slaughtered at the rudimentary wooden "shrine" you can see on the left side of the lake in the forest, and its blood poured into the water for the crocs, themselves considered sacred.' (Derek Schuurman)

An essential part of your stay in Ampijoroa is a visit to the Angonoka Tortoise Programme run by Don Reid, a British herpetologist working with the Jersey Wildlife Preservation Trust. This is one of Madagascar's most successful projects: so successful that Don Reid is leaving in 1997, confident that the conservation work he initiated will be continued by Mamy, the new Jersey-trained head of the project. After many years of research and much trial and error, the *angonoka* or plowshare tortoise – one of Madagascar's rarest reptiles – is now breeding readily and being reintroduced to its original habitat. Equally rare, the attractive little flat-tailed tortoise, *kapidolo*, is also being bred here.

MAINTIRANO AND REGION

Maintirano, a small port due west of Tana, has been somewhat out on a limb, with very few foreign visitors. Bishop Brock, the indefatigable cyclist, provided most of the following information.

The road from Tsiroanomandidy to Maintirano

'I cycled from Tana to Maintirano, thence to Morondava, a distance of about 1,100km, of which only about 250km were paved.' The first part of Bishop's ride is outlined on page 159. He continues 'The ride from Tsiroanomandidy to Maintirano is a difficult trek through a rugged, arid wilderness, that requires a large degree of self-sufficiency. Although there is ample water, it's not always conveniently located and at times I carried up to eight litres. There is no formal accommodation, and only one shop and *hotely* in **Ambaravaranala**, **Beravina** and **Morafenobe**. I camped in the bush, stayed in villages and with a family in Morafenobe. Crossing the Bangolava between Ambaravaranala and Beravina was difficult, and crossing the northern tip of the Plateau du Bemaraha east of Maintirano was brutal riding. The scenery was magnificent and varied, however, at times being so wide-open that the sense of isolation was almost overwhelming. It took me eight days in the saddle to cover this 438km.'

This road is also travelled by *camions* and 4WD taxi-brousses. Bishop recommends that you look for a vehicle in Tsiroanomandidy, rather than Tana. The journey should take two to three days. 'It is a potentially dangerous trip. Crossing the Bemaraha Plateau I came upon a Land Rover which had overturned, spilling all the fuel, and that was before the really difficult part!'

Maintirano

This small western port is attractive for people who want to get off the beaten track. Nothing much happens here. Bishop points out that although it appears to be a seaside town on the map, 'it's as though the town has turned its back on the sea: virtually *nothing* in Maintirano overlooks the ocean.' However, he found it one of the friendliest towns in Madagascar (no doubt its isolation has something to do with this). 'I was constantly entertained by local families (and the Catholic missionaries) and one man *insisted* that I take all my meals with his family during my stay there.' (Which is the reason I have no Bishop-recommended restaurants!)

The best hotel is the **Laizama**, which has rooms for 25,000Fmg (1996). Several years ago a reader wrote: 'the best restaurant is on the outskirts of town on the airport road – its name is **Buvette et Repas Mahateatea** and it looks like a garage. Book your meals in advance.' Whether it is still open, and whether it has been joined by other eateries, is up to you to find out.

Maintirano is one of the places served by Air Mad (Twin Otter) on its Tana-Mahajanga run, so there is an alternative to the overland journey.

FROM MAINTIRANO TO MORONDAVA

Continuing by bicycle, Bishop Brock writes: 'This is somewhat easier than the Tsi/didy to Maintirano stretch, and there are major towns/villages every day or two. Some self-sufficiency is still required, though, and water was a problem south of Bekopaka (all the rivers were dry; I had to get water from village wells). Although this route gives free access to the Tsingy de Bemaraha, in my opinion it is not a very interesting bike ride.'

Again, there is an alternative to cycling this route: 'The road is currently being served by a 6WD taxi-brousse that passes each way about once a week.'

Tsingy de Bemaraha

The Réserve Naturelle Intégrale du Tsingy de Bemaraha lies south of Maintirano, just to the north of the River Manambolo, and is Madagascar's largest reserve at 152,000ha. As with all Strict Nature Reserves tourist visits are forbidden, but areas adjacent to the reserve are now open.

This is one of the hardest protected areas to visit, but your efforts will be rewarded by the splendid *tsingy* and succulents growing in the crevices, not to mention lemurs (sifaka and brown lemurs) and reptiles. The area is now controlled by UNESCO, who are in charge of all tours from the main access village of Bekopaka.

Access to the tsingy

Without a 4WD vehicle access is very difficult, even in the dry season. From the north, the reserve can be accessed from **Antsalova** (see below). Most people, however, approach from the south, where the nearest town accessible by taxi-brousse from Belo Tsiribihina is Ankilizato (not to be confused with the town of the same name east of Morondava) which is 57km north of Belo. From there you must either walk (porters can be hired) or take an ox-cart the 24km to **Bekopaka**.

An alternative access town is **Ankavandra** to the east, on the Manambolo river. Christina Dodwell recommends Eleanore Rahariniarivo, who runs the Toro Hotel in the town and is also headmistress of the school. Eleanor speaks excellent English and her husband, Victor, is a river guide and able to arrange descents down the Becupaca, from where the *tsingy* can be seen in relative comfort (see also *River trips* on page 340).

Organised tours

From the north The man to see in Antsalova is Mr Christoph Randriamananjara, who lives in Antsalovabe, 2km from Antsalova. 'He took me to see the *Grotte Christophe* and some *tsingy mai* (burnt tsingy), about a 2½-hour walk east of Antsalova. The *tsingy* near Betopaka is more spectacular, but the Grotte Christophe is a nice cave. It is a large, above-ground cavern composed of a number of tall, oval chambers, some lit by natural skylights... like being in a cathedral. There were lots of bats, and also many butterflies in this area, particularly at a permanent waterhole at the Tsingy Mai. We also saw lots of sifaka and red-fronted brown lemurs. This trip could be done in a day from Antsalova, but we spent two nights camping by the Antranompasazy ("travellers' house") River. The campsite is very near the river's source: it springs to life beneath a massive limestone boulder in the middle of the forest. Staying with Christophe and his wonderful family before and after our visit to the *tsingy* was the personal highlight of my trip.

From the south Accommodation in Bekopaka is the Hotel Ibrahim. There are seven rooms (bungalows) costing 15,000Fmg (1996) and the food is excellent. All tours are organised through the UNESCO office in Bekopaka, and cost 15,000Fmg for a full-day and 10,000Fmg for a half-day tour.

The Grand Tsingy of Ankinajao is a four-hour walk from Bekopaka, but UNESCO has just built a nice campsite three hours from the village.

'The highlight for us was a trip up the Manambolo River to visit the Vazimba tombs. The *tsingy* forms spectacular cliffs along the river. On arrival at the tombs a ritual had to be performed: I had to ask the ancestors' permission for us to be there, and poured an offering of rum over the bones.' (R Harris and G Jackson)

Belo sur Tsiribihina

Apart from being the town at the end of the river Tsiribihina (see *River trips*), this place has little to offer. The famous Avenue of Baobabs is nearer Morondava and an easy excursion from there. Likewise Kirindy, although travellers coming from the north can visit both attractions on their way to Morondava. Tsiribihina means 'where one must not dive', supposedly because of the crocodiles. Be warned!

There is one hotel, the Menabe. The rooms are comfortable and clean (12,500Fmg), the restaurant...unusual...and the management friendly.

Arriving from the north you have to cross the river by ferry to get to the taxi-brousse station for Morondava.

MORONDAVA

The Morondava area was the centre of the Sakalava kingdom and their tombs – sadly now desecrated by souvenir hunters – bear witness of their power and creativity.

This was evidently a popular stopping-place for sailors in the past and they seem to have treated the natives generously. In 1833, Captain W F W Owen wrote of Morondava: 'Five boats came alongside and stunned us by vociferating for presents and beseeching us to anchor.'

Today Morondava is the centre of a prosperous, rice-growing area and a seaside resort. It is also an excellent centre for visiting the western deciduous forest.

There is not much in the way of sightseeing in the town, but the market is worth a visit: to the left of the main street as you leave town. Also, if you are not going to the south, there is a chance to see a didiera tree here: it's on the outskirts of the town, on the right as you drive in from the north.

Getting there and away
By road Morondava is 700km from Tana and served by a once good road. There are regular taxi-brousses which take about 14 hours. They cost around 20,000Fmg. See also *Travelling between Morondava and Toliara.*

By air There is a regular service from Tana or Toliara, and the Twin Otter calls here after visiting small west-coast towns.

Where to stay
Many readers report – and it is also my experience – that for a seaside resort Morondava has a very relaxed attitude towards its foreign visitors. Some would call it indifference.

Category A
Chez Maggie BP 73. Tel: 523 47. British-owned, by Maggie MacDonald, with very comfortable 2-storey chalets on the beach. About 150,000Fmg (£25/US$38); meals 25,000–40,000Fmg. This is *the* place to stay in Morondava. It's usually full, so book well in advance.

Chez Cuccu BP 22. Tel: 523 19. Similar standard as Chez Maggie. Bungalows 140Ff/ £16/US$25. Next to Les Bougainvilliers, Italian-owned, good food. Visa cards accepted.

Renala au Sable d'Or BP 163. Tel: 520 89. 'We checked out this new hotel. I think it's the nicest place in town. Large, solid wooden bungalows surrounded by landscaped gardens and grass. Prices listed as 240Ff–345Ff, depending on accommodation and beach frontage.' (M Hughes, 1995)

Category B
Les Bougainvilliers BP 78. Tel: 521 63. Beach houses, around 30,000–88,000Fmg, but with various levels of comfort; very good food. Service poor. Visa cards are accepted here. 'Location is great. Our bungalow looks right over the beach. The restaurant also looks over the ocean. It's very relaxing – a good thing, because you spend a lot of time waiting.' (M Hughes)

'Françoise organises excursions, or you can contact the very good guide Joachin Theophile through reception. He's excellent for excursions to Belo.' (Derek Schuurman)

Nosy Kely BP 22. Tel: 523 19. On the other side of the fence from the Bougainvilliers Annexe are several beach bungalows of varying prices.

Hotel les Pirogiers BP 73. Tel: 526 19. French-owned (Pierre Boisard) bungalows in Betania (the beach area) past Nosy Kely. Horse-riding and water sports.

Au Mozambique Beach bungalows near the Bougainvilliers. 90,000Fmg.

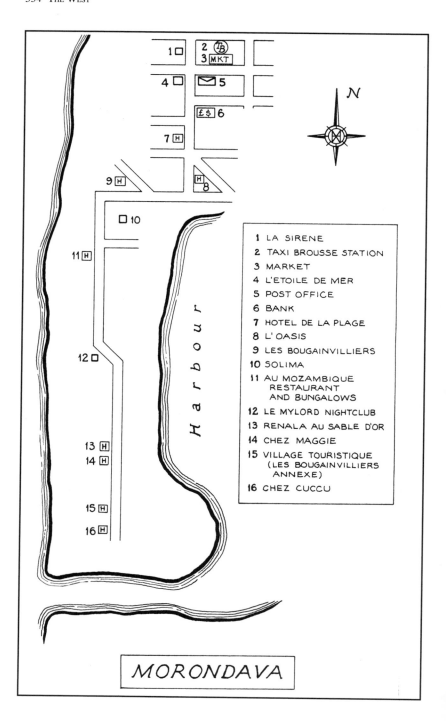

MORONDAVA

1 LA SIRENE
2 TAXI BROUSSE STATION
3 MARKET
4 L'ETOILE DE MER
5 POST OFFICE
6 BANK
7 HOTEL DE LA PLAGE
8 L'OASIS
9 LES BOUGAINVILLIERS
10 SOLIMA
11 AU MOZAMBIQUE
   RESTAURANT
   AND BUNGALOWS
12 LE MYLORD NIGHTCLUB
13 RENALA AU SABLE D'OR
14 CHEZ MAGGIE
15 VILLAGE TOURISTIQUE
   (LES BOUGAINVILLIERS
   ANNEXE)
16 CHEZ CUCCU

Category C

Hotel Central BP 50. Tel: 523 78. On the main street, newish and recently renovated. Hot shower and WC. No restaurant but breakfast served. Rooms about 40,000Fmg.

Hotel de la Plage Tel: 520 31. Not on the plage (100m away). Seven rooms, each with basin and communal WC. Pleasant and clean, with a balcony. Run by Moslems so no alcohol. Indian food (set menu).

The Oasis Tel: 521 60. A near-beach hotel (100m from the shore). Bungalows 45,000Fmg. Mountain bikes available here.

Hotel Menabe 23 spacious, pleasant rooms (30,000Fmg), but a church bell next door tolls all night.

Kismat Basic and clean, but rather noisy.

Where to eat

Renala On the seafront and specialising in seafood.

L'Etoile de Mer An open-air restaurant by the beach serving seafood.

La Serene Standard menu.

Excursions from Morondava

Baobabs are the name of the game here. This is the region of the splendid Grandidier's baobab, *Adansonia grandidieri*, best seen at the Avenue of the Baobabs. Also popular are Les Baobabs Amoureux (two entwined baobabs), and there's a Sacred Baobab as well.

Mountain bikes are available at some of the hotels and are an excellent way to see the baobabs. Beware of the heat, flies, and thorns on the road.

By car, **The Avenue of the Baobabs** is 45 minutes from Morondava. Try to get there shortly before sunset (or – better – sunrise) for the best photos. The **Baobabs Amoureux** are another half hour or so away. Nearby is a lake which is very good for birdwatching. There are two **Baobabs Sacrés** (sacred baobabs), one near the Swiss Forest and one near the turn-off from the main road to Belo. Both are the chunky *Adansonia rubrostipa* not the stately *A. grandidieri*. The former has signs of offerings nearby and lambas tied to the branches. The one near the main road also shows signs of offerings. This is its story: a woman medium or healer was unable to pass her powers on to an heir since her only child, a son, was a Christian and had rejected the traditional beliefs. So the woman was buried under the baobab with her amulets, and the tree became her heir, taking on her powers. So now the people come to the baobab to ask for good crops, a son, or healing – just as they would have come to the woman during her lifetime.

Sakalava tombs: a warning

Although the Menabe region is famous for its tombs, some things of obvious interest to tourists should be left alone. This applies particularly to the famous erotic carvings on tombs in the area around Morondava.

These carvings are fertility symbols, and often depict figures engaged in sexual activities which the Sakalava consider *fady* to practise. One example is oral sex. Erotic carvings of this kind can nowadays be seen in cultural museums in larger towns such as Tana or Toliara, and small replicas are often carved and sold as souvenirs – erotica always has a ready market. In the early 1970s unscrupulous art dealers pillaged the tombs around Morondava, removing nearly all the erotic carvings. As a result, the Sakalava now keep secret the location of those tombs which still have carvings. As one guide reported: 'Some of the graveyards are for the tourists, but most are secret – for the people.'

Derek Schuurman recalls an unsettling experience while visiting a graveyard in the Menabe. Although he was accompanied by a reputable guide, they still had to collect a member of the Council of Elders from the village closest to the graveyard. When they arrived at the secret location, the elder led the way, sprinkling rum on the graves as Derek and the guide followed. Derek could tell from the tone of the elder's voice that he was very unhappy and pleading with the Ancestors for forgiveness at having brought a *vazaha* to the sacred place. There was clear evidence that the tombs had recently been desecrated. Fresh woodchips still lay scattered around where the carvings had been removed... This is why visitors who insist on seeing Sakalava graveyards must be accompanied by an elder from a nearby village. Many will be disappointed, though, because most of the carvings have already been stolen from the sites tourists have managed to locate.

RESERVES NORTH OF MORONDAVA

The dry deciduous forests between the rivers Morondava and Tsiribihina are of great biological importance. Many endemic species of flora and fauna are found here; the area is particularly rich in reptiles such as turtles, snakes and a variety of lizards. The fosa, *Crytoprocta ferox*, is common in these forests and seven species of lemur are found, including white sifaka, *Propithicus verreauxi verreauxi*, and the rare pale fork-marked lemur, *phaner furcifer*, and pygmy mouse lemur. The giant jumping rat, Madagascar's most charming rodent, is unique to this small area.

There are three protected areas between the two rivers: Andranomena, Analabe, and Kirindy (The Swiss Forest). Heading north from Morondava, the first one you come to is **Andranomena**, a Special Reserve. As such it may be visited by tourists but there are no facilities or information. **Analabe** has the same problem, although reports suggest that it will soon be welcoming visitors. It is a private nature reserve owned by M Jean de Heaulme, of Berenty fame. There are, as yet, no facilities for tourists. Analabe lies 60km north of Morondava, to the west of Kirindy by the village of Beraboka. In addition to forest it contains some mangrove areas as well as marshes and lakes typical of coastal plain.

Kirindy (The CFPF or Swiss Forest)

This is one of the most rewarding natural areas in Madagascar, but it is not a reserve. Until recently its sole purpose was the sustainable 'harvesting' of trees, but the Swiss managers have, in the last few years, turned to ecotourism as a way of conserving their forest and its inhabitants. Despite the selective logging that still takes place, the wildlife here is abundant. Indeed, it is probably the best western reserve for seeing Madagascar's endemic dry-forest species such as the giant jumping rat, which is found only here. This is also the best place to see the narrow-striped mongoose and perhaps a fosa.

'A brilliant place, and easily worth a week. Avoid full moon, as a jumping rat doesn't jump, and nocturnal lemurs only come out much later. A *Phaner* visited the camp every night, and we saw all the lemurs except the still-hibernating fat-tailed dwarf lemur (*Cheirogalius medius*).' (Gavin and Val Thomson)

Getting/staying there

Kirindy is about 50km northeast of Morondava – about 1½ hours by good road.

There are now four 2-person bungalows (with mosquito nets, but bring your own sleeping bag) for 15,000Fmg, or you can camp for 5,000Fmg. There is also a small restaurant (cold beer!); simple meals cost 5,000Fmg. To get the most out of Kirindy you should stay the night. Day visitors see far less than those able to observe wildlife at the optimum time of dawn and dusk, and a night-time stroll to look for the giant jumping rat is part of the Kirindy experience.

In the warm season it is *very* hot in the forest during the day.

Information, permits and guides

Permits and some excellent information booklets are available from the CFPF (Coopération Suisse) headquarters in Morondava. The office is on the outskirts of town, on the right as you drive north. There are leaflets covering all aspects of the forest. Probably the most useful over all is *The Menabe Forest: highlights for the visitor*. Leaflets may also be available at Kirindy itself.

Entry to Kirindy is 20,000Fmg per person (1996). A guide will cost you 5,000Fmg per hour (day) or 10,000Fmg per hour (night).

TRAVELLING BETWEEN MORONDAVA AND TOLIARA

There are two slow routes, road and road-and-sea. Or you can fly between the two main cities via Morombe.

This is not a journey to hurry: there are many attractions and places to relax in on the way.

By road In the dry season, from April to the end of November, the venerable *Bon Bon Caramel*, a 25-year-old green Mercedes truck, makes the journey between Morondava and Toliara. It leaves Morondava on Monday at 06.00, arriving Tuesday at about 17.00. The return from Toliara is Thursday at 06.00, arriving Friday evening. The night is spent in **Manja** (where there are bungalows and good food), or at the river some 80km from there (where you can sleep on the beach). 'It is reasonably well organised. The staff is trained on being stuck. Once *Bon Bon Caramel* was with one wheel at least one metre stuck in mud; they fixed it in 20 minutes!' (Luc Selleslagh)

By road and sea You can find road transport between Morondava and Belo Sur Mer, and between Morombe and the Ifaty road-head north of Toliara. The sea stretch in the middle is done by pirogue. John Kupiec took a taxi-brousse as far as the Vezo fishing village of Ankeva Sur Mer, then walked south along the beach for 16km to Belo Sur Mer (there was a pirogue-ferry to cross the river). In Belo John met a pirogue builder called Aime, who speaks English, and who took him to Morombe for 45,000Fmg (1994). It was a rough and rather dangerous trip, made more eventful by rescuing a family whose pirogue had capsized. From Morombe he found a taxi-brousse to Toliara. If you don't find a vehicle going all the way, there is a hotely in Befandriana.

Jim Bond reports that there is a taxi-brousse, owned by the Hotel Brillant (Morombe), which makes the trip about twice a week, or other vehicles which go inland to **Ambahikily**, where you have to spend the night before looking for ongoing transport. 'For the first 60km out of Morombe the road is terrible, but there are some good baobabs (*A. grandidieri*).'

Belo Sur Mer

Not to be confused with Belo Sur Tsiribihina, this little town south of Morondava is the base for visiting a cluster of nine very interesting offshore islands. The main island is **Nosy Andravano**, but there are numerous islets. Derek Schuurman reports: 'The islands themselves are little more than sandbanks. A tour here can be arranged in Morondava because you need to sail here. It takes about eight hours to sail to Belo. The village has an interesting collection of small houses and huts; each family keeps a pig which is allowed to forage at night – Belo's mobile garbage disposals. There are huge vessels among the coconut palms at the Belo lagoon, and these are still built using exactly the same designs as the pirates used centuries back.

'On the islands are temporary Vezo settlements; the people on these barren islands, which are surrounded by magnificent coral reefs, seem to make a living from exporting sea cucumbers to the Far East. These are left to dry in the sun, as are shark carcasses and turtle shells. The local bakery is quite something: a Vezo woman sits cross-legged in front of a small fire and flips a batter-like mixture into black iron pots. In a few minutes she produces delicious pancakes called *mokara*.'

Derek recommends a week to get to and from Belo from Morondava, and to visit the most interesting islands. The best guide in Morondava is Joachim Theophile (Theo). He can usually be contacted through the main hotels. Give him a day's warning and he'll arrange everything.

Morombe

Chris Ballance writes 'Morombe clearly died when the French left, but 9,000 souls remain and they spend their time walking up and down the only street, very slowly, shaking hands with each other and discussing the possibility that someone might build a proper road to them someday.'

Despite this, the town seems to be bursting with (inevitably empty) hotels, as well as having a smart BTM bank so you can pay for them (if it agrees to change money).

Where to stay/eat

Hotel La Croix du Sud BP 33. Tel: 56. Eight spacious rooms with bathrooms and hot water; restaurant.

Hotel Baobab Fourteen concrete bungalows with Legoland-style red, green and blue tiled roofs, on the shore on the south side of the town. Air-conditioning, restaurant. Same management as Hotel La Croix du Sud.

Hotel Le Dattier Inexpensive reed huts, five concrete and airless rooms. No restaurant.

Hotel Mozambic To the right of La Croix du Sud. Six double rooms with shower.

Hotel Brillant Recommended by Jim Bond for people-watching and value for money: 10,000Fmg. 'Mangrove poles under the mattress, but not too bad. Food OK. Good ambience.'

Hotel Kuweit City Very comfortable reed huts; in 1994 it was recommended as the best value in town, but I have had no recent feedback.

Andavadoaka

'The best beach in Madagascar' is 45km to the south of Morombe and has some very comfortable bungalows, **Coco Beach**, under the same management as Hotels Baobab and Croix du Sud in Morombe. Diving/snorkelling available.

An enterprising man who calls himself Monsieur Coco has rooms in the village for 10,000Fmg.

The town has two motor vehicles, both owned by the Catholic Mission. It is sometimes possible to hitch a ride. Alternatively you can take a pirogue from Morombe, which takes about five hours.

Miandrivazo

Said to be the hottest place in Madagascar. The town lies on the banks of the Mahajilo, a tributary of the Tsirihina, and is an important centre for tobacco. 'The name comes from when Radama was waiting for his messenger to return with Rasalimo, the Sakalava princess of Malaimbandy with whom he had fallen in love. He fell into a pensive mood and when asked if he was well replied "Miandry vazo aho" – I am waiting for a wife.' (Raniero Leto)

It's a ten-hour journey from Morondava by taxi-brousse, costing about 10,000Fmg.

Where to stay/eat

Hotel Chez la Reine Rasalimo Tel: 255 32. Concrete bungalows on a hill overlooking the river. Good restaurant.

Le Relais de Miandrivazo BP 22. On the main square. Comfortable rooms with mosquito nets, 27,000Fmg (1995). Reasonable food, good atmosphere. Intermittent water.

Hotel Laizama 'A simple but homely hotel – we often found ducks in the shower – with very helpful management. We ate at the Buvette Espoir in town. Meals must be booked in advance; great value.' (R Harris and G Jackson).

Excursions

David Rasolofoarijaona, who can be found at Le Relais de Miandrivazo, runs a variety of tours. The same hotel can help you arrange a trip down the Tsirihina river – see below.

RIVER TRIPS

Trips down the lazy western rivers of Madagascar are becoming increasingly popular, with many tour operators now offering them. The most popular is down (or up) the Mahajilo and Tsirihina rivers. Several tour operators run this, and you can also organise it yourself.

'The trip took us almost four days but was one of the highlights of our stay. The bird-life is phenomenal on this stretch and we saw many lemurs in the trees on the banks as well as chameleons and snakes. We camped on the beach at night, where it was too hot to use the tent – I simply arranged my mosquito net over my sleeping bag. A mosquito net is absolutely essential for this trip, and you need to bring fresh food and plenty of drinking water from Miandrivazo although of course you can purify or boil the river water. At the end of the wet season the trip changes dramatically: camping on the beach is impossible due to the high river so you walk to the nearest village. The trips are much shorter due to the faster-flowing river. Our guide said he had completed a trip in 2½ days.' (Leone Badenhorst)

Mark Hughes and his companion did the same trip in 1995, and were equally enthusiastic. The Relais de Mandrivazo helped him find a pirogue with two paddlers. The price was 800,000Fmg which Mark thought fair for the 3½ days that the journey took. They had no tent but bought a mosquito net locally and rigged it up on the beaches with bamboo poles. Mark offers the following advice:

- Find out the language of your paddler. Ours did not speak much French.
- Look at the pirogue before agreeing to anything, and go for a test run. We didn't. Three minutes into our trip and we were back on shore – the pirogue was so unstable we would certainly have gone over. The paddlers found another one which worked out fine.
- Don't assume the paddlers are guides and know about the wildlife.
- Do your own food shopping or tell your paddlers exactly what you want.

The journey ended at the taxi-brousse depot across from Belo sur Tsiribihina. To avoid spending a night in the town Mark hired a taxi-brousse to take them to Morondava. This cost 200,000Fmg but saved the cost of spending the night and a separate tour of the Avenue des Baobabs.

Tour operators running river trips

All of the main ground operators listed in *Chapter Four* will organise river trips on comfortable vessels with good food and camping equipment, and experienced guides.

There are some specialist operators such as Mad'Cameleon (BP 4336, Antananarivo 101; tel: 630 86; fax: 261 2 344 20). They run canoe trips on the Manambolo river, allowing you to see the *tsingy*.

An expert on the rivers of Madagascar is Conrad Hirsh of Nairobi. For many years Conrad has been taking small, informal groups down the rivers Manambolo (between Ankavandra – west of Tana – and Bekopaka) and Mangoky (between Beroroha – west of Fianar – to Lake Ihotry, which is east of Morombe). For more information write to Conrad Hirsh, Remote River Expeditions, Box 59622, Nairobi, Kenya. Fax: 254 2 891 307.

REMOTE RIVER EXPEDITIONS

Exceptional calm-water rafting trips to wild and scenic parts of Western Madagascar: April – June

Conrad Hirsh, PO Box 59622, Nairobi, Kenya
Fax: (254 2) 891307

'In the olden days, the [Hova tribe], in their efforts to subdue the whole island, and make one great Hova kingdom, went up to fight against the warrior Sakalava tribe in the west. Expedition followed expedition, but time and again they were beaten. The proud Hova could not bring themselves to imagine that their foes were better fighters; they were convinced that their victory was attributable to the charms they wore. "Give us charms", they demanded. "Very well," said their wily sovereign, Andrianampoinimerina, and, hanging a small piece of wood on his neck, he put a leaden bullet under his tongue; at the same time giving one of his soldiers a rifle filled with blank shot, told him to fire point blank at him, which he did. The king, without a wound, spat out the bullet in the presence of his amazed troops. Then the charms such as the king was wearing were served out to every man, and they rushed into the fight absolutely fearless, perfectly sure no manner of harm could come to them.'
From *Peeps at Many Lands: Madagascar*, 1921

Bradt Publications

Travel Guides

41 Nortoft Road • Chalfont St Peter • Bucks • SL9 0LA • England Fax/Telephone: 01494 873478

March 1997

Dear Readers,

This book is a group effort. If it wasn't for all the wonderful letters I receive correcting, augmenting and updating the guide, I could never bring out new editions with so much fresh information and so many different viewpoints. Apart from the practical aspect, I love hearing from you and travelling vicariously in my favourite country through your descriptions.

I do hope you will write. The guide is updated every two years, so it will not be long before your information can be used.

Letters are welcome in any form (but please use capital letters for place names – and your name and address – in handwritten ones) and give the dates that you were in Madagascar. If you want to be really helpful you could indicate on the maps the location of hotels and other recommended places. Please put your name at the top of each page in case they become separated.

Best wishes,

Hilary Bradt

Appendix One

Historical Chronology

Adapted from 'Madagascar, Island of the Ancestors' *with kind permission of the author,*
John Mack

AD 500	Approximate date for the first significant settlement of the island.
800-900	Dates of the first identifiable village sites in the north of the island. Penetration of the interior begins in the south.
1200	Establishment of Arab settlements. First mosques built.
1500	'Discovery' of Madagascar by the Portuguese Diego Dias. Unsuccessful attempts to establish permanent European bases on the island followed.
1650s	Emergence of Sakalava Kingdoms.
Early 1700s	Eastern Madagascar is increasingly used as a base by pirates.
1716	Fénérive captured by Ratsimilaho. The beginnings of the Betsimisaraka confederacy.
1750	Death of Ratsimilaho.
1780	The future Andrianampoinimerina declared king of Ambohimanga.
1795/6	Andrianampoinimerina established his capital at Antananarivo.
1810-28	Reign of Radama I, Merina king.
1818	First mission school opened at Tamatave.
1820	First mission school opened at Antananarivo.
1828-61	Reign of Ranavalona I, Merina queen.
1835	Publication of the bible in Malagasy, but profession of the Christian faith declared illegal.
1836	Most Europeans and missionaries leave the island.
1861-1863	Reign of Radama II, Merina king.
1861	Missionaries re-admitted. Freedom of religion proclaimed.
1863-8	Queen Rasoherina succeeds after Radama II assassinated.
1868-83	Reign of Queen Ranavalona II.

1883	Coronation of Queen Ranavalona III.
1883-1885	Franco-Malagasy War.
1895	Establishment of full French protectorate: Madagascar became a full colony the following year.
1897	Ranavalona III exiled first to Réunion and later to Algiers. Merina monarchy abolished.
1917	Death of Ranavalona III in exile.
1942	British troops occupy Madagascar.
1947	Nationalist rebellion suppressed with many dead.
1958	Autonomy achieved within the French Community.
1960	Madagascar achieves full independence.
1972	General Ramanantsoa assumes power.
1975	Didier Ratsiraka first elected president.
1991	Demonstrations and strikes. Ratsiraka steps down.
1991	Albert Zafy elected president.
1993	The birth of the Third Republic.
1996	Albert Zafy resigns.
1997	Didier Ratsiraka elected president.

Appendix Two

The Malagasy Language

SOME BASIC RULES
Pronunciation
The Malagasy alphabet is made up of 21 letters. C, Q, U, W, and X are omitted. Individual letters are pronounced as follows:

a: as in Father
e: as in the a in Late
g: as in Get
h: almost silent
i: as ee in Seen
j: pronounced dz
o: oo as in Too
s: usually midway between sh and s but varies according to region
z: as in Zoo.

Combinations of letters needing different pronunciations are:

ai: like y in My
ao: like ow in Cow
eo: pronounced ay-oo
When k or g is preceded by i or y this vowel is also sounded *after* the consonant. For example *alika* (dog) is pronounced Aleekya, and *ary koa* (and also) is pronounced Ahreekewa.

Stressed syllables
Some syllables are stressed, others almost eliminated. This causes great problems for visitors trying to pronounce place names, and unfortunately – like in English – the basic rules are frequently broken. Generally, the stress is on the penultimate syllable except in words ending in na, ka, and tra when it is generally on the last syllable but two. Words ending in e stress that vowel. Occasionally a word with the same spelling changes its meaning according to the stressed syllable, but in this case it is written with an accent. For example,

tanana means 'hand', and *tanána* means 'town'.

When a word ends in a vowel, this final syllable is pronounced so lightly it is often just a stressed last consonant. For instance the Sifaka lemur is pronounced 'She-fak'. Words derived from English, like *hotely* and *banky*, are pronounced much the same as in English.

Getting started

The easiest way to begin to get a grip on Malagasy is to build on your knowledge of place names (you *have* to learn how to pronounce these in order to get around) and to this end I have given the phonetic pronunciation in the text. As previously noted, most place names mean something so you have only to learn these meanings and – hey presto! – you have the elements of the language! Here are some bits of place names:

An-, Am-, I-	at, the place where	*Maintso*	green
Arivo:	thousand	*Manga*	blue
Be	big, plenty of	*Maro*	many
Fotsy, -potsy	white	*Nosy*	island
Kely	small	*Rano, -drano*	water
Kily	tamarind	*Tany, tani-*	land
Mafana	hot	*Vato, -bato*	stone
Maha	which causes	*Vohitra, vohi-, bohi-*	hill
Mainti	black		

When coming to grips with Malagasy it is useful to know that the plural form of a noun is the same as the singular form.

Vocabulary
Social phrases

Stressed letters or phrases are underlined.

English	Malagasy	Phonetic Pronunciation
Hello	*Manao ahoana*	*Mano <u>own</u>*
Hello	*Salama*	*S<u>alaam</u>*
(north & east coast)	*Mbola tsara*	*M'boola tsara*
What news?	*Inona no vaovao?*	*<u>I</u>nan vowvow?*
No news	*Tsy misy*	*Tsim<u>ee</u>ss*

These three easy-to-learn phrases of ritualised greetings establish contact with people you pass on the road or meet in their village. For extra courtesy (important in Madagascar) add *tompoko* (pronounced 'toomp'k') at the end of each phrase.

Simple phrases for 'conversation' include:

English	Malagasy	Phonetic Pronunciation
What's your name?	*Iza no anaranao?*	*Eeza nanaranow?*
My name is	*Ny anarako*	*Ny anarakoo*
Goodbye	*Veloma*	*Veloom*
See you again	*Mandra pihaona*	*Mandra pioon*
I don't understand	*Tsy azoko*	*Tsi azook*
Very good	*Tsara tokoa*	*Tsara t'koo*
Bad	*Ratsy*	*Rats*
Please/Excuse me	*Aza fady*	*Azafad*
Thank you	*Misaotra*	*Misowtr*
Pardon me (ie may I pass)	*Ombay lalana*	*m'buy lalan*
Let's go	*Andao andeha*	*Andow anday*
Crazy	*Adaladala*	*Adaladal*
Long life! (Cheers!)	*Ho ela velona!*	*Wellavell!*

If you are pestered by beggars try:

I have nothing (there is none)	*Tsy misy*	*tsimeess*
Go away!	*Mandehana!*	*Man day han*

Note: The words for yes (*eny*) and no (*tsia*) are hardly ever used in conversation. The Malagasy tend to say '*yoh*' for yes and '*ah*' for no, along with appropriate gestures.

Market phrases

How much?	*Ohatrinona?*	*Ohtreen?*
Too expensive!	*Lafo be!*	*Laff be!*
No way!	*Tsy lasa!*	*Tsee lass!*

Basic needs

Where is...?	*Aiza...?*	*Ize...?*
Is it far?	*Lavitra ve izany?*	*Lavtra vayzan?*
Is there any...?	*Misy ve...?*	*Mees ve...?*
I want...	*Mila ... aho*	*Meel ... a*
I'm looking for...	*Mitady ... aho*	*M'tadi ... a*
Is there a place to sleep?	*Misy toerana hatoriana ve?*	*Mees too ayran atureen vay?*
Is it ready?	*Vita ve?*	*Veeta vay?*
I would like to buy some food	*Te hividy sakafo aho*	*Tayveed sakaff wah*

English	*Malagasy*	*Phonetic Pronunciation*
I'm hungry	*Noana aho*	*Noonah*
I'm thirsty	*Mangetaheta aho*	*Mangataytah*
I'm tired	*Vizaka aho*	*Veesacar*
Please help me!	*Mba ampio aho!*	*Bampeewha!*

Useful words

Village	*Vohitra*	*Voo-itra*
House	*Trano*	*tran*
Food/meal	*Hanina/sakafo*	*An/sakaff*
Water	*Rano*	*Rahn*
Rice	*Vary*	*Var*
Eggs	*Atody*	*Atood*
Chicken	*Akoho*	*Aku*
Bread	*Mofo*	*Moof*
Milk	*Ronono*	*Roonoon*
Road	*Lalana*	*Lalan*
Town	*Tanana*	*Tanan*
River (large)	*Ony*	*Oon*
River (small)	*Riaka*	*Reek*
Ox/cow	*Omby/omby vavy*	*Oomby/omb varve*
Child/baby	*Ankizy/zaza kely*	*Ankeeze/zaza kail*
Man/woman	*Lehilahy/vehivavy*	*Layla/vayvarve*

Appendix Three

Further Reading

Madagascar's historical links with Britain and the current interest in its natural history and culture have produced a century of excellent books written in English. This bibliography is a selection of my favourites in each category. These, and other titles on Madagascar, may be available from the following suppliers:

Discover Madagascar (Seraphine Tierney) 7 Hazledene Rd, Chiswick, London W4 3JB. Tel: 0181 995 3529. Fax: 0181 742 0212.
Seraphine puts out a catalogue of books on Madagascar which are in print but may be hard to find in conventional outlets. She also sells Malagasy music cassettes and CDs.

Mad Books (Rupert Parker) 151 Wilberforce Rd, London N4 2SX. Tel: 0171 226 4490. Email: 100572.2434@compuserve.com. WWW: http://ourworld.compuserve.com:80/homepages/Rupert_Parker/. Rupert specialises in old and rare (out-of-print) books on Madagascar, and will send out his catalogue on request. He will also search for books.

Eastern Books of London 125a Astonville St, London SW18 5AQ. Tel/fax: 0181 871 0880. An antiquarian bookseller with a catalogue of rare and out-of-print books on Madagascar.

Editions Karthala (France) 22–24 Bd Arago, 75013 Paris. This French publisher specialises in Madagascar, both for new titles and reprints.

General – history, the country, the people
Bradt, H (1992). *Madagascar* (World Bibliographical Series). Clio (UK); ABC (US). An annotated selection of nearly 400 titles on Madagascar, from the classic early works to those published in the 1990s.

Brown, M (1996). *A History of Madagascar*. D Tunnacliffe, UK. The most accurate, comprehensive and readable of the histories, brought completely up to date by Britain's foremost expert on the subject.

Covell, M (1987). *Madagascar: Politics, Economics and Society*. Frances Pinter, UK. (Marxist Regimes series.) An interesting look at Madagascar's Marxist past.

Crook, S (1990). *Distant Shores: by Traditional Canoe from Asia to Madagascar*. Impact Books, UK. The story of the 4,000-mile Sarimanok Expedition by outrigger canoe across the Indian Ocean from Bali to Madagascar. An interesting account of an eventful and historically important journey.

Dodwell, C (1995). *Madagascar Travels*. Hodder & Stoughton (UK). An account of a journey through Madagascar's most remote regions by one of Britain's leading travel writers.

Drysdale, H (1991). *Dancing with the Dead: a Journey through Zanzibar and Madagascar*. Hamish Hamilton, UK. An account of Helena's journeys in search of her trading ancestor. Informative, entertaining and well-written.

Ellis, W (1867). *Madagascar Revisited*. John Murray, UK. The Rev. William Ellis, of the LMS, was one of the most observant and sympathetic of the missionary writers. His books are well worth the search for second-hand copies.

Fox, L (1990). *Hainteny: the Traditional Poetry of Madagascar*. Associated University Presses, UK and Canada. Over 400 beautifully translated *hainteny* with an excellent introduction to the history and spiritual life of the Merina.

Lanting, F (1991). *Madagascar, a World out of Time*. Robert Hale, UK. A book of stunning, and somewhat surreal, photos of the landscape, people and wildlife.

Lumley, J (1994). *Girl Friday*. BBC Books, London. The book tie-in for the television programme on Joanna Lumley's experience on Tsara Banjina, near Nosy Be.

Murphy, D (1985). *Muddling through in Madagascar*. Murray, London. An entertaining account of a journey (by foot and truck) through the highlands and south.

Pye, G (1995). *Orchids before Breakfast*. Roots & Branches, Cambridge. Memories of life in Madagascar in the 1970s.

Sibree, J (1896). *Madagascar Before the Conquest: the Island, the Country, and the People*. T Fisher Unwin, UK. With William Ellis, Sibree was the main documenter of Madagascar during the days of the London Missionary Society. He wrote many books on the island, all of which are perceptive, informative, and a pleasure to read.

Ethnology

Bloch, M (1986). *From Blessing to Violence*. Cambridge University Press, UK. History and ideology of the circumcision ritual of the Merina people.

Mack, J (1986). *Madagascar: Island of the Ancestors*. British Museum, London. A scholarly and informative account of the ethnography of Madagascar.

Mack, J (1989). *Malagasy Textiles*. Shire Publications, UK.

Powe, E L (1994). *Lore of Madagascar*. Dan Aiki Publications (530 W Johnson St, Apt 210, Madison, WI 53703) USA. An immense work – over 700 pages and 260 colour photos – with a price to match: $300. This is the only book to describe in detail, and in a readable form, all 39 ethnic groups in Madagascar.

Sharp, L A (1993). *The Possessed and the Dispossessed: spirits, identity and power in a Madagascar migrant town*. University of California Press, USA. Describes the daily life and the phenomenon of possession (tromba) in the town of Ambanja.

Wilson, P J (1993). *Freedom by a Hair's Breadth*. University of Michigan, USA. An anthropological study of the Tsimihety people, written in a clear style and accessible to the general reader.

Natural history
Literature

Attenborough, D (1961). *Zoo Quest to Madagascar*. Lutterworth, UK. Still one of the best travel books ever written about Madagascar, with, of course, plenty of original wildlife observations. Out of print, but copies can be found.

Durrell, G (1992). *The Aye-aye and I*. HarperCollins, UK. The focal point is the collecting of aye-aye for the Jersey Zoo, written in the inimitable Durrell style with plenty of humour and traveller's tales.

Jolly, A (1980). *A World Like Our Own: Man and Nature in Madagascar*. Yale University Press. The first and still the best look at the relationship between the natural history and people of the island. Highly readable.

Preston-Mafham, K. (1991). *Madagascar: A Natural History*. Facts on File, UK and US. The most enjoyable and useful book on the subject. Illustrated with superb colour photos (coffee-table format) it is as good at identifying strange invertebrates and unusual plants as in describing animal behaviour.

Quammen, D (1996). *The Song of the Dodo*. Hutchinson, UK. An interesting account of island biogeography and its implications for nature reserves.

Wilson, J (1990). *Lemurs of the Lost World: Exploring the Forests and Crocodile Caves of Madagascar*. Impact Books, UK. An interesting and informative account of the Ankarana expedition and subsequent travels in Madagascar.

Specialist literature and guides

Bradt, H, Schuurman, D, Garbutt, N (1996). *Madagascar Wildlife*. Bradt Publications (UK); Globe Pequot Press (USA). A photographic guide to the island's most interesting and appealing wildlife, and where best to see it.

Dransfield, J & Beentje, H (1996). *The Palms of Madagascar*. Royal Botanic Gardens, UK. A beautiful and much-needed book describing the many palm species of Madagascar.

Garbutt, N (1997). *The Mammals of Madagascar: a photographic guide*. Pica Press.

Glaw, F, Vences, M (1994). *A Field Guide to the Amphibians and Reptiles of Madagascar*. A thorough guide to the herpetofauna of Madagascar.

Haltenorth, T and Diller, H; trans by Robert W Hayman (1980). *Field Guide to the Mammals of Africa including Madagascar*. Wm Collins & Son, UK. The illustrations are not accurate enough to be of much use in the field.

Harcourt, C (1990). *Lemurs of Madagascar and the Comoros*. IUCN, Cambridge. A Red Data book with scientific descriptions of all Madagascar's lemurs.

Hillerman, F E, & Holst, A W (1990). *An Introduction to the Cultivated Angraecoid Orchids of Madagascar*. Timber Press, USA. The most accessible book covering the orchids of Madagascar, with a good section on climate and other plant life.

Inventaire Écologique Forestier National. Published in 1996 by the Direction des Eaux et Forêts. A brave and welcome attempt to make the island's botany more accessible.

Jenkins, M D, editor. (1987). *Madagascar: An Environmental Profile.* IUCN, Gland, Switzerland and Cambridge, U.K. Descriptions of the nature reserves, with checklists of flora and fauna.

Jolly, A, Oberle, P, Albignac, R, editors (1994). *Madagascar.* Pergamon Press, UK and Canada. This book in the 'Key Environments' series is mainly a translation of the French *Madagascar: Un Sanctuaire de la Nature.* Now a little dated, but nevertheless one of the best overviews of the natural history.

Langrand, O (1990). *Field Guide to the Birds of Madagascar.* Yale University Press, US & UK. A marvellously comprehensive guide to the island's birds and their distribution, behaviour and habitat. 40 colour plates.

Martin, J (1992). *Chameleons.* Facts on File, USA; Blandford, UK. Beautifully illustrated with photos by Art Wolfe; everything a chameleon aficionado could hope for.

Mittermeier, M et al (1994). *Lemurs of Madagascar.* Conservation International. A detailed field guide to all Madagascar's lemurs.

Morris, Peter (1997). *Birds of Madagascar: a photographic guide.* Pica Press.

Nicholl, M E & Langrand, O (1989). *Madagascar: Revue de la Conservation et des Aires Protégées.* WWF, Switzerland. Currently available only in French, but an English edition is in preparation. A detailed survey of the reserves studied by the WWF, lists of species, and excellent maps.

Richard-Vindard, G & Battistini, R (editors) (1972). *Biogeography and Ecology of Madagascar.* W Junk, Netherlands. Largely in English including chapters on geology, climate, flora, erosion, rodents and lemurs. Each chapter includes an extensive bibliography.

Tattersall, I (1981). *The Primates of Madagascar.* Columbia UP, US. A comprehensive description of the biology of Madagascar's lemurs.

℘

'For the ancients, food nowardays looks like slaves'one (boiled meat). Yet under its tropical latitudes, the Wild Island has a lot of culinary treasures... From the royal carp to the goose veranga, including nymphes of the silk, all the flavours delight your palate. Without forgetting frayed zebu or traditional koba... "Ro sihanaka" is, for instance, a typical dish from Alaotra Lake with wide bredes, anguivy and skimmed zebu de fosse... Even if this guest table is not for all purses, it's worth the detour to really taste the enjoyments of Malagasy gastronomy.'
From an article on Malagasy food from *Madactualites*

Other Bradt guides to Africa
and the Indian Ocean

Africa by Road by Bob Swain and Paula Snyder

Backpacker's Africa – East and Southern by Hilary Bradt

Guide to Ethiopia by Philip Briggs

Guide to Eritrea by Edward Paice

Guide to Malawi by Philip Briggs

Madagascar Wildlife by Hilary Bradt, Derek Schuurman and Nick Garbutt

Guide to Maldives by Royston Ellis

Guide to Mauritius by Royston Ellis

Guide to Mozambique Philip Briggs

Guide to Namibia and Botswana by Simon Atkins and Chris McIntyre

Guide to South Africa by Philip Briggs

Guide to Tanzania by Philip Briggs

Guide to Uganda by Philip Briggs

Guide to Zambia by Chris McIntyre

Guide to Zanzibar by Davis Else

And then there's the rest of the world...

For a fast and friendly mail order service, and for a copy of our catalogue contact:

Bradt Publications, 41 Nortoft Road, Chalfont St Peter, Bucks SL9 0LA, England. Tel/fax: 01494 873478

Bradt

Appendix Four

Madagascar's Lemurs
and Where to Find Them

Gavin and Val Thomson

* = Nocturnal lemurs

Scientific name	Common name	Location
Allocebus trichotis*	Hairy-eared dwarf	Forest 16km SW of Mananara
Avahi laniger	Eastern woolly	**Périnet, Ranomafana**
A. occidentalis	Western woolly	**Ampijoroa**; Manongarivo
Cheirogaleus major*	Greater dwarf	**Périnet** (main road), **Ranomafana**
C. medius*	Fat-tailed dwarf	**Kirindy**; Berenty
Daubentonia madagascariensis	Aye-aye	**Verezanantsoro NP, Nosy Mangabe**
Hapelemur aureus	Golden bamboo	**Ranomafana**
H. griseus griseus	Grey bamboo	**Périnet** (by warden's house), **Ivoloina, Ranomafana**: E forests
H. g. occidentalis	Western bamboo	Bemaraha, Manongarivo SR, Sambirano area
H. g. alaotrensis	Alaotran bamboo	Reed beds of Lac Alaotra
H. simus	Greater bamboo	**Ranomafana**
Indri indri	Indri	**Périnet**
Lemur catta	Ring-tailed	**Berenty**; Beza Mahafaly
Eulemur coronatus	Crowned	**Ankarana; Montagne d'Ambre**
E. fulvus fulvus	Brown	**Périnet, Ampijoroa**
E. f. albifrons	White-fronted brown	**Nosy Mangabe, Ivoloina**; Anjanaharibe-Sud, Betampona, NE rainforest
E. f. albocollaris	White-collared brown	**Forest just W of Vondrozo (W of Farafangana)**; Manombo SR
E. f. collaris	Collared brown	**Berenty** (introduced); Andohahela
E. f. rufus	Red-fronted	**Ranomafana, Kirindy**
E. f. sanfordi	Sanford's brown	**Ankarana, Montagne d'Ambre**
E. macaco flavifrons	Sclater's black	**Marovato sud (9km S of Moromandia)**
E. m. macaco	Black	**Nosy Komba**; Lokobe, Tsaratanana
E. mongoz	Mongoose	**Ampijoroa**
E. rubriventer	Red-bellied	**Ranomafana**; Périnet
Lepilemur dorsalis*	Grey-backed sportive	**Lokobe, Nosy Be**; Sambirano region in NW

Scientific name	Common name	Location
*L. edwardsi**	Milne-Edwards' sportive	**Ampijoroa:** dry deciduous W forests
*L. leucopus**	White-footed sportive	**Berenty**; Beza-Mahafaly, Andohahela
*L. microdon**	Small-toothed sportive	Onibe river to Andapa region
*L mustelinus**	Sportive	**Périnet**; Onibe river to Tolagnaro
*L. ruficaudatus**	Red-tailed sportive	**Kirindy**; dry deciduous W forests
*L. septentrionalis**	Northern sportive	**Montagne d'Ambre:** deciduous forests of extreme N
*Microcebus murinus**	Grey mouse	Dry forest/spiny desert of S & W, Tolagnaro to Sambirano river
*M. rufus**	Brown mouse	**Périnet** (main rd & Orchid Garden); E forests Tolagnaro to Sambirano
*M. myoxinus**	Pygmy mouse	**Kirindy Forest, Analabe**
*Mirza coquereli**	Coquerel's dwarf	**Kirindy**; Bemaraha: secondary forests nr Ambanja in NW
Phaner furcifer furcifer	Eastern fork-marked	**Nr Saraka in Masoala**; Betampona
P. f. pallescens	Pale fork-marked	**Kirindy**; Bemaraha
P. f. parienti	Pariente's fork-marked	Beraty forest W of RN6 (45km S of Ambanja)
P. f. electromontis	Amber Mtn fm.	**Montagne d'Ambre**
Propithecus diadema candidus	Silky sifaka	**Anjanaharibe-Sud**
P. d. diadema	Diademed sifaka	**Mantady NP**; Zahamena, Betampona
P. d. edwardsi	Milne-Edwards'	**Ranomafana**
P. d. perrieri	Perrier's sifaka	**Analamera**
P. v. deckeni	Decken's sifaka	**Bemaraha, Katsepy lighthouse**
P. v. verreauxi	Verreaux's sifaka	**Berenty**; Kirindy, Beza-Mahafaly
P. v. coquereli	Coquerel's sifaka	**Ampijoroa, Bush House** (introduced)
P. v. coronatus	Crowned sifaka	**Katepsy**; forests between Mahavavy & Betsiboka rivers, Kasijy SR
P. tattersalli	Golden-crowned	**S of Antsahampano** (11km E of Daraina on RN5A)
Varecia variegata variegata	Black & white ruffed	**Nosy Mangabe, Bush House** (introduced)
V. v. rubra	Red ruffed	**Masoala** (near Ambanizana)

✆

'The baboon grows to an enormous size... at least seven feet high when standing on its hind legs. It is a very savage and untractable animal and its imperfect and hideous resemblance to the human form gives it an horrific appearance'.
Samuel Copland, History of the Island of Madagascar, 1822

MEASUREMENTS AND CONVERSIONS

Madagascar uses metric measurements and so have I throughout this book. These conversion formulae and tables should help you.

Many people will want to convert metres to the more familiar feet. If you remember that 3 metres is 9.84 feet, or just under 10 feet, you can do an approximate conversion quickly: to convert heights shown in metres to feet, divide by 3 and add a zero, e.g. 6,000 m = 20,000 feet.

The error is only 1.5%.

CONVERSION FORMULAE

To convert	Multiply by
Inches to centimetres	2.54
Centimetres to inches	0.3937
Feet to metres	0.3048
Metres to feet	3.281
Yards to metres	0.9144
Metres to yards	1.094
Miles to kilometres	1.609
Kilometres to miles	0.6214
Acres to hectares	0.4047
Hectares to acres	2.471
Imperial gallons to litres	4.546
Litres to imperial gallons	0.22
US gallons to litres	3.785
Litres to US gallons	0.264
Ounces to grams	28.35
Grams to ounces	0.03527
Pounds to grams	453.6
Grams to pounds	0.002205
Pounds to kilograms	0.4536
Kilograms to pounds	2.205
British tons to kilograms	1016.0
Kilograms to British tons	0.0009842
US tons to kilograms	907.0
Kilograms to US tons	0.000907

TEMPERATURE CONVERSION TABLE

The bold figures in the central columns can be read as either centigrade or fahrenheit

Centigrade		Fahrenheit
-18	**0**	32
-15	**5**	41
-12	**10**	50
- 9	**15**	59
- 7	**20**	68
- 4	**25**	77
- 1	**30**	86
2	**35**	95
4	**40**	104
7	**45**	113
10	**50**	122
13	**55**	131
16	**60**	140
18	**65**	149
21	**70**	158
24	**75**	167
27	**80**	176
32	**90**	194
38	**100**	212
40	**104**	

(5 imperial gallons are equal to 6 US gallons.
A British ton is 2,240 lbs. A US ton is 2,000 lbs.)

INDEX